From the Pass
to the Pueblos

El Camino Real de Tierra Adentro National Historic Trail

From the Pass to the Pueblos

El Camino Real de Tierra Adentro Natonal Historic Trail

George D. Torok

SUNSTONE
PRESS

SANTA FE

Sunstone books may be purchased for educational, business, or sales promotional use. For information please write: Special Markets Department, Sunstone Press, P.O. Box 2321, Santa Fe, New Mexico 87504-2321.

Book and Cover design › Vicki Ahl
Body typeface › Minion Pro
Printed on acid-free paper
∞

Library of Congress Cataloging-in-Publication Data

Torok, George D.
  From the Pass to the pueblos : El Camino Real de Tierra Adentro National Historic Trail / by George D. Torok.
      pages cm
  Includes bibliographical references and Index.
  ISBN 978-0-86534-896-7 (softcover : alkaline paper)
  1. El Camino Real de Tierra Adentro National Historic Trail (N.M. and Tex.)--Guidebooks. 2. Historic sites--El Camino Real de Tierra Adentro National Historic Trail (N.M. and Tex.)--Guidebooks. 3. Historic buildings--El Camino Real de Tierra Adentro National Historic Trail (N.M. and Tex.)--Guidebooks. 4. Villages--El Camino Real de Tierra Adentro National Historic Trail (N.M. and Tex.)--Guidebooks. I. Title.
  F802.E45T66 2012
  917.8904--dc23
                    2012028499

WWW.SUNSTONEPRESS.COM
SUNSTONE PRESS / POST OFFICE BOX 2321 / SANTA FE, NM 87504-2321 /USA
(505) 988-4418 / ORDERS ONLY (800) 243-5644 / FAX (505) 988-1025

To Blanca and Jorgito, who enthusiastically travel
with me along El Camino Real de Tierra Adentro

Contents

List of Illustrations.......................8
Notes and Acknowledgements............10
Introduction..........................13

1: North through the Chihuahuan Desert . . .39
2: Ciudad Juárez 71
3: American El Paso....................97
4: The Mesilla Valley 118
5: The Jornada del Muerto 147
6: The Socorro Valley..................171
7: Tiwa Country.......................200
8: The Northern Pueblos 252
9: On to Santa Fe.....................289

Notes...............................317
Bibliography.........................346

List of Illustrations

1. Map: El Camino Real de Tierra Adentro. 14
2. Map: The western segment of the National Trails System.. 15
3. Replica of a Spanish Colonial *carreta*, or ox-cart. 20
4. *The Equestrian*, a portrayal of Juan de Oñate.. 22
5. Map: El Camino Real de Tierra Adentro through the Lower Valley. 40
6. Landscape of the Chihuahuan Desert. 41
7. Manso Indians, as depicted at the El Paso Museum of Archaeology. 45
8. Los Portales, home of the San Elizario Genealogical and Historical Society. 50
9. The Rio Vista Farm Site. 55
10. The Tienda de Carbajal. 61
11. Socorro Cemetery with mission church in background. 63
12. Tigua parishioners at Ysleta. 68
13. The present Senecú church under construction. .79
14. "The Plaza and Church of El Paso" by A. de Vauducourt, c.1852. 82
15. The Palacio Municipal. 85
16. The San José Chapel, on the road south to Carrizal.. 88
17. Gravesites in the San José Cemetery.. 95
18. Map: El Camino Real through American El Paso. 97
19. A Texas Centennial Marker on today's Paisano Drive. 101
20. Gravesite of Juana María Ascárate, at Concordia Cemetery.. 104
21. Butterfield Overland Mail stagecoach. 109
22. Remains of Hart's Mill. 112
23. "Rio Grande-Near Frontera" by James D. Smillie, c. 1853. 115
24. Map: El Camino Real de Tierra Adentro through the Mesilla Valley. 119
25. The Battle of Brazito site. 121
26. Segment of the Taylor-Barela-Reynolds House and shops on Mesilla's plaza.. . .128
27. The *Casa de Descanso*, a processional rest-stop, in Tortugas. 130
28. The Armijo House, once the most lavishly furnished home in Las Cruces. 133
29. The Amador Hotel building.. 135
30. Quiet backstreet in Doña Ana village. 138
31. Melting ruins at Fort Selden, near Paraje de Robledo.. 142
32. Paraje San Diego. 145
33. Map: El Camino Real through the Jornada del Muerto.. 148
34. National Park Service and Bureau of Land Management signs.. 150
35. Grasses sprout in moistened pools near Paraje Perrillo.. 151
36. Deep arroyos cut through the edges of the Jornada.. 153
37. *El Contadero*, the Counting Place, near Black Mesa. 160
38. The Armendaris land grant in the Jornada. 162
39. Twentieth-century grave markers are found at the former village of Valverde. . .164
40. The ruins of Fort Craig, a National Historic Site.. 166
41. El Camino Real International Heritage Center.. 168

42. Remains of San Marcial. 170
43. Map: El Camino Real through the Socorro Valley. 172
44. The buttes of San Pascual and San Pascualito. 176
45. Basaltic outcrops. 177
46. The abandoned San Antonio railroad depot on NM 1. 178
47. San Miguel Church. 184
48. The Baca Store, Socorro, New Mexico. 188
49. Wooden crosses in the second Lemitar Cemetery. 191
50. The present-day settlement of Alamillo. 194
51. Sevilleta de la Joya. 197
52. Map: El Camino Real de Tierra Adentro through Tiwa Country. 201
53. A few adobe ruins survive near Veguita. 202
54. *Las Barrancas*, the Ravines. 204
55. Hiking trails lead to the summit of Tomé Hill. 207
56. The Sangre de Cristo Church in Valencia. 209
57. The nineteenth-century plaza of Bélen was located in this residential area. 216
58. The Chapel of Saint Anthony at Los Lentes. 220
59. Squaws of Isleta, New Mexico, c.1880-1890. 223
60. The Gutiérrez-Hubbell House in Pajarito. 227
61. Cemetery and eighteenth-century community of Atrisco. 231
62. Map: El Camino Real through the Albuquerque Area. 233
63. Los Duránes Chapel. 239
64. Los Griegos Chapel. 241
65. Los Ranchos de Albuquerque. 243
66. The Abencio Salazar Historic District. 251
67. Map: El Camino Real de Tierra Adentro through the Northern Pueblos. 253
68. Santa Ana Church, 1900. 254
69. Historic Route 66 followed a segment of the original Camino Real. 256
70. San Felipe Pueblo Church, 1897. 258
71. Carretta and plow, Santo Domingo Pueblo, n.d 260
72. San Marcos Pueblo was located near today's Cerrillos Hills Historic District. . . 267
73. Bow and arrow dancers on kiva steps, San Ildefonso Pueblo. 272
74. Cloud Dance, Santa Clara Pueblo, New Mexico, c.1925-1945. 276
75. Holy Cross Church. 280
76. Women winnowing wheat, San Juan Pueblo, New Mexico, c.1925-1945? 285
77. Map: El Camino Real through the Santa Fe Area. 289
78. The village and church of La Bajada. 292
79. The San Antonio Chapel at La Cieneguilla. 294
80. El Rancho de Las Golondrinas. 297
81. Agua Fria Village. 300
82. Palace of the Governors, Santa Fe. 309
83. Analco's Oldest House in the United States. 313
84. The San Miguel Chapel. 315
85. Reynaldo Rivera's *Journey's End.* 316

Notes and Acknowledgements

In the mid-1990s I began to learn about the significance of El Camino Real de Tierra Adentro in the development of my new hometown, El Paso, Texas. Over time, as the Royal Road became better identified and studied, and as the National Park Service and the Bureau of Land Management worked toward formal recognition in the National Trails System, my interests became more focused. In 2003, with the formation of the Camino Real de Tierra Adentro Trail Association (CARTA), I was introduced to an amazing cross-section of trail enthusiasts. I had the opportunity to work with historians, archaeologists, interpretive specialists, professors and teachers, to name a few. I also met many people who had a personal or local interest in the trail. I discovered that many communities, often bypassed by modern highways and development, had fascinating histories and committed local people who preserved, protected, and cherished historic sites and structures along this historic roadway. Within a few years, I found myself gathering enough material for a more detailed study, especially of the segment under development as the National Historic Trail. This book is a summary of that work and an introduction to the varied landscape and history of El Camino Real de Tierra Adentro National Historic Trail.

Countless people have helped with this project, from its earliest inception in the 1990s, to the completion of the work in 2011. All have made valuable contributions and added exciting details, criticism, and suggestions. I made use of much of their advice, but I alone am responsible for any errors in the final text. I am sure I have missed a few names along the way, but, from south to north along the trail, I am deeply indebted to:Barbara Angus, Richard Baquera, Ben Brown, Harry W. "Skip" Clark, Marta Estrada, Marilyn Gross, Sheldon Hall, Nick Houser, Terri Jones, Rick Kelly, Leon Metz, Oscar Martinez, Fred Morales, Ben Sanchez, Sam Sanchez, Susan Taylor, Miguel Teran, Gary Williams, and Pat Worthington, of the El Paso area. Francisco Ochoa Rodríguez of Ciudad Juárez, Mexico. Pat Beckett, John Bloom, Jon Hunner, Jean Fulton, and Ed Staski of the Las Cruces area. Tom Harper and Brenda Wilkinson in Socorro. Margaret Espinosa McDonald of Belen. Troy Ainsworth, Larry Castillo-Wilson, Henrietta

Christmas, Mary Deschane, Hal Jackson, Ann Massman, Joseph P. Sánchez, Samuel Sisneros, and John Taylor, of the Albuquerque area. Daniel Kosharek, Rene Harris, Pat Lucero, Aaron Mahr, Joy Poole, Jim Smith, and Michael Taylor of the Santa Fe area. Vice-President Saul Candelas and Dean Susana Rodarte of El Paso Community College also provided much support over the years. Numerous National Park Service and Bureau of Land Management people, and the officers and members of CARTA, the Camino Real de Tierra Adentro Trail Association, helped with many aspects of the work. Robin Russell patiently edited the manuscript and made innumerable valuable suggestions.

A few brief notes about the text. The Mexican segment of the El Camino Real de Tierra Adentro is not part of the United States National Trails System, but sites in the northern Chihuahua borderlands are included here because of their close proximity to, and complex historical connections to, the El Paso area and the Lower Valley. The maps are intended to give the reader a general overview of the trail. They are not to scale, and provide a mere sampling of geographic features and historical detail. Each entry in the book is designed to give the reader an overview, a general account of a site or region, and promote further interest in the varied landscape of El Camino Real de Tierra Adentro. Perhaps someone taking a brief tour with this modest book will be inspired to write the next great work on El Camino Real de Tierra Adentro.

—George D. Torok
El Paso, Texas
2012

Introduction

*E*l Camino Real de Tierra Adentro, the Royal Road of the Interior, was a 1,600-mile braid of trails that led from Mexico City, in the center of New Spain, to the provincial capital of New Mexico, on the edge of the empire's northern frontier. The Royal Road served as a lifeline for the colonial system from its founding in 1598 until the last days of Spanish rule in the 1810s. Throughout the Mexican and American Territorial periods, the Camino Real expanded, becoming part of a larger continental and international transportation system and, until the trail was replaced by railroads in the late nineteenth century, functioned as the main pathway for conquest, migration, settlement, commerce, and culture in today's American Southwest. More than 400 miles of the original trail lie within the United States today, and stretch from present-day San Elizario, Texas to Santa Fe, New Mexico. This segment comprises El Camino Real de Tierra Adentro National Historic Trail, added to the United States National Trail System in 2000, and now under the administration of the Bureau of Land Management and the National Park Service. The National Historic Trail, along with its lengthier and far more elaborate Mexican counterpart, commemorates Hispanic influence and serves to preserve and promote Native-American, Spanish, Mexican, and Anglo-American history and culture in the region. The 1,400-kilometer Mexican segment of the trail, and fifty-five associated sites from Mexico City to the United States border, was designated as a United Nations Educational, Scientific, and Cultural Organization World Heritage Site in 2010, establishing a further awareness of its contribution to our area of the world. In fact, El Camino Real de Tierra Adentro is one of the few historic trails that remains an active transportation corridor today and continues to shape and influence the borderlands and New Mexico, more than 400 years after its founding. But even though the Camino Real remains an energetic, vibrant influence, few people who live along its path are familiar with its history, or have even heard of its name.[1]

United States

San Juan Pueblo
Albuquerque
Santa Fe

El Paso
Juarez

Chihuahua

El Parral
Allende
Corralitos

Sea
of
Cortez

Mexico

Durango

Zacatecas
Aguascalientes
Lagos
Guanajuato
Guadalajara

Mexico City
Veracruz

Acapulco
Oaxaca

Gulf of

cean

Map of El Camino Real de Tierra Adentro. Courtesy National Park Service.

North Country NST

Nez Perce (Nee-Me-Poo) NHT

Lewis and Clark NHT

Oregon NHT

California NHT

Mormon Pioneer NHT

Pony Express NHT

Pacific Crest NST

United   States

Santa Fe NHT

Continental Divide NST

New Mexico

El Camino Real de Tierra Adentro National Historic Trail

Juan Bautista De Anza NHT

Texas

Mexico

The western segment of the National Trails System in the United States. Courtesy National Park Service.

Spain's Caminos Reales

Caminos Reales, or Royal Roads, originated in medieval Spain. They were modeled after the network of ancient Roman roads and were designed to connect the far reaches of the empire for administrative, military, and commercial purposes.[2] As Spaniards conquered the Aztec empire and colonized Mexico in the 1520s, they developed royal roads throughout the Americas. The first Camino Real in New Spain led from Veracruz west to Mexico City. Another reached north from the capital, winding through the colonial mining towns. By the 1540s, it turned north, to the interior, toward the silver boomtown of Zacatecas, and, forty years later, it reached the Santa Bárbara mining district, near modern-day Parral, Chihuahua. Other caminos reales led out of the capital like the spokes of a wheel, to the ocean coasts, and south, into Guatemala. The Camino Real de Tierra Adentro,[3] the Royal Road of the Interior, crossed the Chihuahuan Desert and reached the Rio Grande near today's El Paso, Texas. From there, it followed the Rio Grande Valley, reaching the northern pueblos and Santa Fe, and for almost 300 years served as a vital transportation system for Spanish, Mexican, and American travelers. The Camino Real de Tierra Adentro was a royal road, but most of its path bore little resemblance to the highways of medieval Europe. In the interior of New Spain, and in the immediate vicinity of major cities, the Camino Real sometimes appeared like an ancient roadway of the Roman Empire. Sections were graded and cobbled, bridges spanned waterways, drainage ditches kept the surfaces dry, and the landscape was periodically cleared. But in the countryside, especially in the northern Chihuahuan Desert, the Camino Real was merely a broad pathway, a cleared area that led through the wilderness. Often the trail simply followed the course of the river or moved along gravel benches on the mesas.[4]

Although Spaniards made these roadways an integral part of their colonial empire, many of the trails had been in use for centuries. Spanish explorers often followed well-traveled Native-American footpaths that had evolved over centuries to join villages throughout the Americas. Indians journeyed along these trails for hundreds, and perhaps, thousands of years and developed a web of ancient pathways that eventually connected the Aztec Empire of central Mexico with the Pueblo Indian settlements of the Rio Grande. By 1000 CE, a road network had been established through Chaco Canyon, home of the Anasazi, an Ancestral Pueblo group, in the Four Corners area of the American Southwest.

Like many Native-American trails, the Chaco road network appears to have been primarily a series of short road segments, not long distance corridors of travel and trade, and it is not clear whether Chaco Canyon roads were primarily economic or religious in origin.[5] Casas Grandes, in northwestern Chihuahua, emerged around 1000 CE as a major Native-American trading center. An Indian corridor known as the West Mexican Interior Trail connected Casas Grandes to central Mexico, passing through present-day Zacatecas and Durango, where a second trail crossed the sierra and led to the Pacific coast. Casas Grandes was also tied to the Rio Grande Pueblo Indian Trail, which led from the El Paso area north along the Rio Grande. Along these trails, goods from the interior and coastal areas, such as marine shells, parrots, copper objects, and macaw feathers, flowed north, while turquoise, pottery, salt, and flint were brought south. By the thirteenth century, the northern Rio Grande and Santa Fe River areas were home to sizable, expanding, pueblo-style villages and were the center of distinct Pajarito and Santa Fe cultures. Migrants from the north, especially from the Four Corners area, added to the growth. By the fourteenth century, large Keres, Tewa, and Tiwa-speaking Pueblo settlements dotted the valley landscape and spread along the future path of the Camino Real.[6]

The Piro Pueblo were descendants of the Jornada Mogollon, who shifted from a hunter-gatherer lifestyle to agriculture by the 800s CE. By the 1100s CE, they had spread along the Rio Grande, south of present-day Socorro, New Mexico, and further east and south, toward Texas. They built a series of adobe and masonry pueblos, similar to those in the north. Piro Pueblo settlements thrived for several hundred years, interacting with Anasazi and Casas Grandes people. By the late fifteenth century, the Piro were already in decline; they were far fewer in number, and many villages had been abandoned. The Mansos and Sumas, who lived further south along the river, were probably descendants of the later Piro Pueblo. Navajos and Apaches were latecomers to the region, probably arriving on the periphery by the 1300s CE from the Great Plains. Newcomers to the region often made use of, and added to, the Native-American transportation network in place. Although there is considerable debate about how much long distance travel regularly took place on these trails, they did become active trade corridors and allowed many peoples and their respective agricultural developments, including the first seeds of corn, to make their way into the American Southwest.[7]

During the sixteenth century, several Spanish expeditions explored the northern Rio Grande Valley. After being shipwrecked off the Texas coast, Alvar Núñez Cabeza de Vaca and three companions entered New Mexico and probably came through El Paso del Norte in 1535. In 1540, Francisco Vásquez de Coronado passed through today's Albuquerque area, by way of Arizona, and waged war against the Tiwa Pueblo along the way. The 1581 Rodríguez-Chamuscado expedition, led by Fray Augustín Rodríguez and military commander Francisco Sánchez Chamuscado, scouted the north in search of sites that could be developed as mission settlements. The next year, Antonio de Espejo, a wealthy Spaniard, and Fray Bernardino Beltrán led a similar expedition north along the banks of the river hoping to find precious minerals in the region. These explorers followed the Conchos River north to the Rio Grande and continued up the valley into the pueblos of present-day New Mexico. But unlike central Mexico, the northern pueblos offered no great riches or Aztec empires. They were the home of large agricultural communities and scattered nomadic tribes. Gaspar Castaño de Sosa led an unauthorized colonizing expedition up the Rio Grande in 1590 bringing the first carts and wagons onto what would soon become El Camino Real de Tierra Adentro in the north. The ill-fated expedition suffered many setbacks, and Castaño de Sosa was eventually arrested and imprisoned.[8] Interest in the region waned, and it was not until the mid-1590s that the Spanish took a second look at the far northern frontier.[9]

Don Juan de Oñate

In 1595, the colonial government contracted Juan de Oñate, a wealthy Spanish nobleman from Zacatecas, to extend the Camino Real north and establish another, or "New" Mexico. Oñate was well-respected among the colonial elite, had fought in many campaigns against area Indians, and his family operated some of the most productive silver mines in Zacatecas. He married Isabel de Tolosa Cortés Moctezuma, granddaughter of conquistador Hernando Cortés, and a descendant of the last Aztec emperor, Moctezuma. Although the Oñate family prided itself on its Spanish heritage, the marriage of the two brought the family into the process of *mestizaje*, mixing the white European blood and culture of the conquerors with the Native-American population of the New World. The Oñate family moved into an estate at Pánuco, near the mines and smelter, but spent much of their time in Mexico City. They eventually had two children, a son, Cristóbal, and a daughter, María. Despite his new family and mining enterprises, by the early 1590s, Juan de Oñate was planning to lead an *entrada*, a colonizing expedition, north. He was not alone. Several other influential men placed bids with the viceroy, but circumstances made Oñate the best choice, and a royal contract was signed in 1595. The terms of the contract were typical of Spanish Colonial entradas. Oñate needed to show that he commanded all the resources necessary for the endeavor. He was responsible for securing soldiers, settlers, and supplies, and making full arrangements for exploration. After many delays, in January 1598, the expedition set out from the San Gerónimo area and began its march north toward the Rio Grande. Most of the colonists traveled on foot. The total number of Oñate's followers can only be estimated but the official records of the expedition list 129 soldiers. Many brought their wives and families, but no list of women and children was ever made. The soldiers were mostly farmers, loyal to Oñate, hoping to receive a land grant in the new colony. There were also uncounted laborers, herders, drivers, servants, and slaves. Along with people of Spanish origins, there were many mestizos, mulattos, various Indian ethnicities, and some of African descent. A few were adventurers expecting great riches in the north. A party of Franciscan friars also accompanied the expedition. Altogether, there were perhaps 500 people traveling with Oñate into New Mexico. More than eighty carts and wagons, thousands of head of livestock, and hundreds of people formed a caravan train almost two miles long. *Carretas*, wooden carts drawn by oxen, and *carros*, two-wheeled wagons pulled by mules, were used to transport supplies and equipment.[10]

Oñate hoped to open a more direct route north, so a scouting team, headed by Sargento Mayor Vicente de Zaldívar, Oñate's nephew, led a sixteen-man party through the Chihuahuan Desert, carefully surveying the terrain. Far ahead of the caravan, the scouting party was often delayed and, at times, lost, but they were finally able to capture four natives whom they coerced into leading them to the river. On February 28, more than a month after leaving San Gerónimo, Zaldívar's scouts arrived at the Rio Grande. They returned south by March 10 and directed the caravan east. The Oñate expedition finally reached the banks of the Rio Grande on April 20, somewhere near present-day San Elizario, Texas. Oñate called for a celebration to give thanks for their survival, to formally initiate the colony, and to prepare for the long journey ahead. The Spanish were joined by local Manso Indians and held a great feast, sharing food and gifts. The missionaries performed a Catholic mass and, in a ceremony known as *La Toma* (the Taking), Don Juan de Oñate formally claimed the land for Spain. A few days later, the colonists, rested and inspired, resumed the journey. They crossed the river just above today's downtown El Paso and continued north along the east bank of the Rio Grande.[11]

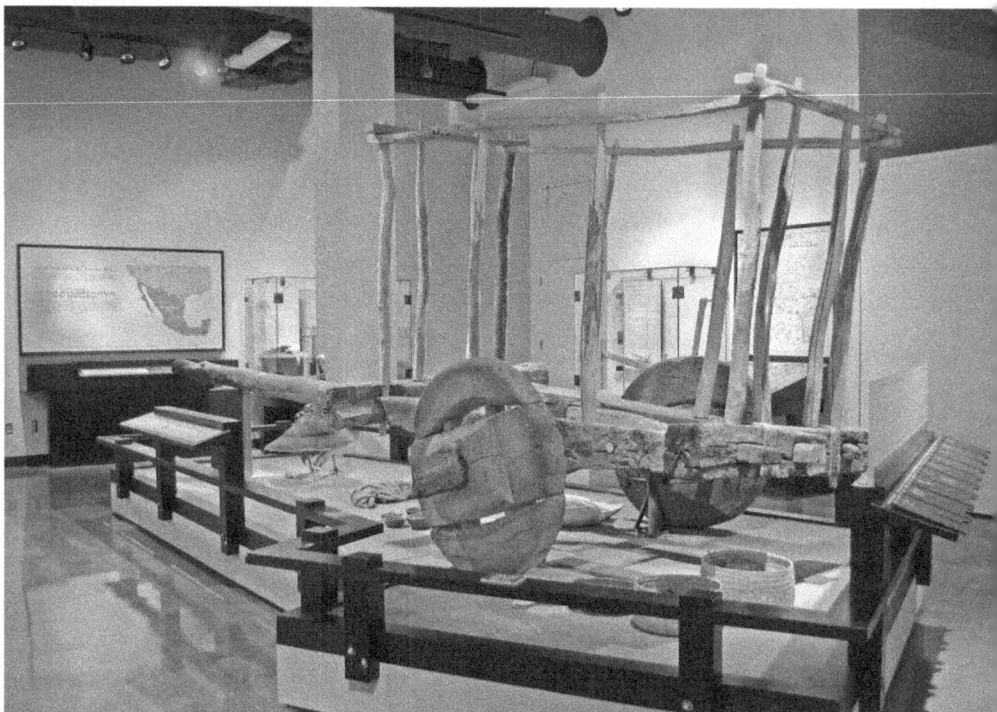

Replica of a Spanish Colonial *carreta,* or ox-cart, at the El Paso Museum of History.

For the next two months they extended the trail further north, finally arriving at the confluence of the Rio Grande and the Rio Chama, and eventually establishing a new provincial capital at the Tewa pueblo of Ohkay Owingeh, which they re-named San Juan Pueblo. But Oñate did not achieve his goal of creating a prosperous, stable colony. Indian resistance, disappointment with New Mexican lands, and dissent among the colonists plagued the expedition for ten years. It was not until 1609, with the founding of the Villa Real de Santa Fe by Oñate's successor, Governor Pedro de Peralta, that New Mexico became a permanent colonial settlement. By then, the Royal Road had been extended more than 650 miles and stretched from Mexico City to Santa Fe, a distance of more than 1,600 miles, thus becoming the lifeline of the northern Spanish Colonial system.[12]

During the entrada, Oñate became infamous for one particular event: the punishment of Indians at Acoma Pueblo. By the winter of 1598, the Oñate colonists were barely surviving, experiencing great hardships and suffering from shortages of food. Some had already deserted; others had growing doubts about the fate of the new colony. Some became desperate, stealing or extorting food from area pueblos, sometimes using force. The Pueblo Indians were increasingly fearful and resentful of the Spanish and began to strike back. At Acoma Pueblo, high atop an isolated mesa, another Oñate nephew, Juan de Zaldívar, and eleven soldiers were lured into the village and killed. In retaliation, Spaniards stormed the mesa, killing an unknown number of native men, women and children. The Indian survivors of the attack, about eighty men and perhaps 500 women and children, were taken prisoner and brought before Oñate. Beginning on February 9, 1599, public trials were conducted and punishments were handed down for the Acomans. All children under twelve were taken away by Franciscan friars, some deep into the interior of Mexico, to be raised in a proper Christian manner. They never saw their parents or homeland again. Both males and females between twelve and twenty-five years of age were condemned to twenty years of servitude. They were soon distributed among the Spanish colonists at San Juan and nearby pueblos. The more infamous part of the sentencing concerned men over the age of twenty-five. Although none were put to death, Oñate condemned each to have a single foot severed. It is unclear how many mutilations were made, but they were a public spectacle, carried out at Santo Domingo and several surrounding pueblos. There was nothing particularly unique or unusual about what Oñate had done. Sixteenth-century Europeans were subjected to the same cruel and unusual punishments on a regular basis. Burnings at the stake, beheadings, and mutilations were common. Native-American warriors also practiced barbarous acts, subjecting their captives to enslavement, ritual sacrifice, and various tortuous acts.[13] But in the twentieth century, the incident took on a far greater and more controversial meaning. The incident at Acoma became the focus of many debates and often created conflict between Native-American and revisionist scholars, and more traditional European-oriented students of history. By 1998, the year of the 400th anniversary of the Oñate expedition and the opening of the Camino Real, the controversy had brought many American Hispanics, proud of their Spanish traditions, into conflict with those of Native-American descent.[14]

The Equestrian, a portrayal of Juan de Oñate, a XII Travelers Memorial of the Southwest monument.

The Colonial Royal Road

By 1600, the Camino Real de Tierra Adentro had become a vital link between the interior of New Spain and the far northern reaches of the empire. But during the seventeenth century, the Royal Road was never a clearly defined, linear roadway. Travelers navigated the trail, watching for changes in the terrain and often choosing alternate routes depending on seasonal conditions. Floodwaters, shifts in river channels, and debris and mud erased segments of the road. Users of the road moved around these obstacles, headed for higher ground, and followed alternative routes that became a net-like series of branch roads, resulting in new routes through the countryside. Small spurs stemmed from the main roads, leading to haciendas, missions, plaza settlements or parajes. Often, trail ruts, swales from previous journeys, and worn patches in the landscape were the only signs of a roadway. Some routes were used for caravans, wagon trains, and mule-drawn vehicles. Others were only suited for small parties traveling on foot or horseback. These *ramales*, or alternate routes, sometimes became major thoroughfares linking new communities and encouraging new trade patterns. Turn-outs on the trail guided travelers around features in the landscape or led them to sources of water at places such as the San Diego paraje or Laguna and Ojo del Muerto in the Jornada del Muerto. A number of prominent landmarks served as beacons and pathways on El Camino Real de Tierra Adentro. Travelers moved north through El Paso Canyon and into the broad Mesilla Valley, west of the Organ Mountains. The Doña Ana and Robledo Mountains guided them along the river, and, after stopping at Paraje San Diego, they aimed for Point of Rocks, an outcrop that led into the Jornada del Muerto. As they crossed the Jornada del Muerto Basin, the Caballo, Fray Cristobal, and San Andres ranges remained in view, and Lava Gate led them toward Black Mesa and the river once again. They crossed the Bosque del Apache wetlands, adjacent to the Magdalena Mountains west of the river. Further north, Tomé Hill became a convenient scouting site, and beyond Albuquerque, the trail led past rugged mesas among ancient pueblos. Travelers entered Tewa country and the Española Valley or climbed La Bajada and continued across the plains to Santa Fe. After Oñate was recalled and a new provincial capital was established at Santa Fe, the main route of the trail shifted east. But few improvements were made on the road, especially in the north along the path of today's National Historic Trail. Occasionally a bridge was built over the Rio Grande, but was quickly washed away. Dams protected a few segments of the trail, and mud and debris were periodically cleared from the roadbed. Overtime, most of these improvements were for naught.[15]

The early Camino Real connected a series of mission settlements. Franciscans accompanied Oñate during the 1598 expedition, and by mid-summer they were assigned to pueblos throughout the new colony. Friars spread out along the trail and began converting, as well as Hispanicizing, the native populations. The Spanish system of *reducción* managed Indians by concentrating them. Whole communities were moved from small, outlying pueblos into mission settlements. Diseases had already greatly reduced their numbers, and new labor systems took their toll on the remaining populations. Once sequestered in the Spanish missions, natives were converted to Catholicism, and, to make the settlements viable, missionaries introduced European agricultural techniques, new crops and livestock, and organized natives to produce food for the Spanish colonists. Missionaries also taught the Indians to speak Spanish and to pursue a "civilized" Christian life. Some missions became large towns with thousands of residents while others remained small, modest settlements, each with a church and a handful of friars. Mansos and Sumas were lured into settlements near the Pass of the North. Missionaries clustered Piros into a small number of pueblos along the Rio Abajo. Further north, where larger Indian pueblos were more common, the friars usually built churches within existing Tiwa, Keres, and Tewa settlements and drew similar ethnic groups into the mission system. In theory, missionaries saw themselves as protectors of the Indians but many abuses were allowed to take place. The *Encomenderos* and many local political officials held rights of *encomienda* entitling them to large land grants and the use of Indian labor. They often mistreated the natives. They moved them to distant locations, forced them to accompany caravans, and put them to work in agriculture and industry.[16]

The Franciscan missionary network of New Spain was based in Mexico City, and, shortly after the settlement of New Mexico, a caravan system was developed to outfit, supply, and communicate with the many missions established in the new province. During the seventeenth century, caravans visited the missions about every three years, transporting basic necessities, sacred ornaments and vestments, supplies and luxury items, as well as news and information from other parts of New Spain. Mule-drawn wagon trains made the trip north in the fall, arrived in the spring, and spent the summer months in Santa Fe before their return. As the members of the caravans and frontier colonists exchanged goods, they helped to develop a trade network along the trail and a system of inter-mission exchange. After outfitting mission sites on the outgoing journey, caravans returned loaded with goods produced in the north. The sale of surplus corn, wheat, cattle, sheep, hides, salt, nuts, and textiles from the north to the south helped to keep the mission system alive. The entire cycle would take more than eighteen months, just enough time to start preparations for the next caravan out of Mexico City. The government of New Spain assisted the Franciscans' caravan system. Friars created a basic infrastructure while the colonial government aided with funding, personnel, and Indian labor.[17] Frontiersmen who lived in Mexico City and were familiar with travel on the Camino Real de Tierra Adentro were often contracted as guards or scouts to accompany caravans north into New Mexico. These *escoltas*, or escorts, were formally organized in the capital, to accompany mission supply caravans, or small parties venturing into the frontier. By the eighteenth century, escoltas led merchant wagon trains north through the mining towns and on to Santa Fe. Military men were preferred for the escorts but anyone who had spent time on the frontier might be considered.[18]

A typical caravan had about seventy people in thirty to thirty-five wagons with teams of wagon drivers, Indian scouts, servants and cooks, friars, and government officials. Over time, merchants joined the caravans. Large-wheeled carretas pulled by oxen made their way along the trail for short trips and long distance hauling was done with mule teams. These covered wagons had four iron-tired wheels and carried loads of about two tons. Eight mules pulled a wagon and a second team followed to alternate with the first. Wagon trains carried an amazing amount of freight, about eighty tons in each caravan, and averaged about twelve miles a day on the northern stretch of the trail. These wagon trains included a great variety of livestock. For example, a 1631 caravan had 544 mules, 72 heads of cattle, 200 sheep, 250 heifers, and numerous chickens. Livestock provided a source of food for caravan travelers and was used to help start new missions or supply residents.[19] Fray Alonso de Benavides (c.1580–1664), served as *custos*, or Father Custodian of New Mexico, in the 1620s. In 1626, he and twelve other friars joined a mission caravan as it made its way north. He placed the twelve friars at sites throughout the province, established new missions among the Piro and Tompiro, built new churches at Socorro and Santa Fe, and founded new *conventos*, or residences for friars, at several sites. During his extensive travels along the Camino Real de Tierra

Adentro and into remote areas of the kingdom, Benavides kept careful notes and compiled a detailed report, the *Memorial*, of his work.[20]

The arrival of a caravan was an exciting event in Camino Real settlements. Lead wagons, covered with decorated *rebozos*, or blankets, rang bells as they entered the town. Other wagons flew colorful banners displaying royal coats of arms. Government officials traveled in luxurious horse-drawn coaches while merchants, ordinary travelers, Indian laborers, and slaves followed. Herded animals stirred clouds of dust that could be seen for miles. Travelers brought news from the interior. Local missionaries looked forward to receiving new items for their churches such as statues, altarpieces, organs, vestments, and paintings. Basic foodstuffs such as beans, bacon, oils, and nuts re-stocked the missions. Caravans also created opportunities for farmers and craftsmen to trade goods and purchase items not available locally. Basic tools, medicines, and kitchen supplies could be purchased along with exotic luxury items such as ceramics, fine cloth, or chocolate. As they headed south along the Camino Real, they gathered mission goods such as wool, piñon nuts, hides, and salt. In El Paso they stocked up on wheat, corn, wines, and brandies. Caravan merchants sold these goods in Parral or Zacatecas, and used the earnings to buy supplies in Mexico City for the next journey. In this manner, supply caravans kept the mission system and the entire province of New Mexico alive for many generations.[21]

Missions also served as campsites along the Camino Real. Travelers faced many hardships as they crossed hundreds of miles of open desert lands with few sources of food or water. Only an occasional spring provided relief. Good campsites, where travelers could find water, rest their animals, or spend the night at missions or haciendas, were few and far between. Campsites became known as *parajes*, places where fresh water, firewood, abundant fish and game were available. The Guadalupe Mission, established in 1659 at the Pass of the North, became the largest and the most important way-station on the Camino Real in the north, the only significant settlement between Santa Bárbara and Santa Fe.

The Pueblo Indian Revolt

Mission life was shattered in August 1680 when the largest Indian revolt in the colonial history of the Americas took place in northern New Mexico. In the decades preceding the revolt, Native-Americans were devastated by European diseases, forced to labor under harsh conditions, and abused by corrupt officials. Following a new wave of epidemics and drought in the 1670s, Spaniards cracked down on a resurgence of traditional native religious practices. On August 10, the feast day of San Lorenzo, many Pueblo tribes united in their assault, killing hundreds of Spanish settlers and missionaries, looting haciendas, and destroying mission churches. The violence and chaos of the rebellion divided the province. One group of Rio Arriba survivors huddled in Santa Fe, overseen by Governor Antonio Otermín and a small garrison of troops. A second group, from the Rio Abajo, gathered by Lieutenant Governor Alonso García, sought protection in the Tiwa pueblo of Isleta. Both fleeing parties escaped and marched into the Jornada del Muerto where they eventually met up at the paraje of Fray Cristobal. From there, the 2,000 Spanish and Indian survivors fled down the Camino Real de Tierra Adentro to the safety of El Paso del Norte. Many were eventually re-settled at a series of missions and civil communities along the Rio Grande, south of the Pass. For the next twelve years, El Paso del Norte was the northern terminus of the Royal Road and the headquarters for efforts to re-gain control of the province. In 1692, Governor Diego de Vargas led a small force from El Paso del Norte into the interior to recapture New Mexico and pacify the native population. At first, Vargas was able to negotiate with individual Pueblo tribes but the intended re-conquest quickly turned into a military operation. It took several years to arrange a peace with various Indian factions and re-establish the Villa of Santa Fe. In 1696, a second rebellion challenged Spanish authority, but Governor Vargas was able to bring the situation under control fairly quickly and finally restore order in the north.[22]

Eighteenth Century Changes

After the re-conquest, eighteenth-century settlement patterns changed along the trail. Many mission settlements were never again occupied. Rather than large *encomienda* grants of land and labor, the colonial government encouraged homesteads and *ejidos*, or community grants. Pioneers settled in remote, isolated areas and attempted to farm and ranch along the river. Many mission settlements evolved into small towns, drawing more Spanish and mestizo residents. Parish churches replaced some of the missionary system, and new *villas*, or official administrative centers, were established at Albuquerque, La Cañada, and Chihuahua City. Spaniards re-organized their presidios and oversaw peace programs to pacify native populations. The mission caravan system faded, and new commercial ventures made use of the Camino Real to transport goods to market. Sheep ranching thrived in the north and livestock were driven south to the mining centers of the interior. Regional trade fairs extended the braid of trails that connected with the Camino Real de Tierra Adentro and created a more intricate network of commerce. Over time, branch roads of the Camino Real de Tierra Adentro reached north into areas beyond San Juan Pueblo and Santa Fe. Routes led northeast from La Cañada through Chimayó, Truchas, and onto the Taos area, and from San Juan Pueblo to the edge of the Great Plains.[23]

Native-American trade had existed for hundreds of years in the Taos area where buffalo hides and dried meats were bartered for corn, squash, beans, and blankets. In the early years of the eighteenth century, a new native empire emerged. The Comanches, who were nomadic hunter-gathers recently arrived from the central Great Plains, displaced Apaches, overran other Native-American and Spanish settlements, and created a vast new imperial system in the northern frontier. These skilled horsemen engaged in hunting, trading, raiding, slaving, diplomacy, and commercial expansion for the next 130 years. Their empire restrained the growth of European and Anglo-American settlements and impacted communities along the northern stretch of the Camino Real de Tierra Adentro. The Comanches remained nomadic, but established relationships with individual towns, presidios, missions, and agricultural communities rather than negotiate formal arrangements with colonial and territorial governments.[24] The Spanish tried to pacify the Comanches, partly because they feared raids on colonial settlements, but also because alienating the Comanches might strengthen the tribe's ties with French or American interests further east. Thus, Spanish Colonial officials often tried to court the natives, supporting trade fairs, exchanging goods, and offering gifts. In the late colonial era, Comanche chiefs routinely visited Santa Fe and were welcomed as guests. In fact, by the 1760s, the Comanches sometimes had better access to firearms and ammunition than Spanish troops or frontier settlers. They obtained weapons in the east, from French traders or through Indian alliances, and sold or bartered them in Camino Real communities. By the 1770s, Comanche expansion sparked wars with the Apaches and drove many back into southern New Mexico and west Texas, making it easier for peace programs to proceed.[25] Trade fairs were major events, and, during the Spanish Colonial era, warring tribes declared truces and cautiously mingled at Taos. Spaniards and Tiwa-speaking Taos Indians traded with Utes, Kiowas, Navajos, Comanches, and Apaches. French and American fur trappers ventured into northern New Mexico and also traded at the fairs. Trade at Taos was less formal than the organized caravan efforts on the Camino Real. Far from Santa Fe and well off the main trail, Spanish customs regulations and official proceedings were lax, if not absent altogether.[26] Over time, conflicts with the Comanches declined, and, by the early years of the nineteenth century, the natives had shifted their commercial activities east, away from the Rio Grande and Taos, and toward the Pecos and Mora Valleys.[27]

Eighteenth-century Spain, concerned with the growing power of France and Great Britain in North America, instituted a series of reforms, including a review of military posts along the frontier. In 1758, engineer Bernardo de Miera y Pacheco (c.1720–1785) mapped areas of New Mexico, noting settlements and parajes along the trail. In 1767, the Marqués de Rubí, a field marshall, conducted a general inspection of the north. Nicolás de Lafora (c.1730–?), the expedition's cartographer, produced maps of the Camino Real, and Joseph Ramón de Urrutia y de Las Casas (1739–1803), a military engineer, drew plans of the villas of El Paso del Norte and Santa Fe. Church officials also traveled the Camino Real in the mid-eighteenth century conducting *visitas*, or official visits, to mission settlements and new parishes in the north. Bishop Pedro Tamarón y Romeral toured the province in 1760, and Fray Atanasio Domínguez filed detailed reports on missions, haciendas, towns, and villas during his extensive 1776 review of New Mexico. Their reports provided details such as population figures, the design and layout of settlements, and general observations about the cultural, economic, and political conditions in the frontier. Pedro Vial, a French-born Indian trader, explored the area east of New Mexico in the 1780s and 1790s, opening diplomatic discussions with the Comanches and other tribes of the lower Great Plains. His travels through the region established a new route across the plains, which became the Santa Fe Trail of the 1820s.[28]

The turn of the nineteenth century brought further international intrigue. French traders continued to penetrate the colonial frontier. When the Louisiana Territory became part of the United States in 1803, Anglo-Americans ventured into Spanish territory. In 1806, Lieutenant Zebulon Montgomery Pike (1779–1813) led an expedition west, but he and his men were arrested by a New Mexican patrol, they were held at Santa Fe, and then escorted south to the command center at Chihuahua City. Colonial officials investigated, and, after interviewing the men, returned them to the United States. A few years later, Pike published his journals, the first Anglo-American account of the Camino Real, and piqued further interest in the Spanish Colonial frontier. By the time Pike's work was in circulation, Spain faced a series of rebellions in its colonies, including one led by Father Miguel Hidalgo y Costilla that led to Mexican independence eleven years later. Even though the Spanish drove foreign traders out of the north and made occasional efforts to enforce commercial restrictions, the days of the Camino Real as a major royal colonial highway were rapidly coming to an end.[29]

The Mexican Era

After Mexican independence in 1821, the Camino Real became the *Camino Nacional,* the National Road, and continued to be the main transportation system through the north, but a second road opened, heading west from the United States. William Becknell, a Missouri trader who ventured into northern New Mexico, was the first Anglo-American to formally establish relations with the new republic and organize traffic across the Great Plains to Santa Fe, through some of the territory explored by Pedro Vial in the late eighteenth century. Pack horses and mule trains carried wares west as traders brought goods from Missouri to New Mexico along the Santa Fe Trail (designated a National Historic Trail in 1987), and then began freighting south along the old Camino Real to Chihuahua City.[30] This northern segment of the trail, linking Santa Fe with Chihuahua, became known as the Chihuahua Trail. Just as the world of New Spain had been transported north, the trail now brought the Anglo-American world south. Mexicans became familiar with United States manufactured goods, especially textiles, woolens, bottles, dry goods, and hardware, and American merchants reaped enormous profits. Goods from the Pass, especially wines and brandies, became popular export items and were purchased by American traders for resale elsewhere. Pack mules were the most common mode of transport, but Anglo-American traders also introduced Conestoga wagons, iron-tired wooden vehicles that were drawn by mule teams. Placing large sheets of canvas over wooden frames created the "covered" wagons common throughout the mid-century American West.[31] In 1844, Josiah A. Gregg (1806–1850) published *Commerce of the Prairies*. It lured adventurers from the Ohio and Mississippi Valleys to the lucrative, but often erratic, overland trade. Anglo-American businessmen frequently worked with Mexican merchants and developed intricate trading networks along the trail. Some married into prominent Mexican families and extended their influence far beyond their commercial ventures. Americans also moved into Mexican territories seeking land grants available under the republic's new colonization acts of the 1820s.

Santa Fe was also the eastern terminus of the Old Spanish Trail (designated as a National Historic Trail in 2002), that connected two Mexican provinces, New Mexico and California, and linked the interior of the northern frontier with international markets in the Pacific. There were several eighteenth-century attempts to blaze a route from the villa, but it was not until 1829 that Santa Fe merchant Antonio Armijo opened a trail that led west through Colorado and Utah and eventually to Los Angeles. Blankets and assorted products from Santa Fe, including goods that came north along the Camino Real and west along the Santa Fe Trail, were taken to California in mule trains where they were traded for horses that were brought back to the Rio Arriba. Increased trade, traffic, and settlement brought further tensions between Mexican settlers and Indians in the 1830s, especially along the trade routes. The Mexican military waged a series of wars against the Apaches, and local vigilante groups often fought their own campaigns. Native-Americans, greatly reduced in numbers and no longer protected by missions, lost more land, trade, and influence.

Although international trade brought benefits to the region, tensions developed as American merchants competed directly with Mexicans in the Chihuahua City area. In the 1830s, some Mexican officials feared that continued American activities in Chihuahua and New Mexico might lead to annexation by Texas. In response, the Mexican government tightened restrictions on foreign trade and enacted new import duties. In 1835, officials established a customhouse at El Paso del Norte. Texas independence raised further concerns and President Mirabeau B. Lamar's ill-fated Texan-Santa Fe Expedition of 1841, suspected of being a plan for invasion, increased tensions between Mexico and the new republic. Journalist George Wilkins Kendall (1809–1867), along with most of the expedition, was captured in northern New Mexico and taken south, as a prisoner of the Mexican army. Kendall's published accounts of the long, cold, trek in the dead of winter at the hands of cruel Mexican soldiers, added fuel to the fire. The survivors did not receive any adequate food or medical attention until they were cared for by Father Ramón Ortiz at El Paso del Norte.[32]

Soon, new documents and mercantile passports were required for foreign merchants. Trade continued, and, in the 1840s, well-stocked American merchants reaped profits of fifty to one hundred per cent. Making the venture even more attractive, Chihuahua, a prosperous mining town, offered payment in silver. American merchants had several advantages over Mexicans: they had better connections to trade centers in the United States, they brought a much greater variety of goods into Chihuahua, and they had more capital available to finance large caravans. Local Chihuahuan merchants also complained that Americans violated many Mexican laws, bypassed regulations, negotiated their own taxes and fees, and stole livestock along the way. As time passed, trade brought many American goods south, but fewer Mexican products were transported north. Americans soon monopolized trade along the Chihuahua Trail.[33]

The old Camino Real played an important strategic role when war broke out between the United States and Mexico in 1846. General Stephen W. Kearny led 1,700 American troops into New Mexico along the Santa Fe Trail, and, after securing the provincial capital, served as its first military governor. In August, Kearny led his Army of the West toward California, and Colonel Alexander W. Doniphan remained in charge of New Mexico. After dealing with Navajo raids in the north and securing a peace with the Zunis and Utes, he led his First Regiment Missouri Mounted Volunteers down the Camino Real toward Chihuahua City. They met up with a large American merchant caravan of about 300 wagons near the paraje of Valverde. Doniphan ordered the caravan to follow behind his army as they made their way south. On Christmas Day, his troops defeated Mexican forces at the campsite of Brazito. They continued on to El Paso del Norte with the merchant caravan in tow, took control of the old villa, and eventually moved down the trail and defeated Mexican troops once again at Sacramento. American forces took possession of Chihuahua City on March 2, 1847. Several people who traveled with Kearny, Doniphan, and the wagon train wrote accounts of their experiences along the trail. Lieutenant James William Abert (1820–1897), joined Lieutenant William G. Peck at Santa Fe and the two explored New Mexico, venturing as far south as Socorro. Abert filed a report that was later published. British soldier-of-fortune George Ruxton and volunteer George R. Gibson also kept detailed notes of their experiences. Susan Shelby Magoffin, the young bride of a Santa Fe trader, kept a diary of her journey south with Doniphan. Friedrich Adolph Wislizenus (1810–1889), was a naturalist and was trained as a medical doctor. His notes on the journey focused on the terrain, geology, botany, and natural environment along the old Royal Road.[34]

In 1848, the Treaty of Guadalupe Hidalgo ceded half of Mexico's territory to the United States, made the Rio Grande an international boundary, and severed the Chihuahua Trail. The northern end of the Camino Real, now located in the United States, served as a route between Santa Fe and American El Paso. The southern segment of the Camino Real in Mexico connected El Paso del Norte with Chihuahua and Mexico City. El Paso del Norte was now an entryway to the Mexican interior. Boundary commissioners and surveyors also published detailed works that described areas along the trail.[35]

The Territorial Trail

During the 1830s, short, regional stagecoach lines operated in Texas. They connected scattered communities in the east and carried mail, light freight, and passengers through the republic. After the war, they ventured further west and segments of the old Camino Real became important links to new western American roads. In 1849, two expeditions scouted routes from San Antonio to the El Paso area. William H.C. Whiting and Lieutenant William F. Smith followed a southerly course through Texas. Major Robert S. Neighbors of the Texas Rangers traveled in the north, across the Pecos River, and through the Guadalupe Mountains. These two new roads met the old Camino Real and became new lines of transport for the military, pioneer settlers, and commercial traders. United States Army Captain Randolph B. Marcy led his men from Fort Smith, Arkansas, to Santa Fe, down the Rio Grande Valley to Doña Ana, and east into the Sacramento Mountains. In 1853, William W.H. Davis was appointed United States District Attorney for New Mexico. He traveled extensively throughout the Territory and published *El Gringo*, an account of his impressions.[36] United States Post Office contracts were signed to serve new western territories, and each month coaches carried mail and passengers along these new routes. Legendary stage drivers such as Henry Skillman and William Alexander "Bigfoot" Wallace commandeered coaches through the wild, West Texas plains and into New Mexico. The route from El Paso north followed much of the path of the old Camino Real and enabled travelers to reach Santa Fe in as few as eight days. Coaches crossed the Jornada del Muerto, endured Apache attacks, camped at Fray Cristóbal, and followed the river north to the old villa. By the mid-1850s, Skillman was supervising mail delivery to San Diego, California. Unlike the slow wagon trains and caravans of the Spanish Colonial and Mexican era, travel in a stagecoach was fast and grueling, and early western roads were primitive and dangerous. Wagons tipped over, horses were injured and abandoned along the way, axles were shattered, and flash floods obliterated the trail. One traveler reported having seen more than sixty wagons, along with many dead and dying animals, strewn along the stretch between El Paso and the Guadalupe Mountains.[37]

James B. Leach was contracted by the War Department to improve the Franklin (El Paso) to Yuma Road through the Gadsden Purchase. In 1857, much of the old Camino Real between the Pass and La Mesilla was cleared, widened and re-routed. Although never constructed, proposals were also made to build bridges across the river at Frontera and La Mesilla. In September 1858, a new long-distance transportation system was pioneered by John Butterfield. His 2,700-mile Overland Mail ran letters, packages, and passengers from the end of the railroad at Tipton, Missouri to San Francisco. Stages pulled by four-or six-horse teams made the one-way trip in about twenty-five days. Approximately every twenty miles along the route, they built stations where passengers could be fed and teams of horses and mules could be watered or changed.[38] Henry Skillman drove the first Overland Mail into El Paso, arriving after ninety-six hours of non-stop driving, on September 30, 1858. The Butterfield Overland followed several routes through Texas, including the Mission Trail of the Camino Real de Tierra Adentro. From El Paso, it continued along the old Camino Real north as far as Fort Fillmore before veering off to the west.[39]

During the American Civil War, the trail provided a path for Confederate troops as they attempted to seize control of New Mexico. In 1861, the Southern army entered El Paso and occupied Fort Bliss before heading up the trail to capture Fort Fillmore, near Las Cruces. In February 1862, Brigadier General Henry H. Sibley led 2,500 Confederate troops further up the Rio Grande Valley where they encountered Union forces, including the First New Mexico Volunteers, at Valverde, a well-known Camino Real paraje. Both sides suffered heavy casualties in the engagement, forcing the Union troops to retreat to Fort Craig. General Sibley continued up the trail, laying plans for the capture of New Mexico, Arizona, and the ports of California. He and his troops seized Santa Fe on March 10 and prepared to move east toward Fort Union. But Sibley's battle-worn troops were defeated at Glorieta Pass, in the Sangre de Cristo Mountains east of Santa Fe, and retreated south to Texas, ending the Confederate army's attempt to gain control of New Mexico.[40]

In the late 1870s, railroads penetrated New Mexico and headed down the Rio Grande Valley toward West Texas. They followed the path of the Camino

Real de Tierra Adentro through the Territory and brought an end to the days of long distance wagon traffic on the trail. The Atchison, Topeka, and Santa Fe Railway left Kansas in 1869 and reached Pueblo, Colorado by 1876. Two years later it entered Raton Pass. The Denver and Rio Grande Railroad followed the Rocky Mountains south from Denver and into northern New Mexico. By February 1880, the Atchison, Topeka, and Santa Fe paralleled the path of the Santa Fe Trail through Las Vegas and into the capital. From there, it cut south into the Rio Grande Valley, along the route of the Camino Real, reaching Albuquerque in mid-April. By the end of 1880, the Atchison, Topeka, and Santa Fe had arrived at the new railroad town of San Marcial, continuing down the east bank of the Rio Grande, and through the Jornada del Muerto. The rails veered west to Rincon where a spur was to meet the Southern Pacific Railroad as it made its way from California. From Rincon, the Atchison, Topeka, and Santa Fe continued south along the trail through the Mesilla Valley toward American El Paso where it was scheduled to meet up with the Southern Pacific and Mexican rail lines. The Southern Pacific line arrived in El Paso in May 1881 and was joined by the Atchison, Topeka, and Santa Fe later in the summer. With El Paso, Texas as a major railroad junction, transportation in the American West was never quite the same. Now, goods and people could move rapidly along a north-south and east-west network which replaced the slow, rutted trails of the old colonial, Mexican and Territorial road systems. Farming, ranching, mining and smelting boomed. At the same time, Mexican rails reached north from Mexico City and headed south from El Paso del Norte. International rail traffic crossed bridges at American El Paso and continued into the Mexican interior. United States Army Captain John G. Bourke (1846–1896), served on the staff of General George Crook, and spent much of the early 1880s traveling the old road and reporting on Indian populations along the Rio Grande and the impact of the rails. With the arrival of the railroads, the old Camino Real was quickly relegated to a secondary route for regional travel and commerce. It served local needs but lost its importance as a major economic, political, and cultural thoroughfare. The days of the great long distance trail had finally come to an end.[41]

Twentieth Century Changes

Though diminished in usage, the Camino Real de Tierra Adentro never quite disappeared. The rails usually followed the route of the trail, often laid directly over the old roadbed. In many areas, the trail was just off the tracks, and functioned as a service road for workers to maintain the rails. The old Camino Real continued to link local communities and connected with other trail networks throughout the region. By the early twentieth century, the path of the Camino Real became the base for new automobile routes through New Mexico, West Texas, and Chihuahua. In 1903, the New Mexico Legislature passed a bill making "El Camino Real" a public highway through the Territory. By 1915, the State Highway Commission had published maps and brochures guiding motorists along its route. The Ocean-to-Ocean Highway, an early transcontinental route, paralleled the old roadway in areas of New Mexico's Rio Abajo. The Federal Highway Act of 1921 authorized federal matching funds to help states improve automobile roads. In New Mexico, the old Camino Real was revived with north-south highway improvements, and segments were used for some of the first federal highways in the region. The road became a branch of US 85 which led from the Mexican border in El Paso, along the Rio Grande, north through the central region of the state, and on to Albuquerque. US 66 crossed through La Bajada, making use of old segments of the trail, and wound through the Rio Arriba. Roadbeds were graded, graveled, and even paved in some areas to allow county and state highways to follow the old trail.[42] A Texas automobile road traced the old Mission Trail of the Camino Real through settlements of El Paso's Lower Valley. In Mexico, the coach road to Chihuahua City followed the old trail along the river in northern Chihuahua. Mexican Federal Highway 45, opened in the 1940s, served as a Pan-American thoroughfare to the interior, following the trail south from Ciudad Juárez. Today's Interstate 25, north from El Paso, Texas, whisks travelers alongside much of the old Camino Real de Tierra Adentro through the Land of Enchantment.[43]

With the expansion and re-numbering of highway systems by mid-century the Camino Real de Tierra Adentro was all but forgotten. Scholars writing of the Spanish Colonial past understood its importance and influence, but seldom examined the trail itself.[44] In many places, the trail was gone, graded, built over, or plowed under. By mid-century, there were few visible traces of the trail left. It was not until the 1980s that the Camino Real de Tierra Adentro drew the focused attention of scholars. Archaeological surveys, conferences, and minor publications began to revive interest. During the 1990s, the National Park Service and the Bureau of Land Management studied the feasibility of including the Camino Real in the National Trails System, as the nation's first historic trail dedicated to Hispanic heritage. By 2000, it was officially designated as a National Historic Trail and placed under the joint administration of the two federal agencies.

In 2003, the Camino Real de Tierra Adentro Trail Association (CARTA), was founded as a citizens' partner organization for the trail. In 2005, El Camino Real de Tierra Adentro International Heritage Center was designated as a New Mexico State Monument and opened its doors to visitors. Since then, local, state, and federal historical markers, trail signs, and wayside exhibits have been erected at sites along the trail in the United States. Today, the 404-mile El Camino Real de Tierra Adentro National Historic Trail winds through West Texas and New Mexico, creating a heritage tourism corridor that parallels ancient Indian footpaths and the old Spanish Colonial roadway. This book describes historic sites and settlements along El Camino Real de Tierra Adentro National Historic Trail and a series of Mexican communities across the river at the Pass of the North. Examining the development of these sites and highlighting their historic landscapes will lead to a deeper experience of the national historic trail, and communities and associations will be able to finally commemorate the rich and complex story of this ancient roadway.

1

North through the Chihuahuan Desert

When the Oñate expedition set out in January 1598, the Camino Real led more than 1,000 miles from Mexico City through the mining towns of Querétaro, Zacatecas, and Durango, and into the northern frontier. The road ended at Santa Bárbara, a small, out-of-the-way mining community of a few hundred Spaniards and Indian laborers. Oñate's colonists camped at nearby Valle de San Bartolomé, now called Valle de Allende, located on the San Gregorio River, a tributary of the Rio Conchos that flowed northeast toward the Rio Grande. Earlier expeditions north had followed the Rio Conchos to the Rio Grande, and then stayed along the river as it meandered west into today's New Mexico. Oñate's scouts blazed a new trail away from the Rio Conchos, directly north, through 200 miles of the Chihuahuan Desert to the Rio Grande. After reaching today's El Paso/Ciudad Juárez area, Oñate's colonial caravan opened another 400 miles of roadway, pressing forward to the Tewa pueblo of Ohkay Owingeh where it established the first provincial capital of New Mexico. The 404-mile segment north of the Pass is now designated as El Camino Real National Historic Trail.[1]

After the founding of New Mexico, the mining frontier continued to advance north. By 1709, Chihuahua City was founded and nine years later it was designated as a colonial villa. Still, the Royal Road north from Chihuahua City remained an open, difficult, desolate, and often dangerous route, and by mid-century, the only inhabited site between Chihuahua City and El Paso del Norte was *Carrizal*, the Reeds, an isolated oasis, established as the last refuge for weary Camino Real de Tierra Adentro travelers. In 1758, the town of San Fernando was founded and by 1774 a new military post, *Presidio de San Fernando de Carrizal*, the Fortress of Saint Ferdinand of the Reeds, had been established there to take the war to the Apache frontier and protect traffic along the trail.[2] Spaniards built a walled fortress-village where as many as 300 soldiers and their families lived. The troops patrolled Apache strongholds and often accompanied large caravans along stretches of the trail that were particularly dangerous. Colonial-and Mexican-era travelers sought refuge at Carrizal, camped outside the post, and listened closely to information gathered by military scouts.[3] The fort remained active until the Mexican-American War, when it was abandoned as Colonel Doniphan's troops invaded the state of Chihuahua.[4] The town of Carrizal continued to have a small population long after its days as a presidio. Today, it is a quiet village, about ten miles southwest of Villa Ahumada, off of Mexican Federal Highway 45. The fortress is no longer intact, but a series of small adobe mounds reveal its outline.[5]

The Lower Valley and Ciudad Juárez

El Camino Real de Tierra Adentro through the Lower Valley and Ciudad Juárez.

The Oñate expedition camped at San Vicente, about fifteen miles north of Carrizal. It became known as *Lago de Patos*, the Lake of the Ducks, named for the water fowl that were often in the area, and it became an important marker on the trail because just beyond, near a site known as *Ojo Lucero*, the Bright Spring, the Camino Real de Tierra Adentro forked, offering two different routes into the Pass of the North.[6] The Oñate expedition had hoped to blaze the trail straight north through the Chihuahuan Desert to the Rio Grande, but after stopping near Ojo Lucero, the desert landscape became more ominous. Advance patrols entered *Los Médanos de Samalayuca*, the Samalayuca Sand Dunes, and discovered a formidable barrier of blowing and shifting sand that covered almost 800 square miles and still challenges modern travelers along Mexican Highway 45.

The harsh, barren landscape of the Chihuahuan Desert presented formidable challenges to trail travelers.

Oñate's scouts reported that it would be impossible to cross the dunes with wagons and carts, so instead they ventured east, possibly guided by area Indians, and found a pass that led to the river. They crossed the mountains through Puerto Presidio and descended to the Rio Grande, somewhere near modern Guadalupe Bravo, Chihuahua.[7] They continued along the southern bank toward today's Ciudad Juárez. It took several days for all the wagons to catch up with the expedition, but by April 27, they were all on the banks of the Rio Grande. The wagon train traveled northwest for two days and set up camp somewhere near present-day San Elizario, Texas. On April 30, 1598, the expedition held a great feast of thanksgiving and a ceremony known as *La Toma*, the formal taking of the land, in which Governor Juan de Oñate took possession of New Mexico in the name of King Philip II of Spain.[8] Although the exact location is unknown, the site remained an important one during the Colonial era and in 1665, a small Franciscan mission, *Las Llagas de Nuestro Seráfico Padre San Francisco*, the Torment of Our Angelic Father Saint Francis, was briefly established nearby.[9]

La Jornada de Cantarrecio and the Mission Trail

By the early seventeenth century, the Spanish had opened an easier route around the Médanos, completely avoiding the sand dunes. Instead of passing through Puerto Presidio, they went southeast of the Sierra el Presidio, through a gap known as Puerto Ancho, a hard dirt area on the trail where some of the best preserved ruts of the Camino Real can still be observed.[10] This route, through the Arroyo de Cantarrecio, continued north toward the river, arriving in the valley between present-day Praxedis G. Guerrero and El Mimbre, Chihuahua. From there, the Camino Real followed the south bank of the river near the path of today's Mexican Federal Highway 2, toward Guadalupe and San Isidro. Until the nineteenth century, when major floods shifted the main river channel to the northeast, travelers could continue along the Camino Real de Tierra Adentro through today's Lower El Paso Valley settlements without having to ford the river. As missions, haciendas, and a presidio were established along the roadway, this "Mission Trail" of the Camino Real connected area settlements and provided a safe, reliable route into El Paso del Norte. The Mission Trail remained in use for centuries and became a segment of the main stagecoach route to Chihuahua City, later serving as the foundation for the first regional automobile road through the valley.

El Paso's Lower Valley

The Mission Trail of the Camino Real de Tierra Adentro led through the El Paso Valley, a broad, flat, fertile area that spreads about eighty miles from the Fort Quitman area to the mouth of a canyon near today's downtown El Paso. The area southeast of the city is locally known as the Lower Valley, a wide floodplain, created by the constant swelling and receding of river waters over thousands of years. Humans were present in the valley 8,000 to 12,000 years ago when they roamed the riverbanks and sand hills as small, nomadic bands of hunter-gatherers. More than 2,000 years ago they lived in pit houses and cultivated fields along the river. Around the time of the first millennium, natives congregated into larger settlements along the Rio Grande where they raised crops in the rich, alluvial soil, but by the 1400s CE the settlements had been abandoned and many of the natives returned to a hunter-gatherer lifestyle. When Spaniards arrived in the valley in the sixteenth century, all of the pueblo-style settlements and any semblance of organized agriculture had vanished. The El Paso Valley became the home of the Manso Indians who lived along the Rio Grande and inhabited an area that spread north toward today's Hatch, New Mexico. They were a gentle, nomadic people who lived in temporary brush huts, hunting and foraging along the oasis created by the river.[11] They were described as having "...long hair cut to resemble little Milan caps, headgear made to hold down the hair and colored with blood or paint."[12] Mansos met the Oñate expedition near the river and guided them to the Pass, and north, to a river ford. The Sumas roamed the area south and west of the Pass, from the Casas Grandes area. They too were nomadic hunter-gatherers who survived by following game and foraging throughout northern regions of the Chihuahuan Desert and the river valley. The Sumas were more suspicious of the Europeans and often kept their distance, frustrating early Franciscan friars. Suma rebellions repeatedly challenged Spanish authority in the seventeenth and eighteenth centuries. The Mansos and Sumas did not fare well under the Spanish colonial or Mexican systems. They rebelled, resisted, and succumbed to a variety of epidemics. By the nineteenth century, their numbers had greatly declined. Today, a few people identify themselves as descendants of Manso and Suma Indians, but most of the language, social customs and practices disappeared more than one hundred years ago.[13]There are no visible ruins or archaeological sites specifically identified as Manso or Suma settlements in the El Paso Valley, and little has been written about their existence. The El Paso Museum of Archaeology, in the northeast area of the city, offers the best overview. The museum is dedicated to preserving and promoting the archaeological and anthropological heritage of the greater El Paso area, and several permanent exhibits portray the ancient Native-American lifestyles of the Southwest.

The sixteenth-century landscape of El Paso's Lower Valley was considerably different than it is today. The wide, meandering, floodplain, surrounding marshes, and river bosque provided travelers with fresh water, fish, fowl, and game. Thick vegetation and large trees dotted the banks and spread throughout the watered fields, offering a variety of edible plants, cool shade, and firewood. In the early seventeenth century, there were a few small, temporary missions established in the Lower Valley. They were modest sites, with a thatch or mudbrick chapel, and one or two missionaries in residence. They had limited success in drawing Mansos and Sumas into a structured, Hispanic Christian life and were soon abandoned. The real growth of the Lower Valley began after the 1680 Pueblo Indian Revolt when Spanish refugees and Native-Americans from northern New Mexico were re-settled south of the Pass. During the next two centuries, the river's course shifted toward the southwest, and much of El Paso's Lower Valley, including the communities of San Elizario, Socorro, and Ysleta, were north of the Rio Grande. Today, the Rio Grande serves as an international boundary and divides the Valley. Its meandering course has been straightened and channeled and stripped of much of its native vegetation. The Mission Trail of the Camino Real de Tierra Adentro remained an important transportation corridor until the late nineteenth century, when the railroad bypassed the Lower El Paso Valley. Even so, the first major automobile roads and highways followed the old trail through the region.

Manso Indians, as depicted at the El Paso Museum of Archaeology.

San Elizario

El Camino Real de Tierra Adentro National Historic Trail formally begins at San Elizario, Texas, a village that traces its origins to an eighteenth-century hacienda and Spanish fortress. With a traditional plaza, a Colonial-era *acequia*, or irrigation system, still in use, and many historic structures, San Elizario is the best preserved town on the Mission Trail. Antonio Tiburcio de Ortega purchased land along the southern bank of the Rio Grande in the 1720s and spent twenty years developing a large hacienda, *Nuestra Señora de la Soledad de los Tiburcios*, Our Lady of Solitude of Tiburcios. The settlement suffered through epidemics, Indian raids, floods, and may have been abandoned several times, but Hacienda Tiburcios survived, and by the 1750s, Ortega's descendants, consisting of an extended family living in the small agricultural hamlet along the river, were producing substantial amounts of maize, grapes, beans, wheat, chile, cotton, and garlic. Most likely, the hacienda was no more than a group of simple adobe houses clustered in the middle of the property, organized for defense, sharing outer adobe walls, and enclosing a plaza. For almost thirty years the pioneers at Tiburcios persevered, but life on the frontier finally took its toll, and by the late 1770s the settlement was abandoned. The site of the hacienda has never been precisely located, but it was most likely within the historic center of today's San Elizario. Tiburcios remained noted on maps, but disappears from the historical record by the early nineteenth century.[14]

In 1774, a Spanish presidio was constructed on the southern bank of the Rio Grande, near present-day El Porvenir, Chihuahua, as part of the Bourbon-era re-organization of frontier defenses. *San Elzeario* was a large, walled fortress named for Saint Elzear, the French patron saint of soldiers. The presidio was active for fourteen years until it was moved up the river to the old Tiburcios site in 1788. The new post at Tiburcios reflected policy changes under the Regulations of 1772, a series of new guidelines for frontier presidios intended to reform the military system and improve frontier defenses. The new walled fortress, modeled after the one at El Porvenir, had troops' barracks, workrooms and storage facilities, a parade ground, a chapel, and livestock pens. It was surrounded by three-foot-thick adobe walls more than twelve feet high, and had two defensive towers placed at each end of the compound. A second outer wall was added later, to protect domesticated animals and enclose areas of the community that grew up around the fortress.[15] The San Elzeario Presidio was primarily established as a settlement for area Apaches. Peace programs offered Indians rations and security in exchange for agreements to cease raids on Spanish settlements and Camino Real caravans. By the early years of the nineteenth century, soldiers and their families, re-settled Indians, and new arrivals from the region formed a small community within, and alongside, the fortress. Early nineteenth-century commercial traffic expanded as presidio soldiers escorted supply caravans north to Santa Fe. In 1807, United States Army Captain Zebulon Montgomery Pike, who was suspected of espionage and taken into custody near Santa Fe, was brought through San Elzeario en route to Chihuahua City. Pike wrote the first Anglo-American account of the village, describing in his journal meetings with local elites and his observations of a Catholic mass at the presidio chapel, and of the resident Apaches.[16] The presidio remained active during the Mexican era, but the Apache population dwindled as the new republic ended peace programs and curtailed rationing. Hostilities increased, and by the 1830s the state of Chihuahua routinely waged war against

Apache bands throughout the region. San Elzeario presidio soldiers, militia from El Paso del Norte, and troops from Janos and Carrizal often joined in the campaigns. By the end of the decade more extreme measures were taken to defeat the Apache, including the use of scalp hunters and mercenary troops. In the 1840s, during the last days of the Mexican presidio, a few Apache were re-settled near the town and received rations once again.[17]

Fewer troops were needed as rationing and re-settlement programs came to an end. The local civilian population increased, and by 1840 about 1,000 people lived at San Elzeario. The opening of the Santa Fe and Chihuahua trade helped the town grow and as agriculture and new commercial enterprises expanded, the presidio became less critical to the survival of the town. In December 1846, when American forces took El Paso del Norte, the military structures and chapel at San Elzeario were in ruins, and Mexican troops had abandoned the site. Americans took formal possession of the town in early 1849, and the old name of "Elzeario" was Americanized as "Elizario."[18] Following the war, American troops were stationed at what was left of the old fortress, and in 1850 San Elizario became the county seat of the newly formed El Paso County. The few remaining presidial structures were dismantled to provide adobe for new residential and business buildings. As a county seat, and the largest community in El Paso County, San Elizario thrived in the 1850s with a post office, stagecoach station, and new mercantile establishments.

The town also became an important junction along new routes through the American West. From 1849 to 1853, the first horseback mail service between San Antonio, Texas, and Santa Fe, New Mexico, passed through San Elizario. Stagecoach lines and freight services used segments of the old Camino Real to link with new trails east and west. The military continued their interest in the Lower Valley, visiting communities and conducting reconnaissance in the area, including novel experiments such as Lieutenant Edward Beale's caravan of twenty-five camels that passed through San Elizario in 1857. The same year, the San Antonio and San Diego mail line came through the valley, and by 1859 the Butterfield Overland Mail had established a station there. The Butterfield station, which later became the area post office, was located near the northwest remains of the old presidio wall. A second building, where teams of horses were changed and meals were served to weary travelers, occupied about a quarter of the block.[19]

The ebb and flow of the Civil War affected valley life in the 1860s. After the war, Texas's role in the former Confederacy allowed Republicans to gain control of the state, but new regional rivalries complicated their rule. In the 1870s, conflicts between area Hispanics and Anglo-American settlers erupted in a violent period that became known as the "Salt War," named for a dispute over the privatizing of salt deposits at the base of the Guadalupe Mountains east of town. Other changes had more long reaching effects on the community. By the 1870s, new stagecoach routes began to bypass San Elizario and head directly into American El Paso. In 1881, the railroad was built through the community of Clint, several miles east of the old Camino Real. American El Paso, thirty miles further up the river, thrived in the late nineteenth century and became the economic and political hub of the region, while San Elizario returned to being a quiet agricultural community. Only in recent decades has El Paso's urban expansion reached into the Lower Valley.[20]

Today, San Elizario is a well-preserved historic village with many examples of Colonial-and Territorial-style architecture. Its central plaza features a series of state and county historical markers that highlight the region's Spanish Colonial past. The streets surrounding the plaza today: Main Street, Alarcón Road, Paseo del Convento, and Socorro Road follow the outline of the old presidio wall. The main gated entrance to the fortress faced Glorieta Road, and the core of several long, rectangular flat-roof adobe buildings, such as the one at 1500 Church Street, was probably the barracks. The presidio walls no longer exist, but a few segments survived well into the mid-twentieth century. The most prominent structure in town is the San Elizario Presidio Chapel, on the south side of the plaza. It is commonly referred to as a mission, but neither the village nor the chapel, was ever part of the colonial mission system. The first chapel was built for Spanish soldiers and their families. It was originally a large adobe building, close to the site of the present church, and served the village for the first few decades. During the 1829 flood, it was badly damaged, and eventually razed. By 1840, a new, more substantial structure was built on higher ground. The new chapel only survived a few years and was in ruins by the time of the Mexican-American War. In the 1850s, the adobe remains and rubble were used to build a temporary church. In 1877, work began on the present structure, which took five years to complete. The new San Elizario Chapel was set on an elevated site, to protect it from flooding, and had plastered adobe walls, strong buttresses, narrowed windows, and a large triangular bell tower. The church is an example of late nineteenth-century adobe construction using a single nave, but by the early twentieth century, the San Elizario Chapel featured Europeanized elements common in Territorial New Mexico. Between 1910 and 1925, the facade was re-designed and by the end of the decade the church appeared much as it does today with a rounded bell tower and curved gable.[21] The San Elizario Chapel was re-plastered throughout the twentieth century with cement mixtures that weakened its structural integrity. Many adobe buildings along the Camino Real de Tierra Adentro National Historic Trail suffered the same fate. Cement plasters prevented the natural adobe compounds from breathing, and trapped moisture within walls. Over the decades the walls weakened, cracked, and sometimes collapsed. By the 1980s and 1990s, many historic adobe structures, which had sometimes survived hundreds of years, were in danger of being lost. In contrast, massive adobe structures in Mexico were in generally good condition because natural lime plasters that helped the adobe materials breath had remained in use, rather than cement which traps moisture causing the adobe to crumble. In the late twentieth century, these traditional methods were re-introduced to communities in the United States and many adobe buildings were subsequently restored. In the late 1990s, the San Elizario Chapel was stripped, repaired, and re-surfaced using traditional lime plaster.

There have also been changes to the interior since the chapel's dedication in 1882. A pressed-tin ceiling was added to cover the original wooden *vigas* or beams. Old wooden columns were boxed in by neo-classical posts and painted to resemble marble. They now have a plain white surface with gold trim. In 1935, a major fire destroyed much of the interior of the church. Following the fire, new pews and altars were installed. Beautiful stained glass windows were added, blending patriotic and religious symbols. In the 1940s, the rear of the church was re-designed to honor local-area soldiers who had fought in the Second World War. A small shrine to the Virgin Mary is located alongside the church. The San Elizario Chapel was added to the National Register of Historic Places in 1972.

Los Portales, home of the San Elizario Genealogical and Historical Society.

On the south side of the plaza, a long, Territorial-style building houses Los Portales Museum and Information Center, operated by the San Elizario Genealogical and Historical Society. It was built in the early 1850s by Gregorio N. García as a private residence. García was a local farmer and landowner who entered politics, serving as captain of the Texas Rangers and a county judge of El Paso in the 1870s. Los Portales is the best example of Territorial-style architecture in San Elizario. The long, one-story building lies on an adobe foundation and is made of adobe bricks. A flat soil-and-clay roof lies over cottonwood vigas interwoven with saplings and thatch. The front of the building faces the plaza and features a long, inset *portal*, or porch, which led to the name Los Portales. In the 1870s, it was donated for use as a school, and the first teacher was Octaviano Ambrosio Larrazolo who later became Governor of New Mexico and a United States Senator in the 1920s. In the twentieth century, Los Portales has served as an apartment building, a school district office, and a general storage facility. In the late 1990s, it was refurbished and became the property of El Paso County, and the new home of the local historical society. The Los Portales Museum offers visitors an overview of the Lower Valley's history and features exhibits that highlight San Elizario's colonial, Mexican, and modern-day American history.

Casa Ronquillo is about 500 feet from the village center, on the edge of the San Elizario Lateral Canal (or the *acequia madre*). The core structure was built in the 1820s and purchased in 1832 by José Ignacio Ronquillo, a prominent official in the El Paso del Norte area, who served as *alcalde*, or mayor, of San Elizario, Prefect of El Paso del Norte, and Captain of the San Elizario Presidio.[22] The house, which is only partially standing, once had twelve or more rooms in three wings, with an interior courtyard surrounded by a portal and enclosed by a high adobe wall. Mexican-era visitors were frequently entertained at Casa Ronquillo.[23] After Ronquillo's death, the land was sold, and in 1869 passed to Charles Ellis and his wife, Teodora Alarcón de Ellis. Ellis was a wealthy merchant and political figure in San Elizario who died at the hands of an angry mob during the Salt War of 1877.[24] Casa Ronquillo remained a private residence for years and became an early twentieth-century motor lodge and restaurant, but by the 1950s it was neglected and lay in ruins. The crumbling remains became known as San Elizario's haunted house and was said to have once been the home of a Spanish Viceroy. Unfortunately, the colorful reputation of Casa Ronquillo helped contribute to its demise as treasure-hunters ravaged the grounds, punctured walls, and ripped up floors, in search of gold and precious gems. Although there was never any treasure found at the site, Casa Ronquillo continued to spark local imagination. Stories of hauntings and ghosts have been told about the house for years, and some residents have even reported seeing the Old Viceroy riding through the plaza after midnight. They say that he gallops through the town, passes Casa Ronquillo, and disappears off into the desert. By the early years of the twenty-first century, Casa Ronquillo was in ruins, a crumbling five-room segment of the original estate.[25] In recent years there has been a renewed interest in Casa Ronquillo. Plans are underway to stabilize and restore the remaining structure.

San Elizario has many other buildings that date from the nineteenth and possibly eighteenth centuries. Over the years, they have been enlarged, modified, or completely re-designed but still bear the markings of the Colonial and Territorial periods. Some believe that the Ochoa Store, Lalo's Grocery, and the Lujan Store, all along Main Street, may date from the eighteenth century and contain segments that were part of the original presidio compound. Further along the street is the Old County Jail, which may date from the 1820s but was probably constructed as a residence after 1860 and later converted to hold prisoners. The small, flat-roofed adobe jail, with its large steel and wrought-iron cages inside, was in use until the 1940s. A popular local legend tells of how Billy the Kid helped his friend Melquiades Segura escape from the jail in 1876. Behind the jail are agricultural fields and an acequia system that have been in use since the colonial era. The private residence at 1500 Paseo del Convento is said to have been a stop on the Butterfield-Overland Mail route. Without United States military protection, the station was built as a fortress, and large, strong gates allowed wagons to enter its *placita*, or enclosed plaza, through thick windowless walls. Numerous archaeological studies have been conducted in the town, and an extensive Historic American Buildings Survey was completed in 1980. With so many structures and sites identified and registered as landmarks, in 1997, the San Elizario Historic District was placed on the National Register of Historic Places.

The First Thanksgiving

San Elizario claims to be the site of the first thanksgiving celebration held in what is now the United States. On April 30, 1598, twenty-three years before the Pilgrim thanksgiving at Plymouth, the Oñate expedition feasted on the banks of the Rio Grande, somewhere between today's Guadalupe Bravo, Chihuahua, and San Elizario, Texas, to give thanks for surviving the dangerous trek through the Chihuahuan Desert. Each April, San Elizario commemorates its "First" Thanksgiving with a history conference, pageant, and festival. The mention of a thanksgiving celebration conjures up images of pious Pilgrims feasting alongside friendly Indians, sharing food and celebrating a rich harvest. But in the twentieth century, the leaders and citizens of several communities asserted that their town was the site of the first such celebration and could document the claim. President John F. Kennedy, a native of Massachusetts, conceded and, in 1963, formally declared the Berkeley Plantation Thanksgiving of 1610 to officially be the "first." The matter was thought to have been laid to rest, but by the 1970s, new claims were made by ten communities in the West and South, areas that had been explored and colonized by the Spanish in the sixteenth century. Thanksgivings were said to have been held during the expeditions of Ponce de León, in 1513; Hernando de Soto, in 1529; and Francisco Vásquez de Coronado, in 1541; and at the founding of Saint Augustine, Florida, in 1565.

The controversy has continued as rival communities claim their "first" status. To make matters more confusing, it has come to light that the Plymouth celebration probably did not bear much resemblance to its usual portrayal, and may not have occurred at all. Even the scholars and interpretive staff at Plimoth (the seventeenth century spelling) Plantation, a living history museum where the Pilgrim and Indian experience is recreated with great historical accuracy, concede that harvest festivals were traditional in both English and Native-American cultures and that it was much later that the term "thanksgiving" was used to describe the event."[26]

San Elizario's claim bears consideration. The Oñate expedition had a difficult, traumatic, journey through the Chihuahuan Desert. The last days of March were particularly daunting as they wandered through the parched landscape in desperate search of water. Finally, on April 1, the skies opened and a deluge rescued the weary travelers. They called the event the *Socorro del Cielo* (Aid from Heaven), when a miraculous shower saved the expedition from ruin. One week later Oñate's scouts led the expedition east to the river, and by April 26, everyone was together on the banks of the Rio Grande, preparing to continue north. The arrival at the river signaled the end of hardships, an exodus, and the beginning of a journey into a "New" Mexico, a Promised Land.[27] Oñate gathered the weary group together and praised them for their loyalty, courage, and endurance. They continued up river a few leagues and made camp where, on April 30, 1598, the expedition gave thanks and celebrated. They built a small chapel under the shade of the trees, held a traditional mass, and performed a play written by one of the officers. A few Manso or Suma Indians, who no doubt had little idea of what was taking place, joined in the festivities. Oñate performed "La Toma," the formal taking possession of all of the land drained by the great Río del Norte, an official claim of the territory in the name of King Philip II of Spain. This act, and the accompanying celebrations, took place somewhere southwest of San Elizario, along the banks of the Rio Grande.

Documents clearly show that Oñate's colonists gave thanks and feasted on the banks of the Rio Grande. Because of the changing course of the river, it is quite likely that they were well within the boundaries of the present-day United States. This was a celebration with strong religious overtones and included area Native-Americans. Unlike many of the other claims for Spanish thanksgivings, this was a celebration among the original pioneer settlers who eventually established a new colony. For these reasons, each spring the people of San Elizario celebrate their "First Thanksgiving."[28]

Hacienda San Antonio

The Camino Real de Tierra Adentro followed the path of Glorieta Road out of San Elizario and continued north along today's Socorro Road. Until flooding shifted the main river channel in the early nineteenth century, Camino Real travelers could pass through each of the major Lower Valley settlements and enter El Paso del Norte without crossing the river. Two other colonial sites briefly existed on the opposite bank, connected by branch trails and a river ford. Although the exact locations of Hacienda San Antonio and Santa María de las Caldas remain unknown, they were somewhere northeast of Socorro Road, between present-day San Elizario and Socorro. After the re-conquest of New Mexico, the El Paso area entered a period of growth and prosperity and the re-opening of the Camino Real offered area farmers, ranchers, and merchants, opportunities to profit from trade along the trail, especially in the lucrative markets of northern New Mexico and Chihuahua. A well-run hacienda could profit from both local trade and demand in distant settlements. Three major haciendas were established in the region, all selling a great variety of agricultural goods including wheat, corn, grapes, wine and brandy, beans, skins, hides, and various textile products. Because of the lack of coins, wines and brandies became major trade goods and often served as a form of currency.[29] Around 1710, Captain Antonio de Valverde Cosío (1680–1728), Commandant of the El Paso del Norte Presidio, established the *Hacienda San Antonio de Padua*, named for Saint Anthony of Padua, a thirteenth-century Portuguese Franciscan. It was a sprawling farm and ranch on the north bank of the river that covered tens of thousands of acres and specialized in wheat, although large quantities of corn were also harvested. A stone grist mill was built at the site to grind grains for local consumption, area trade, and sale along the trail. More than 10,000 vines produced grapes for wine and brandy. Sheep, pigs, and goats were grazed in fields along the river and provided meat and milk. An *obraje*, or textile mill, on the hacienda processed wool. Horses and cattle were raised on the south side of the river, and more than one hundred oxen were available for working the fields.[30] The core settlement was probably arranged as a defensive plaza, with adobe walls enclosing residential buildings and some of the workshops. By the 1720s, Valverde Cosío had been promoted to general, and served as the governor of New Mexico. Over the next two decades, the hacienda flourished, increasing Valverde Cosío's wealth and status in the community. He spent much of his time in El Paso del Norte where he had a large, well-furnished three-story home, surrounded by gardens and orchards. Unfortunately, several mid-eighteenth-century crises ended the great agricultural boom in the valley. As it became increasingly difficult to farm the land, many settlements in the region were abandoned. Indian raids on remote sites, epidemics, and river flooding threatened these enterprises, and Hacienda San Antonio de Padua was abandoned by the early 1750s. El Paso del Norte area agriculture never quite recovered from the decline.[31]

The Rio Vista Farm Site, developed as a movie set in the 1990s, is probably near the site of the Hacienda San Antonio and the "lost" mission of Las Caldas.

Santa María de las Caldas

Another eighteenth-century settlement on the north bank of the Rio Grande was the curacy of *Santa María de las Caldas* (Our Lady of the Hot Springs), located near the Valverde Cosío hacienda. Las Caldas had a brief, stormy history, and, although noted on several eighteenth-century maps and mentioned in a few travelers' accounts, it was soon forgotten.[32] Because there are few records of the settlement, and no ruins or remains have ever been associated with Santa María de las Caldas, it is often referred to as El Paso's "lost mission." In the 1730s, five Franciscan mission settlements had been established in the El Paso del Norte area (Guadalupe, San Lorenzo, Senecú, Ysleta, and Socorro). Spanish missions were run by friars affiliated with religious orders such as the Franciscans, Jesuits, or Dominicans. In New Mexico, all of the early Spanish settlements were under Franciscan control. By the 1700s, the Catholic Church of New Spain wished to expand its authority and reign in missionaries who dominated the empire, by establishing parishes, under the control of a diocese and bishop and supported by the Crown. Parishes covered larger geographic areas and served many different people, including Spaniards, mestizos, Indians, laborers, and town residents. When the Bishop of Durango, Benito Crespo, whose diocese included New Mexico, visited the El Paso area in 1730, he was looking for opportunities to establish new parishes. That same year, a small chapel, Santa María de las Caldas, was built at a settlement called El Capitán, near Socorro. The Franciscans at Socorro and Ysleta were offended by the chapel, seeing it as infringing on their territory and influence in the valley. At about the same time, El Paso Presidio Captain José Valentín de Aganza warned the viceroy that a group of approximately 250 Suma Indians who did not wish to be administered by the Franciscans had struck out on their own and were building a pueblo and farming fields on the north bank of the river. The Suma were the most independent of the area Indians, uncomfortable under missionary control and often rebellious. The diocese saw this as an opportunity to reign in these local Sumas, serve the spiritual needs of Hacienda San Antonio, and create a new parish, centered at Las Caldas, to check the powers of the Franciscan missionaries.

Captain Aganza led the effort at Las Caldas. He purchased the land, built adobe housing blocks, oversaw the digging of an acequia to draw waters from the Rio Grande, arranged the construction of a church, and recruited settlers. While most of the residents at Las Caldas were Sumas, records indicate that some came from far off locations: the interior of New Spain, northern New Mexico, and even Guatemala. They mixed with a few Mansos, Piros, and Apaches. While Hacienda San Antonio and Las Caldas thrived, there was plenty of work in the area, and Indians, along with a growing mestizo population, worked as laborers, farmhands, and cowboys at the nearby hacienda and its extensive operations in the lower valley. There may have been more than 200 families living at Las Caldas in the 1730s, but the chronic problems of the mid-eighteenth century affected the parish settlement as well. Several epidemics swept through the valley, especially impacting the Indian population, and it is estimated that half of the Sumas at Las Caldas were lost to disease. The river ran high in the 1740s, leading to periods of extensive flooding that isolated both Las Caldas and Hacienda San Antonio on the north bank. This left the two settlements highly vulnerable to outside Suma and Apache raiding parties, and when a crisis occurred, the swollen waters made it virtually impossible for presidio troops to render aid.[33]

In April 1745, in the midst of the raging spring floods, the Sumas and Apaches at Santa María de las Caldas rebelled. They ransacked the settlement and fled into the nearby mountains. The rebellion was brought under control and for a few years Las Caldas was quiet until a second uprising in 1749 completely destroyed the site. Parish authority was broken, parishioners abandoned the settlement, and the nearby hacienda was threatened. When the rebellion was over and the remaining Sumas were taken to San Lorenzo and placed with the Franciscans, the parish priest left the area, and, it was more than one hundred years before a new parish was established in the valley. The structural remains, along with memories of Hacienda San Antonio and Las Caldas, seem to have faded fast, and when early nineteenth-century Anglo-American travelers came through the valley, they made no mention of the hacienda or the parish ruins. It was not until the 1960s that scholars re-discovered these colonial landmarks and began to piece together their histories. The re-discovery of the Las Caldas parish led to further research and speculation about the history and location of the settlement. The center of the parish was on the north bank of the river, near Hacienda San Antonio. In the mid-eighteenth century, the Rio Grande ran several miles northeast of its current path through the valley. Las Caldas was located between Socorro and Hacienda San Antonio which were about two leagues (five to six miles) apart. The key to the location of Las Caldas and San Antonio is an ancient area landmark known as Palo Clavado, a high ridge of land near the old river channel of the Rio Grande, sited as a marker for the 1751 Tigua land grant. This would place the two settlements south of today's Interstate 10, in the central area of Socorro, between Americas Avenue and Horizon Boulevard.[34] The Rio Vista Farm Complex, a former processing center for the *bracero* labor program (and a set for the 2000 feature film *Traffic*), along with the Socorro town offices, are probably in the general vicinity of the two sites.

Socorro

The Camino Real de Tierra Adentro continued about five miles along Socorro Road to the site of a community that grew alongside a seventeenth-century mission. A few weeks after the thanksgiving celebration, about 200 miles north of San Elizario, the Oñate expedition was met a by group of Piro Indians from Teypana Pueblo who offered food and assistance to the weary colonists. Shortly after the colony of New Mexico was formally established in late 1598, Franciscan friars began organizing missions for Indian populations along the Camino Real. Missions served as a way to convert the natives to Catholicism and place Indians in concentrated settlements (a process known as *reducción*) where they could be taught to be loyal subjects of the crown and provide useful labor for the colonial system. By the 1620s, a new mission for the Piros of Pilabó, *Nuestra Señora de Perpetuo Socorro*, Our Lady of Perpetual Help, stood at the site of today's San Miguel Church in Socorro, New Mexico, and honored the aid that the Oñate colonists had received. The settlement grew and by mid-century there were as many as 600 people living at the Socorro Mission, mostly Piro Indians and a few Apaches. Disease and drought took their toll, and by the 1670s the population had declined, and the mission was no longer a major center.[35] When Lieutenant Governor Alonso García and his refugee caravan arrived in August 1680 (fleeing the Pueblo Indian Revolt in the north), the few remaining Piro residents, fearing reprisals by the Apaches, joined the Spaniards as they retreated to El Paso del Norte.[36] The mission was re-established near El Paso del Norte as *Nuestra Señora de la Limpia Concepción de los Piros de Socorro del Sur*, Our Lady of the Immaculate Conception for the Piros of Southern Socorro. The temporary mission camp was originally further down river, but, in 1683, it was moved closer to the present site, and by 1690 construction of a permanent church was underway. Franciscan priests oversaw the settlement, several Spanish families were placed in the area, and a group of Indian officers tended to local affairs. In 1692, before returning north to re-conquer New Mexico, Governor Vargas officially granted the land to the mission, and although some Piros returned north with Vargas, most stayed on at Socorro.[37] The Socorro del Sur Mission was re-located several times during the next 130 years as river flooding destroyed a series of churches and forced the community to seek higher ground. With each major deluge, the settlement inched northwest toward its present site on Socorro Road.[38]

During the rest of the Spanish Colonial era, Mission Socorro del Sur remained a small community of a few hundred Piro and Manso residents, administered by the Franciscans. The Piros duplicated some of the architecture from their native communities in the north and built a multi-storied adobe housing-block surrounding a central plaza. Hispanic families settled near the mission, and the town of El Socorro was founded by the mid-eighteenth century. Individual family farms dotted the area surrounded by vineyards, corn fields, and fruit trees. After a major flood in 1829, the river once again cut a new channel, destroying the mission church and most of the nearby residences, and placing Socorro, along with San Elizario and Ysleta, on an island, further dividing the community. By the 1840s, the tribal government of the Piros collapsed and the remaining natives began to disperse as their land was seized. The diocese took control of the church in 1852, replacing the Franciscans. By the 1850s, when a Texas land grant was made to the town of Socorro, it does not appear that any Piro Indians challenged the claim.[39]Much of the indigenous culture was disappearing rapidly, and by the end of the century only a few families identified themselves as Piros.[40] William P. Huff visited Socorro on his way to the California goldfields in 1849 and made no mention of an Indian community. He described a sleepy "Spanish" town with abundant agriculture and was impressed with the vineyards and orchards, especially the grapes which he described as the "largest and most tempting" he had ever seen. He noted that many of the fruits (pears, peaches and apples), were of superior size and flavor and that corn grew especially well in the region.[41] After the Mexican-American War, Socorro was located in the United States, and the Lower Valley attracted Anglo-American settlers, along with a number of unsavory desperados who terrorized the community. During the transition from Mexican to American rule, lawlessness often plagued the border. In one incident, a gang murdered a quartermaster working for Boundary Commissioner Russell Bartlett. Some of the perpetrators had been employed by the commission, but Bartlett insisted that they be apprehended and tried, partly as a way to re-establish order in the Lower Valley. Three were found guilty and hanged from a large cottonwood tree on the plaza, in front of the Socorro Mission Church. A fourth was chased to Guadalupe, across the river in Mexico, and brought back to Socorro to face the same fate. The incident drove many criminals from the area and helped restore order to the quiet farming community.[42]

Socorro maintained a reputation for its abundant harvests in the 1850s but remained a small settlement, a stop on the coach road, between the larger communities of Ysleta and San Elizario. Several residents developed substantial freighting businesses, extending commercial connections made along the Chihuahua Trail, and taking advantage of new American transportation networks linking the east and west. Some of the area's commercial success was dampened when the railroad bypassed the town in the 1880s, and Socorro remained an agricultural town, on the fringe of the boom taking place in American El Paso and Ciudad Juárez in the early twentieth century. Today, little remains from eighteenth-and nineteenth-century Socorro except for the mission church and grounds, and a series of scattered structures along Socorro Road. Unlike San Elizario, its plaza arrangement, narrow winding streets, and much of the adobe architecture in its historic core has been lost to development. A bilingual El Paso County Historical Marker on Buford Road marks the site of the main eighteenth-century mission. The later, nineteenth-century town center was located near today's 10100-10300 blocks of Socorro Road, and, along this stretch of the road, the modern highway narrows and various structures, trees, crumbling adobe ruins, and homes close in on the old Camino Real.[43] Oral tradition tells us that the one-story, L-shaped, adobe brick building at 10245 Socorro Road, a Texas Historical Landmark known as the *Tienda de Carbajal*, Carbajal's Store, was a supply center for freight caravans to Chihuahua City and La Mesilla. The structure was built in the 1850s as part of a hacienda. In the 1870s, the site was abandoned and partially demolished. The remains were then rebuilt and used by an area merchant, Juan Carbajal. In the late nineteenth-century, when segments of the old Camino Real were linked to other regional trade routes, Carbajal saw new opportunities and outfitted wagon trains in order to trade salt as far afield as Chihuahua City and the Mesilla Valley. The tienda's three-foot thick adobe walls, traditional linear plan, and flat roof supported by vigas are typical of the late Mexican and Territorial periods. Over the years, there have been many additions and changes to Tienda de Carbajal, including a major renovation in the 1970s. It is currently a commercial establishment.[44] Casa Ortiz, at 10167 Socorro Road, is another Texas Historical Landmark connected with the merchant trade between Chihuahua, New Mexico and West Texas. The house appears to have been built in the mid-nineteenth century, about the time the last mission church was being constructed. The original owner, José Ortiz, was also a merchant and salt trader who organized wagon trains from Santa Fe to Durango, and northeast into the plains of New Mexico. Ortiz also traded in blankets, clothing, and knives. The U-shaped building is made of adobe bricks, with a typical flat-roof, vigas, and shuttered windows. The original structure was a simple rectangular one. An open porch, adobe sheds, and a nearby *horno* (oven) have been added over the years. Casa Ortiz is presently a giftshop and bookstore.[45]

This building on today's Socorro Road, housed the Tienda de Carbajal.

The most prominent historic structure in Socorro is the 1843 mission church, now known as *Nuestra Señora de la Purísima Concepción*, Our Lady of the Immaculate Conception. The large, gleaming, white-washed adobe facade and stepped parapet face east, overlooking the Socorro Cemetery. La Purísima has adobe walls five feet thick, a twenty-six foot high ceiling, and a main nave measuring twenty-two by one hundred feet. It was built following the 1829 flood, completed in 1843, and has had several major modifications over the years. In the 1880s, a new transept was built, in addition to a front facade, bell wall and sanctuary. The Socorro Mission church remained in use for more than 150 years, but by the 1990s it was in danger of being lost. Most church activities had moved next door, to a new building. Efforts to preserve and re-enforce the old structure (such as cement plastering and collaring along the main walls), had actually trapped moisture and structurally deteriorated the building. The original, thick adobe walls were in danger of collapse. A major five-year restoration project, headed by Cornerstones Community Partnerships of Santa Fe, in cooperation with the Diocese, the Texas Historical Commission, and many area associations and institutions, was completed in 2005, which stabilized the building and returned the church to its original splendor. Extensive interior and exterior work preserved and strengthened the massive adobe walls, refurbished the ornate woodwork and statuary, and made use of 20,000 new adobe bricks.[46]

Inside La Purísima, the altar and nave have been totally refurbished. The interior vigas and corbels, salvaged from earlier seventeenth-and eighteenth-century churches, bear the remains of hand-painted designs made long ago by the Piro Indians of Mission Socorro. The altar appears to be marble but is actually painted wood. Although the Socorro Mission Church is dedicated to the Immaculate Conception, left of the altar is the church's most prominent icon, a beautifully painted wooden statue of Saint Michael, regarded as the patron saint of the community. Records indicate that the statue was donated by the Holguín family in the 1830s and placed in the new church in 1845, but parishioners often tell a very different story about the arrival of Saint Michael. A well-known local legend is that the statue came to Socorro with an early nineteenth-century merchant caravan making its way up the Camino Real. Among the many goods being brought north in an oxen-drawn, two-wheeled *carreta* was a life-size wooden statue of Saint Michael bound for the San Miguel church in Socorro, New Mexico. The caravan camped in front of the church, and, after spending a few days in Socorro, preparations were made to continue the journey north. When the drivers tried to move Saint Michael's carreta, it would not budge. A second team of oxen was hooked up to the cart, but it still could not be moved. The drivers decided that maybe the saint wanted to visit the church, so they carried the statue into La Purísima. The statue paid its respects and was hoisted back into the cart, but once again, the cart, could not be moved. It was then decided that Saint Michael wanted to stay in Socorro, so they donated him to the church. Ever since then, he has been regarded as the protector of the community and has become an important part of local religious tradition. It is said that Saint Michael has appeared in Socorro from time to time, including a miraculous visit during the 1877 Salt War to protect residents from United States troops.[47]

Segments of the Socorro Mission Rectory, a one-story L-shaped adobe building behind the mission church, may also date from the 1840s. The building once contained workshops where wood products such as pews, ornaments, and icons were made for use in the missions, and is one of the few remaining buildings in the area to have a central patio and *zaguán*, or large covered passageway. A cemetery was located behind today's mission church and remained in use throughout much of the nineteenth century, but in the 1890s the present cemetery, directly in front of the church, was opened. One of its unique features is its four *descansos*, or sheltered resting places, at the four corners, a common feature among Spanish and Mexican cemeteries before the twentieth century. The Socorro Cemetery is the last remaining example of this tradition in the El Paso area. The Socorro Mission was designated a Texas Historic Landmark in 1963 and added to the National Register of Historic Places in 1972. Several Texas Historical Commission and Centennial markers are located at the site.[48]

Socorro Cemetery with mission church in background.

Ysleta del Sur Pueblo

Ysleta del Sur Pueblo is a Native-American community located about four miles northwest of Socorro on the Camino Real de Tierra Adentro. The Tigua Indians of Ysleta del Sur trace their origins to Isleta Pueblo, New Mexico, where friars established the mission of *San Antonio de la Isleta*, Saint Anthony of the Little Island, named in 1612 for Saint Anthony of Padua, a thirteenth century Portuguese Franciscan.[49] Isleta Pueblo was located at a strategic site along the trail, near the boundary between Piro and Tiwa territory.[50] For reasons that are unclear, the Isleta Tiwa did not join in the early stages of the 1680 Pueblo Revolt. The written records of the Spanish and the oral traditions of the Tiwa differ, but it appears that the Isletans were divided. Some were loyal to the Spanish and their Franciscan overseers; others saw the rebellion as an opportunity to challenge colonial rule. On August 10, 1680, Lieutenant Governor Alonso García and a small band of soldiers found themselves isolated in the Rio Abajo and in the midst of the rebellion. They received erroneous reports that Santa Fe had been taken by the rebels, and that all the Spaniards in the Rio Arriba had been killed. By nightfall, they moved south to Sandia Pueblo where García gathered area survivors and led a desperate retreat south on the Camino Real. The next day, the refugee train, led by García and his soldiers, entered Isleta Pueblo. If there were any plans to attack the Spanish, they were quickly abandoned as 1,500 men, women, and children overwhelmed the Tiwa. The refugees whom García gathered at the pueblo were a desperate lot. Terrified, they had fled their communities, had few provisions, and were separated from friends and family.[51]

On August 14, with no word from the provincial capital, and amidst growing concerns about impending attacks, García called a general meeting and the decision was made to abandon Isleta Pueblo and seek safety in the south. 317 Indians, mostly Isleta Tiwa, were marched south with the Spanish refugees. They were joined by Piros and Tompiros along the trail. Not all of the Tiwas went willingly; a few remained behind, hiding in the countryside around the pueblo, and some escaped en route. Others fled north to Sandia Pueblo and west into the Hopi lands. Later, when Governor Otermín arrived at Isleta with his Santa Fe refugees, he found the pueblo deserted. He and 500 survivors continued south along the trail and eventually met up with the García party.[52] Together, more than 2,000 Spanish and Indian refugees of the Pueblo Revolt crossed the Jornada del Muerto and arrived in El Paso del Norte in mid-October. They were placed in temporary camps along the river, below the Pass. Isletans were settled at *Santísimo Sacramento*, the Most Holy Sacrament, a refugee camp on the Rio Grande. They quickly constructed a small, temporary chapel of thatch and mud, and on October 12 celebrated a Catholic mass.

Governor Otermín attempted to re-conquer northern New Mexico the next year. On November 5, 1681 he left El Paso del Norte with an army of 146 soldiers, 112 Indian allies, and various missionaries and servants. The troops were poorly equipped and ill-prepared for the venture. Many were armed with only daggers and shields. They secured a few sites, but Pueblo rebels held firm at most of the old mission settlements. Some Tiwa and Piro Indians who had remained behind re-occupied Isleta. Initially, they resisted when Otermín established a camp outside the pueblo, but they soon cooperated with the Spanish. The Governor toured the site and found the church and convent burned and destroyed. Isletans blamed the destruction on Northern Tiwa and Tewa Indians who had raided the pueblo.[53] Otermín remained suspicious, adding to the mounting tensions. A few Isletans probably hoped that the Spanish might offer some protection from rival natives in the region, but others were anxious about their return. As Otermín's men advanced north, they faced intense resistance and gained little ground. By January 1682, the governor concluded that another full-scale attack was imminent, so he ordered a retreat. The Spanish burned Isleta Pueblo and fled, taking 511 Isletans with them. Along the way, 126 escaped. The rest were taken down the Camino Real and were resettled near El Paso del Norte at a new site, *Pueblo de Sacramento de la Ysleta*.[54] It will never be known exactly how many Tiwa were loyal to the Spanish, how many were forcibly brought south, and how many simply tried to avoid being caught up in the conflict.

In the meantime, revolts, food shortages, and desertions had disrupted the refugee camps south of the Pass.[55] By 1691, a new settlement, at *Corpus Christi de la Ysleta de los Tiguas* (or *Ysleta del Sur*, Southern Ysleta), was established and a permanent mission church was completed. The next year, before setting out to re-conquer northern New Mexico, Governor Vargas granted the Tigua formal title to the land, buildings, and furnishings on the site. The grant extended one league north, south, east, and west from the mission church. The settlement was then known as *Misión de San Antonio de la Ysleta*, Saint Anthony's Mission of Ysleta, referring to the Tigua's patron.[56] They constructed an Indian pueblo dwelling, a compact U-shaped multi-story adobe structure that housed several hundred residents, similar to ones that existed in the north. By 1700, it consisted of a series of housing blocks, a *kiva*, or ceremonial chamber, a main plaza, and a cemetery. A devastating flood in 1740 destroyed both the mission church and residential pueblo, and both were rebuilt east of their original sites. Some Tiguas returned north after New Mexico was re-conquered but most remained, and during the eighteenth century about 350 people lived in Ysleta del Sur. Epidemics of the 1780s hit the Tigua population especially hard. The first Spanish census to formally count and list the names of the Tiguas was conducted in 1790 and showed only 55 families, or 191 Indians, residing at the pueblo. At that time, about half of the settlement was mestizo or Spanish.[57]

Ysleta del Sur produced wheat, corn, and fruits, and Tiguas gathered salt at a nearby river channel and at salt flats near the Guadalupe Mountains. Their crafts included rope work, baskets, blankets, and pottery, all commonly traded along the Camino Real. After Mexican independence, Ysleta del Sur attracted Anglo-Americans traders and merchants who worked the Santa Fe and Chihuahua Trails. The American presence greatly increased after 1848, when Ysleta, on the north bank of the Rio Grande, became a part of the United States. Hispanics and Anglo-Americans increasingly dominated the area economy, and Territorial architecture changed much of the appearance of the pueblo. Mexican and Anglo-American influence diluted much of the native culture, but, even so, traditional practices persisted. In 1849, William H.C. Whiting, a United States Army engineer, visited Ysleta while surveying a wagon road from El Paso to the Gulf of Mexico. He described the residents as being:

> somewhat different from the Mexicans…They wear the same wide, flowing drawers, but confine them from the knee with buskins [sic] and moccasins. Their women also wear the buskin. Still speaking their old language, still holding many old customs, time has not diminished their fierce animosity to the Spanish race.[58]

More than thirty years later, in November 1881, United States Army Captain John G. Bourke, who toured many of the Indian pueblos and villages of New Mexico and Arizona, and wrote a detailed account of his journeys, visited Ysleta del Sur. He found Ysleta to be a very active agricultural community, producing apples, peaches, apricots, grapes, corn, wheat, barley, chile, onions, beans, sweet potatoes, and peas. Among the livestock were horses, oxen, cows, burros, mules, pigs, and large herds of sheep and goats.[59] Bourke also noted that the Ysletans had scattered throughout the region: some lived in the nearby town of Socorro and others across the river in Zaragoza. Many complained that the Americans and Mexicans moving into the valley had taken much of their land without any legal claim or compensation. Culturally, he found the pueblo of Ysleta was thoroughly mixed with the Mexican-American town of Ysleta, and that Mexican customs and dress dominated the pueblo. Many of the traditions he had found in the north were absent at Ysleta del Sur, and much of the clan identity had been lost.[60] Even so, at the turn of the century, anthropologist J. Walter Fewkes still found much of the native culture alive. He observed ceremonial dances in the main plaza, the continued use of the Tigua language, and an extant tribal organization.[61]

During the 1850s, Ysleta was connected to other Texas communities by new American roads. One led east toward Hueco Tanks where it junctioned with the upper road of the Butterfield Overland Mail. The lower road, opened in 1859, followed the old Camino Real through the valley with a stop at Ysleta.[62] Travel continued along the old Camino Real with freight, passenger, and mail service north into New Mexico. Ysleta briefly served as the county seat from 1874 to 1883, before the railroad bypassed much of the Lower Valley. Texas Rangers were stationed there in the 1870s and 1880s, during the last stages of the frontier wars against area Apaches, on both sides of the border. The Tiguas, often threatened and harassed by the Apaches and Comanches, served as scouts and organized their local militia to assist the Texas Rangers and the United States cavalry in campaigns against the Apache in the late nineteenth century.[63]

The Tigua land grant has been disputed for several hundred years. In 1854, the Texas legislature recognized a 1751 grant which should have secured Ysleta's claims to large tracts of land around the village. Although the original documents have never been located, the royal grant was well understood by locals, supported by oral tradition, and used in early boundary decisions. Problems arose after 1871, when the legislature approved the incorporation of the town of Ysleta, despite the fact that no local referendum on the matter was ever held. The incorporation allowed for the taxation and sale of land within the grant, which quickly attracted land speculators and dishonest real estate agents. In the coming years, land in Ysleta was purchased for small amounts of money, or in exchange for inexpensive goods, which slowly led to the impoverishment of the Indian population. In some cases, excessive taxes were levied, and when the taxes could not be paid, the land was forfeited. Further losses occurred when the assets of incorporation were sold off by the commissioners' court. The incorporation was dissolved in 1895, but by then much of the land within the original 1751 grant was lost. The tribe filed a lawsuit in the 1960s, which is still working its way through the courts. The Tiguas of Ysleta del Sur still claim large amounts of territory, much of it within the sprawling city limits of contemporary El Paso.[64]

Tigua parishioners at Ysleta. Library of Congress, Prints and Photographs Division, Historic American Buildings Survey, Mision de San Antonio de la Ysleta del Sur, May 25, 1936, HABS TEX,71-YSL,1-3.

Today, Ysleta del Sur is the oldest continually settled site in Texas and the only place in the El Paso area where Native-American culture has been preserved. It has a small historic center, but most of its Colonial and nineteenth-century architecture has been lost. Settlement has shifted east of the church, where the *Barrio de los Indios*, the Neighborhood of the Indians, now blends with the residences of Mexicans, Mexican-Americans, and Anglo-Americans. The Ysleta church has remained the center of the Tigua community for hundreds of years, and the present structure is either the third, or fourth, one built at the site. The 1691 church was greatly damaged in the 1740 flood and within a few years was rebuilt on or near the present site. The basic structure was typical of eighteenth century New Mexican churches: a box-like form, with a single nave, a transept clerestory, and a front facade facing east.[65] In the late nineteenth century, several controversial changes were made. Despite protests from Tiguas in 1870, a picture of Our Lady of Mount Carmel was blessed at the site, and four years later the bishop designated her as the church's official patroness. Her statue became the centerpiece of the church, and the Saint Anthony icon was moved to a side altar. The exterior of the church was remodeled in the 1890s: the front facade was squared, a small gable and two bell niches were added, and new windows were installed. The most dramatic change was the addition of a massive, domed bell tower. In 1907, a major fire destroyed the dome and much of the interior of the church. It was replaced by the smaller, simpler tower that stands today.[66] The central altar remains dedicated to Our Lady of Mount Carmel. A side altar honors Saint Anthony, the patron saint of the Tiguas. The *Santo Entierro* (body in the casket) represents Christ in his tomb before the resurrection. The origins of the icon are unknown, but it is said to be the only flammable object to survive the 1907 fire.[67] While older burial sites existed near the mission church, a nineteenth-century Tigua cemetery is located in a corner of the Mount Carmel Cemetery, on South Zaragosa Road. A rock fence encloses the area in which hand-wrought markers indicate the graves that, unlike the modern arrangements of Mount Carmel, face many directions and are scattered throughout the site.[68]

The layout and design of present-day Ysleta can be seen on eighteenth-century maps. The streets, acequia system, and basic plan of the community have changed little over the years. The Camino Real followed Old Pueblo Road, which served as the southern entrance to the settlement. This portion was known as *La Entrada por el Alto*, the Entrance by the High Bridge, which crossed over the acequia madre. The trail passed between the mission church and the old Ysleta Pueblo located on the west and east sides of the road. Zaragoza Road was an eighteenth-century route to the salt flats near the Guadalupe Mountains. The Camino Real de Tierra Adentro then followed today's Old Country Road, joined Alameda Avenue, and continued northwest. Most of the buildings in the historic center of Ysleta date from the nineteenth and twentieth century, although some may be expanded versions of earlier eighteenth-century structures. Some of the homes feature traditional viga and adobe construction. Various structures along

Old Country Road date from the period and served as stagecoach stations.[69] The Ysleta Mission was added to the National Register of Historic Places in 1972, and in 1986 the El Paso City Council created the Ysleta Historic District to help protect and preserve the community.

The state of Texas recognized Ysleta del Sur Pueblo as an Indian community in 1967. The Tiguas have maintained a tribal government with many Spanish Colonial traditions and more than 300 people were formally recognized as tribal members in the early 1970s, which helped spark a revival of native traditions, a new interest in the Tigua language, and a renewal of tribal ceremonies and customs. Beadwork and pottery traditions have been resurrected, and a small museum, cultural center, and a series of gift shops feature the work of local artisans. Ysleta Pueblo celebrates the feast day of its patron, Saint Anthony of Padua, on June 13 each year with festive activities and traditional ceremonial dances.

2

Ciudad Juárez

After leaving Ysleta del Sur, the Camino Real de Tierra Adentro followed the south bank of the Rio Grande and continued into today's Ciudad Juárez. Although a few Franciscan friars spent time with area Indians at the Pass in the early seventeenth century, no regular missionary work took place until the 1650s, when Francisco Pérez and Juan Cabal built a small, temporary chapel of mud and thatch near the river and began converting the Mansos and Sumas. In 1655, they were joined by Fray García de San Francisco, who had twenty-five years of experience in New Mexico working at the Senecú and Socorro missions. The date traditionally cited for the formal founding of *Nuestra Señora de Guadalupe de los Mansos*, Our Lady of Guadalupe of the Mansos Mission, is 1659.[1] The appellation *Our Lady of Guadalupe* refers to a sighting of the Virgin Mary on the Hill of Tepeyac, just outside of Mexico City, by the Indian peasant Juan Diego in 1531. The image of the Virgin of Guadalupe became a symbol of Christian benevolence and expedited the Catholic conversion of Indians throughout New Spain. By the early seventeenth century, there were numerous chapels, missions, and churches honoring the Virgin along the Camino Real de Tierra Adentro. Rome was slow to recognize the phenomena, and it was not until 1660 that it formally accepted the sighting as the Virgin Mary, and almost one hundred years later before it designated December 12 as an official day of celebration. Since then the Virgin has become a divine symbol of wisdom and motherhood, especially in Mexico. Throughout Latin America, there are devotional societies and cults, as well as local and national celebrations, that have elevated the Virgin of Guadalupe to the role of Patroness of the Americas.[2]

The friars worked with area natives, planting crops, developing an irrigation system, grazing livestock, and overseeing the harvests. They learned the Manso and Suma languages, introduced Christianity, and began to draw settlers into the mission, including some resistant Apaches and Jumanos, and a small number of Piro families from the north. In 1662, Indian laborers began building a larger, permanent mission church. After five years, the temple was completed and was said to rival any of the existing churches in New Mexico. It was built on a gentle rise to avoid floods and still stands at its original site, overlooking today's Plaza de Armas in Ciudad Juárez. The church was dedicated to the Virgin of Guadalupe and opened with a grand celebration in January 1668. To mark the occasion, baptisms and marriages were performed throughout the day, as hundreds of Indians from the surrounding countryside came to view the ceremonies and participate in the festivities. Spanish authority was re-enforced by a grand display of "fireworks, guns, and bombs."[3]

Seventeenth-century mission caravans supplied settlements along the Camino Real about once every three years, and the Guadalupe Mission became a crucial way-station on the Royal Road, standing approximately half-way between the settlements of northern Chihuahua and Santa Fe. Visitors described an oasis in the desert, with flowing irrigation canals, cultivated fields, and vineyards. The Pass provided a respite from the long stretches of desert trail and harsh terrain. It had a reliable river ford and served as the gateway into the New Mexican heartland. For years, travelers camped on the mission grounds and marveled at the stately church, but the calm of daily mission life was shattered in October 1680, when thousands of refugees fleeing the Pueblo Revolt flowed into the Pass. The government-in-exile was headquartered at San Lorenzo el Real, and the civil community of El Paso del Norte became the heart of the Spanish settlement, elevated to the status of a *villa*, a charted settlement with special privileges, in 1683. Missions were re-established downriver and a presidio was built alongside the mission.[4] In 1691, Governor Diego de Vargas used El Paso del Norte as a base for re-establishing Spanish authority in New Mexico, and within a few years several waves of refugees had returned to the north.

By 1700, order was restored, and the Camino Real de Tierra Adentro once again became an active transportation corridor. The Guadalupe Mission, El Paso del Norte, the presidio, and the string of settlements downriver formed a thriving center of agriculture and trade. The population grew and prospered in the first half of the eighteenth century; several large haciendas were organized, and the Pass became an important link in the northern economy. When Bishop Tamarón visited in 1760, he found the country to be "delightful" and described an extensive irrigation system which channeled half of the river's waters into vineyards and fields. He noted plentiful crops of wheat, maize, fruits, and assorted grains.[5] Tamarón also noted the dangers of traveling through the region and was comforted by the presence of a royal presidio with a captain and fifty soldiers. The strategic importance of the Pass was re-enforced by several government reconnaissance surveys that reviewed northern defenses. In 1766, Joseph de Urrutia, a cartographer with the Marqués de Rubí inspection team, produced the first known map of El Paso del Norte. The Urrutia map shows the Guadalupe Mission and convent, the presidio, and an irrigation system that drew water from the Rio Grande. It also pinpoints two branch roads of the Camino Real de Tierra Adentro that wound through the villa. One approached from the east, connecting missions in the Lower Valley and the settlements of Senecú and San Lorenzo. An irrigation canal, *del Rio Grande del Norte*, from the Great River of the North, paralleled the road and carried water to settlements downstream. Today's Avenida 16 de Septiembre generally follows the path of this roadway and canal through Ciudad Juárez. A second road, the *Camino del Carrizal*, led south to the presidio town of Carrizal and onto Chihuahua City. It paralleled the *Acequia de los Indios*, the Canal of the Indians, which flowed southeast through today's San José district. Present-day Avenida Reforma follows the same general path.[6]

Even as the region prospered, typhus and smallpox epidemics, Indian raids and rebellions downriver, and a series of major floods, brought stagnation. Large haciendas were abandoned, and the local economy declined, but by the end of the century the epidemics had subsided, new presidios at Carrizal and San Elizario protected trade along the trail, and agriculture flourished once again. In the Mexican era, El Paso del Norte remained the largest of six area settlements. New land grants opened areas in the north to homesteading, and trade with the United States brought new opportunities to the Pass. Canutillo, Santa Teresa, and what would later become American El Paso were all settled during the 1820s, and the Santa Fe Trail connected Missouri with Santa Fe. Trading patterns changed as the old Camino Real became an international trail, bringing American merchants, traders, and caravans through El Paso del Norte. The northern segment of the Camino Real between Santa Fe and Chihuahua City became known as the Chihuahua Trail. So many goods came through the Pass that Mexico established a customhouse there in the 1830s to regulate trade.[7]Several regional and international conflicts impacted El Paso del Norte.

Sporadic Indian raids continued as Mexico abandoned traditional Spanish peace programs and waged war against the Apaches. In 1841, captured members of the Texan-Santa Fe Expedition were brought to El Paso del Norte and were kindly received by Father Ramón Ortiz. During the Mexican-American War, United States forces under Colonel Alexander Doniphan routed Mexican troops at Brazito and took El Paso del Norte without firing a shot. After spending less than two months at the Pass, they continued south and defeated Mexican forces at the Battle of Sacramento on February 28 and marched into Chihuahua City in March 1847. The 1848 Treaty of Guadalupe Hidalgo moved the international border and brought American settlers to the east bank of the river. After the war, El Paso del Norte gained importance as the flow of American goods increased. It served exile communities along the new international boundary and established new ties with American El Paso.

Many Anglo-Americans were impressed with life at the Pass. George Gibson observed that in the 1840s the town was "different from anything in New Mexico or the United States with its *acequias*, which are almost canals, its fruit trees and shrubbery, [and] its vineyards and orchards handsomely arranged."[8] Several years later Judge Davis noted that:

> The settlement extends down the valley some ten or twelve miles, and the population is estimated at 6,000. The houses are so much interspersed with vineyards, orchards, and cultivated fields, that it presents more the appearance of a succession of plantations than a town. The *Plaza*, as the more compact portion is called, is near the head of the valley, where is situated the old cathedral, customs-house, and other public buildings, and where the trade of the town is carried on…As we rode through the town I was struck with the charming appearance it presented. On every side were vineyards, flower gardens, orchards, and shrubbery, loaded with foliage, flowers, and fruits, and little canals carried the water along nearly all the streets, and through the gardens and yards, adding to the pleasantness of the scene.[9]

He concluded that with a "climate that rivals that of Italy, it can easily be conceived that, as a place of residence, it is almost an earthly paradise."[10] El Paso del Norte grew slowly to about 4,500 residents by the 1850s. Its remote location also provided political refuge when Benito Juárez established his exiled government here in the 1860s, spending almost a year at the Pass.[11]

In the early 1880s, the railroad connected the Pass with the eastern and western United States and reached south to Mexico City, further increasing the flow of goods and people. The old Camino Real continued to be used locally and regionally, but within a few years railroads carried much of the freight. In 1888, El Paso del Norte was re-named Ciudad Juárez, in honor of Benito Juárez, and a new urban elite emerged to oversee the expansion and development of the city. The historic core was transformed, and the basic adobe architecture that had dominated the Pass for 200 years was soon replaced by brick facades, pitched metal roofs, lumber framing, shingling, and posts and porches; all materials that were brought in on the railroads. Downtown Ciudad Juárez and urban segments of the old trail resembled an American main street, streamlined and modernized for the new commercial look of the city. Although still a rather small, compact city, a new municipal building, a customhouse, a commercial center, and American bungalow-style houses were built. The central plaza was re-designed with a gazebo and park, and Comercio Street (Avenida 16 de Septiembre), the path of the old Camino Real, resembled a bustling, urban American commercial thoroughfare.

In the early twentieth century, Ciudad Juárez played a critical role in the Mexican Revolution. Its location on the Mexican Central Railroad, and its close proximity to the United States, made the city a strategic site and a center of revolutionary activity. Ciudad Juárez became the main path of funding, arms, munitions, and people. Mexicans fleeing the fighting in the interior crowded into Ciudad Juárez and often across the border into American El Paso. Revolutionary leaders, including Francisco Madero and "Pancho" Villa, headquartered their operations at the Pass, and several important battles between revolutionary and federal forces took place on the streets of Ciudad Juárez. As the revolution was winding down in the late 1910s, prohibition brought a new surge of tourists to El Paso, Texas, who crossed the bridges and enjoyed the lively nightlife of Ciudad Juárez. During the 1920s, the city gained a reputation as a wild party town with nightclubs and cabarets, saloons, gambling, cockfighting, bullfights, carnivals, and horse racing. An underground economy of prostitution, narcotics, and organized crime developed as well.[12]The boom turned to bust with the Great Depression of the 1930s. Tourism declined, restrictions on trade and travel reduced commerce along the border, and prohibition was repealed. The Ciudad Juárez economy, which had become so dependent on the United States economy, declined rapidly. At the same time, the Mexican government began a campaign to clean up the border towns. There were crackdowns on criminal rings, prostitution, and narcotics. Unemployment soared and city services were stretched to the limit. Inflation, a devalued peso, rationing, and nationalist restrictions added to the stress.[13]

A 1939 visit by President Lázaro Cárdenas signaled a new direction for the city. Cárdenas traveled by train from Mexico City, and, while visiting Chihuahua City and Cuidad Juárez, he personally inspected segments of the new automobile highway under construction between the interior and the border, which paralleled the old Camino Real. Mexican businessmen and their counterparts from El Paso met with the president and discussed major changes that would be taking place as automobile traffic and trucking opened new international trade and tourism opportunities for both countries.[14] By the 1940s, Ciudad Juárez was recovering. The expansion of Fort Bliss and other area military facilities during the Second World War revived the tourist trade. A new, upscale nightlife brought well-known performers and international celebrities to the city. A small industry of "quickie divorces" attracted an entirely new type of tourist. Many came in their automobiles, expanding the travel and tourism industry. The American interstate system and new Mexican federal highways, often along the path of the old Camino Real, dramatically increased traffic. By the 1950s, the economic direction of the republic shifted toward industry and manufacturing and lessened its dependency on agriculture. Many Mexican nationals, who had worked in the United States as *braceros* (wartime laborers), returned to the republic and settled along the border. *Maquiladores*, or twin plants, led to an international manufacturing boom along the border. Ciudad Juárez drew large numbers of migrants from the Mexican interior in search of higher paying jobs, and investments in the Mexican infrastructure aided in the growth. As a result, both Ciudad Juárez and American El Paso experienced dramatic population increases during the second half of the twentieth century. As urban sprawl increased and shantytowns spread across the city's northwest, the population of the small border town reached 131,000 by 1950 and grew approximately ten times as much by the end of the century. Today, Ciudad Juárez is home to approximately 1,500,000 people, and, along with 700,000 residents of American El Paso, is the largest border community anywhere in the world. Although most of Ciudad Juárez has been built during the last sixty years, several significant sites survive from the era of the Camino Real de Tierra Adentro.[15]

Senecú

The Camino Real de Tierra Adentro followed the south bank of the river from Ysleta del Sur into Senecú, now a suburb of Ciudad Juárez. Senecú traces its origins to *Misión San Antonio de Senecú de los Piros*, the Mission of Saint Anthony of Senecú of the Piros, founded in the 1620s about 150 miles north, near today's San Marcial, New Mexico. At the time of the 1680 Pueblo Revolt, it was inhabited by several Franciscans, Piro and Tompiro Indians, and a small number of Apaches. They joined Governor Otermín's refugees in the retreat to El Paso del Norte and were re-settled at *Senecú del Sur*, Southern Senecú.[16] They were first placed further downriver but were moved closer to the Guadalupe Mission in the early 1680s, and by 1706 the first permanent church was constructed, along with a multi-storied adobe pueblo and kiva. The original mission lands spread as far east as Alameda Avenue in El Paso, Texas, but frequent river flooding often shifted the main river channel, dividing Senecú and destroying the community's churches and residences. As the settlement was rebuilt, it moved further to the west.[17] The church in today's Valle de Senecú district is built around the core structure of an early nineteenth-century one, near the site of the original colonial settlement. The acequia madre, which flows from today's downtown, and formerly irrigated the farmlands of the mission, winds through the posh residences, gated communities, and grounds of the Juárez Country Club.[18]

Most of the 700 people who lived at Senecú in the early eighteenth century were Piro Indians, but by 1760 Bishop Tamarón noted many Sumas there as well.[19] During the next few decades, disease, rebellions, and desertions reduced their numbers, and by the early nineteenth century Spaniards and mestizos outnumbered Indians. Fray José Bravo inventoried the site in 1795 and found a poor church, lacking many basic necessities. While it may have been well-furnished at some point in the past, in the 1790s many of the items listed in the inventory were noted as being old, worn, mistreated, or damaged. Although the church was sparsely furnished, it did have two full adobe altars and ten statues, including one of the patron Saint Anthony. Fray Bravo noted that mid-century floods had greatly damaged the adobe church; the walls had substantial cracks, and the transept had been removed because of the weak foundation. The nearby convent was also on the verge of collapse. Fray Bravo also noted that "with another spell of bad weather I fear total ruin."[20] Sometime after 1800, river flooding swept the dilapidated church away, and a new one was built further west on higher ground.[21] Mission Senecú continued to suffer in the early nineteenth century, especially after the 1829 flood, when the new church was apparently badly damaged.

Fewer travelers were mentioning Senecú by mid-century, but, in 1850 Commissioner Bartlett met a group of Indians whom he noted as being descendants of the old Piro tribe. He wrote that they:

> wore short jackets, decorated with innumerable bell-buttons, and dark pantaloons...open at the outside from the hip to the ankle, with large white trowsers [sic] beneath. The women all wore short black dresses reaching just below the knees, with a thin white muslin mantle thrown over their shoulders. A bright red silk shawl was tied around their waists, and they had bunches or bows of gay ribbons in their hair. All their faces were painted alike, with a spot of vermilion on each cheek, surrounded by a border of small white dots.[22]

Bartlett observed their music and dancing, noting that they lived at "Sinecu" which their ancestors had occupied for centuries. He estimated that fewer than eighty Indians remained there and that they were rapidly losing their language and customs. Even so, fifty years later some remnants of native Piro culture had survived after all. In 1902, J. Walter Fewkes described the community as a small cluster of adobe houses near an old church. The few remaining Piros had a tribal organization and performed ceremonial dances during festivals using traditional drums and hand rattles. No one spoke Piro, but older members of the community still knew a few words and phrases.[23] By the mid-twentieth century, these traditions and practices had disappeared, and Senecú remained a small, quiet agricultural settlement, separate from Ciudad Juárez. Within the last fifty years, Senecú has been swarmed by commercial and residential development and is now in the heart of an upscale neighborhood, surrounded by a country club and golf course.

The present Senecú church under construction, sometime after 1912. El Paso County Historical Society Collections.

San Lorenzo el Real

San Lorenzo is about two and one-half miles west of Senecú along Avenida 16 de Septiembre. Although it too was once a small village on the outskirts of the city, it is now simply a continuation of the urban sprawl of Ciudad Juárez, and, like Senecú, has lost much of its identity as a separate community. San Lorenzo was founded in 1680 and named to commemorate the August 10 feast day of San Lorenzo, the day the Pueblo Revolt erupted in northern New Mexico. San Lorenzo (Saint Lawrence) was a third-century deacon in the Roman Church who was persecuted along with the bishop and other high church officials in 258 CE. He suffered a true martyr's fate by being grilled to death on an open red-hot gridiron. After the 1680 Pueblo Revolt, the refugee community established a series of settlements southeast of the Guadalupe Mission, and San Lorenzo was originally located about twelve leagues downstream, near today's Guadalupe.

Because it was near the site where the Oñate expedition took formal possession of New Mexico (during the ceremony known as *La Toma*), it was referred to as *San Lorenzo el Real de la Toma,* The Royal Settlement of San Lorenzo at the Site of the Taking of Possession. It became the home of the exiled government of New Mexico and was comprised mostly of Spanish and mestizo residents.[24]In 1684, San Lorenzo was moved upstream, much closer to the Guadalupe Mission, and "La Toma" was dropped from its name. The 1684 site was probably near the end of today's Camino Viejo a San Lorenzo, among the housing projects that lie about one mile southeast of today's San Lorenzo Church. The lands that comprised the San Lorenzo community spread further east, into what today is the Ascarate area of east El Paso. The center of San Lorenzo shifted northwest during the eighteenth and nineteenth centuries, after the periodic flooding of the Rio Grande.[25]

San Lorenzo's function as a center of government lapsed after the re-conquest of New Mexico and it was virtually abandoned in the mid-1690s, as many of the residents returned north. Later, some Suma Indians were moved to San Lorenzo, and a small Spanish and mestizo population re-settled the site.[26] By the mid-eighteenth century, San Lorenzo was a cosmopolitan settlement composed of Manso, Tiwa, Suma, Piro, and a few Tlaxcalan Indians, who were overseen by Franciscan missionaries.[27] But the Indian population declined during the rest of the century, and an 1814 census registered far more *vecinos*, or mestizo residents, than Indians.[28] Bishop Tamarón described the village as a community made up of Spaniards and Indians with a typically modest church. Located only a few miles away from the Guadalupe Mission, it never became an important agricultural or commercial center, nor a paraje.[29] Camino Real travelers often mentioned, but seldom described, San Lorenzo, and as recently as the 1950s it remained a small agricultural community on the outskirts of Ciudad Juárez.

Of all of the communities at the Pass, San Lorenzo is most associated with the tradition of *Matachines* dancers and is best-known for its feast of San Lorenzo held on August 10 each year. Los Matachines is a religious dance that dates back to the traditions of medieval Spain, depicting the struggle between Christians and Moors. When the Spanish colonized the New World, they brought their ritual dances and incorporated Indian symbols, music, and rhythms. Over time, Catholic and Mexican icons, such as the Holy Cross and Virgin of Guadalupe, were blended, and a distinctly American traditional dance pageant emerged.

Matachines dances are usually held during major religious feast days. Typical performances include ten to twenty dancers who portray characters such as Moctezuma, La Malinche, or El Toro. Because the pageant is lengthy, many observers do not realize that an entire story is woven into the performance. It usually deals with the attempt of a young virgin to defeat paganism and allow Christianity to triumph. Characters representing elders, such as *El Abuelo*, or the Grandfather, or *La Vieja*, the Old Woman, provide comic relief. At San Lorenzo, locals dance the Matachines in the southern style common throughout Mexico, dressed in brilliant red attire and accompanied by drums and violins. The entire sequence can take hours, and sometimes the entire day, to perform.[30]

San Lorenzo's feast day on August 10 has also become famous for its ritual pilgrimages, symbolizing the retreat from northern New Mexico. People walk the four miles from the Guadalupe Mission to San Lorenzo where they encounter the Matachines dancers and a lively day-long fiesta. Throughout the twentieth century these spectacular festivals have drawn tens of thousands of people although their numbers have tempered in recent years.[31] Today's church is located within a mile of the earlier structures and remains the center of the San Lorenzo community. It was rebuilt in the nineteenth century, renovated in the 1950s and 1990s, and bears little resemblance to its colonial predecessors. To the left of the large central interior is a small Sanctuary of San Lorenzo, featuring a modern marble altar and a tiny, gilded Colonial-era wooden statue of the church's patron saint, which is said to have miraculous healing powers. The faithful regularly frequent the sanctuary, praying to San Lorenzo for aid, and making offerings. Modern statuary and furnishings are found throughout the small side chapel.

Our Lady of Guadalupe Mission

The Camino Real de Tierra Adentro continued along today's Camino Viejo a San Lorenzo and Avenida Alanís, and Avenida 16 de Septiembre, about four miles to Our Lady of Guadalupe Mission.[32] Although dwarfed by the modern cathedral alongside, this is the oldest and best preserved colonial site in Ciudad Juárez. When first built in the 1660s, it had typical New Mexican features: basic adobe brick construction, a flat roof, a long rectangular nave, and clerestory lighting. Elaborate vigas, corbels, pews, and doorways were made of area aspens. An *atrio*, or walled yard, surrounded the mission, and a cemetery was located in front of the church. The original altars featured carved wooden *santos* and religious ornaments. A large beautiful canvas, lit by the clerestory window, depicted Our Lady of Guadalupe. Musical instruments were placed in a choir loft, and by the 1700s a small organ provided music for services. A *convento*, a small separate building, served as the friars' residence. The mission bells were probably hung from a wooden frame outside the church.[33] The mission structure remained simple in appearance for almost 250 years. Mid-nineteenth century drawings show the adobe church and convento, a bare open courtyard, and a low wall surrounding the complex. Only the large three-story bell tower, added in the late eighteenth century and separate from the mission, showed any elaborate architectural detail.

"The Plaza and Church of El Paso" by A. de Vainducourt, c.1852. Courtesy of El Paso Public Library, Border Heritage Collections.

Substantial changes were made in the late nineteenth century. A new brick molding façade covered the front of the mission, and a pair of large niches with religious statues, were inset high above the doorway. A small tower and clock were placed atop the church in the 1920s, and a neo-classical and baroque altarpiece, modern statuary, stained-glass windows, and chandeliers were added to the interior. In the early 1940s, the large, imposing modern cathedral, also dedicated to the Virgin of Guadalupe, was built next door, at times literally overshadowing the old mission. As the area around the new cathedral developed, the small church lost its prominence. The destruction of the old convento, the building of a stone parish office, and commercial development downtown crowded the site further, obscuring the view of the church.[34] By the 1960s, the Guadalupe Mission looked quite different than it did in the colonial era and was in need of extensive repair and renovation. In 1967, a major restoration project was begun under the direction of the Juárez Diocese and the Mexican government. Architect Felipe Lacouture oversaw the strengthening and stabilizing of the old mission church, removing most of the late nineteenth-and early twentieth-century additions. Using nineteenth-century images and documentary descriptions, workers meticulously restored the Guadalupe Mission. The elaborate interior woodwork was stripped, cleaned, and refinished.[35] Religious ornaments and statuary were replaced with pieces more reminiscent of the colonial period. The exterior of the church and bell tower were refinished and re-plastered, producing a smooth white finish over the adobe base. Today, Nuestra Señora de Guadalupe is one of the best examples of colonial New Mexico mission architecture along the entire trail.

Plaza de Armas and the Presidio Site

The landscape surrounding the old mission church has also changed considerably since the nineteenth century. For hundreds of years, the open space below the mission was filled with wagons and livestock and served as a campsite, corral, and trading center. Caravans and wagon trains often spent days camped there before continuing on their journey along the Camino Real. In 1881, the arrival of two major railroads at American El Paso on the opposite bank of the river brought sweeping changes to El Paso del Norte. In 1882, the first train crossed from the United States into Mexico and construction of the Mexican Central Railway was begun, starting from El Paso del Norte and reaching Chihuahua City by the year's end. By 1884, Mexico City was connected to the major western railroads of the United States through El Paso del Norte. In 1885, the Mexican government created a free trade zone, and, the old historic center, antiquated with its typical adobe dwellings, vineyards, orchards, and a handful of mercantile establishments, was transformed. Over the next two years, a building and landscaping spree brought modern commercial establishments, elegant department stores, and jewelry, liquor, clothing and curio shops to the center. Factories, mills, and manufacturing establishments followed. The barren, open plaza was redesigned to have the look of a more typical Mexican *plaza de armas*, or parade grounds. It was landscaped as a park with trees, benches, and monuments. Commercial establishments replaced the temporary vendors' stalls and spread up the streets surrounding the church. A bullring and a market were built along Calle del Porvenir (today's Vicente Guerrero). By the early twentieth century, the entire area became a bustling commercial zone filled with shops, craftsmen, and street vendors.[36]

The colonial presidio was located directly behind the Guadalupe Mission, where the old City Hall now stands. In 1683, the exiled New Mexican government established the *Presidio de Nuestra Señora del Pilar del Paso del Rio del Norte,* The Fortress of Our Lady of Pilar at the Pass of the River of the North, about sixteen miles downriver, but it was moved to this site in the new villa of El Paso del Norte the next year. The original adobe-constructed fortress was a series of rooms grouped around two patios. A round defensive tower was located at the southwest corner of the compound. There were living quarters for the captain and his family and a barracks for regular troops. In the eighteenth century, about fifty soldiers were in regular service at the presidio.[37] After 1772, the military and civil systems of the north were re-organized. A company of presidial soldiers from El Paso del Norte was moved south to Carrizal to better protect travelers along the Camino Real, and in 1788 construction began downriver for a second new presidio at San Elizario. Local militia units operated from El Paso del Norte and communities along the river, responding to Indian attacks and providing escorts north along the trail to Robledo. The old presidio building became a militia headquarters and center of government activities. The Lieutenant Governor of New Mexico, based in El Paso, was a military officer but also held the highest position in local civil government. He was responsible for the protection of El Paso del Norte and its neighboring communities. Many historic events during the Spanish Colonial and Mexican eras, such as negotiations with area Apaches, took place at this site. Colonel Doniphan's troops raised the American flag over the presidio during their occupation of El Paso del Norte in 1846–47, and it remained a fortress during the last stages of the Apache wars in the 1880s.[38] The old presidio is the core of today's *Palacio Municipal*, the old City Hall, which stands directly behind the Guadalupe Mission and the cathedral. This large two-story structure with an interior patio was constructed around the old fortress in 1947. Its thick adobe walls are covered with saw-cut lava blocks brought up from the Mexico City Basin. Like the old presidio, it served as the center of civil government, functioning as the city hall until the 1970s. The building was re-modeled in the late 1990s and today houses the Municipal Center for the Arts. The Juárez coat of arms adorns the front façade and a mural illustrating scenes of local history is located in the foyer. Upstairs, the old mayor's office and city council meeting room are enclosed by elaborate hand-carved woodwork.[39]

The Palacio Municipal, behind the Guadalupe Mission, was built around the seventeenth-century presidio.

San José

While most travelers entered El Paso del Norte along the Mission Trail of the Camino Real through Senecú and San Lorenzo, some took a second, more direct route that led straight north through the Samalayuca sands dunes and bypassed settlements along the river. The two branches of the Camino Real de Tierra Adentro spilt at Ojo Lucero, near today's El Lucero, Chihuahua. The Samalayuca route continued north about fifteen miles and then began to enter *Los Médanos*, the Sand Dunes. Within a five-mile stretch, the trail passed through the worst of the dunes, but the next ten miles remained torturous as well and tried even the most experienced travelers. Parties had to be well-provisioned for the journey as there were no settlements, sources of water, or parajes in the dunes, only blowing, drifting sand and the relentless desert sun. In 1846, George F. Ruxton wrote:

> The huge rolling mass of sand is nearly destitute of vegetation…Road there is none, but a track across is marked by the skeletons and dead bodies of oxen, and of mules and horses, which everywhere meet the eye. On one ridge the upper half of a human skeleton protruded from the sand, and bones of animals and carcasses in every stage of decay. The sand is knee-deep and constantly shifting, and pack-animals have great difficulty in passing.[40]

Others had similar experiences. Adolph Wislizenus described his night crossing of Los Médanos as "appalling" and "ghastly." He made a vow that "whenever I should undertake this trip again, I would rather go three days around, than travel once more over the sand hills with a wagon."[41] As late as the 1850s, Bartlett noted that only "persons on horseback, pack-mules, and light pleasure wagons alone attempt to cross the [sand] hills."[42] The trail then reached *Ojo Samalayuca*, a natural spring, just southeast of today's village of Samalayuca.[43] From there, the trail continued approximately twenty-seven miles north to the center of El Paso del Norte. On this entire stretch of the Camino Real, from Ojo Lucero into El Paso del Norte, there were no settlements of any kind. Not one hacienda, presidio, mission, or village is mentioned in any travelers' accounts. Only occasional bandits or small groups of Suma Indians roamed the sand hills.

The path of the Camino Real into the city followed today's Avenida Oscar

Flores and the former Mexican National Railway. Eighteenth-and nineteenth-century El Paso del Norte spread west, above the floodplain, but the lower edge of the city reached only a few miles south into the desert. The Camino Real entered the city through today's San José district, along the path of *Antiguo Camino a San José*, the Old Road to San José, which leads into Avenida Reforma and the Guadalupe mission, about four miles away. San José lies along the *Acequia de los Indios*, the Acequia of the Indians, an irrigation system that has been in use for hundreds of years and still runs through the western edge of the neighborhood. San José remained a rural agricultural area until quite recently but was overrun by development in the 1970s.[44]It appears to have been sporadically settled during the colonial era and abandoned during much of the nineteenth century. Legend has it that a small church or shrine stood there serving as a paraje for weary travelers, and a refuge from bandit and Indian attacks. Today, San José is the site of the San José Chapel, a small late nineteenth-century church that is hidden behind a shopping center and surrounded by industrial and commercial growth. The chapel, also called commonly a mission church, is a basic, well-kept, square structure with a curvilinear parapet wall, a bell tower, parish quarters, and a cemetery secured behind a large iron gate. The interior is quite simple, with modern statuary, woodwork, and furnishings. Three prominent Paseños and members of their families are associated with San José and lie buried in the small cemetery behind the church. Although the chapel was badly damaged in a 2007 flood, efforts are underway to rebuild the structure and restore the cemetery site.

Father Ramón Ortiz (1814–1896), a renowned and revered parish priest of nineteenth-century El Paso del Norte, was born into an established and well-connected Santa Fe family whose ancestors arrived with the Vargas re-conquest. Young Ramón was taken south to Durango and Chihuahua City to study for the priesthood and he was ordained in 1837. In 1838, he was appointed *cura*, or parish priest, for the Nuestra Señora de Guadalupe parish in El Paso del Norte. For sixty-two years, he served as head of the parish and helped establish and oversee churches in Carrizal, Casas Grandes, Janos, La Mesilla, Socorro and Ysleta. After the Mexican-American War, he became a commissioner of *colonias*, new settlements, and helped establish Mesilla, Guadalupe, and San Ignacio. Throughout his life, Ortiz witnessed some of the most turbulent periods of El Paso del Norte's history and played an important role in protecting his parishioners and re-building relations on both sides of the border.[45] Ortiz lived in a large comfortable home surrounded by orchards, vineyards, and corrals, a few miles downriver from the Guadalupe Church. Until the 1860s, he operated a dam and mill at the site. Although he never married or had children of his own, he became the patriarch of a large extended family that included his sisters, their children, and an adopted Tarahumara Indian boy. Ortiz entertained and offered lodging to many visitors, including Mexicans, Anglo-Americans, and some of the first Mormon settlers in the area. He was said to have entertained Benito Juárez during his stay at the Pass. He was known as a "Renaissance man," well-read, comfortable with people from all walks of life, and particularly aware of the great political, social, and economic changes underway in the mid-nineteenth century.[46]

The San José Chapel, on the road south to Carrizal.

In the summer of 1841, a group of about 320 Texans laid claim to New Mexican land along the Rio Grande and tried to annex it as part of the new Republic of Texas. This disastrous attempted-invasion became known as the Texan-Santa Fe Expedition. New Mexico's governor, Manuel Armijo, defeated the invaders and took 172 surviving Texans as prisoners. They were marched down the Camino Real toward Mexico City and along the way suffered the wrath and abuse of their New Mexican captors. They were reportedly tortured, starved, and tormented, and taken through the notorious Jornada del Muerto. When they arrived at El Paso del Norte, José Manuel Elias González, the commanding officer in charge at the presidio, was outraged at the treatment the men had received. Father Ortiz came forward to care for the prisoners. Their wounds were bandaged, they were bathed and fed, and clothing was repaired and replaced. The kindly Ortiz oversaw the entire humanitarian process, rallying his parishioners and providing whatever was needed to save the lives of the tortured men and prepare them for the difficult journey ahead. One prisoner, George Wilkins Kendall, who later became co-founder of the New Orleans *Picayune*, wrote that "if ever a noble heart beat in man it was in the breast of this young, generous and liberal priest."[47]

The next encounter Ortiz had with American soldiers was during the Mexican-American War. As Doniphan's troops headed south along the Camino Real from Santa Fe in December 1846, Ortiz did what he could to resist the invasion. He sent reports to Chihuahua City detailing American troop movements and conditions at El Paso and encouraged his fellow Paseños to support the remaining Mexican troops. Many area farmers and laborers served with Mexican forces but were defeated at the Battle of Brazito (between El Paso and Las Cruces) on December 25, 1846. Later, several militia units headed north to confront the Americans, but desertions and disagreements led to their disbandment. There was no organized effort to defend the Pass. In late December, several local leaders worked out an amicable surrender; Doniphan's army secured El Paso del Norte, and comfortable arrangements were made for the American troops. Ortiz refused to welcome the invaders. Doniphan, fearing that Ortiz might organize resistance, took him into custody and held him hostage as they made their way south to Chihuahua City. After Chihuahua was secured, Ortiz was released, and he returned home to his family in El Paso del Norte.[48]

Within a few years, Ortiz became involved in a third great conflict, this time with the Liberal government of Benito Juárez (1806–1872). President

Juárez, an Indian from the state of Oaxaca who had once trained for the priesthood, enacted a series of reform laws under the Constitution of 1857 that greatly restricted the powers of the Catholic Church. Its properties were limited and often confiscated. While the rights of baptism, marriage, and burial were guaranteed by the new codes, the role of the church was diminished. The powers and privileges of clergy were now closely regulated by the government. Day-to-day church practices and informal religious traditions that had grown up around Catholic beliefs were further controlled. Matachines dances and processions associated with the December Virgin of Guadalupe celebrations were ended. Church fees, supplies, and pleas for support from the community were closely regulated.

Ortiz was greatly disheartened by these reforms, especially when his own nephew, Doctor Mariano Samaniego, serving in the El Paso del Norte government, enforced the new Liberal codes. To make matters worse, a new ruling elite often benefitted from the changes. Governor Luís Terrazas confiscated church property, helping him become the wealthiest landowner in the state of Chihuahua. Ortiz asked to be relieved of his parish duties in 1865 and spent the next eight years in a self-imposed exile, torn between the greater struggle taking place between church and state. He fled to the high sierra and worked with the Tarahumara Indians, served in small rural churches, and tried to stay clear of deepening political conflicts of the day. But he was often witness to the constant guerrilla warfare and brutality of the conflict. Disobeying the church, he stayed away from El Paso del Norte, especially when the exiled Juárez government took refuge there in 1865–66. He briefly allied himself with the French Intervention, hoping this would offer greater protection to the Catholic Church in Mexico. It was not until 1873, when a new government and bishop were safely in power, that Ortiz was allowed to return to his parish at El Paso del Norte.[49] Father Ortiz remained in El Paso del Norte the rest of his life, enjoying his parishioners, his extended family, and friends on both sides of the river. His efforts healed many of the wounds of the Mexican War and often led to cooperation between the developers of American El Paso and El Paso del Norte. Ortiz lived in the Chamizal area until the 1870s when he moved to an estate at San José, near the chapel, on the outskirts of the city. When he died in 1896, the elaborate funeral procession began at the Guadalupe Mission and traveled south to the San José Cemetery,[50]where he was interned.

Ramón Ortiz's widowed cousin, Josefa Delgado Samaniego and her five children were living in Sonora in the 1830s when Ortiz made a dangerous journey through Apache country to bring them to his home in El Paso del Norte. They moved into his estate and became a part of his extended family. Josefa Delgado became a permanent resident at the Ortiz home and oversaw the household for the remainder of the nineteenth century. Her youngest child, Mariano (1831–1905), was tutored by Ortiz, attended the seminary in Durango, and received a degree in medicine from the University of Paris. After returning to Mexico, he worked with Benito Juárez's Liberals, served as a surgeon in Luis Terrazas' republican forces, and once again made his home in El Paso del Norte. He was one of the first doctors and dentists in the area and was well-known for his charity and work with the poor. As his practice expanded, Mariano invested in a variety of financial ventures, becoming one of the wealthiest men in El Paso del Norte, and was soon prominent in local and regional politics. Samaniego is often credited with playing a major role in the transformation of the small border settlement of El Paso del Norte into the modern community of Ciudad Juárez. His lavish funeral, perhaps as large as that of Father Ortiz, attracted thousands of mourners from both sides of the border. On October 4, 1905 Mariano Samaniego was laid to rest in the cemetery at San José.[51]

Mariano's sister, Concepción, married Inocente Ochoa (1824–1909), a prosperous merchant who invested heavily in the freight business, as well as ranching, mining, and commercial development. He eventually became the wealthiest man in Ciudad Juárez, with an estate valued at millions of dollars by the time of his death. He had extensive real estate holdings throughout the city and owned many of the buildings along Calle Commercio (now 16 de Septiembre). His typical court-adobe home, with a zaguán and placita, was the most lavish in the city, and housed presidents and dignitaries (including Benito Juárez) during their visits to the Pass. Although there were sometimes political and social conflicts between the two men, Ochoa and Samaniego were well-connected business partners, investing in new developments and founding the Banco de Minero. Ochoa also owned the Hacienda de Samalayuca and helped make way for the Mexican Central Railway. Inocente Ochoa is said to have bought the chapel at San José and remodeled it for his wife, Concepción, in the late nineteenth century. They lie buried in the same family cemetery as Ortiz and Samaniego, behind the chapel.[52]

Benito Juárez's weary government-in-exile had traveled through Guadalupe and Senecú when they first came to El Paso del Norte in 1865. On their second journey north, they rushed through the Samalayuca area and into San José.[53] Benito Juárez became the first full-blooded Indian leader of Mexico and the first who did not have a military background. He brought a series of moderate reforms to his home state and more effectively managed the government. He opposed the regime of Antonio López de Santa Anna and left the country for a brief time, living in New Orleans. When Santa Anna resigned and fled the republic in 1855, Juárez returned and helped organize a new government, beginning an era known as *La Reforma* (the Reform). A new constitution in 1857 and the *Ley Juárez* (Juárez's Law) abolished special privilege, especially for the church and military, and declared citizens of the republic equal before the law. Juárez served as chief justice in the new government and, following an attempted takeover by conservatives, served as interim president in late 1858. A new civil war, the War of the Reform, erupted between liberal and conservative factions, but after forging alliances throughout different regions of the country, the liberals were able to build support for their cause and re-captured Mexico City in early 1861. Benito Juárez was formally elected president of the republic and set out to restore order and reform the national government. However, Juárez had inherited an empty treasury and insurmountable debts. Commerce was stagnant, the national infrastructure failing, and little currency was in circulation. In desperation, Juárez chose to stop payments on foreign debts. Outraged European creditors launched a plan for the occupation of Mexico.[54] Emperor Louis Napoleon Bonaparte III, nephew of the infamous Napoleon, decided to intervene and sent the army of the Second French Empire, supported by Spain and England in order to enforce repayment of the debt. The foreign troops were temporarily repelled at Puebla on May 5, 1862 (now celebrated as *Cinco de Mayo*) but regrouped and advanced, driving the Juárez government into exile in 1863. The Juárez government took refuge in the north, first at San Luis Potosí, and then continued along the Camino Real to Chihuahua City and El Paso del Norte.[55]

Convinced that the United States would not oppose their strategy, Napoleon III and Mexican conservatives arranged for Maximilian von Hapsburg, brother of the emperor of Austria, to be declared the emperor of Mexico. He arrived in Mexico to assume power in May 1864. Maximilian represented quite a contradiction. He was supported by the conservatives, but his views were closer to those of Juárez. His attempts to implement liberal polices, including an invitation to Juárez to serve in his government, infuriated conservatives but gained him little support from the liberals. Exiles continued to fight the French intervention, even after Maximilian instituted the death penalty for anyone involved in the liberal cause. When the American Civil War ended in 1865, Abraham Lincoln sought to invoke the Monroe Doctrine, which limited European powers in the western hemisphere. He rebuked Maximilian and granted formal recognition to the Juárez government. By then, the Juárez government in exile had traveled north, on the Samalayuca route of the Camino Real, and arrived in El Paso del Norte on August 15, 1865. They stayed in El Paso del Norte for the next ten months.

Word reached El Paso del Norte early on August 15, 1865, that the Juárez government was on its way. By evening, Juárez and his exiled party arrived with a full military staff, 500 troops, and the presidential cabinet with its attendant advisors. Later, General Luis Terrazas, Governor of Chihuahua, brought 300 additional men north to the Pass. The troops camped at the west end of the town, guarding the road south to Chihuahua. Juárez settled into the old post office building, on the main plaza, where he issued dispatches and met visitors. During his time at the Pass, Juárez welcomed many official and unofficial American representatives but chose not to cross the border. Instead, lavish efforts were sometimes made to bring visitors to El Paso del Norte, where they were received and entertained by the exiles and their supporters. By the spring of 1866, the French threat had ebbed, and General Terrazas returned south to guard Chihuahua City, and by May of the same year Maximilian's troops were in full retreat. In early June, with Chihuahua freed, Juárez prepared to return to the interior. On June 17, the entire presidential entourage and army left the Pass and made their way south along the old Camino Real; within a year they were back in Mexico City.[56]

By then the United States was threatening to help the *Juaristas* secure arms and money. Juárez's republican army launched an offensive in the spring of 1866, and by the end of the year France began to retreat and withdraw its troops. In May 1867, Maximilian was captured as he led the last French troops out of the country. In retaliation for his harsh treatment of loyal republicans, Juárez executed the emperor on the Hill of the Bells, outside of Querétaro, on June 19, 1867. Once the French had been driven from the country and the Mexican republic was restored, Benito Juárez was re-elected to the presidency. Juárez implemented a wide range of new programs to develop the national economy and institute basic social and political reforms. The *Ferrocarril Mexicano* (Mexican

Railroad Company) was organized to begin linking Mexico City to Veracruz. Mining was expanded and the economy stabilized. A rural police force, the *rurales*, patrolled the major highways and backroads. Education became a major focus of the liberal administration, and, for the first time, a school system was established and laws were passed to make primary education compulsory. The curriculum emphasized literacy, mathematics, and the natural sciences.

Juárez is often regarded as the Abraham Lincoln of Mexico. Both men led their nations through a traumatic time and helped restore order and stability. Lincoln preserved the Union, Juárez restored the Republic. Both advanced plans for social, political and economic reform. Juárez was re-elected in 1871 but died the next year. He is revered in Mexico and throughout Latin America. Many monuments, memorials, public facilities, and streets and thoroughfares have been named in his honor. In 1888, the name of El Paso del Norte was changed to Ciudad Juárez to honor the beloved leader and signal a new age for the growing city. A marble monument dedicated to Juárez stands as the centerpiece of a park on Calle Vicente Guererro. The monument was commissioned for the centennial celebration of Mexico's independence in 1910. It was constructed in 1909, and two Italian sculptors, Augusto Volpi and Fransisci Rigalt, oversaw the project. Four plaques along the base detail the significant events of Juárez's presidency. The main tourist market in the city, at Avenida 16 de Septiembre and Calle Agustín Melgar, is also named in his honor. Avenida Juárez leads from the old customhouse to the United States border.

Benito Juárez's government was headquartered near the central plaza, east of the Guadalupe Mission, on Avenida de Septiembre. His office was located in the only federal structure in El Paso del Norte, the customhouse, a small building that later became the post office, which survived until the Mexican Revolution, when it was destroyed in the fighting. Today, a small bust of President Juárez and a commemorative plaque are located at the site, tucked in a small space between two buildings on a busy segment of the downtown street. The Victoria Building, at the corner of Avenida 16 de Septiembre and Calle Madero, was built as a theater in 1945 and stands on the site of the home of Inocente Ochoa. In 1865, he provided lodging there to Benito Juárez during his exiled government's stay in El Paso del Norte.[57] Further west, the Museum of the Revolution, housed in the old customhouse on the corner of Avenida Juárez and Avenida 16 de Septiembre, chronicles the history of the city, with permanent and visiting exhibits that highlight the rich cultural heritage of the border region and the state of Chihuahua. The customhouse was built in the late 1880s and is one of the few surviving examples of Victorian architecture (characteristic of the Porfirio Díaz era), in the city. It was remodeled in 1909, and a large interior courtyard was covered to create a central hall. The museum opened its doors in 1990 and is operated by INAH, the *Instituto Nacional de Antropologia y Historia* (the National Institute of Anthropology and History). The recently renovated central hall, where a formal celebration was held in 1909 for United States President William Howard Robert Taft and Mexican President Porfirio Díaz, serves as the main gallery. Exhibits feature artifacts from the pre-Columbian and Spanish Colonial eras, the War of Independence, and the Mexican Revolution.

Gravesites of Ramón Ortiz, Inocente Ochoa, Mariano Samaniego, and other family members, in the San José Cemetery.

In the colonial era, whether travelers entered El Paso del Norte through San José or followed the Mission Trail through the Lower Valley, they arrived at the Guadalupe Mission, the last inhabited site for many miles to come. From the nearby presidio, the Camino Real de Tierra Adentro followed present-day Calle Ugarte, once known as *El Camino de la Presa y del Nuevo Mexico*, The Road to the Dam and New Mexico, north toward the river. The trail led to the Rio Grande, near the intersection of today's Boulevard Fronterizo and Calles Alumino and Platino, where a dam diverted water to the local acequia system. It continued along the west bank for just less than a mile to a narrow and shallow point with a hard, rocky surface. This was *el paso*, the main river ford, where travelers crossed to the east bank and continued north through El Paso Canyon.[58]

3

American El Paso

The Camino Real de Tierra Adentro continued north from the Guadalupe Mission to *el paso*, the main river ford, and crossed over into today's downtown El Paso, Texas. There were no missions, presidios, or haciendas on the north bank during the Spanish Colonial era, but by the early nineteenth century at least one settler, Ponce de León, established a homestead there. American El Paso was settled after the 1848 Treaty of Guadalupe Hidalgo designated the Rio Grande as the international boundary between the United States and Mexico. The new border severed the 1,500 mile Camino Real, but segments of the old trail provided the underpinnings for vast new road networks on both sides of the river. While most traffic was still north and south, American travelers now came west across Texas, arrived at the Pass, and made their way into New Mexico or along new routes that linked the area with Arizona and California. New coach roads led through the Lower Valley, often following the path of the old Camino Real de Tierra Adentro.[1]

El Camino Real through American El Paso.

The first road surveys conducted after 1848 in the Southwest were carried out by the military. Texans recognized the advantages of connecting the eastern part of the state with American El Paso and sought an all-weather route through the Pass, and on to Arizona and California. The town of San Antonio led the effort to blaze a new wagon road and outfitted a private expedition to explore possible routes, while the United States War Department sent several scouting parties through the region. The Corp of Engineers and the Topographical Engineers also ventured west, following the Pecos River and the Rio Grande. But while treaty negotiations were still underway, gold was discovered in the new American territory of California, and countless prospectors and entrepreneurs from all over the world made their way west. These emigrants blazed their own trails through West Texas.

Beyond the Pecos, water was scarce, roads were badly rutted, and Indian attacks common. After surviving the trek, many found that El Paso lived up to its mythical reputation as an oasis in the desert. By mid-1849, thousands of emigrants were camped on the American side of the Rio Grande, and many crossed the river and visited El Paso del Norte, the only place where they could re-supply. A few of these travelers recognized new business opportunities and decided to stay. They created a series of small homesteads along the north bank of the river, spaced a mile or two apart. These pioneer settlements laid the foundation for a new community, American El Paso.[2] The California gold rush created a surge of traffic through Texas, and by 1853 regular mail service was contracted between San Antonio and Santa Fe, via El Paso. Most of the 49'ers traveled in their own caravans, but regular passenger service soon followed. In the mid-1850s a San Antonio to San Diego route was also opened. A line known as the Jackass Trail, because of its use of mules along segments of the route, connected the east with the west coast. By far the most famous and successful of the early stagecoach services was John Butterfield's Overland Mail, which began operations in September 1858 and carried the United States mail from the end of the rail line at Tipton, Missouri, to San Francisco, California, in twenty-four days. A Lower Road of the Butterfield Overland Mail, opened in 1859, made use of segments of the old Camino Real, as it wound through San Elizario, Socorro, and Ysleta, and entered American El Paso, roughly along the path of today's San Antonio and Overland Avenues. The El Paso station, located midway along the 2,700 mile route, was the dividing point between the Overland Mail's

Eastern and Western divisions. It was the largest and best equipped on the line, serving hundreds of passengers annually, and helped spur the development of businesses, housing, and land tracts along the north bank. The stagecoach lines joined the old Camino Real once again at Hart's Mill, continuing north toward Las Cruces. Just beyond Fort Fillmore, they left the old trail and veered west toward Arizona.[3]

The opening of mail routes and stagecoach service in West Texas and New Mexico brought a new breed of rough frontiersmen into the region. Henry Skillman (ca. 1814–1864) was one of the best known. He first came through New Mexico with a wagon train on the Chihuahua Trail in the 1840s, served as wagon master for the Doniphan expedition, and commanded a scouting party as American troops moved into Chihuahua during the war. In 1849 and 1850, he was one of the first to carry mail between San Antonio, Texas, and El Paso. He received the first United States postal contract for the route in 1851 and expanded it to include passenger service the next year. Twice a month Skillman's coaches ran passengers on the nineteen-day journey from San Antonio to Santa Fe. From El Paso, they traveled the path of the old Camino Real. The stages crossed the Jornada del Muerto, endured Apache attacks, camped at Fray Cristóbal, and followed the river north to Santa Fe. These new coach services were designed for speed. Unlike the ox or mule drawn wagons of the Spanish Colonial era, these light canvas-covered, horse-drawn vehicles raced along primitive roads, and made stagecoaching a dangerous venture. Wagons tipped over, horses were injured and abandoned along the way, axles shattered, and flash floods obliterated the trail. One traveler noted more than sixty wagons, along with many dead and dying animals, strewn along the stretch between El Paso and the Guadalupe Mountains. By the mid-1850s, attention had shifted west, and Skillman was supervising mail delivery to San Diego, California. He drove the first stage west into El Paso on the Butterfield Overland Trail, arriving after ninety-six hours of grueling, non-stop travel, on September 30, 1858. Skillman survived numerous Indian attacks and was known for spinning yarns about his many adventures along frontier trails. During the Civil War he became a spy for the Confederates and was killed by the California Cavalry in 1864.[4]

Meanwhile, there were problems establishing the new international boundary created by the Treaty of Guadalupe Hidalgo. The treaty transferred half of Mexico to the Unites States, opening much of today's American Southwest, but the specific boundary was difficult to pinpoint. A bi-national commission was established to determine its exact location. John Russell Bartlett (1805–1886) was appointed United States Boundary Commissioner, and Pedro García Condé (1806–1851) led the Mexican delegation. Bartlett, a publisher from Rhode Island and a well-connected Whig party leader, had a keen interest in the Southwest but little interest in his job. His appointment allowed him to travel throughout the newly acquired territories and write about his experiences, and, being a well-read gentleman, Bartlett was able to comment on geography, climate, terrain, and culture. García Condé, born in Sonora, joined the Corp of Engineers in 1828, and rose to the rank of general. He had been stationed at San Elizario in the 1820s, had a good working knowledge of the area, and in 1834 completed a map of the state of Chihuahua. The two men met at El Paso in late 1850 to resolve some of the inaccuracies in the original treaty agreement.[5]

The treaty's provisions ignored the problems presented by a major meandering river flowing through a dry, arid region. The river, particularly active in the early 1850s, often flooded and carved entirely new channels. As a result, the valley communities of Ysleta, Socorro, and San Elizario were left on an island, surrounded by two major branches of the river. The commissioners established that the main river channel ran west and south of the island, placing these communities within the United States. Senecú and San Lorenzo, west of the island, remained in Mexico. A second problem concerned the boundary above El Paso, as it led west through New Mexico and Arizona. Bartlett and García Condé resurveyed the area, compromised, and set the line forty-two miles north of the Pass (well above present-day Las Cruces). Assuming their work was complete, the commissioners prepared their reports. Bartlett set out to tour California and later traveled throughout northern Mexico. The United States Congress, however, rejected the line drawn by Bartlett and García Condé, and a few weeks later James Gadsden, a railroad man from Charleston, was appointed as the new United States Minister to Mexico. Gadsden began negotiations with President López de Santa Anna for the purchase of territory south of the boundary, so that an all-weather year-round transcontinental railroad could connect major southern cities with Pacific ports. In 1853, the Gadsden Purchase dropped the international boundary to the 32nd parallel, its present-day location, adding 30,000 square miles to the United States and creating the desired right-of-way for the proposed railway.[6]

A Texas Centennial Marker on today's Paisano Drive indicates the site of "the Pass of the North," the main river ford.

By then, five new frontier settlements had been founded at the Pass. A business district developed in today's downtown area, even though San Elizario and Ysleta remained larger, more developed communities and still served as the seats of county government. The arrival of the Southern Pacific Railroad in May 1881 changed American El Paso forever, as stagecoaches were replaced by locomotives, and the city became a regional hub for railroad traffic. Nearby agriculture, ranching, mining, and manufacturing added to the growth. By the mid-1880s, there were newspapers, churches, schools, hotels, countless commercial enterprises, and a municipal government. From a population of less than 1,000 in 1881, it numbered 10,000 by the next decade. It doubled again several times during the next forty years. In the early twentieth century, commerce and trade expanded rapidly, and the 1910 Mexican Revolution brought large numbers of refugees into the city. This led to a build-up of military activities in the region. Fort Bliss became an important element in the local economy as thousands of troops and their families came to the city. By the 1920s, there were more than 100,000 people living in El Paso. The Second World War, which spurred a federal interstate highway system, and a major shift in immigration and international trade agreements, added to the explosive growth in the second half of the twentieth century. In the early twenty-first century, El Paso has become a major western city with a mostly Hispanic population of about 700,000 people. A mixed economy has emerged based on trade, transportation, military contracting, light manufacturing, and retailing. Today, the expansion of the city has spread far beyond the path of the old Camino Real, or the stagecoach routes of the 1850s, but several sites scattered throughout the area reveal the transportation heritage and ties to the nineteenth-century past of American El Paso.[7]

Concordia

One of the earliest pioneer settlers in the El Paso area was Hugh Stephenson (1798–1870), who founded Concordia, at the junction of the trail north from the Lower Valley, and the coach road to San Antonio. Stephenson was born in Kentucky but spent his youth in Missouri. He came west as a trapper and trader, and may have been the first Anglo-American to spent time at the Pass, arriving with a Chihuahua Trail wagon train in 1824. He struck up an acquaintance with the Ascárate family, prominent merchants in El Paso del Norte, and by 1828, purchased land near the Ponce de León grant.[8] The same year, he married Juana María Ascárate, an heir to the family's ranching, farming, and mining properties. Stephenson also acquired a Mexican land grant of 23,000 acres in the Brazitos tract, south of present-day Las Cruces, and later purchased a mining claim in the Organ Mountains. The Stephensons had business ventures in El Paso del Norte, Chihuahua City, and Janos. It appears that during the late 1820s, they lived in the Las Cruces area, but, by the early 1830s they had moved back to the Pass where they operated a mercantile store.[9] By 1840, the Stephensons had established a large ranch known as Concordia, named for Concordia, Missouri. Hugh Stephenson enjoyed the life of a Kentucky gentleman and entertained local elites and travelers who came through the Pass. He kept a low profile during the Mexican-American War and may have left the area during the 1840s. In 1848, he opened a silver mine in the Organ Mountains and operated a furnace near Fort Fillmore where the ores were smelted. Stephenson's family stayed on at Concordia and, by 1850 the estate had grown considerably. They built a small chapel and opened a family cemetery by 1854. *San José de Concordia el Alto* was the first Catholic church built in American El Paso and was blessed by Father Ramón Ortiz of El Paso del Norte. The first person buried in the new cemetery was Stephenson's wife Juana, who died after being gored by a pet deer in 1856. By 1859, there were ninety-five houses with more than 400 residents. Stephenson spent increasingly more time in Las Cruces, especially after the death of his wife, but by the 1860s he was back. He pledged loyalty to the Confederacy during the Civil War and, because of his work with the Rebels Stephenson suffered after the war, losing property that took years for his family to recover. In his later years, Hugh Stephenson lived at La Mesa, New Mexico, where he died in 1870.[10]Following a major flood in 1867 that washed away most of Fort Bliss, the United States Army established Camp Concordia on the Stephenson property. The small family cemetery was expanded in the 1860s, and Stephenson's descendants opened sections for public burials. In the late nineteenth and early twentieth centuries, it grew into a large, diverse cemetery, the final resting place of many of early El Paso's pioneers. Today, Concordia Cemetery is all that remains of the old Stephenson homestead. The fifty-four acre site, which contains more than 65,000 graves, is the most historic cemetery in the region, with innumerable ethnicities, religions, and nationalities, represented within its walls. Anglo-Americans, Hispanics, African-Americans and Chinese share a large presence. Sections have been opened for Catholic, Protestant, Masonic, and Jewish residents. Prominent historical figures, from both American El Paso and Mexico, are buried at the site. Probably the best known Concordia resident is West Texas gunfighter John Wesley Hardin, who was gunned down in El Paso in 1895. Since 1990, it has been overseen by the Concordia Heritage Association. Concordia was designated as a Historic Texas Cemetery in 2005.[11]

Gravesite of Juana María Ascárate, at Concordia Cemetery.

Magoffinsville

Magoffinsville was settled in 1849, just west of Concordia. James Wiley
Magoffin (1799–1868) was born in Harrodsburg, Kentucky, into a frontier family
who ventured into land sales, merchandising, and banking. During the 1820s, he
made his way south to Matamoros, Mexico, where he became a merchant, active
in the booming Texas-Mexico trade. In 1832, Magoffin traveled to Chihuahua
City where he established himself as a successful entrepreneur, became fluent
in Spanish, and accumulated enough wealth to become known in local circles

as *Don Santiago*, Sir James. He married into a prominent San Antonio de Béxar family, taking María Gertrudis de los Santos Valdez de Veramendi as his bride. Magoffin's commercial enterprises expanded, and the family made their home in Guererro, west of Chihuahua City. Magoffin developed new merchandising efforts and participated in the lucrative Chihuahua Trail trade, aided by his wife's relatives: Santa Fe trader Gabriel Valdez, and Albuquerque merchant and future governor of New Mexico, Manuel Armijo.[12] In 1844, James Magoffin moved his family back to the United States, so that his children could attend American schools.

James Magoffin was commissioned as a United States colonel of cavalry at the outbreak of the Mexican-American War because of his influential position among northern Mexican elites. He accompanied American forces into New Mexico and helped to arrange the peaceful surrender of Santa Fe. In September 1846, separated from his troops, Magoffin and four others were detained by Mexican officials at Doña Ana, taken south to the presidio at Carrizal, and later transferred to Chihuahua City. In the meantime, Doniphan's Missouri regulars were making their way south through New Mexico. They were followed by hundreds of merchants and traders, in more than 300 wagons, headed down the trail behind the American forces. James's brother Samuel and his wife Susan, who kept a diary of the journey, were among the travelers. Their ox-drawn caravan brought forty-five wagons of goods and supplies south. Doniphan's troops routed Mexican forces at the battle of Brazito on Christmas Day and entered El Paso del Norte in January 1847. They continued south, followed by the caravan, defeated the Mexicans again at Sacramento on February 28, and entered Chihuahua City in the first days of March. Magoffin, considered to be an important hostage and scheduled to be tried for espionage, was taken under heavy guard to Durango, where he was held until a release was negotiated in June.

At the end of the war, Magoffin returned to Missouri where he organized a wagon train along the Santa Fe Trail into the new western territory of the United States. Following the Chihuahua Trail, he arrived at the Pass of the North in April 1849 but soon found that trade with Chihuahua had been complicated by new Mexican taxes and customs regulations. Instead of continuing south, he settled along the Rio Grande and established Magoffinsville in June 1849, midway between Santa Fe and Chihuahua City. The original homestead was in the area of today's Magoffin Avenue and Willow Street, south of downtown El Paso. An irrigation canal, extending from Ponce de León's original acequia, provided water for the fields and powered a grist mill at the site. Goods from San Antonio stocked the stores and warehouses that surrounded a small plaza. Magoffin also dealt in livestock and sold mules to California emigrants on their way west. As more settlers moved to the area, Magoffin prospered and entered new business ventures. In August 1850, he married Dolores "Lolita" Valdez, the younger sister of his deceased wife. He expanded his trade in merchandise and livestock with a ranch fifteen miles north, known as Canutillo.[13]

Magoffinsville became a thriving commercial center, one of the most important in the early American Southwest. James Magoffin bought fine textiles from New York City distributors and re-established trade with Mexico along the old Chihuahua Trail. He partnered with Chihuahua City businessman José Cordero who maintained ties with the mining, ranching, and commercial elites of northern Mexico. When Judge Davis visited Magoffinsville in the 1850s, he found the family "living quite in nabob style in a large Spanish-built house that reminded [him] somewhat of an old mansion of the feudal ages."[14] In 1854, the United States Army's first base in the area, the Post Opposite El Paso, was moved to Magoffinsville and named Fort Bliss, in memory of William Wallace Smith Bliss, a Mexican-American War veteran. The Magoffins were Confederate supporters, and in 1862, when Union forces secured El Paso, they fled east to the safety of the Southern government, where his sons served as officers in the Confederate Army. During the war, much of his property was confiscated, the site was badly looted, and his family took refuge across the river in El Paso del Norte. In 1867, he was amnestied by the Andrew Johnson Administration but by then the remains of Magoffinsville had been destroyed by the raging floodwaters of the Rio Grande, including most of Fort Bliss. The post was then moved to Concordia. James Magoffin became ill in early 1868, transferred his remaining properties to his son, Joseph, and died in San Antonio later that year.[15]

Joseph Magoffin (1837–1923) returned to El Paso, rebuilt the family's fortune, and began a new homestead in the early 1870s. He became a prominent citizen of American El Paso, holding many political offices, organizing utility companies and city services, working with the Mexican government on flood control projects, and opening schools. Magoffin and his family built a new home, now a Texas State Historic Site, located at 1120 Magoffin Avenue. The

Magoffin Home is a sprawling, nineteen-room adobe-brick structure, modeled after the original Magoffinsville residence, which was located about ten blocks to the east. The U-shaped single story home is an interesting example of the Territorial-style of architecture, blending Southwest, Mexican, and Victorian features. Plastering and scoring give the exterior walls a modern, masonry appearance, with Greek Revival details. The southern part of the house is the original structure, which included a central hallway, parlors, sitting rooms, and bedrooms. A northern section was added in the mid-1870s, and a third section, connecting the earlier two, was completed in the 1880s. The interior of the home is filled with family heirlooms, original and period furnishings, and memories of generations of Magoffin descendants. Carpets, wall paper, and papered and plastered ceilings throughout the house are typical of those found in turn-of-the-century residences. Historic photographs and original works of art are prominently displayed.[16]

The Magoffin Home was added to the National Register of Historic Places in 1971. Family members lived at the site until 1976, when it became the property of the Texas Parks and Wildlife Department. The area around the Magoffin Home developed into El Paso's premier residential neighborhood in the 1880s. Large Victorian-style houses spread along Magoffin Avenue, and El Paso's wealthiest and most prominent families entertained, socialized, and planned the development of the city from these stately mansions. In 1985, the city of El Paso designated the area as the Magoffin Historic District, leading to the renovation and restoration of many properties along Magoffin Avenue. The Fort Bliss Replica Museum, located on base in northeast El Paso, is housed in a replica of the first Fort Bliss at Magoffinsville, which was occupied from 1854 to 1867.

Franklin

Franklin was located north of Magoffinsville, at the center of today's downtown El Paso. In January 1827, Juan María Ponce de León, a wealthy and influential citizen of El Paso del Norte, petitioned for a land grant on the north bank of the Rio Grande, about one mile from the plaza. This land formed the base for the Ponce de León Hacienda, the first settlement in what would later become American El Paso.[17] Ponce de León completed an acequia system, with the mouth located just above a dam, near the main river ford known as *el paso*. At the time, the Rio Grande followed the path of today's Paisano Drive, and the main acequia ran from the river to the ranch, on a path close to that of San Francisco Street and Texas Avenue.[18] It watered fields and vineyards that were located south of Texas Avenue, near today's United States Courthouse. He built an adobe home near the river, but it was destroyed in the spring floods of 1830. A second home, fortified with a watchtower to help guard against Apache attacks, was completed a few years later and became the center of a small settlement known as Ponce's Rancho,[19] located on the site of today's Mills Building, on the north side of San Jacinto Plaza.[20] There was a tannery and flour mill west of the hacienda, near the site of an earthen dam.[21] With the signing of the Treaty of Guadalupe Hidalgo in 1848, lands north of the Rio Grande became part of the United States. American merchant Benjamin Franklin Coons bought the Ponce de León grant and leased part of it to the United States Army's Third Infantry in 1849. The settlement became known as Coon's Ranch, and was later called Franklin. Coons defaulted on his payments, and the land was sold by his family to other Americans after his death in 1852.

In early 1857, while the Butterfield Overland operation was still being planned, Anson Mills (1834–1924) was appointed district surveyor for the state of Texas.[22]During the summer, he was hired by the Overland Mail Company to design and build a stagecoach station at Franklin, located midway across the 2,700 mile route. By September, the Butterfield Overland Mail was in business, and Mills' Franklin station was the largest and best equipped on the entire route. It spread over a two-acre site, with corrals and a large prominent building that dominated the small frontier settlement.[23] After completing the station, Mills was contracted by the United States Army to conduct surveys of several military installations in the west, including Fort Bliss.

A group of land speculators, who called themselves the El Paso Company, hired Mills to survey the town of Franklin, which at the time was no more than a modest ranch site owned by a Kentuckian, "Uncle" Billy Smith. Smith had been selling small lots to new settlers that were randomly parceled and spread along winding, irregular streets.[24] Mills negotiated with property owners to reach an agreeable survey, and in 1859 he created a plat, or sketch, of the new town. Mills' plat shows the basic outline of the today's downtown El Paso, with many of its early urban features still in place.[25] Missouri Street was the northern edge of the

Butterfield Overland Mail stagecoaches, such as this one leaving the San Francisco station, regularly stopped at Franklin. *Harper's Weekly,* December 11, 1858, Author Collection.

settlement, and Second Street (present-day Paisano Drive), along the river, was the southern boundary. South of San Antonio and San Francisco Streets were rich agricultural lands, including vineyards, orchards, wheat, and cornfields. The main street names indicated the direction that the roads headed from the center of town. The stage route to San Antonio was named San Antonio Street. El Paso Street ran south to a river crossing and El Paso del Norte (today's Ciudad Juárez). Public squares at today's Pioneer Plaza and San Jacinto Plaza can also be seen on the plat. Mills is also responsible for changing the name of the settlement from Franklin to El Paso. He noted in his autobiography that Franklin was located at the only feasible crossing of the Rio Grande and suggested that the name "El Paso" would emphasize the importance of the location.[26] Mills stayed on after his work and played a major role in the development of the new city. He served in the United States Army during the Civil War, invested in commercial properties, and became an important promoter and developer of El Paso. In 1913, the city changed the name of Saint Louis Street to Mills Avenue, in his honor. Mills died in 1924 at the age of ninety and is buried in Arlington National Cemetery. His plat continued to generate controversy, and, in the late nineteenth century, there were numerous efforts to once again determine the original outline of the grant and settle disputes over boundaries. The waters of the Rio Grande carved new channels, and the general position of the river continued to move south toward Mexico, after extensive floods in the 1860s and 1870s. The dispute over these lands and the actual boundaries of the Ponce de León Land Grant were not finally resolved until the Chamizal Treaty was formally implemented in 1967.[27]

Hart's Mill

From Franklin, the coach road continued north along the east bank and met the old Camino Real at *el paso*, the main river ford. The 1598 Oñate caravan had spent several days traveling north along the west bank, through today's downtown Ciudad Juárez, and into El Paso Canyon. Oñate's scouts searched the river bank for several leagues, looking for a suitable crossing for the caravan, and on May 4 they reached a place they called the "the pass of the river and the ford," referring to a narrow point in the canyon where the Franklin Mountains sloped down to the river bed.[28] They called the point *Los Puertos*, or the entrance to the canyon, and the site of the crossing, *el paso*. The Pass was on a well-worn Indian trail that had been followed by countless Native-American travelers and several earlier Spanish expeditions. It was situated where the river bed was hard and rocky and the current a bit gentler than further upstream. There, the carts were least likely to get stuck in the river's thick mud. Manso Indians helped ferry carts, wagons, and livestock across the river, allowing the expedition to continue north through the canyon along the east bank. The records of the Oñate expedition are the first reference to the site as "el paso."[29]

Simeon Hart (1816–1874) was born in Kentucky, raised in Missouri, and came to the Southwest during the Mexican-American War with the Missouri Cavalry. After the hostilities ended, he made the acquaintance of Chihuahua merchant Don Leandro Siqueiros and married his daughter, Jesusita Siqueiros. The newlyweds moved into American territory on the north bank of the Rio Grande and watched for new business opportunities, as trade patterns shifted after the war. Hart had ambitious plans for the region, and in 1849 opened a small mill, where he ground corn and wheat into flour and meal. He later expanded his operations to include a much larger gristmill, a sawmill, and two fanning mills. Hart provided milled products for people living as far away as San Antonio, Santa Fe, and Tucson. He also outfitted wagons, sold livestock, and contracted for mail delivery. Hart's Mill, or *El Molino*, located at the river crossing, became an important meeting place and center of commerce along the trail. Stagecoaches and wagon trains made their way through the settlements of the Lower Valley, followed the east bank into today's downtown area, and continued on the old trail to the mill.[30]

Hart's home was one of the earliest residential buildings in American El Paso. It was constructed in 1850, shortly after the mill was operating, and was later enlarged. The Hart homestead served as a restaurant, providing food and comfort to weary stage-and wagon-train travelers. Over the years, his commercial enterprises thrived; Hart became the wealthiest man in the Pass, and his residence was a prominent social center.[31] Judge Davis noted:

El Molino (the Mill), the residence of Judge Hart, is rather romantically situated upon the east bank of the Del Norte, three miles above the Mexican town of El Paso, and a short distance below where the river forces its passage through the mountains. The house is built in the Mexican style, is large and convenient, and within were found every luxury and comfort of home.[32]

However, by the 1860s Hart's erratic and sometimes violent personality, along with his fierce loyalty to the Confederacy, made him several bitter enemies. During the war, he helped outfit the Southern army, was given the rank of major, and used his homestead as a launching point for the invasion of New Mexico. As a result, at the end of the war, his property was confiscated. Hart then entered the newspaper business and founded the El Paso *Sentinel*. His son, Juan, later became the founder and first editor of the El Paso *Times*. In the early 1870s, the family recovered the property. The mill operated until 1895, and Hart's relatives and descendants lived at the site until the 1930s.

In 1881, part of the Hart homestead became the fifth site of Fort Bliss, located alongside the river, on the international boundary. Many of the borderland's Indian wars were orchestrated from there, including campaigns against Geronimo and Victoria. Fort Bliss stood on leased land and covered more than 135 acres. There were six officers' quarters, enlisted men's barracks, a large parade ground, hospital and many smaller structures. In 1881, the railroad cut through the property, along the path of the old trail. A few years later, a fire destroyed much of the fort, operations were scaled back, and only a handful of men remained stationed there by the late 1880s. Today, a pair of two-story wooden buildings (once officers' quarters), are all that remain of the old Fort Bliss complex.[33] Although the ruins of the mills, commercial enterprises, and most of the military structures are long gone, Hart's residence still sits quietly in a busy area of the United States-Mexico border, just north of downtown El Paso. The one-story sprawling adobe home, a prominent landmark along Paisano Drive, is known throughout the area as La Hacienda Café. It has a flat roof with a parapet and a wide arched porch across its front. It has three-foot-thick adobe walls and a roof made of sycamore and willow branches. A grand salon area runs through the center of the building, connected to a series of a dozen rooms. High ceilings, fireplaces, and large windows complete the interior. As one of the few places in the area that still has a western-style bar, it has recently served as the site of re-enactments and celebrations of wild west shoot-outs. Enlarged and renovated over the years, the building served as a restaurant, meeting place, and entertainment center for most of the twentieth century.[34] Hart's Mill and the site of old Fort Bliss were added to the National Register of Historic Places in 1972.

Remains of Hart's Mill. Library of Congress, Prints and Photographs Division, Historic American Buildings Survey, West Elevation of Old Grist Mill, May 25, 1936, HABS TEX,71–ELPA,1–1.

There is a small park just south of the old mill site with a series of Texas Historical Commission and Texas Centennial markers commemorating its importance. North of Hart's Mill, on the opposite side of the river, accessible by a wooden bridge under the railroad trestles, is another that lies on the international boundary between the United States and Mexico. Within the park is Boundary Marker Number One, a white limestone obelisk, the first boundary marker set in place after the new border was established in 1856. It marks the point where the international boundary leaves the Rio Grande and heads west to the Pacific. It is also the spot where the three states of Texas, Chihuahua, and New Mexico meet. Today, there is a small park on each side of the marker, one in the United States and one in Mexico, where people from both nations can gather.

North through the Pass

Hart's Mill was located at the mouth of El Paso Canyon which extends almost five miles north to Sunland Park. The Franklin Mountains, the southernmost part of the Rocky Mountain chain, are east of the river. The highest point at North Franklin Peak reaches 7,192 feet above sea level, about 3,000 feet above today's riverbed. The Franklins are actually an uplift and the gray peaks reveal the limestone bed of an ancient sea that once covered the area. The Sierra de Juárez, of similar composition, lies to the west. The steepest, rockiest part of the canyon route reaches about three miles beyond Hart's Mill. Mount Cristo Rey, a failed volcano, is the oldest mountain in the area, and hems in the trail on the west side of the river.[35] From the river ford, the Camino Real de Tierra Adentro continues along the east bank through El Paso Canyon, close to the path of Paisano Drive. Until the twentieth century, this narrow river canyon was one of the more challenging segments of the trail. The Oñate expedition spent two days working its way through the narrow pass and was so exhausted after the ordeal that they took another day just to rest their animals. Little changed during the next 250 years, and in 1851 Commissioner Bartlett still described this segment of the trail as "difficult and tortuous" through "wild, rugged, and hilly country."[36] Caravans moved up to the sand hills whenever possible, where the former smelting complex and the railroad tracks are today. Some improvements were made after this stretch of the old trail became a common stagecoach route, but even so it was still cited as "one of the steepest and stoniest" passages on the road.[37] Beyond Mount Cristo Rey, the trail exited the canyon and the old channel

of the Rio Grande continued north, rather than making as sharp a bend to the
west as it does today. The Camino Real followed the riverbank, about one mile
east of its present location, approximately along the path of Doniphan Drive.
Today, much of the landscape in this area is considerably different than it was in
the early nineteenth century, extensively leveled and graded to make way for the
railroad and industrial development.[38]

Seasonal flooding and the tortuous terrain of El Paso Canyon caused some
travelers to stay on the west bank of the river, bypass the ford, and move around
the far side of Mount Cristo Rey. In 1760, Bishop Tamarón commented that "it
would not be difficult to open a road on the west side of the river,"[39] and by the
early nineteenth century this had apparently been done. Josiah Gregg noted that
many travelers on the Chihuahua Trail followed the west bank and made use of
another ford about six miles north of El Paso.[40] In the 1840s, Adolph Wislizenus
described two commonly used routes through the Pass, one on each side of the
river.[41] The west-bank trail through today's Anapra, Chihuahua, was cited on
nineteenth-century maps as the *Camino de los Muleros*, or the Mule Boys' Road.
There were also attempts to build bridges across the Rio Grande north of El Paso.
At one site in 1797, massive cottonwood logs were floated down the river and
used to build a seventeen-foot wide structure that spanned more than 500 feet
across the river. Although the bridge was supported by caissons and cross poles,
it did not hold up well under the powerful currents of the Rio Grande and was
washed away in 1798. Sometime after that it was rebuilt and used, until 1815,
when it was once again destroyed by flood waters.[42]

Frontera

Frontera, the first permanent American settlement on the river, was
located at the northern river ford, about six miles beyond the Oñate crossing.
It became known as the "upper crossing" of the Rio Grande, located near the
Texas-New Mexico border, west of the intersection of today's Frontera Road
and Doniphan Drive, at the entrance to the Mesilla Valley.[43] In August 1848, T.
Frank White built a trading post at the upper ford. There, the river was wide and
shallow, allowing for a much easier crossing of horses, mules, and wagons. When
the waters were high, canoes were used to float cargo and wagons across.[44] White
called the site *Frontera*, the Border, because it was located near the new borders
of Texas, Chihuahua, and New Mexico.[45] It also became known as Mule's Ford

because mule trains often used the west bank road.[46] Although the end of the Mexican-American War and the signing of the Treaty of Guadalupe Hidalgo established the river as an international boundary, White expected regular trade and travel to resume along the old Chihuahua Trail. He soon found, however, his river crossing was located along another important route: the road west to the California goldfields. The El Paso area was one of the few oases located along the trail after hundreds of miles of dry, hot West Texas desert. By mid-1849, thousands of emigrants were camped in the area and White's Frontera became the main trading post. It thrived as White sold supplies and pack animals, and arranged river crossings. Frontera also drew the attention of Lieutenant William H.C. Whiting, who recommended it as the location for a military post on the Rio Grande.[47]

"Rio Grande-Near Frontera" by James D. Smillie, c. 1853. Courtesy of El Paso Public Library, Border Heritage Collections.

White became the first successful merchant in the area and was soon the first magistrate and collector of customs. Typical of the confusion over boundaries at the time, White was appointed Prefect by the Military Governor of New Mexico, Colonel John M. Washington, even though Frontera was located in Texas. During 1849, he removed several area residents from their positions and extended his jurisdiction over the Lower Valley settlements of Ysleta, Socorro, and San Elizario.[48] White soon found himself competing with four other settlements in American El Paso, and Frontera fell on hard times. The military post was established further down the river, near the main ford. In November 1850, White tried to sell his land to the United States Boundary Commission, but instead they only leased some of the land for use as an observatory. As the trading post declined, White lost much of his political influence. Shortly after making arrangements for the observatory, White left El Paso. His brother, Charles W. White, apparently managed the property until the mid-1850s. A few years later, the ranch and trading post were in ruins and abandoned.[49]Today, the site of White's Frontera is located in a quiet residential area of west El Paso. A marker, placed by the Boundary Commission, on White's property, lies buried along Frontera Road near the railroad tracks. The river tamed, channeled, and narrowed, lies almost one mile west of its nineteenth-century course.[50] Nearby Keystone Heritage Park, a certified National Historic Trail site, is on the lower floodplain of the Rio Grande, west of Keystone Dam, along Doniphan Drive. Studies in the 1970s revealed that the site may have been occupied by Native-Americans as far back as 4,000 years ago. It is one of the oldest known village sites in the American West with evidence of substantial settlement in the late pre-historic era, about 200 to 1400 CE, as Native-Americans were making the transition from nomadic hunter-gatherers to a more sedentary, agricultural, village lifestyle. Keystone is designated as a State Archaeological Landmark by the Texas Historical Commission, and Keystone Heritage Park, a fifty-two acre site, is overseen by the El Paso Museum of Archaeology and the Museum and Cultural Affairs Department of the city. While the Keystone site was long abandoned and forgotten by the time Europeans made their way through the Pass in the sixteenth century, perhaps some of the earliest inhabitants of this primitive village made their way along the river banks on foot trails that later became part of the Camino Real de Tierra Adentro. Today, the park is one of the few sites in the area that preserves and protects the native wetland and Chihuahuan Desert environment.[51]

La Salineta and Salinera

La Salineta and *La Salinera* were located further north on the Camino Real de Tierra Adentro. These two parajes were often confused, since both names referred to salt deposits found in the marshes of the Rio Grande. Their exact locations are uncertain, but La Salineta, north of Frontera, was the larger and better known site, located at another river ford. Accounts of the Pueblo Revolt describe great drama at La Salineta and reveal some of the hazards faced when traveling along the old colonial road near the Pass. In September 1680, Governor Antonio de Otermín and more than 1,900 Spanish and Indian refugees (who had just survived a long, harrowing march down the Camino Real de Tierra Adentro) gathered at La Salineta. While they set up camp along the river, Father Francisco de Ayeta was leading a twenty-five team supply caravan north from the Guadalupe Mission. The swollen waters of the Rio Grande prevented the supply caravan from crossing at El Paso, the usual ford, so it moved up the west bank, toward Mount Cristo Rey, and continued north to La Salineta. As they entered the water, the powerful currents drew the wagons under, scattered frightened animals, and stranded Father Ayeta in the middle of the river. Ayeta almost drowned but was rescued at the last minute by several of Otermín's men. The surviving supplies and livestock were brought to the camp, and for awhile La Salineta functioned as a temporary site for the exiled government. The refugees stayed at La Salineta until October, when a decision was made to settle the El Paso Valley south of the Guadalupe Mission, a safer and more secure area on the trail.[52] La Salineta was abandoned, but it remained a popular campsite, noted by Rivera, Pike, Magoffin, and others in their journeys over the next 150 years.[53] La Salinera was located somewhere further north along the trail[54] and appears to have been the site where several efforts were made to build a bridge across the river in the 1790s. Although the exact location is still unknown, a New Mexico Highway Department Camino Real marker located along Doniphan Drive tells the story of La Salinera.[55] From there, the Camino Real de Tierra Adentro National Historic Trail continues north through the Mesilla Valley.

4

The Mesilla Valley

After exiting El Paso Canyon, the Camino Real de Tierra Adentro entered the Mesilla Valley, a broad, flat, fertile area created by the meandering of the Rio Grande over thousands of years. The modern river has been straightened and channeled and lies far to the west, but the trail followed the old riverbed, close to the path of today's railroad tracks through the valley. The Mesilla Valley is widest in the south and is hemmed in on the east by the Tortugas, Organ, and Doña Ana mountains. Other smaller volcanic outcrops dot the landscape. The valley ends near Radium Springs, where several small mountain ranges close in on the Rio Grande, as the river enters a narrow, rocky canyon.[1]

Small bands of hunter-gatherers wandered through the Mesilla region as far back as 10,000 BCE, and there is some evidence of agriculture 2,000 to 4,000 years ago, but when the Spanish came through the valley in the sixteenth century, it was home to the Manso Indians, who lived quietly in primitive villages along the river. Franciscans established a mission there in the late seventeenth century, about twenty-five miles above El Paso del Norte, but it disappears from the records by the 1690s. Poor relations with Gila and Chiricahua Apaches, who had been driven into the wilderness and were desperate to survive, hindered settlements in the valley. While there appears to have been occasional farms or ranches along the trail during the colonial era, there were no substantial communities established there until the mid-nineteenth century. Only one village, Doña Ana, existed along the trail in the Mesilla Valley, at the time of the Mexican-American War in 1846.[2] After the war, United States troops brought some stability to the region, and new towns were founded on both sides of the border, but it was not until the 1880s that Mexican and United States military campaigns eliminated the threat of Indians and their attendant problems were finally brought under control.[3]

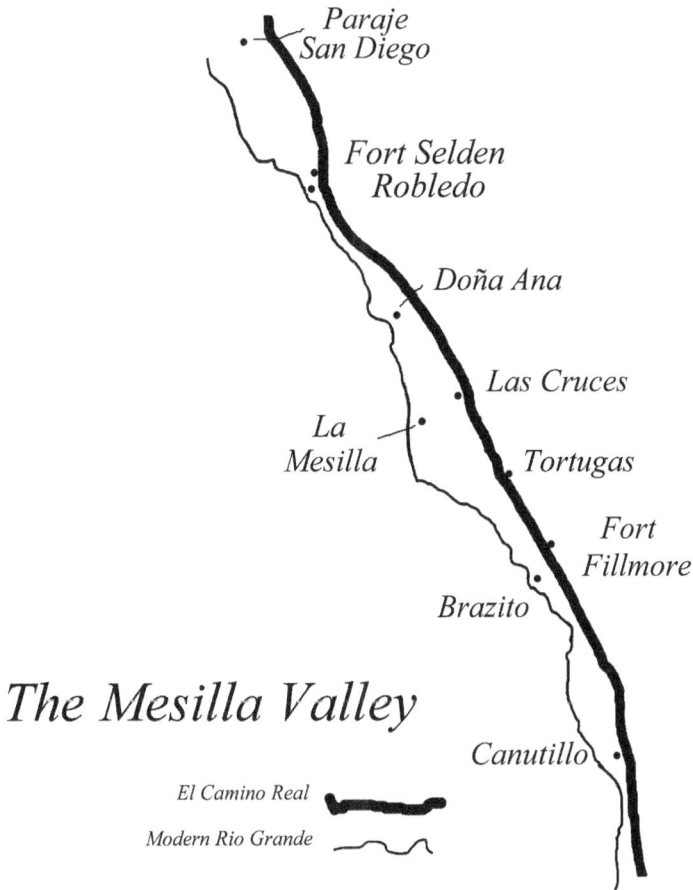

El Camino Real de Tierra Adentro through the Mesilla Valley.

Canutillo

Canutillo was a paraje north of Frontera, named for a crescent-shaped lake near the Rio Grande, where a small eighteenth-century Spanish military outpost and corral served the presidio at El Paso del Norte. The first people to settle at Canutillo were a group of Paseños who petitioned for a land grant in 1823. Led by Juan Ponce de León, twenty-nine residents requested farm land at the paraje, on the east bank of the river, below a series of sand hills. In early 1824, Canutillo was formally founded, with about one hundred pioneers living at the site by the end of the year. They plowed and planted their fields, grazed livestock along the riverbanks, and built an acequia system to water their crops.

The small agricultural hamlet did not survive very long as frequent Apache raids drove most of the settlers back to the safety of El Paso del Norte. The situation worsened in the 1830s when the Mexican government declared war on renegade Indian tribes along the frontier. By 1833, the few remaining residents had abandoned Canutillo, and the homesteads and corrals melted into the landscape, or were swept away by the river. After the Mexican-American War, James W. Magoffin began ranching near the lake and rebuilt the old irrigation system. Even though the land was now part of the United States, Spanish and Mexican landowners held certain rights under provisions of the Treaty of Guadalupe Hidalgo. As Magoffin poured thousands of dollars into improvements at the site, some of the original 1823 grantees and their heirs challenged his right to the property. In 1854, the Rio Grande Commission only recognized a small portion of the claim. Anson Mills was hired by the original landowners to produce a more detailed, accurate plat, but he found many discrepancies and was unable to identify the Mexican surveyors' markers. The new Mills survey further limited the Mexican claims.[4] In the meantime, Magoffin organized businesses along the trail at American El Paso, La Mesilla, and Las Cruces, and expanded his ranch at Canutillo.[5]

There were two sites along the old trail beyond Canutillo that became stagecoach stations in the 1850s. The Cottonwoods Ranch was located in present-day La Tuna, just short of today's New Mexico state line. In 1851, Commissioner Bartlett referred to the site as the *Alamos*, or Cottonwoods, and it served as a way-station on the Santa Fe Mail, and the San Antonio and San Diego Mail, lines. In 1858, Cottonwoods was the last settlement on the road between El Paso and Fort Fillmore, and became a regular stop on the Butterfield Overland Mail. Waterman L. Ormsby, who rode the Butterfield Overland in the fall of 1858 and wrote of his adventures in the New York *Herald*, described the station as lying in a "pretty grove of cottonwood trees." These stations were built to provide "a change of mules, a moment of rest, and a simple meal - bread, coffee, meat, and beans."[6] A second station was located near today's town of Vinton. It was called *Los Tres Hermanos*, or the Three Brothers, and was on a ranch owned by El Paso's Mills brothers. The Tres Hermanos station was merely a small adobe building where teams of horses were changed, and stage passengers were occasionally served meals. By 1860, a few people lived around both stations. The real growth of La Tuna and Anthony came with the railroad in 1881.[7]

Brazito

Further north was a site known as the *Vado*, the river ford, settled in the mid-nineteenth century, and beyond the Vado was the *brazito*, or little arm, of the Rio Grande, noted by colonial and Mexican travelers as an important campsite on the Camino Real de Tierra Adentro. The brazito was a large bend in the river that created a small wooded island, with tree-shaded areas along the banks, firewood, and abundant fish, wildlife, and vegetation. In 1805, Juan Antonio García de Noriega retired from the presidio at El Paso del Norte and applied for a land grant at the Brazito. He built a small adobe house, dug an acequia, and moved his family and friends to the site. In the early 1820s, Apache attacks made it impossible for the García clan to live at the Brazito. A few hardy pioneers remained, but after García died in 1828, the handful of remaining homesteaders abandoned the area and returned to El Paso del Norte.

The Battle of Brazito took place at a bend in the Rio Grande, near the site of this restored twentieth-century schoolhouse.

The campsite is best known as the site of the Battle of Brazito, during the Mexican-American War. In the late fall of 1846, the First Regiment Missouri

Mounted Volunteers, under the command of Colonel Alexander W. Doniphan, were ordered south along the old Camino Real, to meet up with Brigadier General John E. Wool's forces at Chihuahua City.[8] They rendezvoused at Valverde, where they met up with a large merchant-caravan that had been camped at the paraje for more than a month, fearful of traveling further into Mexico. Doniphan ordered the 300-wagon caravan to follow behind his troops as they made their way south. They proceeded in several detachments, entered the Jornada del Muerto on December 14, and re-grouped at Doña Ana on December 23. By Christmas Eve, about 400 of Doniphan's men made camp at Brazito.[9]

Meanwhile, Mexican forces, under the command of Brevet Lieutenant Colonel Antonio Ponce de Léon, left El Paso del Norte and headed north to block the American invasion. An American advance party noticed a cloud of dust to the south, and alerted the Doniphan camp, which quickly organized for a confrontation with the Mexicans. The Mexican forces were well-equipped and outnumbered Doniphan's army. Among their ranks were Veracruz lancers in scarlet coats and brass helmets, a battalion of Chihuahua infantry, and hundreds of El Paso militia. The Mexican charge should have easily surrounded and overwhelmed the Americans, but Doniphan's men held fire until the last minute and were able to break the Mexican line, secure their howitzer, and throw the troops into confusion. The battle lasted less than a half-hour. Eleven Mexicans were killed, and seventeen were wounded. Seven Americans were injured in the assault. As Mexican forces scattered, Doniphan's troops advanced.[10] On December 27, they met with a delegation of Paseños, marched into El Paso del Norte, and raised the American flag on the central plaza, all without firing a shot. The army went on to defeat Mexican forces at the Battle of Sacramento on February 28, 1847, and by March 2 they had taken Chihuahua City. Doniphan was celebrated as a hero, and several of his men, and a few merchants who followed the army, wrote popular accounts of their experiences.[11]

After the war, Hugh Stevenson purchased two-thirds of the Brazito grant from the García heirs, an area of more than 23,000 acres, and he and his partner Joseph Bennett opened a small silver mine at the bend in the river.[12] Among the laborers who came to work at the mine and smelter were a few Tigua and Manso Indians from the El Paso del Norte area.[13] In the 1860s, flooding shifted the Rio Grande west and the meander became landlocked, surviving only as a marsh. Twentieth-century flood control projects drained the marsh and created a series of irrigation canals for area farmers and one branch, the Brazito Lateral, follows the path of the old river bend. Although there has been considerable debate over the exact location of the battlefield, most evidence points to the site of the old Brazito Schoolhouse, an early twentieth-century brick structure along the east side of NM 478. A New Mexico Highway Department Camino Real Historical marker is located just south of the site.[14]

Fort Fillmore

The few remaining ruins of Fort Fillmore lie between NM 478 and Interstate 10, north of Brazito. In 1851, the United States Army leased land from Hugh Stevenson and brought troops from garrisons at Doña Ana, El Paso, and San Elizario to construct Fort Fillmore, named for President Millard Fillmore. The original fort was a series of simple mud and branch *jacales*, or shacks, but troops were soon making adobe bricks for larger, more permanent buildings. Fort Fillmore was first established to oversee the frontier on the new international boundary which, in 1851, ran along the river just west of the post. Shortly afterwards, the garrisons at Doña Ana and Fort Bliss were abandoned, and troops were transferred to Fort Fillmore, the new headquarters of the Third United States Infantry. Fort Fillmore was a large U-shaped site with enlisted men's barracks, officers' quarters, administrative centers, a hospital magazine, and supply centers. A corral area, northwest of the fort, housed horses and livestock, and an acequia supplied water from the river.[15]

During the early 1850s, Fort Fillmore troops engaged in limited campaigns against area Apaches, provided escorts for Captain John Pope's mapping expedition, and oversaw traffic on the old trail and new wagon roads that crossed the valley. La Mesilla was the nearest settlement of any significant size, so it provided most of the supplies, materials, laborers, and entertainment for the fort and its troops. In 1853, the Gadsden Purchase dropped the international boundary south, placing La Mesilla within the United States and Fort Fillmore more than forty miles away from the border. The old Camino Real continued north through Las Cruces and onto Santa Fe, but about four miles north of Fort Fillmore a new wagon road branched off to the west. This placed the fort near a major regional crossroad. In 1858, the Butterfield Overland Mail built a station and corral at the post.[16]

Fort Fillmore expanded as more American settlers moved into the new territory. Lydia Spencer Lane, the wife of a United States Army officer, visited the post just as the Civil War erupted in 1861. The experience was unsettling. She noted Confederate sympathies in the region and feared that, in case of an attack, the small garrison could offer little resistance. She was unimpressed with Fort Fillmore, describing it as "most dreary and uninviting," with rows of "shabby adobe quarters" and grounds that suggested "neither beauty nor comfort."[17] When war broke out, Fort Fillmore's federal troops were under the command of Major Isaac Lynde. He abandoned the post after a skirmish with Confederates at La Mesilla on July 25, 1861. Rebel soldiers arrived with Lieutenant Colonel John R. Baylor and occupied the site. They negotiated a new lease with Hugh Stephenson, a Confederate sympathizer. Baylor's men stayed on for about a year, but as the Southerners' campaign in New Mexico collapsed in the summer of 1862, they abandoned the post. The First California Infantry Volunteers, known as the California Column, a Federal army under the command of James H. Carleton, arrived during the fall months and found the fort in poor condition. Materials had been taken away for construction at other sites, and many of the remaining structures had been looted. The California Column left Fort Fillmore on November 13, 1862, the last troops to ever make use of the post. The lease expired, and after the war the United States Army was no longer interested in the site.[18]

For years, the ruins of Fort Fillmore stood quietly alongside the main road between El Paso and Las Cruces, and locals laid claim to much of the debris, arguing over doors, frames, and windows. By the early twentieth century, much of the site had been ransacked and combed for artifacts. In 1931, when the Conklings made their epic survey of the Butterfield Overland Mail route, they visited Fort Fillmore and noted "some crumbling walls and washed down mounds of adobe."[19] Fort Fillmore was placed on the National Register of Historic Places in 1974, but efforts to make it a state monument ultimately failed. Today, there are only a few low crumbling wall-segments hidden by the surrounding pecan groves. Because so much of the land around the old post has been plowed and planted, the outline of the fort, or the location of buildings, is almost impossible to determine. Fortunately, the current landowners have guarded and posted the area, helping to preserve what little remains.

La Mesilla

La Mesilla is located north of Fort Fillmore along NM 28 and is probably the best known Hispanic village in southern New Mexico. *La Mesilla*, the Little Mesa, was settled after the Mexican-American War as a refuge for area Hispanics who wished to remain in their homeland. Rafael Ruelas worked with El Paso del Norte's Father Ramón Ortiz, who was serving as a commissioner of *colonias*, to issue Mexican land grants to pioneer settlers.[20] The Camino Real de Tierra Adentro continued along the east bank as it headed north through the valley, but the village of La Mesilla was established on a low, west bank plateau, accessible by several river fords in the area.[21] After the Gadsden Purchase, the new international boundary placed La Mesilla within the United States.[22]

La Mesilla was originally situated on the northern frontier of Mexico and had its share of Indian problems. As the Apaches struggled, slowly exterminated by disease, lack of food, and harassment by Mexican and United States military campaigns, they engaged in attacks on new settlements in the area. The natives usually stole livestock and ran off horses, but when confronted, they fought back, sometimes killing farmers and herders. Northern-Mexican frontier settlements often organized a *guardia móvil*, a small volunteer militia, to maintain order. The Mesilla Guard, mostly Hispanic residents of La Mesilla, led numerous attacks on Apache camps in retaliation for raids made on area farmers and herders.[23] Tensions increased in the 1850s, and the Guard became more aggressive, launching bolder, often unprovoked attacks, and committing several acts of violence that shocked many in the Territorial government. On February 7, 1858, about thirty Mesilla Guardsmen brazenly rode out from the town plaza to a nearby camp, where they scalped three Apaches and mercilessly attacked women and children. Residents of nearby Doña Ana, who had fairly good relations with the Indians, were horrified by the Guardsmen's behavior and protested to local officials. After a second raid, the entire Guard was arrested and taken to the Third Judicial District Court in Socorro. Public opinion favored the Guard, and in the October 1858 trial all were acquitted. In order to prevent future incidents, officials disbanded the organization and created a new militia, placed under Territorial control.

In the meantime, La Mesilla became a county seat and transportation hub. In 1858, the Butterfield Overland Mail forded the Rio Grande into today's Mesilla Park. Coaches were ferried across the river and continued west into La

Mesilla station, the best equipped between El Paso and Los Angeles.[24] By 1860, La Mesilla had also become the junction for Butterfield's Santa Fe Mail, a branch line that used the old Camino Real path north. Even so, La Mesilla was still a small frontier town, with crudely constructed adobe stores and houses. About 2,000 residents lived in simple jacales, grouped around the village plaza.[25]

La Mesilla had numerous Confederate sympathizers, and, in late July 1861, southern troops, led by Lieutenant Colonel John R. Baylor, left Fort Bliss and followed the old Camino Real north into New Mexico.[26] Baylor secured La Mesilla, declared it part of the Arizona Territory of the Confederacy, and proclaimed himself governor.[27] As the Anglo-American presence increased, new businesses, building materials, and architectural styles changed the appearance of the village. During the 1860s, flooding changed the course of the Rio Grande, shifting the river channel west of La Mesilla. It was no longer necessary to ford the river to reach the village.[28]

La Mesilla grew until the railroad arrived at nearby Las Cruces in 1881. Then, no longer a hub of regional transportation, it was eclipsed by its neighbor and became a quiet agricultural settlement once again. With limited growth and development in the twentieth century, it remained one of the best preserved Hispanic villages in southern New Mexico, and by the mid-twentieth century was recognized for its historic plaza, many architectural and cultural resources, and compact village setting. La Mesilla may be the best preserved village in the area, but little of what a visitor sees today resembles the simple frontier town of the nineteenth century. Most of the structures in the historic center have been greatly modified, re-surfaced, and "New Mexicanized" over the years. The present design, with an open square and bandstand, dates from the 1970s and re-creates a setting that existed in the 1930s. The La Mesilla Historic District was added to the National Register of Historic Places in 1982. The town's commercial buildings are grouped around the plaza, and residential areas radiate out from the center. Most are adobe-based but have been modified over the years with brick, concrete, and wooden features. The most prominent building on the plaza is San Albino Church, a yellow brick structure, built in 1906, with many turn-of-the-century architectural features that stand in sharp contrast to the Territorial designs that dominate the village.

Several prominent structures in the village center are directly related to its past as a regional crossroads. The area just below the plaza was the heart of the transportation district. The Miranda-Bean Building lies along the southside, facing the gazebo and church. Guadalupe Miranda, the land commissioner who followed Ramón Ortiz, first built part of the structure in the 1850s, and a few years later it was greatly expanded. All four sides of the long, adobe and brick building fronted the street, filling an entire village block. The interior was a *placita*, or open patio, and once served as the Mexican customhouse. After the Gadsden Purchase, the rear section of the building housed freight offices and served as a waiting room for passengers waiting for the San Antonio Mail. The large area behind the bar served as the Mesilla station of the Butterfield Overland Mail. The northeast section of the building was lost in a fire in the 1910s, and by the 1920s a brick facade and parapet was added.

The Bean-Butterfield Building is across the street, at the southeast corner of the plaza, on Calle de Parian. A house was located at this site as early as 1854, and segments may have been incorporated into the present structure. The one-story stuccoed adobe building once had a spacious, open patio that has since been enclosed and is now part of the interior. In the 1850s, Sam Bean and his brother Roy (Judge Roy Bean) ran a freight and passenger service west to Pinos Altos from there and by the 1870s John Davis had converted the station into the Corn Exchange Hotel, one of the best in the Southwest. His family operated the inn until the early twentieth century. Brick trim and a brick-stepped parapet were added later, modifying the Territorial design. The hotel business declined as the railroad diverted traffic to Las Cruces, and in 1939 the building was re-modeled and has been one of the more popular restaurants in La Mesilla ever since.

Dominating the west side of the plaza is the Taylor-Barela-Reynolds building, constructed in the late 1850s. In the early 1860s, Rafaela Barela lived there with her son, Sheriff Mariano Barela. She operated a store in what today is the northern portion of the structure and a narrow passageway led from the storefront back into the living quarters. William Charles Reynolds later purchased the property, expanding and renovating the site in the early twentieth century. He added decorative changes popular at the time, such as the pressed metal facade on the front of a new store. In 1953, the Barela-Reynolds building became the residence of J. Paul and Mary Taylor, prominent La Mesilla residents who over the years became very active in area agriculture, politics, history, and preservation. They further enlarged the structure to thirteen rooms and filled the sprawling home with historic art and furnishings. In 1978, the site was listed in the National Register of Historic Places. Major conservation work was conducted in the 1980s, through grants from the State Historic Preservation Office, and in 2006 the Taylor family donated the property to New Mexico State Monuments, which became the Taylor-Barela-Reynolds Mesilla State Monument. Plans are for the site to eventually become a state museum.[29]

Segment of the Taylor-Barela-Reynolds House and shops on Mesilla's plaza, part of a series of nineteenth-century adobe buildings modified and renovated over the years.

La Mesilla's plaza, re-landscaped in the twentieth century, was originally an open, dirt-filled area frequented by wagon traffic, livestock, local vendors, and troops. It was also the site of the formal transfer of the Gadsden Purchase to the United States. On December 30, 1853, troops from Fort Fillmore gathered on the plaza, while the Mexican flag was lowered and removed from the post, and replaced by the Stars and Stripes. Today, several historical markers located around the lively plaza detail some of the significant events in La Mesilla's history. The backstreets of La Mesilla have many examples of small, historic adobe-based buildings that have been renovated and restored over the years. Along Calle de Guadalupe there are several "contiguous" adobe structures that share common walls and date to the nineteenth century. A neighborhood northwest of the plaza was known as the California district, made up of larger, Territorial-style homes built by Anglo-Americans.[30] The old acequia system still runs through the village and supplies water to surrounding fields, orchards, and gardens.

Tortugas

Tortugas is east of La Mesilla, off of NM 28. It originated as a small mid-nineteenth-century settlement on the old trail and is the only surviving Native-American community in southern New Mexico. *Tortugas* is named for Tortugas Mountain, just east of the village, which rises about 700 feet above the plain and is said to resemble a turtle.[31] Several Native-American groups are represented in the village, including Tiwa, Piro, Manso, and a few other native cultures of northern Mexico. Over the years, many of their indigenous traditions have been blended together into the cult of the Virgin of Guadalupe. Tortugas is neither a pueblo nor a reservation, although there have been some attempts by various groups in recent years to formally recognize the indigenous heritage of the village.

Tortugas was founded after the Mexican-American War, when laborers from the El Paso Valley moved there to work at the nearby Stephenson mine and smelter. It first appears on Brevet Captain John Pope's 1854 map of the Mesilla Valley. Tortugas is divided into two smaller communities, each with a different heritage. Guadalupe, the southern section of the town, was established by Indian families from Ysleta del Sur, Senecú, and Isleta, and has traditionally identified with its Tiwa past, despite a great deal of intermarriage with New Mexican Hispanics. Residents of El Paso del Norte, who came north to settle in the Mesilla Valley, brought many customs and traditions with them, including a devotion to Our Lady of Guadalupe, Mexico's most popular religious and cultural icon. A Las Cruces group known as the *Inditos*, or Little Indians, continued some of these traditions and were joined by other families who migrated north from Ysleta del Sur and Senecú. Indigenous ceremonies and dances from the Guadalupe

Mission in El Paso del Norte were performed at Saint Genevieve's Church in Las
Cruces until the 1910s, when the Inditos moved the performances to Tortugas.
A few people of Manso descent came from Ciudad Juárez in the early twentieth
century and also participated in the ceremonies.[32] Some probably had Manso
or Piro blood, but by the late nineteenth century they had lost much of their
language and cultural customs. Tortugas was able to preserve some of the Indian
traditions that were lost in Ciudad Juárez during the twentieth century, and,
even though English and Spanish are the common languages in the villages,
some Tiwa is still used in their ceremonies. The second neighborhood, San Juan
de Dios, Saint John of God, spreads across the northern part of the village and is
more ethnically mixed.

The village of Tortugas with its two neighborhoods, Guadalupe and San
Juan de Dios, lies between the Las Cruces Lateral, which irrigates the village,
and Interstate 10. The original 1887 chapel and village center was near Eugencio
Street, just south of Tortugas Drive. The Tortugas Catholic Church, an early
twentieth-century adobe structure, still in use today, is located on Parroquia
Street, south of Tortugas Drive.[33] At the east end of Guadalupe, there is a Casa
del Pueblo, a contemporary version of a Pueblo Indian clan house: a rectangular,
adobe, one-story building with a large hall and small room in back. A small
oratorio, or private place for prayer, dedicated to Our Lady of Guadalupe, is
alongside. A large square block of land is set aside for ceremonial purposes, and
two small community structures are at the east end. Remains of nineteenth-
century adobes dot the area around the village center.

The *Casa de Descanso,* a processional rest-station, in Tortugas.

The village of Tortugas is best-known for its Lady of Guadalupe celebrations held December 10–12 each year. During the ceremonies, the image of the Virgin is carried from the small chapel to the Casa del Pueblo. *Danzantes,* or dances that follow the Tiwa tradition, matachines performances, and rosaries are conducted throughout the night. The next day a procession up Tortugas Mountain, a limestone block about four miles east, takes place. A mass on the mountain, ceremonial fires, and the placing of *luminarias,* or festive lights, concludes the second day of festivities. On the last day, December 12, the image of the Lady of Guadalupe is paraded through the village and then returned to the chapel, where it remains until the next year.[34]

Las Cruces

Las Cruces may have been the location of a Manso Indian village near a river ford known as *La Ranchería,* the Hamlet, mentioned by a few travelers in the early seventeenth century.[35] As Spaniards entered the area, the Mansos fled to the nearby Organ Mountains, until missionaries persuaded them to move south to the Guadalupe Mission in El Paso del Norte. After that, the future site of Las Cruces remained an open paraje, a mere campsite along the river. The name *Las Cruces,* or, the Crosses, is said to refer to crosses marking the site of a killing or massacre, but there is no historical documentation for any of the stories. The only reference was made by Susan Magoffin, who noted a "solitary white cross" on the Chihuahua Trail nearby in 1847.[36]

In 1848, Doña Ana's Justice of the Peace Pablo Melendres requested that the United States Army help build a new town south of his village. Doña Ana had become overcrowded, the presence of American troops made many locals nervous, and new settlers were encroaching on residents' properties. The Army agreed and offered Doña Anans the opportunity to move to a new tract, laid out by Lieutenant Delos Bennett Sackett. When Sackett arrived to survey the new town site, more than one hundred people were already camped there, to be among the first to choose *suertes,* or numbered papers, from a hat, and receive one of the best lots. Sackett marked out an area for the plaza and church, and laid out a grid of streets. After the eighty-four block tract was opened, the rush of settlers caused confusion, resulting in street and property lines that were often crooked or poorly measured, and a shortage of good soil for adobe bricks led to the random digging of holes along the streets and unassigned properties. One of the early main thoroughfares was Water Street, which followed the path of the acequia. The old Camino Real ran along today's Mesquite Street, the eastern edge of the new town.

The pioneers who moved to Las Cruces made sure that their new community was adequately fortified. Two general stores were constructed, and, as the tallest buildings in town, they also functioned as lookout posts where sentries kept a watchful eye for any signs of Apache activity. The outer walls served as protective barriers. They had thick adobe surfaces with a few small portholes, in which they could aim their guns, in the event of an attack. Freight wagons that made their way along the old trail were corralled in town, protected by the defensive walls. The residents were well-prepared, but by 1851 Fort Fillmore had been established south of town, and, unlike nearby La Mesilla or Doña Ana, Las Cruces was seldom attacked.

In the 1850s, Las Cruces remained small, with only a few hundred inhabitants. Farming, freighting, and trading were the main enterprises and a handful of mines operated in the nearby Organ Mountains.[37] Missouri freighters and Chihuahua Trail traders settled in the community and expanded their commercial operations. Gregoria Rodela de Amador, a widow from El Paso del Norte, opened a small store on the corner of today's Amador Avenue and Main Street. One of her three young children, Martin, worked at Fort Fillmore, where he learned English and later received a trading-post commission. He expanded his mother's store to take in teamsters and travelers on the old Chihuahua Trail. In 1866, he built a one-story house for his family, which was later converted to a rooming house for drivers and freight agents. By the 1880s, the structure had become the city's best hotel and the social center of the community. Nestor Armijo, nephew of the last Mexican governor Manuel Armijo, was born into a wealthy Albuquerque merchant family, and first passed through Las Cruces during an 1853 drive that herded more than 50,000 sheep west to the California goldfields. He returned the next year, established a store and saloon, and, by the time of the Civil War, greatly expanded his business. In the late 1860s, he had sold the store and concentrated on freighting into Mexico, trading along the new western trails, and ranching. Armijo's home became one of the most lavish in Las Cruces.

The Armijo House, on Lohman Avenue, was once the most lavishly furnished home in Las Cruces.

Even so, Las Cruces remained a small village throughout the 1870s, cut off from much of the commercial activities of American El Paso and La Mesilla. When La Mesilla refused to sell the right-of-way to the Santa Fe Railway, William L. Rynerson and a group of Las Cruces investors donated land for a depot and track line through the western edge of the village. The railroad opened new markets and replaced most of the overland freight business along the old Chihuahua Trail.[38] Las Cruces grew, and, by 1900, it boasted a regional college in addition to agricultural, commercial, and transportation services. The population remained largely Hispanic, with a growing influx of Anglo-Americans and a small African-American population. East of town, in the Organ Mountains, a mining boom brought further development in the 1890s. Most of Las Cruces's growth followed the Second World War, and, by the 1950s, 12,000 people lived in the city. A second spurt of growth began in the 1990s and continues today.[39]

The original town site covered much of today's downtown, but about half of the old settlement was lost to mid-twentieth century urban renewal projects. The surviving segment of old Las Cruces (the southeast corner of the original town site) lies east of Campo Street. Campo, San Pedro, and Mesquite Streets, which run north to south and parallel to the old trail, were some of the earliest streets in the village. The oldest surviving structures, tucked away among the narrow streets, are found in the area north of Kansas Avenue, especially in the 200 to 600 blocks.

The Mesquite Historic District, established in the 1980s, contains much of the original village site. Scattered throughout the district are many examples of nineteenth-and early twentieth-century adobe houses with typical Mexican and Territorial features. A handful of long, low rectangular buildings, whose outer walls lie close to the narrow streets, may date from the founding of the town. Small door and window openings, irregular contours, and rough exteriors are common. Some have almost solid outer walls, which were necessary for defense. Territorial and Hip-Box style residences are also found. Many others represent common Santa Fe, Pueblo Revival, and Mediterranean styles of the twentieth century, but may be expanded or modified versions of earlier structures. The Mesquite Street Original Town Site Historic District was added to the National Register of Historic Places in 1985.[40]

A few early Las Cruces structures survive west of the historic district. The Armijo House is located on the southside of Lohman Avenue, just east of Main Street. In 1877, Nestor Armijo bought the house from Missouri trader, Bradford Daily, and greatly expanded it, remodeled the interior, and added a second floor. Armijo was a prominent rancher, freighter, and merchant, and as the family prospered they lavishly furnished the site and remodeled areas to suit their needs. Although the original house was built in 1868, Armijo's extensive changes dramatically altered its appearance and made it the first two-story home in Las Cruces. The Armijo family luxuriously furnished the home, with fine French chairs, marble-topped tables, and elaborate Victorian décor. Greek Revival detailing and lavish artworks flowed through the interior. A two-story veranda made of milled lumber, and featuring Queen Anne trim, was added in the 1880s. The home was surrounded by corrals, vineyards, pasture land, barns, and gardens, making it one of the most impressive residences in the city. Family members lived in the home until the late 1970s, when the property was finally sold and underwent a major restoration. The once sprawling estate is now hemmed in by a shopping center and parking lot.

The Amador Hotel was a thriving inn, on a major New Mexican coach road.

The Amador Hotel is located on Amador Avenue, west of Main Street. In 1878, when Martin Amador's family moved into a new, larger house across the street, their old residence became a rooming house and hotel. The old property also served as warehouse space for Amador's freight business and was expanded when the railroad replaced stagecoaches and wagon trains. In 1885, the hotel was enlarged; a second floor was added, and a balcony and lobby were built. A livery, patio and bar were later added. A social hall stood alongside the rooming house, and the two structures were combined in 1887 to become the Amador Hotel. The lobby of the hotel had a central stage, on which theatrical and musical troupes performed, making the Amador the center of Las Cruces' social life. The Amador Hotel earned a reputation as one of the best places to stay in the Southwest, and the Amador family continued to operate the inn until 1970. By the 1980s the building had been listed on the State Register of Cultural Properties. After that, its adobe exterior was stuccoed to create a Spanish-Pueblo Revival look, and it became a local bank and, then, county offices. Since 2006, the Amador Hotel building has been vacant, but a local foundation is currently attempting to restore the building for use as a museum.

Doña Ana

Doña Ana is located about five miles north of Las Cruces on NM 320, off Interstate 25. It was a trail paraje during the colonial period: a large area on a plateau fifty or sixty feet above the bottom lands, between a small mountain range and the river. In the eighteenth century, there may have been a ranch briefly settled nearby, leading to references of Doña Ana as a *ranchería*. It was first mentioned by the Otermín party during their 1680 retreat and appears on several colonial-era maps.[41] One of the few documented references notes a Mesilla Valley ranch owned by Doña Ana María de Córdoba that was attacked by Indians in the 1690s and is more likely the source of the name.[42]

Today's village of Doña Ana dates from the Mexican era. In 1839, José María Costales, and 115 others filed for *El Ancón de Doña Ana*, or the Doña Aña Bend Colony Grant which extended from the paraje on the trail (near the present-day village) south into today's Las Cruces. By early 1843, the first settlers had arrived and began constructing an irrigation system to draw water from the Rio Grande. Doña Ana grew slowly. Apache raids disrupted spring planting, and some of the first colonists returned home in frustration to El Paso del Norte. Mexican troops rode through Doña Ana in the spring and were appalled by the poverty and destitution they observed, so they issued the settlers uniforms, horses, and mules. The presence of Mexican troops quieted Indian raids and planting resumed. The fall of 1843 brought a good harvest of corn, beans, and vegetables. Peace and prosperity drew new settlers to Doña Ana, and, by the next year, the village had more than 250 residents.[43]

The Doña Ana Bend Colony was formally surveyed in January 1844. A census disclosed that, of the 261 settlers, forty-seven families and twenty-two single men were entitled to land grants. The original fourteen settlers were given their first choice of farmland, and a public drawing allocated lots to the others. The town site had a public plaza, a lot for a church, and space for public buildings. A grid of streets, each thirty-five feet wide, was laid out, and lots about 137 feet square were designated. Many of these were later divided, creating long rectangular wedges throughout the village. Grazing lands and wooded areas along the river were marked for common use, and any remaining lands within the grant were set aside for future settlers.[44] Early dwellings were simple jacales, or small adobe buildings, and rooms were usually added one at a time, often resulting in an extended rectangular structure or an "L" shape, when reaching a corner or lot line. Settlers were encouraged to build houses close together, often connected to their neighbors' homes, to form a protective wall along the village streets. Few windows faced the street and doors were heavily fortified. The long front facades of the buildings placed close together made the main streets into walled corridors. Outside of the village center, dwellings were less formally arranged.[45]

Within a few years, the Mexican-American War disrupted life in the Mesilla Valley. In December 1846, Doniphan's Missouri Volunteers spent several days in Doña Ana. They camped near the river, prepared defenses, and bought large stores of corn, grain, and livestock from the locals.[46] Doniphan's ragtag army was a sorry sight and frightened many of Doña Ana's residents. The soldiers spent their time drinking, gambling, chasing women, and generally raising hell throughout the town. Most Doña Ana residents were glad to see them depart.[47]

When the war ended in 1848, Doña Ana was still the only settlement in the Mesilla Valley. Doña Ana became the first county seat and a county courthouse was built along the main street.[48]Although improvements were made, many residents of Doña Ana remained wary of the Americans. Conflicts continued, and in 1849 lots were offered to Doña Ana residents in the new settlement of Las Cruces, a safe distance away from the soldiers. Others, preferring to return to Mexico, crossed the river and joined loyal Mexicans at La Mesilla. About 600 people remained in the village in the 1850s.[49]

The settlement of Las Cruces and La Mesilla, the establishment of Fort Fillmore, the Gadsden Purchase, and the arrival of the railroad in 1881 all diverted attention south, and soon left Doña Ana a quiet agricultural village once again. It stayed that way throughout much of the early twentieth century and has only recently experienced spurts of growth and development.[50] Today, the historic center is located just south of NM 320 away from much of the commercial activity along the highway. The most prominent landmark in town is the *Nuestra Señora de la Candelaria* Church, also known as Our Lady of Purification, the oldest church in the Mesilla Valley. This appears to be the second church in Doña Ana, built after 1844, with a nave of high adobe walls, simple lines, and small windows. It was probably constructed in several stages over a period of many years. By the end of the nineteenth century, a wooden belfry was erected above the nave, and carved woodwork imported from France, graced the interior. After 1900, several additional changes were made, including parapet walls, decorative curved brick copings, and new tall windows. A new floor was added, and the supporting wooden vigas were hidden under a plastered ceiling. The roofing was replaced, and a concrete bell tower made the church appear more typical of the New Mexico Territorial-style.[51]

El Camino Real de Tierra Adentro passed along this quiet backstreet in Doña Ana village.

By the 1960s, the old church was in poor shape, so a nearby parish hall was used for services until a new church could be built. The new church, opened in the 1970s, soon became the center of the community's activities, and, on several occasions, residents considered demolishing the old Candelaria Church. In the early 1990s, plans were made to stabilize and restore the Candelaria Church. Over the course of several years, the roof was repaired, traditional *latillas*, or little sticks, were once again installed over the vigas, water damage was repaired throughout the structure, and the cement plaster was stripped from the exterior.

More than 17,000 adobe bricks were used to repair and strengthen the walls.[52] Research and study of the church created interest in other aspects of the town's heritage.[53] Although development changed much of the town center in the mid-twentieth century, the 1990s brought a renewed interest in preservation and restoration. Nuestra Señora de las Candelaria Church was added to the National Register in 1985 and the Doña Ana Village Historic District was listed in 1996.

Today, Doña Ana retains much of the ambience of a nineteenth-century Hispanic village on the old Camino Real and many structures in the historic center remain much as they were in the mid-nineteenth century. Although windows and doors have been replaced with modern fixtures, many buildings are still flat-roofed, irregularly-walled, one-room wide structures. Early Doña Ana buildings are still commonly used as residences, and decades of plastering and repairing have not modified the rough, hand-hewn designs of these basic adobe dwellings. Little of the Territorial or eastern-Anglo style of architecture is found in the village today. In back of the dwellings, the corral-courtyard areas can still be seen. In the village itself, and in the surrounding cultivated fields, the basic grid pattern, laid out more than 150 years ago, remains evident. Homes are spread along the original grid of streets, often connected to one another, and persist as remnants of the fortified system devised in the original town plan.[54]

Cristo Rey Street was the old Camino Real. It passed along the east side of the church and served as the main village thoroughfare in the nineteenth century. The original acequia, dug in 1843, remains in use just west of the plaza. North of the church, the trail followed Abeyta Street north to *El Alto*, the upper end of Doña Ana. Along both sides of Cristo Rey Street are some of the oldest buildings in Doña Ana, dating from the Territorial period. When the United States Army stationed troops there after the Mexican-American War, they constructed larger, more permanent buildings. Many became private residences and businesses when troops were removed to Fort Fillmore in the 1850s. The first two buildings, south of the church, on the opposite side of the street, became residences.

In the late nineteenth century, the second building became a general store, owned and operated by Herman Wertheim. In 1954, Harvey Fergusson (1890–1971) used Doña Ana as the setting for his novel, *The Conquest of Don Pedro*, and the lead character, Leo Mendes, a Jewish merchant from New York, is loosely based on the life of Herman Wertheim. Mendes traveled the old trail south from Santa Fe, exploring settlements along the way and interacting with a wide variety of nineteenth-century New Mexicans.[55] After years on the trail, he settled in Don Pedro (Doña Ana) and opened a general merchandise store, similar to the one operated by Wertheim. Like many traders along the Chihuahua Trail, Mendes hauled local hides, pelts, dried chilis, and grains north, to exchange for knives, firearms, metal tools, religious icons, statues, and exotic herbs, spices, and medicines.[56] Mendes's life in Don Pedro, although highly dramatized and romanticized, allows readers to get a glimpse of life in a small Camino Real town and understand some of the many conflicts present in the New Mexico Territory in the late nineteenth century.

The large adobe building on the southeast corner of Cristo Rey and Gutiérrez is typical of nineteenth-century Hispanic village architecture in New Mexico. The home dates from the 1840s and is L-shaped, with adobe walls, vigas, and latillas. The next building was the first Doña Ana County courthouse, where officials oversaw an area that extended west to the Colorado River, and east to Texas. The street ends abruptly two blocks south, and a path winds down toward the acequia below. Cristo Rey was the old Camino Real and main thoroughfare through the village. In the nineteenth century, the road continued from this point down to an area known as *El Bajo* (the lower end of town), along the main acequia, and on to Las Cruces. In 1901 a flash flood destroyed much of El Bajo, and the road was later diverted.[57]

The old Catholic and Methodist cemeteries, both badly damaged by developers beginning in the 1960s, lie at the east end of Joe Gutiérrez Street. Most of the remaining tombstones and markers date from the early twentieth century. Near the highway, on the east side of Abeyta Street, is a home with a curved segment of wall, the remains of a *torreón*, or tower, once used for village defense. It later served as the Abeyta Oratorio (a chapel inside a home), and was dedicated to the *Santo Niño de Atocha*, the Holy Child of Atocha, honored in Fresnillo, Mexico, and Chimayo, New Mexico. A statue of the Holy Child, still remaining in the home, is believed to have been brought up the Camino Real in the early years of the settlement. For many years, the child was seen as the protector of Doña Ana residents, especially those who served in the First and Second World Wars.[58]

Paraje de Robledo and Fort Selden

This campsite was named in honor of one of the 1598 expedition's elders, sixty-year old Pedro Robledo, who died at the site of natural causes, no doubt brought on by the many hardships of the trip north. The site became known as the *Cruz de Robledo*, Robledo's Cross, and, later, the Paraje de Robledo. The massive, dark, bleak mountain that looms 1,500 feet above the river, just west of the trail, bears the name Robledo Mountain.[59]

In the seventeenth century, Cruz de Robledo became an important Camino Real paraje for trail travelers. In August 1766, Captain Lafora was relieved to reach Robledo, which he described as an *ancón*, or an open area, on the trail, after traveling nine leagues north along the "serpentine" course of the river through "woods of mesquite, huizache, etc., so thick that the vehicles had great difficulty in passing through."[60] But while Cruz de Robledo offered a welcome respite, it also made travelers vulnerable to Apache attacks, so the Rubí inspection team recommended that a detachment of troops be posted at the paraje. Bishop Tamarón experienced some "anxiety" when he stopped there in 1760, as his party observed smoke signals coming from the nearby Doña Ana Mountains. They later found a small black cross alongside the road and a sack of fresh venison and deerskin. At first, they thought this signaled a warning, but native guides explained that the Apaches were peaceful, and were offering gifts. Tamarón's men left a knife, pieces of bread, and tobacco at the site and continued along the trail. When they were almost out of sight, two Indians on horseback came into the clearing, returned to the cross, and retrieved the gifts. Tamarón continued through the Jornada without incident.[61] Through most of the Mesilla Valley, Camino Real travelers stayed along the east bank of the Rio Grande, but beyond Robledo the river twists and turns, veering off to the west in a large arc. There is no longer a wide floodplain as the river cuts its way through rocky banks, deep arroyos, and steep escarpments. Travelers faced days of treacherous travel, so Oñate's Indian scouts steered the expedition away from the river and onto a pass, which offered a more direct route north, through a flat desert prairie that became known as the Jornada del Muerto. Robledo was the last campsite before the move east and functioned as an oasis on the trail.

Melting ruins at Fort Selden, near Paraje de Robledo.

Mexican-era policies drove the Apaches back out into the hinterland, and by the 1830s there were renewed attacks that further disrupted settlement in the region. After 1848, when American troops were stationed at Doña Ana, and, with the establishment of Fort Fillmore a few years later, Apache attacks decreased. After the Civil War, new plans were made to secure the frontier and protect trade along the wagon and coach roads that passed through the Mesilla Valley. Western military posts were spaced about fifty miles apart on the frontier, the approximate distance a cavalry could move in one day. Lieutenant Colonel Nelson H. Davis surveyed the Robledo campsite in 1865 and reported it to be an ideal location for a new fort. The site he suggested was located on a high ridge about one-half mile from the river and offered a panoramic view of the Mesilla Valley. Just to the west, the peaks at Robledo Mountain provided troops with a good lookout post and sweeping views of the Jornada.[62]

In 1865, Fort Selden, honoring Henry H. Selden, a Union officer who helped defend Fort Craig during the Civil War, was constructed at Paraje de Robledo. The original fort was built of adobe and was designed for one company of cavalry, but by the 1870s there was also a company of infantry, bringing the total to about 170 men. Troops from the 125th Infantry, comprised of African-American soldiers, commonly known as "Buffalo Soldiers," manned the post and conducted campaigns against area Apaches after 1866. The fort was a rectangular parade ground, lined with single-story adobe buildings. Officers' quarters were at the north end of the compound and enlisted men's barracks opposite them. The fort had shops, corrals, a small hospital, guardhouses, and offices. Eventually about fifteen square miles of land were designated as the Fort Selden Military Reservation, public lands closed to most settlement.[63] Scouting parties and escort patrols took most troops out into the field and usually left few men at the post.[64] Supplies often came from La Mesilla, the nearest town of any significant size, and Adolph Lea's homestead, near the reserve, became the site of Leasburg, a typical small frontier community of saloons and dance halls.

Military campaigns and the coming of the railroad brought changes to the frontier during the 1880s. The western United States Army was re-organized, and in 1887 a decision was made to close Fort Selden. In the 1890s, Forts Cummings, Marcy, and Union were also closed, while Fort Bliss was greatly expanded. The Department of the Interior and a handful of troops remained to strip Fort Selden's facilities and oversee the remains. A few people lived at the site from time to time, but it was usually abandoned, visited only by a few locals and occasional looters. The properties were sold and transferred several times during the early twentieth century. In 1963, the Bailey family donated the property to the New Mexico Parks and Recreation Department, and, ten years later it became a New Mexico State Monument. Major surveys and preservation works were conducted in the mid-1970s and 1990s to stabilize the site. Today, there are no complete structures remaining at Fort Selden, just a series of wall segments, but a visitors' center interprets the fort's history and displays military equipment and excavated artifacts.[65] The Camino Real passed along the main acequia and the east edge of the fort. Two branches of the trail led north, across the railroad tracks, and remained east of the interstate.[66]

Paraje San Diego

Paraje San Diego, about ten miles north of Robledo, was located near the Upham exit of Interstate 25, an area where the trail came up onto a flat, level surface before entering the desert plain. Although it was well west of the trail, Paraje San Diego offered one last chance to drive cattle down to the river and fill caravans' water jugs. The campsite was the last stop before heading into the Jornada del Muerto. It was never a fixed location, but simply a broad area extending along the river escarpment, possibly as far north as Rincon.[67] Archaeological surveys conducted in the 1980s and 1990s at San Diego produced a wealth of information about the site.

The 1598 Oñate expedition camped there[68] and Paraje San Diego appears to have been regularly used by the mission-supply caravans of the seventeenth century, especially in the period before the 1680 Pueblo Revolt.[69] Many of the artifacts found at Paraje San Diego are from the seventeenth-century caravans. Northern New Mexico was fairly isolated during the early colonial period. There were no settlements along the 560-mile stretch of the trail, between Santa Barbara, Mexico and Mission Senecú, New Mexico, until the establishment of the Guadalupe Mission at El Paso del Norte in 1659. Rio Grande-glazed pottery, a northern style of Pueblo painted pottery, common before the Revolt, was found scattered around the area. These ceramic works were brought back on the return trip from Santa Fe, often acquired at northern missions, and popularly traded in settlements further south. Rio Grande-style pottery became less commonly produced after the re-conquest, and the style was fairly rare by the mid-eighteenth century. *Majolica*, a soft paste ceramic with a lead-tin glaze, was a decorative style that originated in Sevilla, Spain and was produced in Puebla and Mexico City. Many majolica pieces were common among those collected at San Diego. By the 1560s, the Manila galleons had opened trade between the Spanish and the Orient. Exotic luxuries such as spices, fabrics, ivory, and porcelain goods arrived through the Pacific ports of Mexico and made their way north along the Camino Real. The San Diego site yielded pieces of Ming Era Chinese porcelain, probably some seventeenth-century traveler's prize possession. It was somehow broken at San Diego, and the owner left the remains of this rare artform that had traveled thousands of miles around the world, there, at this desolate campsite on the northern stretch of the Camino Real de Tierra Adentro.[70]

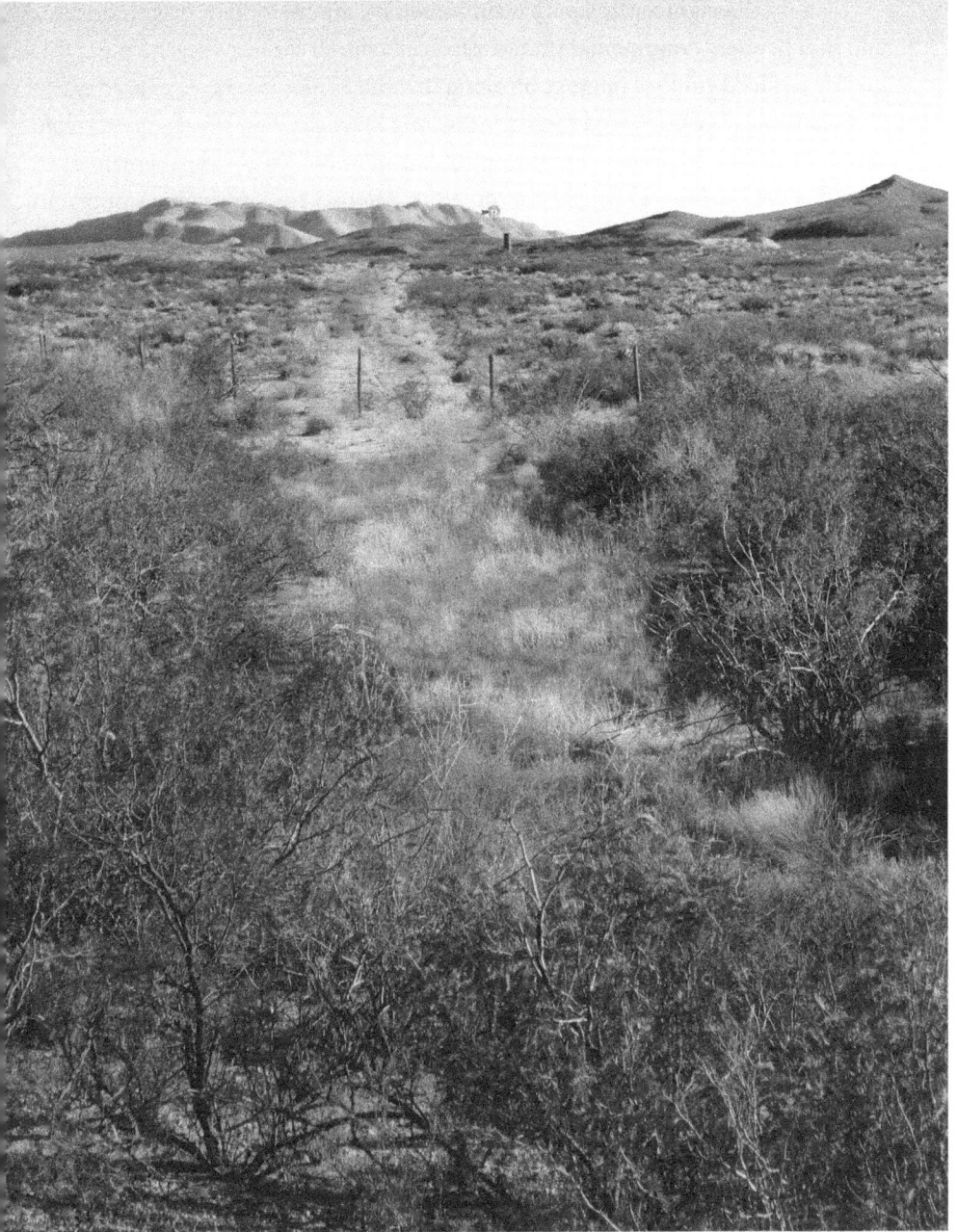

Paraje San Diego was west of the main trail but provided one last source of water before entering the Jornada del Muerto.

By the eighteenth century, the mission-caravan system was in decline, and independent commercial traders replaced church caravans on the trail. This greatly reduced cultural interaction along the trail as merchants purchased wares at distant sites and packaged them for the long journeys. Fewer local goods were acquired or traded from community to community.[71] The paraje remained in use after the Pueblo Revolt and was noted in colonial and Mexican accounts. In the nineteenth century, Anglo-American traders traveled the trail, but there was never any attempted settlement at San Diego. The dry desert terrain high above the river offered little hope for farming or grazing.

5

The Jornada del Muerto

*A*fter resting at Paraje San Diego, the Oñate expedition left the steep and rocky terrain along the river. An advance party, perhaps following the advice of Indian scouts, took the governor due north onto a high, flat desert plain east of the river. The colonists followed with their carts, wagons and livestock and made their way slowly through a ninety-mile stretch of the trail that became known as the Jornada del Muerto. The Jornada is hemmed in by the Oscura and San Andres Mountains on the east side, and the Caballo and Fray Cristóbal Mountains on the west. The path of the Camino Real de Tierra Adentro through the Jornada del Muerto generally followed the flat desert landscape, occasionally broken by gullies, arroyos and rock outcrops. Most of the Jornada is dry, with frequent blowing, shifting dust.[1] There are few trees, but the sparse vegetation includes greasewood, tumbleweed, tall-growing yucca, and short grama grass when water is present, especially after the summer rains. Only three Jornada parajes were commonly used, and, only two, Paraje del Perrillo and Laguna del Muerto, were considered a reliable source of water. North of the Fray Cristóbal range is an area of *malpaís*, or badlands, termed for the line of rugged volcanic basalt outcrops that separate the trail from the river.[2] The old Camino Real avoided the malpaís by passing between the Fray Cristóbal range and the lava beds through an area known as Lava Gate. From the Gate, the trail descended and met the river once again at paraje Fray Cristóbal. The last stretch of the trail entered the Socorro Valley through today's Bosque del Apache National Wildlife Refuge. After 1598, most caravans, wagon trains, and military expeditions followed the Camino Real de Tierra Adentro through the Jornada, and the first railroads and automobile highways through the region continued along the same path.[3]

The Jornada del Muerto was Apache territory. Mescalero Apaches lived among the San Andrés and Sacramento Mountains to the east, and Warm Springs Apaches inhabited the area west of the Rio Grande. Roaming Utes and

Navajos also occasionally entered the region. There were no Indian pueblos or missions in the Jornada, and caravans and small parties were always vulnerable, as clouds of dust from their wagons and herds could be seen from miles away on the flat landscape. Even the light, fast American stagecoaches that roared through the region in the mid-nineteenth century were subject to attack. After the Mexican-American War, the United States military established posts in the Jornada to protect travelers and settlers, but the Apache were one of the last tribes in North America to be brought under control.[4]

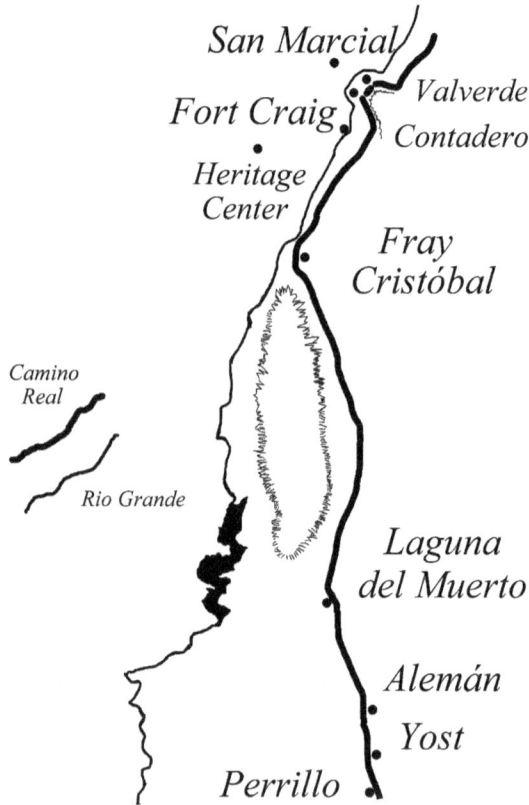

El Camino Real through the Jornada del Muerto.

Jornada del Muerto is often translated as the Journey of the Dead, but it is more accurately translated as the Journey of the Dead Man, referring to a tragic incident that occurred in the late seventeenth century. In the 1660s, Bernardo Gruber, a German trader from Sonora, was reported to the Holy Office of the Inquisition in the Jurisdiction of Las Salinas, east of the Jornada, in the Manzano Mountains. He was accused of superstition and immorality, and imprisoned at Sandia Pueblo. The case against him moved slowly, and, after a year of captivity, Gruber became despondent, especially as he lost most of his livestock and trading goods to local frontiersmen. After a second year passed, he planned an escape. Gruber was assisted by his loyal servant, an Apache named Atanasio, and several area traders who offered to help. On June 22, 1670, after removing the bars of his cell, Gruber and Atanasio made their way out of the Manzanos and down the Camino Real toward the Socorro Valley.[5]

Nine days after the escape, Atanasio appeared alone at Mission Senecú, near today's San Marcial. He told how he and Gruber had ridden south for two days and camped at Fray Cristóbal. The next morning they continued through the desert basin but were soon desperately short of water. By evening, Gruber, exhausted and parched from thirst, sent Atanasio ahead to scout the pools and springs and search for any signs of moisture. He rode as far south as paraje San Diego, filled a large gourd and came back looking for Gruber, but before he arrived, the gourd broke and the water was lost, so Atanasio returned to San Diego once again. This time he used a blanket to soak up river water and galloped back up the trail to rescue Gruber. When he returned to the camp, Gruber and his horse were gone. Atanasio spent the next two days looking for his German master and finally, exhausted, gave up and decided to turn himself in to authorities at Mission Senecú. Another ten days passed before Gruber's body was found. A group of traders stumbled across the grisly remains near a site that became known as *Alemán*, the German. His dead horse was tied to a nearby tree and Gruber's corpse had been ripped apart by animals and scattered around the site. The death of Gruber sparked some of the first references to the area as an "jornada del muerto" and by the end of the century the name was commonly cited in travelers' journals and maps.[6]

National Park Service and Bureau of Land Management signs guide visitors through sites in the Jornada del Muerto.

The notorious reputation of the Jornada del Muerto reached Anglo-Americans through the writings of George Wilkins Kendall, a journalist who joined President Mirabeau B. Lamar's ill-fated Texan-Santa Fe Expedition of 1841. Kendall, along with most of the expedition, was captured in northern New Mexico and taken south, as prisoners of the Mexican army. Some of the worst treatment they received was during their forced march down the Jornada del Muerto. Kendall described a long, cold, cruel trek in the dead of winter. Food was scarce, and the troops quickly became weakened and exhausted. The starved, weary men begged for rides on merchant wagons and traded whatever they had for a few minutes of relief. Those too weak and sick to continue were reportedly shot dead by the guards. The survivors did not receive any adequate food or medical attention until they were cared for by Father Ramón Ortiz at El Paso del Norte.[7]

Today, the Jornada del Muerto is one of the most remote, isolated regions on the Camino Real de Tierra Adentro National Historic Trail. The railroad cuts a lonely path through its center, following much of the old roadbed, and unpaved roads and trails crisscross the plain. Only a few public roads wind through the region, but north of Engle, a small ghost town, the Jornada del Muerto is closed to public traffic. Locked gates prevent travel through the area, and only primitive jeep trails allow access to the river. Elephant Butte Reservoir, and the Rio Grande, lie along the western edge of the Jornada, further isolating it from the interstate and area communities.

Paraje del Perrillo

County Road A-013 parallels the Camino Real de Tierra Adentro National Historic Trail through the Jornada del Muerto. The Oñate expedition left Paraje San Diego and traveled north to Point of Rocks, a large basaltic outcrop rising hundreds of feet above the desert plain.[8] They camped miles from the river and had to carefully conserve the little water they had left. One morning, a small dog traveling with the expedition wandered away from the Point of Rocks camp and returned in the afternoon with mud caked on his paws. Mud meant water, so Captain Villagrá and Father Salazar followed the little dog's tracks back through the desert and found two small pool of water left from a recent rainfall. They called the pool *Los Charcos del Perrillo*, Pools of the Little Doggie, and the nearby campsite became known as the Paraje del Perrillo.[9]

Grasses sprout in moistened pools near Paraje Perrillo.

The area around Paraje del Perrillo became a routine campsite on the trail, but travelers had to exercise caution, because it was also a popular Apache watering hole, and the nearby formation of Point of Rocks provided good cover for a surprise attack.[10] Indians closely observed travelers as they made their way through the Jornada del Muerto from nearby mountain peaks and used smoke signals to alert each other of approaching parties. Long continuous columns of smoke meant that someone had entered the area; short puffs signaled that they were well-armed. At night, lone torches and flames let travelers know they were being watched. The flat, empty landscape of the Jornada made for an easy strike, as the natives could hide in the mountains and quickly gallop down to the desert floor. A wagon train was helpless; no one could outrun the Apaches. Camping near Point of Rocks meant being vigilant; at any moment an attack might take place. During the Spanish Colonial era, Perrillo became an important rendezvous point for caravans, and escort troops from Santa Fe were relieved by soldiers who accompanied the wagon trains south to Chihuahua City.[11] Today, the Point of Rocks Trail, a one-half mile hiking trail off of A013, developed by the Bureau of Land Management and the National Park Service, is located near Paraje del Perrillo and overlooks the Camino Real. It features three interpretive signs that describe travel along this stretch of the trail.

Yost Escarpment Trail

North of Perrillo and Point of Rocks, along the Yost Draw and the Yost Escarpment, is a small pullout and parking area on the east side of County Road A-013. The escarpment landscape features are named for Hiram Yost, a close acquaintance of western writer Eugene Manlove Rhodes. The trail follows one of the best preserved segments of the Camino Real in the Jornada, where several well-defined road segments, clear of any vegetation, wind north toward the escarpment. Runoff water has allowed vegetation to grow more freely at the south end of the roadway, while the north end, near the escarpment, has several long stretches of the old Camino Real that stand in sharp contrast to the creosote and tar brush alongside. Rock surfaces and boulders along the roadway are polished and worn, evidence that livestock and wagons were often driven along this stretch of the trail.[12] The National Park Service and Bureau of Land Management have developed the Yost Escarpment as an interpretive site, with parking, a short hiking trail that parallels the Camino Real, and signage explaining the history and significance of the roadway. Five interpretive signs describe travel and transport along the trail, and life in the Jornada del Muerto. The Yost Escarpment Trail is a one and one-half mile hiking trail that leads east from the highway to the Camino Real roadbed which runs south to north along the rise, and continues up to the escarpment overlook. From the edge of the escarpment, at the northern end of the trail, traces of the old roadway can be seen continuing across the plain to Alemán Ranch. Sweeping views of the Camino Real corridor through the Jornada del Muerto are visible from the rise. East of the trail, a spaceport complex, currently under construction, can be seen in the distance. Metal, glass, and pottery fragments have been found along the corridor, but this particular segment of the Camino Real appears to be a later roadway, perhaps originating in the era of the Chihuahua Trail. In order to avoid the small rise in the landscape to the north, there may have been parallel road segments, yet undiscovered, nearby.[13]

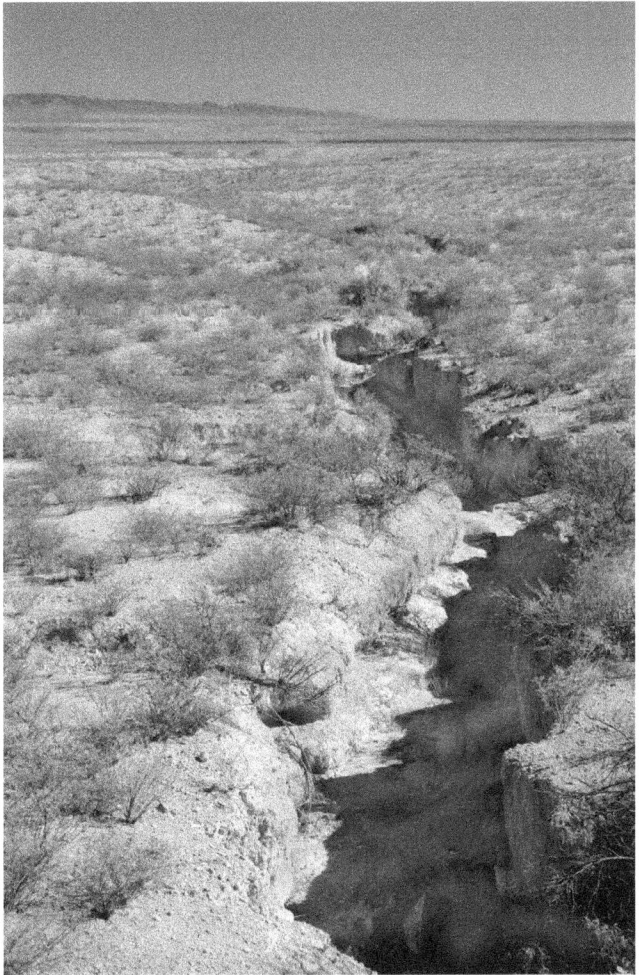

Deep arroyos cut through the edges of the Jornada.

La Cruz de Alemán

A few miles north of the Yost Escarpment was a much less reliable source of water at a site called *Alemán*, the German, said to be the place where Bernardo Gruber's body was found in 1670. Although this was a commonly visited paraje, like other sites on the Jornada, no one attempted to settle there until the nineteenth century. Following the Mexican-American War, the New Mexico Territorial Legislature requested funding from the United States Congress to develop the old trail between Santa Fe and Doña Ana and dig wells in the Jornada, but few improvements were ever made. Only one small, isolated hamlet, San Ygnacio de Alamosa, existed in the area in the 1860s, but drought, along with the constant threat of Apache and Navajo attacks, made life extremely difficult. By 1867, Alamosa had been abandoned and the remaining settlers moved west to present-day Monticello.

John "Jack" Martin came to New Mexico during the Mexican-American War as a drummer boy. In 1849, he traveled west to the California goldfields and, twelve years later, when the Confederate Army moved into the Jornada, Martin joined more than 2,000 California volunteers to protect the territories of the west. Martin was stationed in Arizona but moved to Las Cruces after the Civil War. He served in military escorts for stagecoaches delivering the mail along the old Camino Real and became well-acquainted with the Jornada del Muerto. In 1867, he and his wife moved to Alemán, where they established the first ranch in the Jornada. In 1868, without assistance or funding from either the Legislature or the United States Congress, Captain Martin dug the Jornada's first successful well, striking ground water 164 feet below the surface. The Martins established a cattle ranch, which became known as the Alemán Ranch. Jack, ever the entrepreneur, began charging travelers for the use of his water and gained a tax-exemption for the business. He offered the military free water and arranged for troops from Fort Selden to be posted at Alemán to protect travelers through the region. He also helped arrange for the first telegraph lines to reach Las Cruces. The Alemán Ranch was never a large operation but was described as a one-story adobe building that fronted the main road with corrals, stables, and outhouses. Martin, convinced the Jornada was on the verge of great development, brought the first post office to the remote site and opened a modest hotel. Alemán continued to be a stagecoach stop until the 1880s.[14]

Laguna del Muerto

About sixteen miles north of Alemán is *Laguna del Muerto*, Dead Man's Lake, near today's NM 51 and the ghost town of Engle. Laguna del Muerto is a wet-weather lake, a depression in the basin that gathers run-off, especially after the summer rains. Because it allows a considerable amount of water to be absorbed within its rim, tall prairie-grass sprouts and continues to grow long after the waters have disappeared from the surface. The tall, greenish grass often makes the site stand out in the barren landscape. Oñate's colonists stopped at the Laguna, and it soon became the most important campsite between Robledo and Fray Cristóbal. Five to six miles west of the Laguna was *Ojo del Muerto*, Dead Man's Spring, the only other source of water in the area when the lake was dry. Like Paraje del Perrillo, Laguna del Muerto and the nearby Ojo del Muerto were favorite sites for Indian raids, and the common soap-weeds and yucca stalks near the Ojo, along with the tall grass growing around the Laguna, provided ample cover for Apache attacks.[15] The lake was often dry, prompting campers to get what little water was available from the nearby spring, but driving horses, mules, and cattle to the spring was a difficult, and sometimes dangerous, undertaking.[16]

After the Mexican-American War, stagecoaches transported mail and passengers through the region along the old Camino Real. Even though the coaches were faster, making treks of fifty miles a day (rather than the twelve to eighteen miles that wagon trains and caravans had traveled), their small entourages of guards were easy prey for the Apaches. They tried to race through the Jornada and stopped only briefly for water. The guards who accompanied coaches were usually veterans, scouts, or former Texas Rangers, well-prepared for trouble, and, by the early 1850s, they were aided by faster, more accurate weapons that gave them a decisive advantage over Indian raiders. Drivers and guards preferred newly available Sharps rifles and carbines (from the Sharps Rifle Company of Hartford, Connecticut). Accurate and easy to handle, these high-powered, repeating rifles and smaller, lighter, carbines were used to ward off attacks. In 1852, after several mail carriers and guards were killed near Laguna del Muerto, legendary driver Henry Skillman armed his men with Sharps weapons. Skillman's party was attacked while crossing the Jornada in 1853, and, after arriving safely at El Paso, he penned a letter of appreciation to the Sharps Rifle Company. Skillman stated that "after having been a frontier man for fourteen years…I have found no arm that in all its attributes begins to compare with the Sharps." He called their weapons "far superior" for their "range, accuracy, and rapidity of firing." The quote was later used by the Sharps Company in their catalogs and promotional literature.[17] Continued Apache attacks led to the 1863 founding of Fort McRae, about three miles from the Rio Grande, near Cañon del Muerto, which is a gap between the Fray Cristóbal and Caballo Mountains. The Laguna del Muerto remained a remote campsite until it became the town of Engle in 1881, named for railroad engineer Robert L. Engle.[18] Stagecoaches connected mining centers in the Black Range with Engle. By then, the entire area was undergoing a cattle-ranching boom. As the railroad brought regular traffic through the Jornada along the path of the old Camino Real, Laguna and Ojo del Muerto provided water to re-fuel steam locomotives at Engle.

For many late nineteenth-century readers, the romantic image of the cowboy personified the American West. Texas ranchers organized long cattle drives north to the railheads as the demand for meat products grew dramatically in eastern markets. Some cattle trails led northwest into New Mexico as they followed the Pecos River, crossed the Tularosa Basin, wound through the Organ Mountains, and led into the Jornada. From there, some followed the old trail north toward Colorado; others continued west to Arizona. Sheep grazing along the old Camino Real declined but was replaced by a cattle boom that lasted until the early years of the twentieth century. The heirs of Pedro Armendáriz sold large tracks of land around Engle to cattle barons who were establishing ranches in the Jornada. New Mexico had about 57,000 head of cattle in 1870 and by 1880 the herds had increased to more than 348,000. The cattle boom brought prosperity, but it was an erratic, uncertain, and sometimes violent business. The expansion of the railroad, soaring cattle prices, range wars, and contested land titles made the late nineteenth-century an unstable time in the Territory. Engle gained a reputation as a violent "wild west" town and in nearby Lincoln County, the 1877 range wars made William Bonner, more famously known as "Billy the Kid," a living legend throughout the region. Much of this drama was immortalized in the western writings of Eugene Manlove Rhodes (1869–1934), the Jornada del Muerto's greatest promoter, and "the cowboy chronicler."[19] His family moved to New Mexico in 1881, and he experienced firsthand the great changes taking place in the Tularosa Basin and the Jornada del Muerto. Rhodes worked as a cowboy, stone mason, and road builder (opening the first road from Tularosa to Engle) in the 1880s, gaining a great appreciation for the region and its people.

He left the Territory in 1888 and spent more than twenty years away, a period of time when he produced most of his western novels. Rhodes was self-educated, with a great eye for detail and colloquial character, and his works portrayed the people he lived and worked with in the Jornada, presenting more diversity than was common in the typical "western" novels of the time. Rhodes' *Paso por Aquí* is often cited as his best work and was later made into the Hollywood feature film, *Four Faces West*.[20]

During the great boom of the 1880s, the Bar Cross Ranch was an immense, sprawling operation that extended from Doña Ana County north to San Marcial, with approximately 20,000 cattle on the Jornada. A Michigan syndicate, the Detroit and Rio Grande Livestock Company, owned the property which, by the mid-1880s, included the old Alemán Ranch. The manager's headquarters was located at Engle, but, by the 1890s it had moved to Alemán. Rhodes worked the Bar Cross Ranch more than any other outfit and developed a fascination with cowboy life, memorializing the ranch in his writings.

Fray Cristóbal and Paraje

One of the best known campsites on the Camino Real de Tierra Adentro was Fray Cristóbal, also known as Paraje. This secluded spot appears in journal entries and documents throughout the colonial, Mexican, and American era of the trail, and was named for Fray Cristóbal de Salazar, a cousin of Juan de Oñate and a member of the 1598 expedition. Today, the mountains west of the paraje are known as the Fray Cristóbal Range, and a series of serrated peaks in the center are said to bear a resemblance to the old friar.[21]

The campsite was located in an area north of the Fray Cristóbal Mountains where the lava flows smooth out, and the Jornada slopes down toward the Rio Grande. Basalt (or lava) flows, in an area known as the *malpaís*, separated the trail from the river and a few miles before reaching the paraje, the roadbed became sandy and gradually descended. Fray Cristóbal was a green oasis with abundant cottonwood trees and sprawling patches of prairie grass. It was known for its lush vegetation, easy access to river water, and rolling terrain that allowed for easy camping and corralling. When the trail was busy, the constant grazing of livestock depleted the grasses and forced many travelers to move further east, away from the river. The exact location of the campsite, a broad area along the east bank, changed over time, especially with seasonal flooding and receding waters. For those heading south, Fray Cristóbal was the last place to graze and water animals before leaving the river and entering the worst stretches of the Jornada del Muerto.[22]

By the mid-seventeenth century, Fray Cristóbal was regularly visited by supply caravans, military expeditions, and missionaries. During the Pueblo Revolt, it became the rendezvous point for two large parties of refugees escaping the chaos and fighting in the north. Governor Antonio Otermín and Lieutenant Governor Alonso García met at the paraje and led thousands of people on the long march south to the safety of El Paso del Norte. It remained an important landmark after the rebellion and served as a meeting place for caravans, military escorts, and mail service throughout the Spanish Colonial period. Military escorts traveled south from Santa Fe with mail pouches (*valijas*) and exchanged them with correspondence brought north by government couriers from Chihuahua City.[23]

Several sites around Fray Cristóbal, including Valverde, La Mesa, and Bosque Bonito, were settled after Forts Conrad and Craig were established in the early 1850s, and the village of *Paraje*, the Campsite, was founded at Fray Cristóbal by 1857, with almost 200 residents.[24] When the Civil War broke out and Confederates threatened the region, Fort Craig stationed about 140 men at Paraje.[25] After the troops departed, Paraje remained a fairly self-sufficient agricultural village, trading with nearby Fort Craig. Although most residents were poor Hispanics, Paraje's best known residents were Swiss immigrants who ran the local general store and post office. August Rouiller, a merchant and land speculator, was one of the few in the community to live a comfortable life and acquire any wealth. The village enjoyed a brief period of prosperity, but by the end of the century it began to decline. In the 1890s, as plans were made to build a dam and reservoir on the Rio Grande, Rouiller bought nearby tracts of land and later sold them to the Reclamation Service. Although Rouiller profited, Paraje's fate was sealed by the reclamation project. People began leaving the area in the 1910s, and by the 1920s Paraje was a ghost town. A few years later, it was entirely abandoned. In 1942, Elephant Butte Reservoir was filled for the first time, completely submerging the village. Adobe walls melted, and many remaining artifacts were washed away, scattered along the sandy shores of the lake. After a few months, the waters receded, exposing the site once again. For most of the mid-twentieth century, Paraje was a remote, isolated site, seldom visited by anyone. It was occasionally washed by flooding in later decades until a dispute over water rights led officials to fill Elephant Butte Reservoir once again in 1985, leaving Paraje completely submerged, this time for almost three years.[26]

Today, the ruins of the village of Paraje lie along the east bank of the river, at the northern end of the Elephant Butte Reservoir. It is located far from any area highways, in thick river bosque, off a primitive ranch-road on the edge of the reservoir. The site is on federal land, and no public roads lead directly into the area. Although Paraje has seen few visitors, it has been well-studied, especially in the 1980s when much more of the village still existed. While there is a wealth of scattered debris, much of it has been washed ashore from surrounding areas with the changing level of the reservoir. Hidden in the brush are some of few remaining ruins and artifacts of Paraje; many are covered with thick mud, a result of being exposed and re-submerged with each seasonal cycle. Because many structures were made from area basalt, sections of walls and foundations are common among the ruins. Scattered metal fragments and ceramic pieces can be found in the brush. An occasional large piece of debris, such as a fireplace mantel, or machine part, is exposed in the vegetation.[27] Behind locked gates and lying on the eastern edge of Elephant Butte Lake, boaters occasionally stumble upon the remains of this once thriving village, but there is less to discover with each passing year.

Black Mesa and El Contadero

Black Mesa and the paraje of El Contadero lie along the east bank of the river, about nine miles north of Fray Cristóbal. The black basalt mesa rises 300 feet from the river bottom and has a steep, rocky face along its western, northern, and southern side. It is visible from many miles around, particularly to motorists moving along NM 1 and Interstate 25. Black Mesa was mentioned by the Oñate expedition as being of "black rock" and was later noted on maps as "Mesa de Senecú" because of its proximity to the old Senecú pueblo. The large basaltic lava mesa was known by many names, especially in the nineteenth century. It was called the "Mesa de San Marcial," "Table Mountain," and "Black Mesa." El Contadero, the Counting Place, noted on several eighteenth-century maps, was located along the west edge of Black Mesa, a long and narrow passageway that wound between the mesa's steep sides and the banks of the river. The Spanish used it as an inventory site, since it was an easy place to herd and count livestock as they passed along the narrow trail.[28]

El Contadero, the Counting Place, near Black Mesa.

El Contadero was especially important for herding sheep in the eighteenth and nineteenth centuries. The Spanish brought *churro* sheep to New Mexico, scattering them in northern pueblos as early as 1540. Oñate drove thousands of sheep up the trail along with cattle, mares, colts, and goats. Livestock from New Spain thrived in New Mexico, and during the seventeenth century large landowners (especially the governors of the province) established extensive ranching operations north of the Jornada, using Indian laborers. Raising sheep became a profitable business, and the Parral mining district, located hundreds of miles to the south, became the main market for mutton and wool. The Pueblo Revolt temporarily ended the livestock trade, but, by the mid-eighteenth century, it recovered and became the region's most important industry. Troops from the presidios of Carrizal and San Elizario often met large livestock caravans in the Jornada and escorted them south to Chihuahua City.[29] For example, in 1800, ranchers and traders joined the governor and his wagon train headed south from Santa Fe to Chihuahua on official business. Almost 150 regular troops, militiamen, and Indian laborers followed, bringing hundreds of heads of cattle and close to 20,000 sheep along with them. While Mexican independence brought some interruptions, large drives resumed and expanded by the 1820s. Churro sheep remained the preferred stock, but after 1848 American traders often found them to be a disappointing product. Their wool was adequate but coarse, and typical New Mexican sheep carcasses were smaller, producing half of what was common in the east.[30]

Several Mexican-era corrals and pens were constructed at the mesa and used to herd livestock during drives through the Jornada. After Mexican independence, El Contadero became less important and is only occasionally mentioned in later travelers' accounts. A settlement called Contadero was founded in the 1860s and was a small but active community for about twenty years, thriving until Fort Craig was abandoned. The population of about 140 residents included several European immigrants, who earned a living as merchants and craftsmen, and lived in the village along with area farmers until the 1890s, when the community declined. In 1920, only about sixty people remained at Contadero. They stayed a few more years, but the rising waters of the reservoir flooded area-farmland and eventually destroyed the settlement. Today, a few structural remains survive west of the railroad tracks, believed to be the old church and the foundation of a residence. The passageway is hidden in the brush along the base of the outcrop, on the east bank of the river. Nothing remains of the settlement but a few Mexican-era rock corrals that surround the site.[31]

Valverde

Valverde, the Green Valley, was about six miles north of El Contadero, where a good river ford allowed access to the west bank. The earliest reference to Valverde appears in 1805 medical records in which it was noted that children from nearby Sevilleta were vaccinated there. In 1819, Pedro de Armendáriz obtained the only colonial land grant in the Jornada del Muerto, which included the land around Valverde. Armendáriz had served as a first lieutenant at the San Elizario presidio and was a senior administrator in the New Mexican government. He maintained his connections with the presidio and had goods shipped regularly from San Elizario to Valverde with the annual caravans of the 1820s.[32] Whether Pedro Armendáriz ever lived at Valverde is uncertain, but members of the Armendáriz family appear to have settled there shortly after petitioning for the land. Records indicate that a hacienda, corral, and outbuildings had already been constructed by May 1820, the time of the second request, but the settlement lasted only a few years. Navajo attacks increased and had driven the Armendáriz clan out of the area by 1824.[33]

The Armendaris land grant was one of the largest grants made during the early nineteenth century.

In 1832, Valverde was considered as a site for a Mexican presidio, a fortress to protect new settlers and serve as a customhouse where duties could be collected from traders on the Chihuahua Trail. It was hoped that once the area was secure, large numbers of homesteaders would be drawn to the Jornada.[34] But the presidio and port of entry were never established, and the ruins of old Valverde, abandoned and without the protection of troops, slowly melted away into the landscape of the Jornada. Its adobe mounds and piles of rubble became a landmark and a commonly used campsite along the trail, where traders and travelers erected small, temporary shelters.[35] In 1851, Fort Conrad was established on the west bank of the river, near the present-day Tiffany siding, and was named for Secretary of War Charles M. Conrad. Soldiers garrisoned at Socorro were moved to the new fort, a small settlement of cottonwood structures, jacals, and tents. A few settlers returned to Valverde and built their mud and thatch homes south of the old village site. In 1853, Colonel Robert Stapleton opened a ranch near the ruins that became a popular retreat for officers. Fort Craig was established the next year, eventually replacing Fort Conrad. By then, about ninety people lived at the village, cultivating more than 800 acres of farmland and selling goods to the two military posts.

Valverde is best known as the site of one of the West's major Civil War battles. In 1862, Texas Confederates from Fort Bliss were joined by troops under the command of General Henry Hopkins Sibley. Sibley's general plan was to secure New Mexico and Colorado, and continue west until a great transcontinental Confederacy was established. By early February, the two armies, consisting of about 2,600 men, headed north along the trail toward Fort Craig, which was guarded by about 1,000 Union troops under the command of Colonel Edward R.S. Canby. As the Confederates advanced, northern New Mexico militia units were mobilized and brought down to support Canby's men and defend the Union fortress.[36] As the Rebel troops approached, volunteers from nearby villages gathered at Fort Craig. About 3,800 men helped prepare the post for attack by building a moat at the perimeter, and a large ten-foot earthen wall around the fortress. Since it was well-manned and fortified, taking Fort Craig would require a massive effort by the Confederates.

Sibley realized the potential costs of a direct attack on the fort. Instead, he kept his Confederate troops on the east side of the river and planned to sneak past Fort Craig, cross the river north at the Valverde ford, break communications between Fort Craig and Albuquerque, and continue onto Santa Fe. The Rebels camped at Paraje and made their way around the east side of Black Mesa. As they continued north, hidden by some of the rolling uplands along the river, the troops were spotted by Union scouts.[37] Canby moved his men up to meet the Confederates at Valverde, and, on February 20, 1862, Union troops confronted the Rebels and advanced on their ranks. In the early hours of the fighting, Canby's Union men took the lead but by midday the Confederates had struck back. Captain Alexander McRae tried to unite with the First New Mexico Volunteers, but Confederate troops broke through his lines and took control of Valverde. After McRae was killed, and the Union troops were routed, the Confederates launched an attack into the Union lines and seized their howitzers. The fighting never reached Fort Craig. At Valverde, Sibley's men charged through the Union forces and continued north into New Mexico. Scattered Union troops returned south to the fort. Although Sibley's Confederates were able to get past Fort Craig and make their way north through the Rio Grande Valley, they were eventually defeated by troops from Fort Union on March 28 at the Battle of Glorieta Pass, and their plan to take control of the American West collapsed.[38]

A handful of twentieth-century grave markers are found at the former village of Valverde.

Valverde survived and by the 1880s the village was connected by a bridge to San Marcial, located along the railroad tracks on the west bank of the river. The small agricultural settlement thrived for a few years but the abandonment of Jornada posts and a series of fierce river floods in the late nineteenth century brought decline. By the 1920s, only a few residents remained, and a 1929 flood finally brought an end to the town. A handful of people hung on until the 1940s when the river removed the last traces of the village. By the mid-twentieth century, Valverde had all but disappeared.

Not much remains of Valverde today. Its ruins are located along a wet and marshy area of the river, opposite San Marcial, overgrown with tamarisk. Black Mesa looms in the background. The original hacienda was north of the village ruins, but the area was flooded several times in the twentieth century.[39] A few walls and a segment of an old schoolhouse survived until the 1990s but have been reduced to crumbling adobe mounds swept over by the shifting sand. East of the village, on elevated ground, is a cemetery where the Confederate army buried their dead after the Battle of Valverde. Weathered wooden crosses mark the graves and a handful of modern twentieth century iron markers are scattered among the brush.

The Valverde battlefield lies about three miles southwest of the old village site, in an area that has been flooded several times over since the 1860s and is now divided by the railroad right-of-way. Changes in the course of the river and new vegetation patterns make it almost impossible to identify the location of the battlefield, although many artifacts have been found nearby. The battlefield, old hacienda site, and village are all on private land and can only be reached on a primitive ranch road that leads down the east side of the river. Locked gates limit access to the sites. On the opposite side of the river, at the intersection of NM 1 and the gravel road from Interstate 25 to San Marcial, a United Daughters of the Confederacy historical marker commemorates the Texas Mounted Volunteers who fought at Valverde.[40]

Fort Craig

Fort Conrad was mistakenly built on private, not public, land and in a low, marshy area, an unhealthy environment that led to repeated problems with malaria. By late 1853, a new post was under construction about eight miles south, on a wagon road that followed the old west bank trail of the Camino Real. Fort Craig was opened in 1854 and named for Captain Louis Craig who was killed by California deserters during the war. One company of the Third Infantry and one of First Dragoons from Fort Conrad were moved south to man the new post which was located on a mesa, surrounded by scattered brush and cacti, overlooking the west bank of the Rio Grande. By summer, Fort Conrad was abandoned.

Forts Conrad and Craig were established to protect trade, traffic, and homesteaders in the Middle Rio Grande region. Merchant caravans and livestock herds were routinely raided by Indian parties, so post troops scouted the Jornada, routing natives, and freeing hostages and cattle. Throughout its history, Fort Craig soldiers fought, pursued, negotiated with, and contained Apaches, Navajos, and Comanches in the Jornada. As the threats subsided, new regional roads opened the area to more commerce and encouraged the settling of a handful of villages nearby.[41] Fort Craig was a large complex of twenty-two flat-roofed adobe and stone buildings, surrounded by a ten-foot high adobe wall. East to west, the fort measured more than 1,000 feet. The largest structures included the commanding officer's quarters, enlisted men's barracks, officers' quarters, warehouses, sheds, stables, stores, and a hospital. As an important and formidable frontier post, at one point Fort Craig held almost 4,000 troops.

The ruins of Fort Craig, a National Historic Site.

In the 1850s, Mescalero Apaches from the Bonito Valley raided Pecos River settlements and committed numerous robberies on the San Antonio-El Paso road and the old Camino Real. By the time of the Civil War, civilian militias were outfitted and organized to contain the Apache and Navajo threat. In one incident, the militia killed twenty men and brought twenty Indian captives back to Fort Craig. Ironically, at a time when the federal government was preparing to fight Confederates troops over the issue of slavery, many members of the militia hoped to keep the Navajo captives as servants, a timeless practice common in the Middle Rio Grande Valley. After the Civil War, Fort Craig troops continued to wage war against area Indians. They killed Apache leader Mangas Coloradas, pursued renegade Indians, and kept the region open to settlers, herders, and traders.[43] By the late 1870s, the Indian threat was under control, and Fort Craig was less important to new settlement, trade, and traffic. In 1878, it housed only a small group of caretakers. Although temporarily re-activated when Victorio led his Apache raiders through West Texas and New Mexico in 1879–80, Fort Craig was finally abandoned in 1884. It was sold at auction ten years later and remained private property until 1981, when the Archaeological Conservancy purchased the land and donated it to the Bureau of Land Management. By then the harsh desert climate had eroded much of the fortress, and visitors and vandals had greatly damaged the remains. Digging into walls, excavating dirt floors and scouring the grounds in search of buried relics, treasure hunters took the few artifacts left at the site.

Even so, much of the fortress remains. Today, the ruins of Fort Craig lie on Bureau of Land Management property off NM 1, south of San Marcial. A trail leads from the visitors' parking area through the ruins, where a few high walls remain from the commanding officer's quarters. A guard house, built of basalt rocks, is also visible. Segments of several structures, including the officers and enlisted men's quarters, shops, and hospital, are still in place, but are difficult to identify without a map. The Fort Craig site is one of the few easily accessible spots where visitors can experience the isolation and solitude of the Camino Real. Its remote location, miles from highways and settlements, allows for sweeping views of the surrounding countryside, which remains much as it was during the eighteenth and nineteenth centuries. Fort Craig is also located near El Camino Real International Heritage Center, a joint project of the New Mexico State Monuments and the United States Bureau of Land Management. Rather than simply telling the story of an historical event or describing the life of a particular person, the Heritage Center celebrates more than 400 years of the cultural exchange among Mexico, the United States, Spain, and other regions of the world. The Center is more than just a museum building; it is a unique architectural structure, standing in sharp contrast with the area desert environment. The Heritage Center is located about three miles off of NM 1 and offers visitors a variety of exhibits, public events, re-enactments, and celebrations that highlight the trail's role in developing this region of the world.

Exhibits at El Camino Real International Heritage Center detail the rich history of the Royal Road through Mexico and the United States.

San Marcial

San Marcial lies on the west bank of the river, about six miles north of Fort Craig, across from Valverde. An Interstate 25 exit leads to NM 1, and a graded road continues another two miles east to the ruins of the village. Striking views of Black Mesa, on the opposite bank, are found along the road to the ruins and at the nearby interstate rest area. By the early 1850s, around the time that Fort Conrad and Fort Craig were established, Pascual Joyla homesteaded on the east bank and began trading hay, wood, and other supplies at Fort Craig. In the 1860s, others joined him and a small community grew up at the site known as *La Mesa de San Marcial*, located just north of Black Mesa, honoring the third century French saint. In 1865, the area flooded, so Joyla and many of his neighbors moved across the river to higher ground and established a new village near the Fort

Craig Reservation called simply San Marcial.[43] Some trail travelers stayed west of the river and followed a path close to today's Interstate 25, rather than enter the Jornada. This route was occasionally used during the Spanish Colonial and early Mexican era, but American settlement opened the old roadway to more traffic. San Marcial was located along this improved western road and benefitted from trade among several new communities and Fort Craig. Soon, regional roads cut through the military reservation, and stagecoaches connected the San Marcial area with the Black Range. By the 1870s, San Marcial was a village of several hundred residents.[44]

Anglo-Americans began acquiring tracts from the old Armendáriz grant and developing the land around San Marcial. Wilson Waddington, who headed the San Marcial Land and Improvement Company, prepared the town for the arrival of the Atchison, Topeka and Santa Fe Railroad in the late 1870s, and schools, churches, and businesses were built by the time the railroad arrived. San Marcial became an important railroad junction with a freight depot, telegraph building, engine roundhouse, and various shops. The town underwent a construction boom as businesses, new residences, groceries, bakeries, dry-goods and clothing stores, tobacco shops, saloons, churches, and schools sprung up along its main streets. In 1881, a major fire destroyed most of San Marcial, and a new town, about one mile away, was constructed. Mining in the Black Range, lingering problems with Indian attacks, and the usual frontier rowdiness and lawlessness earned San Marcial a reputation as a "wild west" town. But it also prospered and grew with the expansion of transportation. More than 1,000 people lived in the town by the end of the century.[45]

San Marcial became an important regional hub but was plagued by flooding. The railroad tracks and a two-mile dike separated the town from the river, but the waters often spilled over the levees. Major floods in 1884 and 1904 greatly damaged the town. In the 1920s, with a population approaching 1,500, the floods became more severe. In 1929, summer storms dumped record amounts of rain in New Mexico, and the swollen river waters of the Rio Grande filled the reservoir at Elephant Butte. In August and September, disaster struck at San Marcial as two major storms, five weeks apart, inundated the town. Residents were evacuated as the waters rose to frightening heights. The dikes crumbled and waves crashed through the town, destroying most of the homes and businesses. No one was killed, but San Marcial was gone, and with it the entire railroad operation and more than fifty miles of track. The damage was so extensive that the railroad abandoned the site and transferred workers to other facilities, some as far away as California. The town was buried under river silt, and the community never recovered. Although a handful of people stayed and attempted to re-build, most left the area. Many moved sixty miles north to Belén which was becoming the railroad's new division headquarters.[46] Today, not much remains of San Marcial. At the end of the road, from NM 1, there are a few crumbling rock and adobe walls on an elevated site overlooking Black Mesa. A few graves lie north of the ruins. The river, now tamed and channeled east of the town, separates San Marcial from the northern end of the Jornada del Muerto.

Almost nothing remains of San Marcial except for a few scattered, crumbling structures.

6

The Socorro Valley

The Camino Real de Tierra Adentro exited the Jornada del Muerto beyond Fray Cristóbal, led into the Socorro Valley, a fertile floodplain with occasional mountain ranges to the east and west, and continued on to the Belén area. The northern end of the Jornada del Muerto, and much of the Socorro Valley, were home to the Piro Pueblo Indians, descendants of the Jornada Mogollon people, who moved into the region in the 1100s CE and spread throughout an area from present-day San Marcial north to La Joya de Sevilleta. From the mid-fourteenth to mid-sixteenth centuries, the Piro population grew substantially and congregated into large, plaza-type villages along the river, often near arroyos and canyons. The Spanish called these Indians *pueblo*, because they lived in settled dwellings and villages. The villages were usually elevated, on top of buttes, on high ground along the riverbanks, or on benches along the floodplain. Irrigation systems allowed for the channeling and collection of water for agriculture and community uses.[2]Spaniards named this area of the Rio Abajo the Province of the Piros.

Most Piro pueblos had single-story, linear roomblocks, but a few featured multi-storied terraced buildings with hundreds of rooms. Piro housing blocks often served as defensive walls and were clustered around plazas and open community spaces, used for social, ceremonial, and political activities. San Pascual, the largest settlement in the region, served as a regional capital and may have been home to thousands of Piros. Some Piro pueblos were placed at defensive sites and were heavily-fortified, suggesting that in the period before the Spanish arrived there was frequent conflict and warfare. The Piro farmed the surrounding countryside and hunted in the river bosques. They grew maize and gathered mesquite, yucca, prickly pear, and cactus fruits. The Piro hunted deer, rabbits, and hares, and caught many kinds of fish in the river.[2] Geese, ducks, and cranes complimented the diet. The Piro also traded with Plains tribes who brought buffalo products such as meat, hides, and tallow to area villages.[3]

La Joya de
Sevilleta

Alamillo

Lemitar   Sabino

La Parida
Socorro

Teypana
Luis López   San Pedro
San Antonio   Carthage
            Qualacú

San Pascual

Modern Rio Grande

Bosque del Apache
National Wildlife Refuge

San Marcial

Senecú

El Camino Real   Fort   Black Mesa
International Heritage   Craig
Center

San Felipe   *The Socorro Valley*

El Camino Real de Tierra Adentro

El Camino Real through the Socorro Valley.

In the early sixteenth century, just before extensive Spanish contact, there were about 7,000 Piro Indians living in as many as twenty pueblos[4] but European illnesses and epidemic diseases, especially smallpox, reduced Indian populations quickly. The Spanish also disrupted native lifestyles and began consolidating people through the process of *reducción*, or resettlement. They established four missions and six *estancias*, or ranches, among the Piro, where hard labor caused further decline among the weakened Indians who had survived the epidemics.[5] *Encomenderos* held grants of *encomienda* which entitled them to land, a periodic payment of goods produced on the land, and the use of Indian labor. Legally, laborers were to be paid when forced to work, but many area landowners, missionaries, military officials, and even governors of the province frequently abused the system. Forced labor had been outlawed in New Spain during the sixteenth century, but the practice persisted in New Mexico. To make matters worse, many Indians were forced to pay tribute, an assessed payment in goods to the Crown, often collected by the encomendero. After establishing missions and haciendas along the Camino Real, the Apaches resented Piro cooperation with the Spanish, and raids became more common. Disease, re-settlement, drought, raids, and forced labor took their toll. By the 1605, the natives had been further consolidated into three settlements. The Piro were scattered during the 1680 Pueblo Revolt and never returned to their homeland. Some fled the region; others were relocated to the Pass of the North where they mixed with Hispanic, Tiwa, and Mexican populations. By the nineteenth century, the Piro had lost their cultural identity. The Piro language is extinct today and no Piro villages have survived. Despite several archaeological studies and surveys, no Piro ruins are open to visitors.[6]

San Felipe Pueblo

When traveling north along the trail in the seventeenth century, the first Piro pueblo that came into view beyond Black Mesa was San Felipe. It had already been abandoned when the Rodríguez-Chamuscado expedition passed through there in 1581, but they noted forty-five houses of two and three stories, built around a central plaza. Although the pueblo no longer exists, it was the site of a significant event in the early colonial history of the province. On August 21, 1581, Captain Chamuscado took formal possession of the land and named the region *San Felipe del Nuevo Mexico*, to honor Philip II, the King of Spain. The name was later shortened to *Nuevo* (New) Mexico. Despite the importance of the site, it was never re-settled and was only occasionally mentioned by Camino Real travelers in later years. Today, San Felipe is an isolated archaeological site on the old trail, hidden and protected by the desert landscape. It was added to the National Register of Historic Places in 1981.[7]

Mission Senecú

Beyond San Felipe was Senecú, the southern-most inhabited Piro settlement in 1598, located somewhere near today's San Marcial. Little is known about the original Piro pueblo, but two friars, Antonio de Arteaga and García de San Francisco, arrived there in the late 1620s and founded the convent of *San Antonio de Padua*, named for Saint Anthony of Padua, a thirteenth-century native of Lisbon who joined the Franciscan order.[8] Fray García introduced European-style agriculture to the area: irrigation systems, fruit orchards, livestock grazing, and vineyards. He remained there for almost thirty years until he moved south to the Guadalupe Mission at El Paso del Norte.

Senecú Piro harvested salt and transported piñon nuts from surrounding orchards for shipment south along the trail. When caravans or military escorts were in the region, the Piro were often required to provide horses or draft animals from their stock, and some were forced to accompany wagon trains and livestock herds as far south as Parral. Senecú's Indians also labored for New Mexico's governors, producing textiles such as stockings. Conditions at the mission were harsh as mid-seventeenth century drought destroyed many crops, especially mission staples such as corn and wheat. Severe shortages of food followed, and travelers along the trail occasionally came across Indian and Spanish homes where the residents had simply starved to death. By the 1670s, Spanish control of the region declined, and area Apache became a more serious threat. The inability to protect and care for the Indians at Senecú probably played a role in turning some of the Piro against the Spaniards.[9]

It is not clear whether Senecú was continuously inhabited. It disappeared from the records in the 1650s and 1660s. In 1674, Fray Alonso Gil de Ávila was transferred from the Tompiro mission at Abo to Senecú and brought members of his former congregation along.[10] Although Mission Senecú survived a 1675 attack, and a few Piro may have remained at the site, it never fully recovered. The friars and many area natives joined Governor Otermín during the 1680 retreat and were eventually settled at Senecú del Sur near El Paso del Norte.[11]

Otermín returned to Senecú the next year with Fray Francisco de Ayeta and forty Spanish soldiers. The chapel and convent had been burned and demolished leaving only a few segments of the walls standing. Two church bells were recovered from the site and another from the cemetery. They were promptly taken across the river and hauled away in the expedition's wagons. Otermín set fire to the remaining structures at Senecú, crossed back to the east side of the river, and continued north along the Camino Real.[12] By the time Vargas arrived in 1692, river flooding had damaged the few surviving ruins. What little was left disappeared during the eighteenth century, and, as the remaining ruins slowly melted away, the mission location was forgotten. Despite numerous efforts in the twentieth century, Senecú has never been found.[13] From Senecú, the Camino Real de Tierra Adentro continued north through today's Bosque del Apache National Wildlife Refuge, the winter home to tens of thousands of birds, including sandhill cranes, arctic geese, and several species of ducks. The refuge land was once the site of several Piro pueblos, and unspoiled segments of the old trail still pass through the eastern edge of the reserve.

San Pascual

The Piro pueblo of San Pascual was on the opposite side of the river, within sight of Senecú. It was the largest Piro pueblo and may have been home to as many as 2,000 people in the sixteenth century. Just north of San Pascual is a small summit which rises about one hundred feet above the river where the remains of a much more compact, but well-fortified, fourteenth-century Piro pueblo called *San Pascualito*, or Little San Pascual, is found today. The red-brown sandstone pueblo, which consisted of about forty rooms and a kiva, was surrounded by a defensive wall made of stacked rocks.[14] San Pascual has a mysterious history. Although it was an important pueblo, it was not mentioned by any colonial chroniclers until after it had been abandoned. The settlement was thriving in the late sixteenth century, and remained occupied well into the next, but neither the Oñate expedition records nor the Benavides *Memorial* made any reference to the site. The first mention of San Pascual was in 1681 when Otermín referred to it as a "ruined pueblo."[15] There is no evidence that any Spaniards ever lived at San Pascual, but Bishop Tamarón added to the confusion by describing "traces of the church and houses" found at the site when his party camped there in 1760.[16] The remains of San Pascual and San Pascualito are located in the Little San Pascual Mountains on the eastern edge of the Bosque del Apache National Wildlife Refuge.[17]

The buttes of San Pascual and Pascualito were the site of large Piro settlements before Spaniards arrived in the sixteenth century.

Qualacú

The ruins of Qualacú also lie within the Bosque del Apache Wildlife Refuge, just north of San Pascual. This Piro pueblo was once a large, extensive complex of adobe structures built around a northern and southern plaza. There were about 250 ground-level rooms, with perhaps another eighty with second or third stories, large communal rooms, and several ceremonial kivas.[18] It was probably established in the mid-1300s as a small Piro village, but during the fifteenth century it was greatly expanded. Oñate and his scouting party camped across from Qualacú in 1598, awaiting the main wagon train making its way north through the Jornada. The Piro at Qualacú, perhaps already wary of the Spanish from previous contact, fled the pueblo as the expedition approached. Oñate noted that "we reassured them with gifts of trinkets. In order not to frighten them we went to the bank of the river, where we remained, living in tents for a month."[19] Eventually, the residents of Qualacú returned to their pueblo and traded with the Spaniards.

The pueblo may have been abandoned in the mid-1670s when Apache raids destroyed nearby Senecú. Otermín noted it as a ruined pueblo, and by the eighteenth century Qualacú is no longer cited.[20] Over the centuries, floodwaters have destroyed much of Qualacú, and several mid-twentieth century canal projects caused further damage. The site was extensively studied during 1980s and was later nominated to the National Register of Historic Places.

Basaltic outcrops provided basic building materials for Piro pueblos and Spanish settlements.

San Antonio, San Pedro and Carthage

The Camino Real de Tierra Adentro continued north of Qualacú and exited today's Bosque del Apache Refuge. San Antonio, situated on the west bank of the river along NM 1, was named for the Piro mission San Antonio de Senecú. An estancia was briefly established nearby in the seventeenth century and may have helped carry the name north, creating some confusion about the location of the old mission. Present-day San Antonio was not actually settled until the mid-1840s.[21] During the war, American troops and traders referred to the village as a new settlement. George Ruxton described it as a "little hamlet of ten or twelve log-huts, inhabited by pastores and vaqueros-shepherds and cattle-herders."[22] During the next decade, American settlers moved into San Antonio. The town grew with the increased use of a new west-bank branch of the trail that ran from Fort Craig to Socorro. San Antonio's sister village, San Pedro, was just a few miles east, on the opposite side of the river, along the old Camino Real. Carthage, a new coal town, lay east of San Pedro. Ferries and a small bridge connected San Pedro and San Antonio. Wagons hauled coal and goods back and forth between the towns and brought new commercial ventures in to the area. All three communities grew by the 1860s, and expanded further after the disruptions of the Civil War had passed.

The abandoned San Antonio railroad depot lies along NM 1.

By the 1880s, San Antonio had grown from a small agricultural settlement to a thriving commercial one, with blacksmiths, cobblers, silversmiths, a telegraph station, saloons and boardinghouses, and legal and financial services. Transportation continued to be an important business as wagon roads led to the rails, and new trails connected mining and ranching settlements nearby. River flooding was a constant problem in San Antonio, and several major deluges washed out roads and bridges. When a new bridge was built for US 380, San Antonio's commercial and residential center shifted north. The old town center was located about one-half mile south of the federal highway. Today, along NM 1 there is a cluster of about ten buildings remaining from the era. The post office building faces the weathered remains of a foundation that was once a general merchandise store run by Augustus H. Hilton, whose son Conrad went on to establish the Hilton Hotel Corporation. The old Hilton mercantile in San Antonio was destroyed by fire in the 1940s, but the intricately crafted wooden bar was saved and placed in the Owl Bar and Restaurant (a New Mexico Registered Cultural Property) on US 380 where it is still in use today.[23]

San Pedro is opposite San Antonio, on the east bank of the Rio Grande along the main route of the old Camino Real de Tierra Adentro. Today, the entrance to the town is off of US 380, just beyond the New Mexico State Highway Department Camino Real Marker. San Pedro was settled at about the same time as San Antonio by small farmers who planted corn, wheat, barley, oats, and beans around the village. San Pedro also benefited from mining at Carthage, about ten miles to the east. Prehistoric Indian populations in New Mexico mined coal for use in their firepits as early as the fourteenth century, and when Spaniards settled the region small amounts were locally mined for blacksmithing and heating. Coal mining did not begin on a large scale until 1861 when United States troops from Fort Craig opened a government mine at Carthage to supply coal to forts Selden, Bayard, and Stanton. Demand for coal sharply increased in the 1870s. As the railroad followed the old Camino Real south, the demand for coal soared, and New Mexico was soon supplying tens of thousands of tons yearly to fuel locomotives. The mining of metals added to the increase in coal production, as smelters used bituminous coal and coking coal for cleaning, separating, and purifying ores. In the 1890s, homes, businesses, and offices in urban areas of the southwest commonly used coal for heating.[24]

After reaching San Antonio, a branch line of the Atchison, Topeka, and

Santa Fe Railway extended east through San Pedro and into Carthage. San Antonio and San Pedro prospered as the Carthage coal fields were developed and zinc, silver, and copper mining in the Magdelena Mountains, west of Socorro, created an even bigger demand. For the next fifteen years, Carthage fueled the local economy, offsetting some of the losses from river flooding and declining agriculture. San Pedro profited from the coal boom, and the San Pedro Company Store sold general merchandise, along with mining supplies, equipment, and provisions. The boom turned to bust when the Panic of 1893 collapsed silver prices and a national depression followed. By 1894, the mines at Carthage were closed. In the early years of the twentieth century, mining at Carthage resumed. It became a coal company town, owned and operated by the Carthage Coal Company which worked the mines until 1925. By the 1930s, almost all of the mines around Carthage had been closed. A few small independently-owned operations survived until the 1960s. Only the ruins of a few building foundations remain in Carthage today.[25]

Even though agriculture, mining, and commercial ventures attracted people to San Pedro in the late nineteenth century, major floods took their toll on the community. In the 1930s, the railroad and several highway bridges were brought down by raging river waters. After a new bridge was built over the Rio Grande in the late 1930s, the highway no longer went through the center of San Pedro. The new road passed north of town, near the cemetery, and the old road became just another village street. In the 1950s, San Pedro had less than one hundred residents and by the 1960s, it had become a ghost town. Only recently have a few people moved back into the village, living in mobile homes or the few habitable structures that remain.[26]

Today, Camino San Pedro leads south into the village from US 380, just east of the Rio Grande. The remains of San Pedro lie to the west, between the road and the river. Most adobe structures in the village were simple flat-roofed buildings, with vigas, wooden windows, and doors. A few show evidence of Territorial influence: brick copings, porch columns, or pitched roofs. San Pedro, like many Mexican-era villages on the trail, had houses and farms clustered around plazas. An acequia drew water from the Rio Grande, and two irrigation ditches carried it through the village fields. The northern plaza, which lies to the west of the access road, has a few crumbling ruins of adobe buildings and two intact adobe structures that are still in use. The first village church was located there along with a small school and general merchandise store that existed until the early twentieth century. An adobe wall once enclosed the plaza to guard against Indian attacks, and some small portions remain in the surrounding fields.[27] Several houses and the second village church fronted the southern plaza. One of the most prominent buildings in the village was the San Pedro Mission Church, a basic rectangular flat-roofed adobe building that had been modified over the years and served many functions. Area residents recall it being a dance hall and community center in the early twentieth century. At some point, a pitched tin roof, front and back gables, and a wooden copula were added, as it became the village church. The church building, long abandoned, collapsed in the 1990s.[28]

Luis López

From the San Pedro area, the Camino Real continued north, along the east bank of the Rio Grande into the *Vueltas de Luis López*, the Rough Turns at Luis López, steep and sandy ravines near present-day Bosquecito. The vueltas extended over seven miles and made travel quite difficult for colonial carts and wagons.[29] The road through the vueltas was a particularly rough stretch, full of gullies and rocky surfaces. Las Vueltas de Luis López was named for a Spanish captain who was the *alcalde mayor* (mayor) of the Piro Indians at Mission Senecú. He later built a house near present-day Luis López, along the main route of the Camino Real. Although there are no contemporary descriptions of the site, a few travelers noted passing the abandoned ruins of the settlement after the Pueblo Revolt.[30] Nineteenth-century Luis López was founded on the west bank of the river during the late 1830s, and there is some evidence to suggest that it was built around a part of the old López estancia. This Mexican-era settlement was arranged around two large plazas. Houses were built around the plazas, to pen livestock and provide some protection against Indian attacks for the few hundred residents.[31]

Not much of old Luis López remains today. Sagging adobe mounds run along the outer edges of the plazas and the faint outline of the church and cemetery are visible. The railroad cut through the edge of the village and frequent flooding has washed away many foundations and building remains. By the 1880s, old Luis López had apparently been abandoned, and the settlement shifted west, to the present village site, on higher ground. Since the late nineteenth century, Luis López has maintained a population of about 200 to 300 people clustered along NM 1. The San Jose Mission Church, located on the highway in the center of town, dates from the late nineteenth century, probably built when the old settlement was abandoned.[32]

Teypana

The Piro pueblo of Teypana was located near Luis López. On June 14, 1598, the Oñate advance-party camped nearby, and, much to their surprise, the Indians of the village were quite accommodating, providing the Spanish with information about other pueblos along the river and furnishing a good supply of corn to the weary travelers. The Spaniards called the pueblo *socorro* (help or succor), and the story was recorded in the official itinerary, making it the first, and only, reference to the pueblo of Teypana.[33] Missionaries no doubt spent time at Teypana in the early years of the seventeenth century, but there is no record of any church being built or any note of the settlement in missionary documents.

Several sites in the region have been tentatively identified as Teypana, but, with only a brief note by the expedition, it has been difficult to pinpoint its location. Some archaeologists now believe that a previously overlooked Piro site near Luis López may be ancient Teypana. The Plaza Montoya Pueblo was known to locals for years, but it was not until the 1980s that any serious investigations took place. Recent survey work in the early twenty-first century has resulted in a much fuller understanding of the site and produced a considerable amount of evidence that this was indeed Teypana, the pueblo that provided *socorro* to the Oñate expedition in 1598.

Situated near the west bank of the Rio Grande, this rectangular pueblo village was organized around a central plaza with access through a northeastern gateway. The pueblo was substantial at one time, with more than 250 ground-level rooms and perhaps another 150 on the upper stories. It appears to have been originally constructed in the late 1400s and was expanded for several hundred years. The first rooms built at Plaza Montoya fronted the plaza. They contained a central hearth, storage bins, and living quarters. By the seventeenth century, rooms were built out onto the plaza, sheltering old mixing basins, roasting pits, storage and refuge pits. There is some scattered evidence of European influence in the pueblo. Molded adobe bricks were used, fireplaces were moved away from the center of rooms to the walls or corners, and European-style doorways were added.

Plaza Montoya Pueblo was a victim of the epidemics that swept through the region, and, with a small surviving population, the native Piros of Teypana were most likely moved to nearby Pilabó which later became known as Mission Socorro.[34]The *socorro* story probably followed. When Plaza Montoya Pueblo was excavated, no common Piro household items were found at the site, and there were no extant ceramic vessels, only fragments and broken pieces. Nor were any utensils, grinding stones, or tools found in the rooms. There were no personal or ceremonial articles, such as shells or bones, found anywhere at the extensive site. Even large objects such as roof timbers were missing. (With the scarcity of wood in the region, roof timbers were often removed and used at other sites). Furthermore, there is no evidence of any natural disaster, collapse of construction, or calamity of any sort. All of this suggests that Teypana was abandoned and evacuated in an orderly manner, as the Spanish consolidated mission sites in the Rio Abajo.[35]

Socorro

The City of Socorro is six miles north of Luis López on the west bank of the Rio Grande. It was the site of Pilabó Pueblo, near the center of the Piro province, about halfway between Senecú and Sevilleta. When the Teypana Piros were relocated in the early seventeenth century, the name *Socorro* moved as well and became part of Pilabó mission's formal title. Franciscan friars dedicated *Nuestra Señora de Perpetuo Socorro*, Our Lady of Perpetual Help, and named it in honor of the assistance that the Oñate expedition had received at Teypana. Fray García de San Francisco visited Socorro and introduced some of the same agricultural practices and crops that he did at Senecú.[36] In the late 1620s there was a small chapel, a convent, and several resident friars. The mission grew quickly and soon became a Franciscan administrative center, supervising the smaller sites at Alamillo and Sevilleta. By 1630, they had built a larger church, replacing the tiny chapel.[37]A small number of Spaniards lived with the Piros at Nuestra Señora de Socorro. The settlement grew, and by mid-century there were as many as 600 people at the Socorro Mission. Little is known about life there in the 1650s or 1660s, but epidemics, droughts, and Apache attacks created some of the same problems that plagued other nearby pueblos. By the 1670s, the population had declined, and the mission was no longer a major center.[38]

Today's San Miguel Church was built on the remains of the seventeenth-century mission church. Teypana Pueblo was located just north of the church, in today's parking area.

On August 24, 1680 Lieutenant Governor García and his refugee caravan arrived at Socorro, having fled the Pueblo Revolt. García reported that the Piros were anxious to leave, fearing reprisals by the Apaches, and most joined the Spaniards as they made their escape south along the Camino Real. They were eventually settled in the El Paso del Norte area at *Socorro del Sur*, Southern Socorro, southeast of today's El Paso, Texas. A few Piros remained at the site and may have been killed later in fights with Apaches. When Governor Otermín returned to the Socorro mission the next year, he found it in ruins, so he burned the rest of mission village.[39] Although New Mexico was re-conquered in the 1690s, the Spanish did not return to re-settle Socorro. Throughout the eighteenth century, Camino Real travelers noted the ruins of the mission, but no one returned to live in the area for more than one hundred years.[40]

By the early nineteenth century, pioneer settlers began moving back to the site of the old mission. It is not clear when they first arrived, but by 1816 baptisms were recorded and in 1817 Xavier García, Manuel Trujillo, Anselmo Tafoya, and José Montoya secured a land grant for seventy families. They cleared away the rubble and debris from the old church and used remaining segments of the walls to construct a new one, dedicated to *San Miguel*, Saint Michael. The church, which stood alongside the remains of Pilabó pueblo, was completed in 1821, and a small village grew up around the site. Somewhat isolated on the west bank, away from the main traffic on the Camino Real de Tierra Adentro, Soccoro remained a poor, isolated community where most people survived by raising livestock, farming, or bartering. When Mexico opened trade with the United States, the Chihuahua Trail brought Santa Fe traders south through Socorro on their way to the interior of the republic. As American wagon trains passed through the area, the Baca and García families of Socorro expanded their commercial activities along the trail.[41]

Apache attacks remained a serious problem in the Rio Abajo, and in one dramatic raid forty-eight Socorrans were killed while defending the town. Poor relations with the natives often disrupted trade and thwarted efforts to mine silver in the mountains west of town, but Socorro survived. It became a county seat in the newly established Territory of New Mexico and had about 500 residents, many of them soldiers who were soon assigned to Valverde. A branch of the old trail connected Socorro with new communities along the west bank, which increased trade and traffic through the town. Following the Civil War, villagers sold goods to Fort McRae, Fort Craig, and shipped products as far south as Fort Selden. The new forts brought economic growth and stability in the 1870s and, with more than 1,000 people, new mills, businesses, smelters, residences, a courthouse, and the city's first jail were built.[42] Socorro's real boom began with the arrival of the Atchison, Topeka, and Santa Fe Railway in August 1880. The Anglo-American population increased, and Chinese and European immigrant workers came to lay the tracks and labor in the yards. Agriculture remained steady, as area wineries, flour mills, and breweries prospered. Livestock also added to the local economy. A mining boom in the 1880s brought people to the nearby hillside mines and smelters.

In the twentieth century, some of New Mexico's first regional highways followed segments of the old trail, maintaining Socorro's importance as a transportation hub and rest stop for travelers. The commercial center of the town shifted several times, eventually moving to California Street by the 1960s. Today,

Socorro is an active commercial center and college town with a population of about 9,000 residents. Agriculture is still a mainstay, but interstate travelers regularly stop there and frequent its many hotels, restaurants, and shops. The historic center of Socorro has a great variety of nineteenth-century architecture, much of it related to its days as a regional commercial center along the old trail. The buildings range from simple adobe structures to the stately Victorian homes and territorial dwellings common throughout the town. Many have been recorded as New Mexico Cultural Properties or added to the National Register of Historic Places.

Mexican Socorro grew around the ruins of the old mission church. Pilabó pueblo, a multi-storied adobe Piro settlement, was located just north of the church, beyond today's parking area. The ruins survived into the nineteenth century but were cleared away as the new village expanded. The first houses around San Miguel were small, flat-roofed adobes with tiny doorways and window openings, defensively clustered around a series of small plazas. None of the original dwellings remain, but some of the houses and buildings near the church may have been built around early nineteenth-century structures. Behind the church are several examples of Spanish and Mexican period architecture typical of the early nineteenth century; basic rectangular buildings with adobe walls and flat roofs supported by vigas.[43] Houses south of the church are grouped close together along the narrow roads that wind through the old village center. One of the oldest existing structures may be El Torreón, the Tower, in the 200 block of Park Street. The central part of this greatly-modified and expanded building dates from the 1820s, and the tower-like feature at the end could be the remains of an observation post that stood at the outskirts of the village.[44]

The most prominent building is San Miguel Church, dedicated to the Archangel Saint Michael who, according to local legend, intervened during an early Indian raid and saved the town from destruction. The original building was a simple cruciform design, made of adobe. Vigas held a layer of branches and a flat, packed earth roof was laid over the top. A few small windows provided light for the altar, but, for defensive reasons, the walls of the church were solid. The front façade was plain with a simple bell tower. Since the 1820s, San Miguel has undergone many renovations. Several floors have been laid over the original hardened earth. A transept, peaked roof, and large twin wooden bell towers were added, and by the end of the century the church had a decidedly Gothic look. A major restoration took place in the early 1970s, removing layers of paint and plaster, and revealing some of the original woodwork. Imitation doors and arched nichos in the towers were removed, and a simpler traditional look was restored. The interior received a makeover as well. Several layers of old flooring were removed, and pews and interior woodwork were refurbished. A tin ceiling was removed to expose old vigas and corbels.[45]

In the mid-nineteenth century, an open area south of the church was used as a community plaza. The United States Army camped there in the 1850s, and, by the 1870s, two large mercantile buildings fronted the east side of the plaza. Today, the Juan José Baca House remains standing on Bernard Street, facing the old plaza. The Baca family moved to Socorro from Belén, and Juan José was the grandson of one of the town's first settlers. This home was built about 1860 and was expanded to include a general merchandise store. The Baca family lived in part of the dwelling while the front portion facing the plaza was used for business. Its basic structure had adobe walls eighteen inches thick and a flat roof. A large false-front façade was added to the building. In the 1880s, as lumber became more readily available, a second story was added to the building, and a pitched metal roof covered the front portion of the structure. An elaborate overhanging balcony was added as well. Today, this historic structure has been thoroughly restored and houses several businesses.[46]

Across the street, also facing the old plaza, is the Juan Nepomucero García House. It is a large one-story flat-roofed building originally consisting of a rectangular series of adobe rooms around a courtyard, or *placita*. It is the only surviving placita-style building in Socorro dating from the 1860s. Its long *portal*, a traditional covered walkway, still faces the plaza, and features white squared posts and large windows, typical of the Territorial style. Juan García was the half-brother of Juan José Baca. He was a descendant of one of the founding families of Socorro and developed extensive commercial enterprises in the area. After Juan García died in 1886, his widow, Francisca, inherited the property and built the García Opera House, east of the site. Both the Juan Nepomucero García House and the García Opera House have been added to the National Register of Historic Places and have been thoroughly renovated. They continue to be used as commercial outlets and a theater today.[47]

The Baca Store, Socorro, New Mexico. Library of Congress, Prints and Photographs Division, Historic American Buildings Survey, 1946, NM, 27–SOCO, 1–1.

Much of Socorro's nineteenth-century architecture dates from the boom era of the 1880s. The railroad brought new construction materials and skilled tradesmen who soon changed the look of the town. Anglo-American merchants built one-and two-story houses with eastern American features, pitched roofs, front porches, picket fences, and front and back yards. The best examples are in the Park Street area, especially the Antonio Abeytia House, also known as the *Casa de Flecha*, House of the Arrow, an elaborate Queen Anne-style residence.[48] Kittrel Park, the town plaza, has been the center of life in Socorro since the Territorial period. West and south of the plaza are residential areas; commercial growth has spread east toward the railroad depot. Manzanares Street, which runs east from the park, was the main commercial thoroughfare of the city until California Street was extended for automobile traffic in the early twentieth century.

Bosquecito and La Parida

The main path of the Camino Real de Tierra Adentro stayed on the east bank of the Rio Grande where two small Mexican-era settlements were located, opposite Luis López and Socorro. *Bosquecito*, the Little Forest, first appears in travelers' journals of the 1840s and on a few Territorial-era maps. It was never a significant settlement, probably just a cluster of houses and farm buildings. Bosquecito disappears from maps and documents by the 1870s and then re-appears about fifteen years later. By 1900, less than one hundred people lived at the site. A 1937 flood washed away most of the adobes, and today there are a few scattered homes in the area, all dating from later in the twentieth century.

La Parida, the Birth, is first listed on the Santa Fe-Chihuahua mail route in the 1830s. After years of flooding washed away orchards and cornfields, it was moved to a higher elevation. Lieutenant Abert stopped at La Parida in 1846 and described the locals, many of them descendants of the Baca family, as kindly and courteous people. He noted how they gently tipped their hats when offering tobacco, formally addressed him, and rose to their feet as an old village patriarch entered the dwelling.[49] By 1850, La Parida had attracted more settlers and had orchards, vineyards, and fields of corn and wheat. About 150 people lived in the area, trading with settlements on both sides of the river. La Parida and Bosquecito were located near Parida Hill, considered a particularly difficult segment of the trail that ran along the east bank, often covered with sandy patches that bogged down carts and wagons. There are a few remains at La Parida, scattered adobe mounds and rubble, near the far edge of the floodplain.[50]

Lemitar

Lemitar is located on the west bank of the Rio Grande, about six miles north of Socorro, just beyond La Parida. Until the early nineteenth century, an abandoned Piro pueblo stood at the site but it was probably destroyed when the village was founded. Settlers came to Lemitar in 1831, after the nearby communities of Socorro, Polvadera, Sabino, and La Parida had already been established. The new village, named for the *lemita* plant, attracted poor farmers from Atrísco, Albuquerque, and Belén, who received small land grants. Simple adobe houses were built in a typical frontier plaza arrangement, and within a year work was begun on a new church, *Sagrada Familia de Lemitar*, the Sacred

Family of Lemitar Church. Records indicate that it was in regular use by 1835 when the first burials were made in the adjacent cemetery. The families of Juan Armijo, Pablo Sánchez, and Salvador Gonzáles, the founders of Lemitar, lived in houses clustered around the plaza, just east of the church.[51]

During the 1830s and 1840s, Lemitar was a small agricultural village, occasionally visited by travelers on the Chihuahua Trail. Local farmers grew wheat and corn, and grazed sheep in the surrounding countryside. Anglo-American travelers passed through Lemitar during the Mexican-American War, and the village received brief mention in some of their journals. After the war, the west bank trail connected the settlement with Socorro and Polvadera and one of New Mexico's most controversial governors, Manuel Armijo (c.1793–1853), retired to Lemitar. Armijo was a prominent, prosperous merchant in Albuquerque who made a fortune in ranching and the Santa Fe-Chihuahua trade. When the war broke out, the governor liquidated many of his personal assets and arranged for friends to guard his remaining properties. Although Armijo called for a defense of New Mexico against the invading American forces, his actions remain highly suspect. Contemporary accounts described a reluctant Armijo, pressured by militia officers and priests to resist. In early August 1846, American trader James Magoffin (a distant relative) met with Armijo and regular army commander Diego Archuleta, to convince them not to fight the American forces. Supposedly, Armijo refused but did offer protection to American traders in Santa Fe. He then moved his troops about ten miles south of the city to prepare a defense. After an argument with his officers, Armijo abandoned the defense and fled to Chihuahua City. His troops returned to Santa Fe where they surrendered to Kearny.[52] As the war came to a close, Armijo returned north and settled on a small ranch in Lemitar where he lived until his death in 1853.[53]

During the 1860s, almost 700 people lived in Lemitar. Farmers, merchants, ranchers, and a few Navajo servants resided in the village. They built a school, expanded area farms and ranches, and developed a small merchant community.[54] After the war, a "new" Lemitar was built as the town spread southwest of the church. A post office was established and new houses and commercial sites were developed. By the end of the decade, Manuel Vigíl, Luis Baca, and Juan Montoya had become the town's more successful merchants. As Lemitar grew it attracted carpenters, blacksmiths, shoemakers, freighters, a deputy sheriff, and school teacher among its residents.[55]

Wooden crosses are scattered in the second Lemitar Cemetery.

The mining boom of the 1870s in the Magdelena Mountains west of town drew some residents away from Lemitar, but the arrival of the Atchison, Topeka, and Santa Fe Railway in 1880 brought daily service to Santa Fe and El Paso, and new life to the village. By then, the Rio Grande had shifted further to the east, and the new rail bed served as a levee, offering some protection from seasonal flooding. Lemitar saw more traffic, but most residents remained small farmers and ranchers, producing corn, wheat, cotton, and beans in the surrounding fields. After the mining boom, cattle ranching expanded but employed few people, so some locals moved to nearby Socorro as it began to prosper. A powerful hailstorm damaged many properties in 1924, and a devastating river flood in 1929 broke through the levees, destroying much of old Lemitar, especially the area north of the church.[56]

The Sagrada Familia de Lemitar Church, also known *as Los Dulces Nombres de Jesus, María, y José*, the Holy Names of Jesus, Mary, and Joseph, was located about one-half mile east of Interstate 25. It faced south and was sited along the edge of the old floodplain, near the original village settlement. The church, which resembled the San Miguel Church at Socorro, was constructed in the 1830s. A small cemetery, located just in front of the church, was enclosed by an adobe wall. The Sagrada Familia had a typical cruciform plan and was originally covered with a flat earthen roof. Its massive vigas, dating from the 1830s, remained intact throughout the twentieth century. In the nineteenth century, a small cross was hung above the entrance and two church bells were added to the front corners of the structure. Few changes were made to the church until the 1940s when a galvanized metal roof was added, and some of the interior and exterior features were modernized. Walls were plastered, hand-carved doors were set in the front entrance, stained-glass windows were installed, and a new gas heating system replaced the old stoves. Twin bell towers were added, along with a raised front façade, in 1955. The sacristy was rebuilt and new *santos* were placed in the church in the 1960s.[57] The church remained in use for decades, but, after continued deterioration, it was razed in 2010.

The original village site lies just east of the church. Some of the adobe structures of the nineteenth century have been enlarged and modified and are still in use today as residences. Others have crumbled and eroded over the years. A few segments of the old Armijo ranch remain standing in Lemitar. There is no existing contemporary description of the house or grounds, but some residents remember being told of a lavish, sprawling estate that stood at the site with as many as thirty rooms surrounded by a long adobe wall. The southern end of the estate and the outline of about ten rooms, are still standing and sections of the outer wall, complete with timber vigas, remain.[58]

The second Lemitar cemetery, known as the *Camposanto Viejo*, is located about one quarter mile southwest of the church, on an elevated site. It was originally surrounded by an adobe wall, but today it is enclosed by a wire and post fence. It was probably opened by 1850 and remained in use until the early years of the twentieth century. Only a few wood and stone markers remain although more than one hundred graves have been identified at the site. Most are typical of nineteenth-century Hispanic cemeteries with carved pine boards or rock slabs used as grave markers. Small wooden picket fences sometimes enclosed the burial plots, and in one case an ornate Victorian-era cast-iron fence surrounds a gravesite. A third cemetery, opened in 1907 and still in use, lies just east of the interstate along the frontage road.[59] Other areas of Lemitar date from the mid-nineteenth century, especially the period following the Civil War. The 1866 post office may have been located in the large residence that is just southeast of old church site. Across the street from the church is the site of "new" Lemitar. Some of the commercial buildings and houses near the present post office and NM 408 became the center of village activities by the 1870s.

The smaller village of Sabino was on the east bank of the Rio Grande, opposite Lemitar. It was settled in the 1830s and survived as a modest agricultural community for about forty years. By the 1860s, there were about one hundred people living at Sabino, but sometime before 1870 the village was abandoned. The ruins of the hamlet appeared on maps for decades, but Sabino was never re-settled.[60] From Sabino, the old Camino Real ran along the east bank about twenty-two miles north to La Joya de Sevilleta. After the 1830s, a west branch of the trail followed the path of Polvadera Road and the Lemitar Frontage Road north to Polvadera, a small Mexican-era settlement noted on mid-nineteenth century maps and mentioned in a few accounts of Navajo raids.

Alamillo Pueblo and Alamillo

About five miles north of Lemitar, also on the west bank of the Rio Grande, is the village of *Alamillo*, the Little Cottonwood, located near the site of the old seventeenth-century Alamillo Mission. It was an important landmark on the Camino Real in the period before the Pueblo Revolt, but efforts to locate the site of Alamillo have been unsuccessful despite the fact that it was frequently noted by travelers and served as a paraje during the colonial era.

In 1680, the Piro Indians of Alamillo joined the Spaniards as they fled south. When Otermín returned in 1681, he found the pueblo "entirely deserted, and the church, convent, and crosses burned." The remaining houses were set on fire.[61] Alamillo may have been damaged or destroyed by later flooding of the Rio Grande, and it disappears from travelers' accounts by the nineteenth century.[62] After 1800, a new settlement called Alamillo was founded northwest of the old pueblo, on the opposite side of the river. It did not survive for long, and its few residents may have moved to nearby Sevilleta. Later, there was a small territorial village called Alamillo opposite La Joyita, on the west bank of the river.[63] Present-day Alamillo, which was settled when the railroad made its way through the river valley, is located just west of Interstate 25, opposite San Acacia.

The present-day settlement of Alamillo, west of Interstate 10 near San Acacia, is probably near the site of the seventeenth-century mission.

La Joya de Sevilleta

The Camino Real de Tierra Adentro continued north from Alamillo through today's Sevilleta National Wildlife Refuge, toward *La Joya de Sevilleta*, the site of the northernmost Piro pueblo, known as *Selocú*. The pueblo was noted by soldier-chronicler Hernán Gallegos of the 1581 Rodríguez-Chamuscado expedition and was later referred to as *La Joya*, the Jewel, a village of about ninety houses.[64] The Oñate expedition first saw the modest pueblo, rising above a marshy area on the east side of the Rio Grande, and thought of Sevilla, Spain, so they called it *Sevilleta*, or Little Sevilla.[65] Franciscans arrived in Sevilleta in the 1620s and founded the *San Luis Obispo Mission*, dedicated to Saint Louis, a thirteenth-century French bishop. Sevilleta pueblo and the San Luis Mission became a major center, serving the Piro population of the northern Socorro Valley.[66] The pueblo village expanded over an open, level area on a gravel bluff, rising about one hundred feet above the valley floor. Benavides called Sevilleta one of the crown's "best pueblos" in New Mexico and described it as a "pleasant" place, "growing more and more each day." A branch road of the Camino Real led directly into the southern portion of the village.[67]

San Luis Obispo Mission survived for almost thirty years despite epidemics and occasional Apache raids. By mid-century, several Spanish encomenderos had moved into the region, and colonial governors ordered the Piros to work for these Spanish landowners so they re-settled them outside of Sevilleta. At one point, the pueblo itself was sold to a local settler. Workers were described as being "enslaved" at the hacienda of Captain Don Diego de Guadalajara, who used them to haul salt from the Salinas area and help carry the shipments as far south as Parral. Piro laborers also reported abuses by Gerónimo Márquez who operated an estancia near Alamillo. Some never returned to Sevilleta. To make matters worse, the increased contact with Spaniards and other Indian laborers introduced more disease and helped reduce the native population even further.

When Lieutenant Governor García's refugee party arrived there in 1680, the remaining Piros joined the Spanish on their way south. Their decision influenced other settlements in the region, and Piros from Socorro, Alamillo, and Senecú joined García's weary exiles. Governor Otermín returned to the region the next year and found Sevilleta in ruins.[68] Although New Mexico was re-conquered and settled in the 1690s, and trade and travel resumed along the Camino Real de Tierra Adentro, no one returned to live at Sevilleta pueblo during the eighteenth century.[69] The Sevilleta Piros were re-settled at Socorro del Sur and Senecú, near El Paso del Norte,[70] and eventually absorbed into the communities of El Paso's Lower Valley. By the 1920s, a small barrio in Ciudad Juárez was home to about fifty remaining Piros who still had a basic tribal structure and spoke some of their native language.[71]

By the early nineteenth century there was renewed interest in opening the Rio Abajo to settlement, but it is not entirely clear when people first moved back to La Joya de Sevilleta. There may have been a few pioneers there by the 1790s, as landless farmers from the north, especially from Santa Fe, Santa Cruz de la Cañada, and San Juan Pueblo, settled just below the old pueblo ruins, along the east side of the river. It appears to have grown fairly quickly. Zebulon Pike described "Sibilleta" as the "neatest most regular village" he had seen and estimated that perhaps 1,000 people lived in the village. He noted the fortified town as a square, with a large mud wall. Pike also noted that many caravans camped near the village.[72]

By the 1810s, formal applications were prepared, and in 1819, the La Joya de Sevilleta land grant, comprising more than 220,000 acres, was authorized for sixty-seven grantees. The Sevilleta grant was an *ejido* grant, a community grant for a group of family-settlers. The original grantees included the Benavides, Montoya, Tafoya, Sisneros, and Trujillo families, whose descendants still live in the area today. The first settlers at La Joya built a small church and simple, flat-roofed adobe dwellings grouped around the plaza. They formed their own local government and were responsible for managing ejido lands for the benefit of the community.[73]

The 1820s and 1830s were a turbulent time in the Rio Abajo as independence from Spain disrupted caravans and livestock drives, limited troop escorts, and brought about a resurgence of Apache and Navajo attacks in the region. After becoming part of the Territory of New Mexico, the town once again became known as *La Joya*.[74] After the Civil War, a post office was established, and the Court of Private Land Claims confirmed legal title to the heirs of the original Sevilleta settlers. The town lost its prominence as a major stop on the old Camino Real when a west-bank branch of the trail diverted traffic to Socorro and other new communities on the opposite side of the river. The railroad, which also passed west of La Joya, reduced traffic even further. Although the mining boom brought thousands of Anglo-Americans and immigrants to the Socorro area, La Joya remained somewhat isolated, away from the main action. The overwhelming majority of residents were native-born New Mexicans and, as a result, La Joya maintained much of its Hispanic cultural heritage and traditions.[75]

Sevilleta de la Joya lies at the southern end of NM 304.

The Sevilleta land grant was confirmed by the United States government in 1907, and by 1920 the town officially became *La Joya*. During the 1920s and 1930s, it was a bustling community with three stores, a saloon, dance hall, school, and prominent church, frequented by area farmers. But in the 1930s, the main automobile highway through New Mexico followed the west bank, near the path of today's interstate. NM 304, which leads south from US 60 and follows much of the old Camino Real, became a dead-end at La Joya, limiting visitors and commerce.

Today, Sevilleta de la Joya lies at the southern end of NM 304. The ruins of Sevilleta pueblo are located between Contreras and La Joya, north of the town, on a bluff overlooking the river. The Camino Real entered La Joya along the bottomlands and a New Mexico Highway Department Camino Real Historical Marker stands at the town's entrance. The area west of the marker was the heart of the old nineteenth-century village. The original *acequia madre*, the main irrigation ditch through the village, dates from the early nineteenth century and was reconstructed in the 1970s. Our Lady of Sorrow's Church may be built upon segments of the original, early nineteenth-century structure. East of the church, the outline of the old village can be detected. The broad, open area was the plaza, once surrounded by flat-roofed adobe dwellings in a defensive arrangement. Crumbling adobe ruins in wooded areas south and west of the church, and the remains of a small cemetery to the east, indicate the extent of the old village. The late nineteenth-century and early twentieth-century settlement spread beyond the old village confines toward NM 304, and along the old Camino Real south to La Joyita. The rutted roads through the floodplain north and south of the town are probably segments of the old trail. The later commercial and residential center of town is further south, on the open flatlands. A twentieth-century cemetery is located on the eastern edge of the town near NM 304.

A few miles below Sevilleta, on Sevilleta National Wildlife Refuge land, are the remains of *La Joyita*, the Little Jewel. It was settled late in the Mexican period and was first noted in the accounts of Lieutenant Abert and Doctor Wislizenus. The village was located on a broad area near the river, on one of the few sites not threatened by the shifting sand banks, and was home to a cluster of red sandy clay dwellings in the mid-nineteenth century. Nothing is left of La Joyita except a few low earthen-mounds and the remains of a handful of adobe houses. One large structure appears to have been the typical casa-corral complex, about ten rooms centered around a courtyard and corral. Artifacts recovered at the site indicate that the village was occupied in the Mexican and Territorial periods. By the 1870s, few people lived at La Joyita, and a major flood destroyed the settlement in 1884.[76]

During the 1930s, General Thomas Campbell purchased much of the old Sevilleta land grant and introduced large-scale cattle ranching to the area. Over a period of thirty years, the enterprise took its toll on the land, and in the 1960s, the Campbells, interested in protecting what remained of the natural environment, started a foundation dedicated to preserving much of the ranch as a wildlife refuge. The Campbell Family Foundation oversaw the refuge until 1973 when it was placed under the United States Fish and Wildlife Service. The Camino Real de Tierra Adentro passed through the edge of the refuge. A great variety of wildlife is found at the Sevilleta National Wildlife Refuge including desert bighorn sheep, pronghorn, mule deer, mountain lion, and bear. Birds are plentiful with occasional bald eagles, peregrine falcons, northern shovelers, pintails, American coots, wood ducks, canvasbacks, redheads, great blue herons, black-crowned night herons, sandhill cranes, killdeer, long-billed dowitchers, red-tailed hawks, kestrels, and burrowing owls. Much of the Sevilleta National Wildlife Refuge has limited access, but a visitor center, hiking trails, and organized field trips provide opportunities to enjoy the site.

7

Tiwa Country

Beyond La Joya de Sevilleta, the Camino Real de Tierra Adentro entered the land of the Southern Tiwa Pueblo. By the 900s CE, Ancestral Pueblo Indians of the Rio Grande Valley, who probably migrated from the northwest, had developed pueblo-style settlements and cultivated maize and assorted crops. They were later joined by people from the Mogollon cultures of the south. The Southern Tiwa dialect, rooted in the Tanoan family, emerged during the twelfth century and was probably a blending of the two languages.[1] By the 1300s CE, the Tiwa lived in a series of large, well-built multi-storied adobe dwellings with an architecture and design similar to the Piros. When Spaniards arrived in the sixteenth century they called the natives *Tigua*, which became Tiwa in English. There may have been as many as twenty Tiwa pueblos in the area, but the natives were consolidated into four mission settlements, Puaray, Sandia, Alameda, and Isleta. During the 1680 Pueblo Revolt, Puaray and Alameda were destroyed, and only two missions, at Sandia and Isleta, were formally re-established after the revolt Today, Sandia, Isleta, and Ysleta del Sur (near El Paso, Texas) survive as Tiwa communities.

Las Nutrias

Today's US 60 approximates the ancient boundary between Piro and Tiwa Pueblo Indian settlements. North of the highway, NM 304 parallels the path of the Camino Real de Tierra Adentro along the east bank of the Rio Grande. *Las Nutrias*, the Beavers, is the first settlement, about four miles north of the federal highway. A *nutria* is actually a South American rodent whose name was applied to the North American beaver. In 1680, as the Spanish fled the Pueblo Revolt, Lieutenant Governor García met Governor Otermín and his refugees near Las Nutrias, and, when Otermín returned north the next year, he noted passing *La Vega de las Nutrias*, the Meadow of the Beavers. By 1766, Las Nutrias was a newly formed town of thirty families. In 1776, Fray Domínguez described the area as fertile, well-irrigated farmland, and suitable for livestock but noted that the Apaches had driven all of the settlers away from the site.[2] Las Nutrias was re-settled about fifty years later, and San Isidro Mission Church, a mission of Our Lady of Sorrows Parish in La Joya, is probably close to the site of the nineteenth-century settlement.

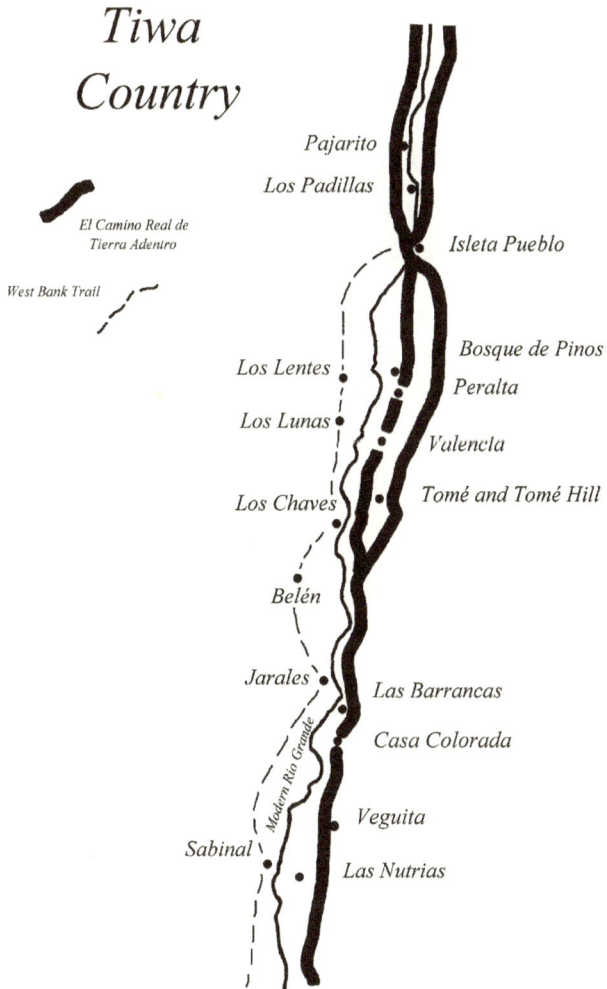

Tiwa Country

El Camino Real de Tierra Adentro

West Bank Trail

Pajarito

Los Padillas

Isleta Pueblo

Los Lentes

Bosque de Pinos

Peralta

Los Lunas

Valencia

Los Chaves

Tomé and Tomé Hill

Belén

Jarales

Las Barrancas

Casa Colorada

Modern Rio Grande

Veguita

Sabinal

Las Nutrias

El Camino Real de Tierra Adentro through Tiwa Country.

Veguita

Veguita, the Little Meadow, is about three miles north of Las Nutrias on NM 304. Little is known about Veguita and it does not appear in any colonial or Mexican-era documents or travelers' accounts. A few adobe ruins are strung along the highway near the Veguita post office, and an open area east of the highway may have been the center of the old community. Just beyond the post office is the San Juan Church, a nineteenth-century structure affiliated with Our Lady of Sorrows.[3]

A few adobe ruins survive near Veguita.

Turn (Casa Colorada)

Turn is about four miles north of Veguita. This was the site of Pueblo Casa Colorado,[4] one of the larger Tiwa pueblos in the area, occupied from the mid-fourteenth century to the end of the sixteenth century, and possibly a few decades beyond. There may have been an estancia there before the 1680

Pueblo Revolt, but there are no records of the settlement, and the only colonial-era reference is from 1760 when Bishop Tamarón noted the ruins of a "house they called Colorada."[5] *Casa Colorada*, or the Red House, probably referred to the reddish mud and clay in the area used to make adobe. Settlers from Las Nutrias were said to have moved to Casa Colorada after a series of Indian attacks drove them away from their community.[6] In 1821, there was a request to build a small chapel there, and in 1823 a petition was made to Mexican officials for a community land grant, but the surviving documents do not show that the grant was ever awarded. Later testimony indicates that a small town was established by the 1830s. In the 1840s, the name Casa Colorada regularly appears in lists of New Mexico towns and was mentioned by Santa Fe Trail trader Josiah Gregg. Doctor Wislizenus' party camped there on July 22, 1846 and noted "Casas Coloradas" as a town with high sand hills near the river.[7]

Nineteenth-century stagecoaches ran along the old Camino Real and a depot was housed in a large general store at Casa Colorada.[8] By the early twentieth century, Casa Colorada was still a small hamlet with a church and several clusters of residences. In the 1920s, the name of the local post office was changed to "Turn" because of the bend in the road nearby. Turn is still officially the name of the settlement, although the name Casa Colorada is more commonly used. Today, it remains quite small, with a population of less than one hundred people. A New Mexico Highway Department Camino Real Marker is located on the east side of the highway, in front of the Casa Colorada School, a restored early twentieth-century schoolhouse. Just north of the marker is a small twentieth-century church, affiliated with the Tomé parish. The nineteenth-century Hispanic settlement of Casa Colorada was located between Veguita and Turn, along the west side of the highway. It was a settlement of adobe dwellings built in a U-shape, around an open plaza on high ground, above the eastern flood plain of the river. There are scattered mounds, worn down by decades of erosions and wind, and the outlines of a few roomblocks.[9]

Las Barrancas

About two miles north of Turn, where the Burlington, Northern, and Santa Fe Railway tracks cross today's NM 304, is an area known as *Las Barrancas*, or the Ravines. It was the site of the Estancia de Barrancas in the 1660s and appears on several colonial era maps. Those who lived at Las Barrancas fled during the

1680 Pueblo Revolt, and there were no attempts to re-settle the site after the uprising. Nonetheless, both Otermín and Vargas noted this break in the landscape of the Rio Abajo when they passed through the area. The precise location of the old estancia is unclear; it was merely noted as being somewhere between Sevilleta and Isleta, and it disappears from maps and documents by the late nineteenth century. A New Mexico Highway Department Camino Real Marker, on the west side of the road, just south of the tracks, describes Las Barrancas.[10]

Las Barrancas, the Ravines, was the site of a seventeenth-century hacienda until it was abandoned during the Pueblo Indian Revolt.

Tomé

Tomé is located about ten miles north of Las Barrancas, on the east side of the Rio Grande. This quiet, historic village has structural remains from the eighteenth and nineteenth centuries and is located near the base of Tomé Hill, a basaltic hill that towers over the area landscape and is rich with ancient and historic petroglyphs. Before the seventeenth century, the Rio Grande ran further to the east, very close to the base of Tomé Hill, but by 1740 the river channel had shifted west, opening the area around today's plaza to settlement. The Camino Real was west of the hill and passed through the plaza of Tomé, closely following the path of today's NM 47 through the valley.[11]

Early Spanish expeditions came through the Tomé area, and scouts probably climbed Tomé Hill to observe the surrounding countryside, but, curiously, made no mention of it in their journals. The site was first settled around 1660 when Tomé Domínguez de Mendoza received a grant of encomienda, west of Tomé Hill, and secured Indian laborers from nearby pueblos. In 1680, the Domínguez family joined Spanish and Indian refugees as they fled south during the Pueblo Revolt to the safety of El Paso del Norte. When Otermín and Vargas returned to re-conquer New Mexico, they camped near Tomé Hill, noting the ruins of the old hacienda. The Domínguez family never returned to their home,[12] but thirty-nine years later settlers from Albuquerque petitioned for the old hacienda land and formally founded *Nuestra Señora de la Concepción de Tomé Domínguez*, Thomas Domínguez's Our Lady of the Immaculate Conception, which became known as Tomé. The settlement was a fortified site around a plaza, about one mile south of the old hacienda ruins, near the remains of a small Indian pueblo. Many of the settlers were *genízaros*, Hispanicized Indians, who as children had been sold or bartered to Spanish families. These pioneers constructed adobe homes and corrals, and plowed the fertile land along the floodplain just west of the Camino Real. They built a small chapel and during the 1740s began work on a larger, more permanent, church.[13]

Annual caravans made their way through Tomé in the eighteenth century, and the village prospered as farmers raised cotton and corn; sheep and cattle grazed in the fields, and local artisans produced textiles, blankets, and clothing products.[14] Truce periods were occasionally arranged with the Comanches, allowing the Indians to enter Tomé and trade. Townspeople would venture out into nearby tipi villages and exchange goods among the natives, but when the truce ended, Comanches sometimes returned and raided the settlements, carrying off agricultural goods, livestock, and captives. One of the best known stories in Tomé (similar to ones told in other New Mexico communities) relates how a marriage was arranged between a Comanche chief's son and one of the town's prominent families in the 1770s. When the marriage was called off, the Comanche chief felt betrayed, and his people returned to Tomé, attacking the church, killing twenty settlers, and carrying off area women and children. The massacre, verified in church records, earned Tomé the name "town of broken promises." While the attack did occur, there is no historical evidence that any marriage had ever been arranged.[15]

Tomé recovered and in 1807 when Lieutenant Zebulon Pike and his party camped nearby, he estimated that about 500 people lived in the village. The opening of the Chihuahua Trail brought new business to Tomé, and large caravans, including American and Mexican traders, carried a whole new array of textiles, hardware, and foodstuffs from the eastern United States. Pelts, buffalo robes, and woolens became commonly traded goods along the route. Local livestock were driven down the trail as far south as the mining towns of Durango. The Otero family, herders and traders of the Tomé-Valencia area, ran a thriving freight business. They sold and exchanged corn and wheat with area farmers and milled grains at a nearby hacienda.[16]

Today, the most prominent building on Tomé's historic plaza is Our Lady of the Immaculate Conception Church, which dates from the 1740s. River flooding in the 1760s greatly damaged the church and by the 1820s it was in danger of being lost. In the 1830s, a new roof was added, and extensive repairs were made to the walls. The biggest changes came after 1859 when Jean BaptisteRalliére, a young French immigrant priest, arrived at Tomé and dedicated the rest of his life to the parish. He arranged for a major renovation of the church, emphasizing a new nineteenth-century Gothic design. Carpenters and carvers re-roofed the structure, added confessionals, new doors, a choir loft, and railings to the interior, and redesigned the entire church in the Greek revival-style of the day. Wooden belfries with louvers and large iron bells, similar to those at the San Felipe Neri Church in Albuquerque, were constructed in the 1860s. Another flood in 1884 destroyed much of the village, but the church remained intact. After the waters receded, repairs were made, and, despite more severe floods in the early twentieth century that collapsed parts of the nave and façade, Immaculate Conception survived and flourished. The church was re-furbished once again in the 1970s when the bell towers were removed, the interior restored, and a new museum and churchyard were built facing the plaza.[17]

The open plaza opposite the church has a few structural remains of eighteenth-and nineteenth-century buildings, including the old jail. Tomé Hill is located one mile northeast of the plaza along NM 47 which follows the path of the Camino Real north toward Valencia. The hill rises 500 feet above the river valley and has been a sacred and strategic site along the river for centuries. Small Pueblo shrines and early Christian symbols are common along its slopes. Three crosses have been erected on its summit, part of the local Penitente tradition, a nineteenth-century Catholic organization active in New Mexico. In recent years, Good Friday pilgrimages have taken place at the site. In 1996, the hill was placed on the State Register of Cultural Places and the National Register of Historic Places. Tomé Hill Park protects much of the area and has a series of historical markers and a sculpture celebrating the site.

Hiking trails lead to the summit of Tomé Hill, a prominent landmark on the Camino Real de Tierra Adentro.

Valencia

Valencia is about five miles north of Tomé on NM 47. Blas Valencia came to New Mexico with the Oñate expedition in 1598. In the 1630s, his son, Francisco de Valencia, received a grant of encomienda and built a hacienda and small chapel on the site of an old Tiwa pueblo. His descendants took over the hacienda in the 1660s and lived at the site until the 1680 Pueblo Revolt. When Vargas passed through in 1692, he noted the "outpost and ruined estancia of Juan de Valencia."[18] The family never returned to the old hacienda, but by the 1740s a group of settlers from the Albuquerque area, including many genízaros, farmed the land around the former homestead.[19] The settlement was organized around two plazas and Valencia was listed as a *puesto*, or post, along the Camino Real in the 1802 census.[20]

Valencia remained a small agricultural village on the Chihuahua Trail, opposite Los Lentes, during the Mexican era.[21] The Otero family came to Valencia in the nineteenth century, and three brothers, Juan José, Antonio, and Manuel, became successful ranchers and merchants and soon dominated the local commercial and political scene. The Oteros intermarried with members of the Luna family, further consolidating their power and privilege, and the two eventually becoming the wealthiest families in the region. Antonio José Otero worked with American troops after the Mexican-American War and was later appointed to the Superior (or Supreme) Court of New Mexico.[22]

Today, Valencia is a small but thriving community with a variety of commercial and agricultural activities. Not much remains of the old settlement, although several archaeological surveys have revealed portions of a Tiwa pueblo and possibly the walls of the nineteenth-century plazas. The pueblo and hacienda were on the west side of today's NM 47, at the site of the Sangre de Cristo Church, which stands on the foundation of the old pueblo.[23] The second plaza of Valencia was close to where NM 47 meets El Cerro Loop. In 1800, the new church, *Sangre de Cristo*, Blood of Christ, was constructed to commemorate the end of a bloody feud between two brothers. During the late nineteenth and early twentieth centuries, it was enlarged and renovated with the addition of a pitched roof, twin towers, and a covered front entrance. Flooding damaged the church over the years, and in 1941 large segments of the walls collapsed.[24] Much of the structure was demolished and rebuilt, following the original design and layout as closely as was possible. The foundation and some of the wall segments were preserved, and some interior furnishings and materials were re-used.[25] The present building, with its sheet metal-covered roof and twin bell towers, was re-dedicated in 1942 and continues to serve the Valencia area.

The Sangre de Cristo Church in Valencia stands near the site of the seventeenth-century Tiwa pueblo and Spanish hacienda.

Peralta and Bosque Farms

Peralta is about three miles north of Valencia on NM 47, and is also at the site of a seventeenth-century Tiwa pueblo. The area became a popular campsite because of the abundant vegetation, timber, and a river ford. The Peralta family name arrived in New Mexico with Pedro de Peralta, Oñate's successor as governor in 1609, but, locally, people believe the settlement's name originated from *peras altas*, for the large pear trees grown in the area.[26] The first known settlers were members of the Gutiérrez family, who received a land grant in 1739. Within a few years, several small farms spread out along the river. In 1769, a major flood shifted the Rio Grande westward almost two miles and divided the original grant. The Gutiérrez descendants relocated to an area that became known as *Bosque de Pinos*, the Forest of the Pinos family, a fairly long stretch on the river, which includes today's Bosque Farms. Members of the Otero and Chaves families arrived in the early nineteenth century, and by the 1830s José Mariano Chaves lived on a large hacienda near the bosque and constructed a small chapel on the grounds. Peralta is first listed as a community in 1835,[27] and eleven years later Lieutenant Abert described it as a village "on the southern skirt of a large round grove of cotton-wood trees." He noted several flour mills in the area in addition to well-built houses, especially the one belonging to Señor Otero.[28]

About one mile further north, between today's Peralta and Bosque Farms, was *Los Pinos*, a hacienda that Wislizenus thought "bore a striking resemblance to a southern plantation."[29] In the 1850s, Judge Davis visited the estate when it was the home of Doctor Henry Connelly, a Kentucky-native who had studied medicine at Transylvania College, and came to New Mexico as a Santa Fe trader in 1828. He settled in Chihuahua City, married into a local merchant family, and became a successful businessman on the Chihuahua Trail. After his wife died, Doctor Connelly returned to New Mexico and based his business in the Albuquerque area. By the time of the Mexican War, he had re-married, taking Dolores Perea, the widow of Peralta rancher José Mariano Chaves, as his bride. Through the marriage, Connelly became related to the Armjo family and moved into his wife's estate, *Los Pinos*, the Pines, a large hacienda on the east bank of the Rio Grande. Susan Magoffin considered it to be one of the most impressive and lavish in New Mexico and described the house as "very large" and "well furnished with handsome Brussles [sic] carpet, crimson worsted curtains, with guilded rings and cornice, white marble slab pier tables-hair and crimson worsted chairs."[30] Doctor Connelly moved much of his mercantile business with him and established several stores near Peralta. In the 1850s, Davis found Connelly living in a spacious, Spanish-style home on a large hacienda near the river, surrounded by thick river bosque, mostly of cottonwoods.[31] Lieutenant Edward Beale brought his famous camel brigade across Texas and into New Mexico in 1857 and camped at the cottonwood grove near Connelly's hacienda. He and his men were invited into the Connelly home for a glass of cognac and when they offered to pay for the hospitality, Connelly would not accept any money, insisting that the unusual sight of the camels was "ample compensation."[32]

When the Civil War broke out, Connelly was asked to organize New

Mexico's militias, most of which had collapsed in the 1850s, and prepare for a possible Confederate invasion from Texas. As governor, Connelly toured the Territory throughout the war, visiting installations and recruiting troops. When Confederates passed Fort Craig, Connelly headed north, encouraging Rio Abajo farmers and ranchers to move their livestock to the mountains and hide whatever property they could. On April 15, 1862, the Confederates were marching down the river valley, retreating south along the trail after their defeat at Glorieta Pass. A skirmish occurred between Union and Confederate forces near Los Pinos. During the "Battle of Peralta," the Rebels encountered Federal troops and engaged in a lengthy artillery duel that greatly damaged many of the walled structures and homes around the village. The Confederates moved to the west bank of the river and took advantage of a sudden dust storm to continue their retreat south. After the war, US troops used Los Pinos as a supply center and military post. Connelly never returned to the estate and died in 1866. His widow Dolores stayed at the hacienda until her death in 1890.[33]

Today's church at Peralta, dedicated to Our Lady of Guadalupe, was constructed on property donated by another widow, Mercedes Otero, in 1879. It took many years to complete the structure, and it was not consecrated until 1892. Peralta remained a small agricultural village until the late twentieth century. The entire structure was renovated in 1987. Our Lady of Guadalupe, with its three gleaming white crosses and tan-stuccoed exterior, stands near the site of the original community.[34]

The West Bank Trail

NM 116 runs close to the path of the Camino Real de Tierra Adentro's west bank trail, a colonial roadway that passed through a series of small agricultural villages founded during the eighteenth century, opposite Las Nutrias, Casa Colorada, Tomé, and Valencia. Abeytas, a mid-nineteenth century settlement, is about four miles north of US 60. There are several large adobe ruins on an elevated site in back of the church, beyond the acequia. A few late nineteenth-or early twentieth-century adobe buildings lie in the brush along the east side of the highway.

Sabinal

Sabinal is about three miles north of Abeytas and was founded in 1741 on an open area along the river. *San Antonio de Sabinal*, Saint Anthony of the Junipers, as noted on colonial maps, was considered a strategic frontier site when the Gila Apaches were brought there in the 1790s and clustered in a series of eighteen adobe dwellings near the town. The Gila briefly cooperated and tended small farm plots around the village, but within a few years hostilities resumed. There were plans for a presidio at Sabinal, but one was never established. By 1800, the Gila had returned to the surrounding countryside and a local militia regularly patrolled the area. This led to a concentration of the Hispanic population at Sabinal, by then a large plaza settlement of several hundred residents. *La Capilla de San Antonio*, the Chapel of San Antonio, was established in the 1820s, but an 1853 flood swept away most of the village and cut a new, straighter river channel through the area. In the 1860s, another village was built on higher ground, about one-half mile east of the old settlement. The San Antonio Church, a twentieth-century structure along NM 116, is probably near the site of the old village.[35]

Jarales

Jarales is another west bank agricultural community, located on Jarales Road which runs parallel to NM 304. The name Jarales may result from the willow thickets along the river, which were sometimes called *Jaralosa*. Oral histories claim that a family called Jaral lived nearby and that the settlement became known as *Los Jarales*, the place where the Jarals live.[36] It never developed into a sizable town and in 1776, Fray Domínguez described Jarales as a small, poor settlement of forty-nine families, mostly genízaros from nearby Belén. He noted that "some of them have small plots of arable land, and others have nothing, supporting themselves as their luck helps them."[37] There is a restored mid-nineteenth century church, dedicated to Saint Francis Xavier, and a 1930s-era schoolhouse which now serves as a community center, in the present-day village.

Belén

Belén lies about four miles north of Jarales on the west bank trail. In 1740, Captain Diego de Torres, his brother-in-law Antonio Salazar, and thirty-one Spanish settlers from the Albuquerque area petitioned the governor for a community land grant in the Rio Abajo. They named the site *Nuestra Señora de Belén*, or Our Lady of Bethlehem.[38] Belén became an agricultural hamlet on the frontier, a plaza settlement with tight clusters of homes and buildings with narrowly-slitted windows that could quickly be sealed and barricaded. Immediately outside of the plaza were cultivated fields and common grazing grounds and open, unallocated land for future settlers.[39] They built a modest mud-brick chapel where a priest from Isleta Pueblo occasionally performed the basic sacraments. In the early 1790s, the community constructed a larger church and in 1793 Belén was designated as a parish.[40] About 600 Belén villagers produced corn, wheat, squashes, chilis, sugar cane, and, as ranching expanded, alfalfa became a mainstay. In the Rio Abajo, a system called *partido*, a form of sharecropping where a herder (the tenant) obtained a breeding herd from a *partidero* (owner), and entered into a contract, dominated the sheep industry. The owner supplied the breeding stock. The tenant absorbed all of the costs and losses, sold wool and lambs to the owner, and sometimes paid rent for grazing when communal lands were not available. The partideros were powerful and wielded substantial political, economic, and social power throughout the entire region.[41] Grazing livestock put herders at risk, and Belén had its share of Navajo and Apache raids in the eighteenth century, so a small military garrison was established here in the 1760s. Disputes over land sometimes divided the community. A group of genízaros claimed that they had inhabited the land before the original petition was filed, making the grant void. No records exist detailing the outcome of the case; however, the original petitioners' families remained on the Belén grant and a small community of genízaros continued to live in the area for the rest of the eighteenth century.[42]

In the early 1850s, river floods destroyed much of Belén, including the 1793 church, so a new village was built west of the original town site. Several men played an important role in the re-building and new commercial development of the region after the 1850s, especially Felipe Chávez, a descendent of New

Mexico's political elite, who was the first prominent merchant in the Belén area. He moved from Los Padillas in 1860 and continued the family business of trade on the Santa Fe and Chihuahua trails. He operated a store in Belén, built a large wholesale enterprise, and became an influential merchant, financier, and patrón. John Becker, a German immigrant who moved to Belén in 1871, became one of the region's major commercial developers, with the financial backing of Chávez. Becker opened a general merchandise store, acquired American military contracts, and brought many family members to New Mexico from Germany to work in his enterprises. He opened and operated the first post office there and eventually became a leading financier and banker.[43]

By the 1860s, the west bank trail had become an important trade route for freight caravans and stagecoaches. The rails entered New Mexico in the 1870s through Raton Pass, and new routes were surveyed in order to streamline traffic across the nation's heartland. The Eastern Railway (later purchased by the Atchison, Topeka, and Santa Fe) cut a line through Kansas, Oklahoma, the Texas Panhandle, and into the rolling plains of eastern New Mexico. It skirted the Manzano Mountains and headed toward the main north-south line of the Atchison, Topeka, and Santa Fe which followed the route of the old Camino Real through the Territory. The tracks were destined to meet somewhere between Jarales and Belén, but in 1902 it was still not clear which was the better route. John Becker, hoping to bring the line to Belén, donated all of the land needed to lay track into the town and construct a large railroad yard. He also covered much of the project's costs and encouraged area farmers to sell land for the right-of-way. The tracks passed well east of the town limiting the immediate impact, but dramatic changes came after 1900 when a new rail cut-off transformed the region and made it a major railroad hub for the Southwest. The completion of the Belén Cut-Off in 1908 brought explosive growth, tripling the population by 1920, and making it a major transportation and commercial center. Machine shops, coaling stations, miles of track, a roundhouse, and a depot created hundreds of new jobs. Commercial outlets expanded and new undertakings serving travelers appeared. Wage labor drew people from the surrounding communities, and new specialty businesses, such as drug stores, newspapers, cafes, saloons, and food markets, followed. Belén, became known as a hub city, where "the rails meet the trails."

The historic center of old Belén was south of the intersection of Wisconsin Street and Ross Avenue. Almost hidden among the tight cluster of homes in the area today is a wooden sign indicating the site of the old plaza. Little else remains of nineteenth-century Belén. West of the site, across the railroad yard and Main Street, is one of the few surviving buildings from the era of the trail, the Felipe Chávez House, a sprawling adobe Territorial-style home located on Lala Street. Chávez was born in 1834, and, after being educated in Guadalajara, returned to the Rio Abajo. He developed a very meticulous approach to the mercantile trades, carefully following small amounts of money and continually re-investing profits. In 1856, he took over the family's freighting business, moving goods in and out of the Territory. Chávez traded in fine cloth, shoes and boots, tailored clothing, and miscellaneous luxury goods. He arranged for extensive shipments of dry goods such as sugar, brandies, whiskies, candles, soaps, and cigars, which drew a good price in the west.

Chávez hired agents to represent him in Missouri and New York. They arranged special prices and organized freighting caravans that followed branches of the old Santa Fe Trail. As railroads penetrated the American West, Chávez increased his shipments and took advantage of drastic cuts in transportation costs. He supplemented his business with military contracts, providing locally produced meats, grains, and hides for Fort Craig. In the 1870s, he grew corn and wheat, opened a mill, and shipped livestock to markets east and west He became the area's leading wholesaler and retailer, competing with, but also supplying, many of his rivals. As he built his commercial empire, he also became a leading financier, creditor, and patriarch, overseeing an extended family of commercial and social networks. He also worked with other area entrepreneurs, including John Becker and Antonio José Otero. He was one of New Mexico's leading nineteenth-century mercantile capitalists and lived on a comfortable estate in Belén. He became known as *el millonario*, the millionaire, because of his tremendous wealth. Chávez built the house in 1860. Along with his many commercial ventures, he was also active politically and served as a judge. He even built a small jail on the grounds. Chávez died in 1905, and family members inherited the estate. The property passed through more than a dozen owners during the twentieth century, and by the 1990s it was neglected, and surrounded by commercial growth. Still, it was listed as a state cultural property in 1980 and added to the National Register of Historic Places. In the early twenty-first century, some of its original splendor was restored. The large home, now obscured by commercial development along Main Street, has had several renovations, including a second story added to the north part of the structure.

But from several angles, the Felipe Chávez House still appears to be a sprawling nineteenth-century estate.

The nineteenth-century plaza of Bélen was located in this residential area, off of Wisconsin Street.

Los Chaves

Further north along the west bank branch of El Camino Real de Tierra Adentro is Los Chaves, on present-day NM 314. Don Nicolás Durán y Chaves is considered to be the founder of *Los Chaves*, the place where the Chaves[44] family lives, a small eighteenth-century settlement. He was the son of Fernando Durán y Chaves II who escaped the 1680 Pueblo Revolt and returned with the Vargas expedition. In 1738, Nicolás Durán y Chaves petitioned for a land grant citing his large family, which included nine sons, and the need for new pastureland. He noted that he had already established a small fortress on the land and hoped to offer protection to shepherds and ranch hands were living on the site. Nicolás

Durán y Chaves was awarded the grant in 1739 and moved his family to the Los Chaves Land Grant, on the west bank of the Rio Grande, opposite Tomé.[45]

By 1790, Los Chaves was listed as a series of six plazas with seventy-eight households. Most of the residents were farmers, ranchers, and weavers, but each plaza had a *comandante* who oversaw the day-to-day operations and defense. Typical of the commandants was José Francisco Pino, a thirty-five year old Spanish livestock rancher who was married to twenty-five year old Juana María Baca. Together, they had five children and a six-year old Apache servant. Along with the Chaves clan, there were several other eighteenth-century extended pioneer families whose descendants still inhabit the area today. Common surnames include Baca, Sánchez, Gabaldon, Pino, and Romero.[46] Los Chaves remained a small agricultural settlement, producing basic staples and grazing livestock. Few visitors passed through the sleepy hamlet. Los Chaves is rarely mentioned in any of the standard eighteenth-and nineteenth-century accounts of the region and is one of the few sites not listed in the 1776 Domínguez survey.[47]

Today, Our Lady of Guadalupe Church lies along a quiet country road in Los Chaves near the site of the original settlement. The first chapel was located on present-day Camino de Los Chaves and appears to have been dedicated to *San Juan Bautista*, Saint John the Baptist. It is not clear when the present structure was completed, but the first time the church is specifically mentioned is in an 1857 inventory. Twenty years later, a major renovation gave the church a decidedly French-Gothic appearance as new steeples, similar to those added to churches at Los Lunas and Los Lentes, were added and the interior was refurbished. By 1880, it was called Our Lady of Guadalupe Church. Some of the present-day interior furnishings and icons, including an altar with a sculpture of the Last Supper, came from Our Lady of Belén when it was torn down and rebuilt in the 1960s. In 1973, a new north wing was constructed. After a powerful hailstorm damaged the church in 2003, a red tin roof was added. Celebrations of both San Juan Bautista and Our Lady of Guadalupe are held each year.[48]

Los Lunas

Los Lunas, located approximately six miles north of Los Chaves on NM 314, is another example of the tradition of naming settlements after the founding families. About 1750, Domíngo de Luna purchased a parcel of the 1716 San Clemente land grant from the Baca family, and in the late eighteenth century, members of the Luna family moved onto the property.[49] The tiny farming hamlet survived into the Mexican era when Antonio José Luna, considered the "father" of Los Lunas, recruited new settlers and expanded commercial activities in the area.[50] Antonio José married into the Baca family of Belén and became a prominent cattle and sheep rancher, and by the early 1850s he had made a fortune with Antonio José Otero of Valencia by driving large flocks of sheep west. After the Civil War, Antonio José Luna became an important civic leader and politician, active in New Mexico's Republican Party, and used his influence in the Territorial government to have the seat of Valencia County moved from Tomé to Los Lunas in 1876. Even so, Los Lunas experienced limited growth during the early twentieth century. It was incorporated in 1928 but still had a population of only about 500 residents at the time. In recent decades it has been affected by the rapid growth of Albuquerque and the Interstate 25 corridor, but, aside from a few nineteenth-century structures near Main Street, nothing much remains of old Los Lunas. The best known historic structure is the Luna-Otero Mansion, a registered National Historic Landmark, located at 110 West Main Street. The sprawling, southern colonial-style home, made of adobe, was built by the railroad for Antonio José Luna in exchange for the right-of-way to the Luna family property.

Los Lentes

Los Lentes is just beyond Los Lunas, about one mile north of Main Street on Los Lentes Road. It was built on the remains of a Tiwa Indian village known today as Los Lentes Pueblo, established in the fourteenth century and occupied for approximately 300 years. It was a moderately-sized pueblo with perhaps one hundred rooms in a multi-storied adobe, apartment-style complex. A second pueblo, just east of today's chapel site, known as Rainbow Village, was larger and more extensive than Los Lentes. Both appear to have been abandoned when the Spanish consolidated native-settlements in the seventeenth century. Most likely, the natives were moved to the nearest Tiwa settlement, Isleta Pueblo, and placed under the supervision of the Franciscans.[51]

The two abandoned pueblos were on elevated sites near the river and by the early 1700s had attracted the interest of several Isletans. Members of the Candelaria family acquired part of a 1718 land grant, and Matías el Ente, a genízaro who lived near Isleta, purchased some of the Candelaria property by 1760. Like Los Lunas, it was named for the pioneer family that settled the area. Matías el Ente of Isleta Pueblo established a homestead that became known as *Los Lentes*, the Lentes People, for the extended family that lived in this small agricultural hamlet.[52] By 1790, they had built a tiny chapel, dedicated to Saint Anthony of Padua. The site was known as the *Plaza de San Antonio de los Lentes*. There were twenty-two households, occupied by farmers, ranchers, herders, laborers, and weavers. The residents were mostly Tiwa and genízaros, with only a few noted as mestizo or Spanish.[53] The plaza remained small, never more than a village, with less than a few hundred residents throughout the nineteenth century. In the early twentieth century, several generations of the Lentes family still lived in the area, but an influx of Anglo-Americans, European immigrants, New Mexican Hispanics, and various Native-Americans diversified the population.

Today, *La Capilla de San Antonio de Los Lentes*, the Chapel of Saint Anthony at Los Lentes, is all that remains of the old colonial settlement. It lies on a one and one-quarter acre site near Trujillo Road, within a fenced area that roughly approximates the boundaries of the old Los Lentes Pueblo. Rainbow Village Pueblo was east of the fenced area. The core structure was built in 1790 as a small rectangular building, with typical vigas and corbels, a flat roof, and clerestory lighting. The main walls were made of *terrones*, unfired sod bricks, rather than the traditional adobe ones found in most similar structures. During the nineteenth century, the chapel was renovated several times and Territorial and Gothic features changed the exterior appearance in the 1870s. The most significant changes came after a 1906 flood damaged the chapel and destroyed much of the sacristy. Many of the changes were similar to those made to the churches at nearby Tomé and Isleta Pueblo. A pitched gabled roof, a central belfry, and two towers with coned steeples greatly altered the simple adobe exterior.[54] The chapel has undergone several restorations and bears little resemblance to its colonial appearance. The small white-washed southern-facing church has a central wooden belfry and two short square towers at each end, with three prominent white crosses pitched atop each. The Chapel of San Antonio at Los Lentes remains one of the earliest Spanish Colonial churches in continuous use in the Middle Rio Grande, and, each June, the San Antonio Fiesta draws hundreds of participants for special prayers, processions, and celebrations.

The Chapel of Saint Anthony at Los Lentes lies near the site of two sixteenth-century Tiwa pueblo villages.

Isleta Pueblo

The east and west bank branches of the Camino Real de Tierra Adentro led a few miles further north to the Southern Tiwa pueblo of Isleta. The native name for Isleta Pueblo, *Shiewhibak*, means "flint kick-stick place," said to refer to the shape of the land where the pueblo is built.[55] According to oral tradition, Tiwa ancestors came from the northwest, most likely descendants of the Anasazi culture in the San Juan Basin, and merged with another migration of people from the south, probably the Mogollon. The two cultures blended at Shiewhibak, which was founded in the mid-1300s. In the sixteenth century, the main channel of the Rio Grande veered west about a mile north of the pueblo while a second one ran east of the settlement along the modern alignment. When both river channels were full, the pueblo became an island, leading the Spanish to name the site *Isleta*.[56] In 1612, a Franciscan missionary, Juan de Salas, established the mission of *San Antonio de la Isleta*, Saint Anthony of the Little Island, named for Saint Anthony of Padua, a thirteenth-century Portuguese Franciscan. Agriculture flourished on mission lands, and the pueblo's strategic site, in the borderlands between Piro and Tiwa territory and a gateway to the Rio Abajo, made it an important settlement along the Camino Real.[57]In the 1670s, several dozen Tompiro Indians left the Salinas area and were re-settled in Isleta Pueblo.[58]

Isleta did not join the 1680 Pueblo Indian Revolt, a decision that has sparked considerable debate and controversy over the centuries. On August 10, 1680, Lieutenant Governor Alonso García and a small force found themselves isolated in the Rio Abajo, below the Villa of Santa Fe. By nightfall they had moved south to Sandia Pueblo, where they began gathering survivors of the attacks, and made a desperate, hasty retreat down the Camino Real. García received reports that Santa Fe had been taken by the rebels and that all Spaniards in the Rio Arriba had been killed. He spent the next day leading everyone south to the safety of Isleta. By Sunday evening there were approximately 1,500 refugees gathered at the pueblo, including seven missionaries.[59]

On August 14, García called a general meeting of political and military officials, including the seven surviving missionaries, and a unanimous decision was made to abandon Isleta Pueblo. He led the refugee train, including the Isleta Tiwa, down the Camino Real, hoping to meet up with a mission supply caravan that was making its way north. By September 13, they were camped at Fray Cristóbal, in the heart of the Jornada del Muerto, and were re-united with Governor Otermín and the survivors of the Rio Arriba. When the Spanish retreated south along the Camino Real, Piro and Tompiro Indians joined the Isletan Tiwa on the road to El Paso del Norte where all were re-settled in a series of new missions. Why Isleta did not participate in the revolt, and why so many Tiwa fled south with the Spanish, remains unexplained. Some historians have argued that the loyalties of the Isleta Tiwa had been suspect, and that Popé (the organizer of the revolt), intentionally did not include them in the rebellion. Others have pointed out that when the revolt began, Spanish soldiers were already present at Isleta, deterring any planned or spontaneous attacks. Were the Isletans "friendly" Indians, loyal to the Church and the Crown, or captives taken south against their will and re-settled in the Pass of the North? Or were they acting expediently, following the Spanish because they were comfortable in their world and offered a degree of protection from the rebellion?[60]Not all of the Tiwa joined the Spanish. Some scattered as the fighting intensified and others escaped. A few Tiwa remained behind, hiding in the vicinity of the pueblo. Others fled north to Sandia Pueblo and west into the Hopi lands.[61]

Governor Otermín attempted to re-conquer northern New Mexico the next year. The Spanish secured a few sites, but Pueblo rebels held firm at many of the old mission settlements. Some Indians who had remained behind and re-occupied Isleta (mostly Tiwas and Piros) offered little resistance when Otermín established a camp at the pueblo. A few hoped that the Spanish might offer some protection from rival natives in the region, but others were anxious about their return. Otermín found the church and convent had been destroyed and burned. Crosses were scattered around the village, and the churchyard was being used as a cowpen. Isletans blamed the destruction on Northern Tiwa and Tewa Indians who had raided the site.[62] As Spaniards ventured into nearby settlements, they faced intense resistance and gained little ground, and, by January 1682, Otermín realized that another full-scale attack was eminent. He ordered a retreat south and when the Spanish fled they burned Isleta Pueblo and took 511 captives. Along the way, 126 escaped. The rest were taken down the Camino Real and placed near El Paso del Norte at Ysleta del Sur.[63] It will never be known exactly how many Tiwas were loyal to the Spanish, how many were forcibly brought south, and how many were simply trying to avoid being caught up in conflict.

Ten years later, Vargas found Isleta deserted and most of the mission in ruins, but by 1710 Fray Juan de la Peña had gathered scattered Tiwa from surrounding communities and established Mission *San Agustín de la Isleta*, Saint Augustine of the Little Island, named for the fourth-century bishop of Hippo, who served as its patron saint. Some of the returning Tiwa had fled west after the revolt and brought Hopi wives back to the pueblo, which added a new cultural dimension to the settlement. Isleta also had a growing Spanish and mestizo population in the eighteenth century.[64] In 1776, Fray Domínguez described the pueblo as a community of "three beautiful blocks of dwellings" located in front of the church and convent, with a very large plaza to the south. Outside of the plaza were newer houses "very prettily designed," made of adobe, but of Spanish, rather than Pueblo, design. He observed extensive agriculture around the village, including fields of wheat, maize, green vegetables, and orchards of fruits and vineyards. Livestock grazed in the lands along the river. Domínguez counted 114 families at Isleta, with a total population of 454 people.[65] Nineteenth-century

Anglo-Americans often visited Isleta Pueblo. Wislizenus described it as a "small village, with its church, green fields, and cluster of cotton and orchard trees, [which] looks quite picturesque in the desert around us."[66]

Squaws of Isleta, New Mexico, c.1880–1890. Ben Wittick, Courtesy Palace of the Governors Photo Archives (NMHM/DCA), Neg. No. 015917.

John Gregory Bourke, a United States Army captain who toured many of the pueblos of the Southwest and wrote prolifically of his experiences, visited Isleta in November 1881. He found it to have a significant amount of Hispanic influence, comparing it more to a plaza settlement than the pueblos he had seen further north.[67] Bourke viewed the church and was also welcomed into the ceremonial kiva which he described as a circular, plastered structure above ground. Heavy pine beams supported an earthen roof, antelope horns were hung along the walls, and a central fireplace provided heat and light.[68] The Atchison, Topeka, and Santa Fe Railway came through Isleta in 1880, making the pueblo a popular destination for rail travelers. It gained further fame through the writings of Charles F. Lummis, an eccentric newspaperman who lived there in the 1880s and had unprecedented access to some of the sacred sites and ceremonies of the pueblo.

In the twentieth century, Isleta Pueblo maintained many of its cultural, spiritual, and social traditions. Today, approximately 3,200 Isletans live on the more than 200,000 acres of reservation land around the old pueblo. Agriculture is still an important source of income, but many tourists visit Isleta, and the area is now well-integrated into the Albuquerque economy. The centerpiece is the Saint Augustine Church which faces the pueblo's large central plaza and may be the oldest continually used church in the United States. During the eighteenth century, repairs and improvements were made to the church. Major renovations were carried out after the 1850s as Territorial, and, later, Gothic and Anglo-American features, were integrated into the structure. The facade was re-plastered and two wooden towers were added at the east and west end of the church. Boards covered the bare wooden floors and new icons and fixtures were placed throughout the interior. By the 1920s, a tin roof and prominent Gothic turrets were added, making the church an eclectic mixture of designs and styles. After 1959, the church was restored to a more cohesive, traditional adobe-style as many of the Gothic exterior features, such as the pitched roof, wooden steeples, crosses and spires, were removed. Cement plaster was applied to the exterior walls and belfries.[69]

The structures in the immediate area of the church are the heart of the old seventeenth-century village. Spreading east, west, and south of the plaza are later residences dating from the last three centuries. Most reflect the simple one-story, adobe-style linear dwellings that were common in pueblo villages.

Isleta's great kiva, a single, round structure south of the main plaza, is reserved for rituals and ceremonial dances, and is typical of Rio Grande Pueblo kivas. It is entered from the top, down through a ladder.[70] Isletans have tribal and social divisions common to many of the Rio Grande pueblos. Isleta Tiwa have both patrilineal and matrilineal traditions, but men have customarily held more power and prestige in the pueblo. Aside from the family, children are placed in Corn groups, social and ceremonial associations that guard and promote rituals and ceremonies in the pueblo. Children are also members of moieties and are alternately placed in the father's or mother's moiety. As a member of a moiety, they are responsible for participating in and preserving tribal rituals, especially an annual dance. Two medicine societies also serve the pueblo.[71]

Tiwa is still spoken throughout the reservation, although English is the most commonly used language. In the mid-twentieth century, there was another revival of pottery, turquoise, silver, and gemstone traditions. Today, artisans from the pueblo produce a variety of fine vessels and jewelry, available in shops around the pueblo and in area galleries. Isleta Pueblo remains a popular tourist destination, especially in the summer months. The inner core of the settlement remains much as it was in centuries past, and, as a well-preserved village, it was added to the National Register of Historic Places in 1975. The main celebration at Isleta Pueblo is on August 28, the feast day of Saint Augustine. A harvest festival follows in the early days of September.

Los Padillas

From Isleta Pueblo, the two branches of the Camino Real continued north. The west bank trail followed today's Isleta Boulevard, NM 314. Los Padillas was a tiny, eighteenth-century agricultural village, just north of the Isleta Pueblo boundary. According to local tradition, the Padilla family farmed there in the mid-seventeenth century and returned in the 1690s after the re-conquest of New Mexico. The Padillas settlement was formally established sometime before 1790, and, soon after, many members of the Chaves clan also moved to the village. By the end of the century, *San Andrés de los Padillas*, Saint Andrew of the Padillas, was home to about 170 people, who tended family farm plots and grazed sheep and cattle in the surrounding fields. The village supported a number of carders, spinners, and weavers. Trade in wool, cloth, hides, and livestock along the

Camino Real created a local merchant elite, and several Padillas and Chaveses lived a comfortable life on their estates, using the titles of *don* and *doña* and housing Indian domestic servants.[72] Nothing remains of the original colonial era settlement. Although Los Padillas has some examples of Spanish Colonial and Pueblo Revival architecture, most of the houses and structures along Isleta Boulevard are typical of early twentieth-century Anglo-American architecture that came to the area with the railroad.[73]

Pajarito

Just north of Los Padillas on Isleta Boulevard is *Pajarito*, the Little Bird. The origins of the name are not clear, but it may refer to birds in the cottonwood groves along the river. References to the Pajarito site date back to 1643 when the resident priest at Isleta Pueblo obtained a small ranch site a few miles north of the Tiwa village. A 1659 document mentions a cattle ranch in the same area, and a 1663 trial before the Inquisition in Mexico City described a violent dispute over the estancia of "Paxarito." Pajarito also became a common Tiwa Indian surname.[74] The García family, probably descendants of Andrés de García of El Paso del Norte, starting raising livestock along the river by the late eighteenth century, and the site became known as *Puesto de San Isidro de Pajarito*, the Post of Saint Isidore of the Little Bird. Saint Isidore (San Ysidro or San Isidro) was a twelfth century laborer and the Spanish patron saint of farmers.[75]

Although abandoned during the 1680 Pueblo Revolt, a few people returned to the area by the early years of the eighteenth century. The Baca family acquired title to the land in the 1740s, but within ten years much of the Pajarito grant, including Los Padillas and Pajarito, had been passed to Clemente Gutiérrez, whose family herded sheep and cattle along the river. By 1790, it had 145 residents and was formally noted as *San Ysidro de Paxarito*. Good pastureland along the west bank led to a thriving business in hides, meats, and wool products. Similar to Los Padillas, Pajarito was home to carders, spinners, and weavers who processed the wool and made homespun cloth that was sold and traded in nearby settlements. Don José Mariano de la Peña, a Mexico City entrepreneur, married into the Gutiérrez family and became the area's main merchant, trading goods along the Camino Real. Pajarito also had a number of residents using the title of *don* or *doña*. In fact, Pajarito had numerous families with servants, including Apaches, Utes, and Comanches, who were purchased or traded through the custom of *rescate* (a charitable rescue). Some were in-house domestics, and others were listed as heads of households who worked as laborers for the Baca and Gutiérrez families.[76]

Pajarito's best known historic site is the Gutiérrez-Hubbell House, located at 6029 Isleta Boulevard. The large Territorial-style home and ten-acre site have been restored and expanded in recent years and represent New Mexico's nineteenth-century agricultural and commercial heritage. Sections of the house date from about 1825 when it was built by the Gutiérrez family. In 1849 James L. Hubbell (known as don Santiago), who had come west during the Mexican-American War, married into the Gutiérrez family. His bride, Julianita Gutiérrez, was the young daughter of a prosperous trading and ranching family whose lineage included the Baca and Chaves clans. Hubbell developed extensive commercial connections with the east and organized freighting caravans from Kansas into New Mexico. After James and Julianita were married, they enlarged the home, adding a hall and parlor, five rooms on the north end, and kitchen, dining, and pantry facilities on the southwest. As their family grew and their businesses expanded, they built corrals, storage rooms, a retail store, and a post office. By 1900, the massive Territorial home was the showpiece of the region, the site of many social and political functions.

The Gutiérrez-Hubbell House in Pajarito, along Isleta Boulevard, the path of the Camino Real de Tierra Adentro

James died in 1885, but Julianita lived at the site until 1899. The Gutiérrez-Hubbell House was added to the New Mexico State Register of Cultural Properties in 1976. Hubbell descendants resided at the home until the 1990s, but in 2000 Bernalillo County purchased the property. Collapsed walls, doors, and windows were repaired and replaced. A new roof was added, and the exterior walls were extensively repaired. Today, the house is a blend of traditional adobe construction, with simple doors and windows visible in the south wing, and Territorial features and a sprawling front porch. The 5,800 square-foot residence sits on a rural site which now includes cultivated farmland and the development of the natural environment. The old irrigation system has been restored, and wildlife has returned to the site. Vineyards and orchards, and fields of oats, alfalfa, and chili surround the property. In 2008, the Gutiérrez-Hubbell House was designated as a certified site along the Camino Real de Tierra Adentro National Historic Trail, and the next year some of the first federal trail signage was erected on the property. A New Mexico Highway Department Camino Real marker telling the story of Pajarito is located on Isleta Boulevard.

Atrisco

Atrisco is just north of Pajarito, on the west bank. The name Atrisco is derived from the Nahuatl word *atlixco*, which refers to a body of water, and may have been carried north by Indians from the valley of Atlixco in central Mexico.[77] Pedro Gómez Durán y Chaves came to New Mexico with the 1598 Oñate expedition. His eldest son, Fernando Durán y Chaves I, inherited his father's encomienda grant and served as the lieutenant governor, overseeing the Rio Abajo district. By 1680, the Durán y Chaves family had settled in the area and the family's landholdings extended from Atrisco north to San Felipe Pueblo.

During the 1680 Pueblo Revolt, Atrisco was abandoned and the Durán y Chaves family fled New Mexico. One member, Fernando Durán y Chaves II, a native-born New Mexican, returned with Vargas in 1692 and requested two tracts of land that his family had occupied prior to the revolt. The two requests were granted and Durán y Chaves formally received possession in 1703.[78] One tract was at San Antonio de Angostura, near the narrows of the Rio Grande and the Rio Santa Ana, and a second was at Atrisco.[79] Atrisco became a small village of individually-owned land grants that spread along the river valley and became known as *Ranchos de Atrisco*. Farmers produced enough corn, beans, wheat, and alfalfa for the community's needs. The ranching boundaries were often vague, and Atrisqueños used common grazing lands west of town to herd sheep and other livestock. Apache and Navajo raids, especially in the 1770s, limited growth.[80] A 1790 census listed Spanish residents as ranchers, farmers, and weavers. Mestizos and genízaros were noted as laborers, shoemakers, shepherds, and carpenters. By the early nineteenth century, Atrisco had four principal plazas, named after families who inhabited separate areas of the grant: Nuestra Señora de Guadalupe de los Garcías, San Fernando de los Chaves, San José de los Sánchez and San Andrés de los Ranchos de Atrisco.[81]

Land was frequently divided, subdivided, and transferred among the extended families of the district, especially the Durán y Chaves, Sánchez, and Baca clans. By the late eighteenth century, many of the original surveys and documents had been misplaced or destroyed. There was occasional litigation involving disputes among family members and neighbors, especially over boundaries, water, and grazing rights. Most community land rights were honored during the Mexican era, but during the Territorial period Atrisco became the center of lengthy and controversial disputes. The Court of Private Land Claims acknowledged the original 1692 grant and recognized it as a community grant, rather than a private one, vesting residents with certain legal and economic rights. The town of Atrisco was incorporated in 1892, and 82,728 acres were formally surveyed and confirmed by a US patent in 1905. In the first decades of the twentieth century, grazing and agriculture still dominated the area, but, by the 1930s, other activities began to encroach on the Atrisco site. Oil and gas drilling, right-of-way easements for US 66, ash mining, and the development of a small regional airport led to lease arrangements with the Town of Atrisco.[82]

The legal question was whether an heir to the grant owned a specific amount of land and was entitled to lease it, sell it, or give it away, or whether the Town of Atrisco held the land in trust for them. Several rulings re-asserted that Atrisco was a community grant and did not allow for the individual parceling of land for lease, sale, or gifting. Most efforts to distribute and sell parcels of land during the 1950s were blocked by the courts.[83] By the mid-1960s, state law permitted community land-grant corporations that could distribute stock and dividends to heirs. Townships were often ordered to relinquish authority over community land grants to these new corporations. In 1968, the owners and heirs of the original Atrisco land grant incorporated as the Westland Development Company, a publicly held company created to manage the vast tracts of unoccupied land in the original grant. The heirs to the Atrisco grant became shareholders and received a stake relative to the amount of land their families once owned. By the early years of the twenty-first century, pressure to allow the expansion of Albuquerque west was mounting, and Westland considered proposals to open Atrisco to more extensive, planned development. In December 2006, the heirs of Atrisco voted to sell their shares to SunCal Companies, a community development corporation, which would oversee a new series of well-planned residential, business, and recreational projects in the area. An Atrisco Heritage Foundation was created, to be funded at 1,000,000 dollars annually, to preserve and promote local heritage and culture and provide essential services to the community. In December 2006, under the new terms of incorporation, one of the last surviving Spanish land grants came to an end.[84]

Today, much of Atrisco is a suburban extension of Albuquerque, indistinguishable from the growth along Bridge Street on the west side of the river. The older section of the village is north of Bridge Street, hemmed in between Atrisco and Foothills Drive. The original acequia, paralleled by an old branch road of the Camino Real, winds through a secluded area just below the mesa. There are still a few small agricultural properties in Atrsico, but industrial, commercial, and residential development and housing are rapidly encroaching on the community. A number of modest adobe houses are strung out along the acequia remains, and a nineteenth-century cemetery, just at the foot of the mesa, is enclosed by a colorfully muraled wall and contains many unmarked headstones. Some are encased in iron fences; others are simply wooden markers. New housing developments loom above the mesa, overlooking the old colonial site. Some of Atrsico's land became part of Petroglyph National Monument, a 7,200-acre site opened in 1990 and managed by the National Park Service.

Housing developments loom over the old cemetery and eighteenth-century community of Atrisco.

Barelas

Barelas is north of Isleta Pueblo, on the east bank and the main colonial route of the Camino Real de Tierra Adentro, opposite Atrisco. The Varelas family settled there in the 1660s and remained until the 1680 Pueblo Revolt In 1707, one year after Albuquerque was founded, some of the family returned to the site.[85] The Barelas river ford connected the Camino Real with a series of cart and wagon roads along the west bank that led to Atrsico and Corrales, or south to Los Padillas and Pajarito.[86] At the Barelas ford, horses and mules dragged wagons through the water or swam alongside their cargo as it was floated across. The unpredictable waters of the Rio Grande often made river crossings difficult, dangerous, and sometimes impossible. In 1856, Major James Carleton, commander of the American military post at Albuquerque, established the area's first ferry service at the Barelas ford, near today's Barelas Street Bridge. The ferry hauled people, farm goods, livestock, wagons, and stagecoaches through the muddy waters.[87]

When the Atchison, Topeka, and Santa Fe Railway arrived in Albuquerque in 1880, it brought major changes to the small farming village of Barelas. The tracks followed the old river channel at the east edge of the valley, dissecting the farmland and cutting it off from the acequia system. The railroad brought opportunities as the nearby Atchison, Topeka, and Santa Fe yards and shops employed many new workers, including Mexican, German, and other immigrants from the east coast. Almost 900 men were employed in the immediate area, and the small farming village tripled in size. Unlike many small rural villages of the Rio Abajo, Barelas was intersected by a grid of new roads and rapidly developed in the late 1800s. It quickly became a crowded industrial neighborhood, a working-class area of downtown Albuquerque.[88]

The village of Barelas was wedged between the Rio Grande and the railroad tracks, and, today, little remains of the older, southern section of the town except for a few nineteenth-century adobe buildings. Further north along Barelas Road, once the main thoroughfare, are many structures from the late nineteenth-and early-twentieth century railroad era. "Shotgun" houses (small, simple, inexpensive houses that were one-room wide and two-to-three-rooms deep) and larger Victorian-style homes (the residences of railroad supervisors and the new commercial elite), can be found between 2nd and 7th Streets.[89] In recent years, Barelas has experienced a revival, and several major initiatives have helped preserve and celebrate the neighborhood's rich history. The National Hispanic Cultural Center, located at 1701 4th Street SW, opened its doors in 2000 and has hosted a variety of exhibits, concerts, and performances that promote Hispanic culture, arts, and humanities. One of the first exhibits showcased the development of Barelas.

El Camino Real through the Albuquerque Area.

Albuquerque

In the mid-seventeenth century, Francisco de Trujillo and his wife Doña Luisa farmed a small tract of land along the east bank, in a cottonwood bosque, near today's Old Town Albuquerque. After Francisco passed away in the 1670s and left the farm to his wife, the site became known as the *Hacienda de Doña Luisa de Trujillo*, and the thick grove of cottonwoods was called the *Bosque Grande de Doña Luisa*.[90] The area was abandoned during the 1680 Pueblo Revolt, and the survivors joined the García and Otermín refugee parties as they escaped south. On April 23, 1706, New Mexico Governor Francisco Cuervo y Valdés informed the Crown and royal officials in Mexico City that he had founded a new villa, and a few days later he wrote to the Viceroy, Francisco Fernández de la Cueva, Duke of Alburquerque. Governor Cuervo stated that the villa had been established in accordance with the Royal Laws of the Indies and was duly sworn. He reported that thirty-five families, consisting of 252 adults and children, were residing at the new township and that a church, priest's residence, and *casas reales*, or government buildings, were under construction. The villa and church honored San Francisco Xavier, a sixteenth-century Spanish Jesuit missionary and saint, who had spent most of his life in Asia and the Pacific, and was known as the Apostle of the Indies. Ten soldiers from the presidio at Santa Fe had been dispatched to escort the settlers down the trail and stand guard at the villa.[91]

The founding of Alburquerque, as described in documents prepared by New Mexico Governor Francisco Cuervo y Valdés, was based in fact, but was actually quite an exaggeration. Questions were raised early on, and by 1712 Alburquerque was still a small settlement with little apparent growth. It did not appear to match Cuervo's glowing description, and an official investigation was undertaken. Testimony revealed that in fact far fewer people had settled at the villa and that many of the legal requirements had been overlooked or ignored. There were perhaps nineteen founding families, no more than 130 people altogether. The villa was essentially a series of farms spread out along the river, not the organized urban settlement hinted at in Cuervo's reports.[92]

Many years passed before the settlement expanded. In 1732, New Mexico's governor announced that the annual trade caravan would begin assembling at Albuquerque each fall, with a military escort, before beginning its trip south down the Camino Real de Tierra Adentro. This created a burst of commercial activity in Alburquerque's plaza during the autumn months. Area residents became carders, weavers, and spinners, and sheep ranching boomed and livestock trade increased. Coopers, blacksmiths, and shoemakers traded their wares on the plaza, and New Mexican goods made their way along the royal road to missions and mining centers in the south. Even so, in 1776, the villa still lagged behind El Paso del Norte and Santa Fe. Fray Domínguez described it as a fairly modest settlement of small ranchos and hamlets scattered along the river. He noted 157 families living in the villa.[93]

During the Mexican era, the Santa Fe and Chihuahua trails brought additional commercial activity to Alburquerque. The population of the old villa doubled to almost 1,500 people, and the number of craftsmen and merchants increased substantially. By the 1840s, a few families, such as the Armijos, had dominated the local mercantile economy. Vicente Armijo had been involved in commercial activities since the 1790s and his sons expanded his businesses. The Armijos emerged as a commercial and political elite, and built some of the most impressive homes around the church. In September 1846, American troops under General Kearny marched into Albuquerque and took the villa without opposition. At first, the arrival of American troops frightened residents, but many soon benefitted from the occupation. The army finally provided protection from Indian raids; soldiers spent money, and new businesses developed to serve the military's needs. The Armijos, Montoyas, and Bacas expanded their commercial operations and amassed considerable wealth during the 1850s.

Albuquerque continued to grow in the 1860s and 1870s and became an important agricultural outlet for the American West. Anglo-Americans dropped the first "r" in the name and called the town Albuquerque. Links to herding trails, new military roads, and stagecoach routes that followed the path of the Camino Real increased its connections to California, Texas, and the East, but the greatest change for the old villa was the coming of the railroad. When engineers surveyed the route in 1879, they followed a straight line through the eastern edge of the valley, about one and one-half miles east of the plaza. Local entrepreneurs scrambled to buy up land in the east and develop roads and services around the new depot and yards. A "New Town" was already booming when the Atchison, Topeka, and Santa Fe laid its last rails at the site in April 1880. The commercial and new industrial base of the city followed, and New Town's population boomed. Old Town remained an important link on the wagon and stagecoach roads, but the entirely new city in the east quickly eclipsed the old villa site.

Old Town became an isolated, archaic village, cut-off from much of the new boomtown action. Anglo-American New Town repeatedly outbid, outspent, and outmaneuvered Hispanic Old Town. Old Town tried to compete, but business waned, shops closed, and people sought work in the booming neighborhoods along the railroad. Some of the old Hispanic elite, such as the Armijos and Bacas, seized the opportunity and became part of the new commercial and political world of New Town. Working-class New Mexicans had new opportunities as urban, commercial industrial work offered better prospects and a chance to break free of the life of an agricultural laborer. Old Town and New Town followed very different paths of development in the twentieth century. Old Town languished as a nineteenth-century Hispanic, Catholic area with narrow, unpaved streets and low adobe houses and shops, standing in sharp contrast to the booming city in the east. In the 1930s, a small artist colony emerged in Old Town, inspired by the influence of Taos and Santa Fe. To a degree, Old Town benefited from being near the main east-west thoroughfare, Central Avenue and US 66.

The Second World War brought even greater growth and expansion as military training, wartime industries, aviation, and research created a population explosion and a surge of development further east. From 35,000 residents in 1940, Albuquerque reached a population of more than 175,000 by 1955. A wave of suburban developments, shopping centers, and commercial outlets pushed right up to the Sandia Mountains. Old Town remained outside of the city limits until 1949, but a renewed interest in the old villa followed annexation. The plaza area was declared a historic zone in 1957, and a wave of rebuilding and renovation followed. The quaint artist-hangouts of the 1930s became the curio shops and tourist centers of the 1960s.[94]

The colonial Villa de Alburquerque was centered in today's Old Town, just east of the Rio Grande, near Central Avenue and Rio Grande Boulevard. The most prominent structure on the plaza is the San Felipe de Neri Church. The first church was built early in the eighteenth century on the west side of the plaza and was dedicated to San Francisco Xavier, but shortly after the villa was founded its patron saint became *San Felipe Neri*, Saint Philip Neri, the sixteenth-century Roman founder of the Oratorians, an informal organization of priests and lay-brothers.[95] After a series of heavy rains in 1790, the building collapsed, and work was begun on the present church, on the north side of the plaza. It was completed three years later. It had a basic cruciform design and a set of twin towers alongside the front façade. By the 1850s, the church had two large bell towers that dominated the single-story homes and shops around the plaza. A new roof, front entrance, floorboards, paintings, pulpit, and sanctuary were also added. Many renovations took place in the 1870s as Italian Jesuits introduced a "folk" Gothic-style to the church. A new front entrance was added, and wooden towers were squared with Gothic-style moldings, louvered windows, and trim. Elaborate wood and tin-work was completed throughout the interior.

The entire parish-complex blended with the new Anglo-American design of the plaza, with white picket fences and a bandstand. San Felipe Neri has been well maintained over the last 130 years. The church was added to the National Register of Historic Places in 1969. A small parish museum is dedicated to the historic church. Although it has lost most of its colonial-era appearance, it is the best remaining example of the drastic Victorian-era renovations that were made to New Mexican churches in the Territorial period.[96] The Rectory, an Italianate-style building just east of the church, was also constructed in the 1790s. The inner adobe-core was a long, one-story, rectangular structure when it was first built as a home for the parish priest. Major changes were made in the 1880s, as a second story, gabled roof, brick façade, and Queen Anne features were added.[97]

The oldest houses, with the fewest alterations, lie southeast of the plaza along Romero and San Felipe Streets, above Lomas Boulevard. There are examples of row houses, long, adobe-based structures with single or double rooms that over the years have been expanded and modified. The Armijos were the most prominent residents. They came to New Mexico with José de Armijo of Zacatecas in 1695. By the mid-eighteenth century, his descendants were farming in the Middle Rio Grande Valley. His grandson, Vicente Ferrer Armijo, was a prosperous rancher who owned land around the villa in the 1790s. Vicente married into the Chávez family, and, with his wife Bárbara, raised eight sons who became militia leaders, merchants, and political figures during the Mexican era. The best known of the sons was Manuel Armijo, who served as the province's last governor under Mexican rule and played a role in many of the conflicts of the 1830s and 1840s, including the Texan-Santa Fe Expedition, and the Mexican War. Manuel, and his brothers Ambrosio and Juan, were pioneer merchants in the Santa Fe Trail trade.

The brothers, cousins, and later their descendants had become some of the wealthiest of Albuquerque's commercial elite by the 1860s. Juan Cristóbal Armijo, the governor's nephew, ran a large store on the southeast corner of the plaza and lived on today's San Felipe Street. Salvador Armijo operated freight and commercial outlets throughout the Territory. In the 1850s, Manuel and Rafael, cousins of the governor, had the largest store of goods in Albuquerque. Casa Armijo, at 200 San Felipe Street, dates to the 1840s and is the best example of a classic, Territorial building in Old Town. It was built as the home of Ambrosio Armijo who dominated many of the trade, freighting, and merchandising enterprises along the Chihuahua Trail. It was built as a traditional, square, placita-style structure with frame portales and a large zaguán.

The Armijo family had businesses and residences throughout Old Town in the nineteenth century but it is not always clear who lived where. Casa Armijo is often confused with Governor Manuel Armijo's lavish hacienda further south, which was razed in 1909. In the 200 block of San Felipe Street is the sprawling Ambrosio Armijo House and Store which dates from the early 1880s. It was once connected by a walkway to Casa Armijo. The House and Store incorporated features typical of the 1880s including a gabled roof and porch. It has been a popular New Mexican-cuisine restaurant for the past 80 years. The large, two-story house on South Plaza was the home of Cristóbal Armijo, a wealthy capitalist, who invested in agriculture, banking, and merchandising. Built as a Queen Anne-style home in the 1880s, it was modified in the Pueblo Revival tradition during the 1950s.[98] The Albuquerque Museum of Art and History, just east of Old Town on Mountain Road, is dedicated to the preservation, study, and celebration of the city's history and the greater history of the Middle Rio Grande Valley.

Los Duránes

North of the villa, the Camino Real followed the path of today's Edith Boulevard, and an alternate route, closer to the river, paralleled today's Guadalupe Trail. Both wound through a series of small agricultural hamlets, settled by extended families in the eighteenth century, each with their own unique character. The first hamlet was Los Duránes, the home of the Durán family, established sometime before 1790 near today's interstate. Not much remains of old Los Duránes except for an occasional nineteenth-century building or an adobe segment that has been incorporated into a later, modern structure. Commercial development has destroyed much of the southern part of Los Duránes, but north of the interstate there are still areas that are semi-agricultural, with a few old farming structures, houses, fields, and irrigations ditches evident. Los Duránes Chapel is at 2601 Indian School Road, west of Rio Grande Boulevard. The small square adobe church, with a wooden steeple sitting atop a pitched metal roof, is located in the old village center. The modest, two-room building was originally a house but was donated to the parish around 1885 and remained in use until the 1960s. After years of neglect, the small chapel was renovated and added to the National Register of Historic Places in 1984. Just east of Rio Grande Boulevard, at Indian School Road, is a popular local restaurant, a large adobe Territorial-style house that dates from the mid-nineteenth century, although it has been extensively remodeled over the last one hundred years. It has irregular adobe walls and windows, a flat roof with exposed vigas, low narrow doors, and a wooden floor.[99] Local tradition identifies the site as a stagecoach stop on the road to Santa Fe.

Los Duránes Chapel, just east of Rio Grande Boulevard, at Indian School Road.

Los Candelarias

Los Candelarias is just north of Los Duránes. The old village center was near Rio Grande Boulevard and Candelaria Road, but settlement eventually extended east to Edith Boulevard. Los Candelarias may have been founded as early as the 1750s but is first documented in the 1790 census in which twenty-six families are listed as living in the *Plaza de Los Candelarias*, with six households headed by a Candelaria. Two of the Candelaria families were prosperous enough to own servants. Today, the only surviving building in the area is Los Candelarias Chapel, also known as the San Antonio Chapel, located at 1934 Candelaria Road. It was built as a one-room church in the mid-nineteenth century but has been remodeled and is currently a private residence. The small adobe building has typical Territorial characteristics, such as window moldings and a gabled roof, and was probably constructed after the 1870s. The chapel was added to the National Register of Historic Places in 1984.

Los Griegos

The heart of the old village of Los Griegos was along today's Griegos Road, between Rio Grande Boulevard and Guadalupe Trail. In the nineteenth century, the settlement spread east toward Edith Boulevard. About 1708, Juan Griego received a land grant for his service in the re-conquest of New Mexico, and by 1750 his descendants founded Los Griegos. The 1790 census listed twenty-five families living in the *Plaza de Nuestra Señora del Guadalupe de los Griegos*, the Plaza of Our Lady of Guadalupe of the Griegos. There were probably never more than twenty-five buildings in Los Griegos in the eighteenth century, and most of the village was washed away in mid-nineteenth-century flooding. It remained a small agricultural hamlet, and by the 1840s much of land around the village came under the control of the Armijo family. Only one Greigo, José Tomás, a grocer, was noted as having any significant wealth in 1860. When the railroad arrived, Los Griegos still had only about 300 residents.[100] Even so, some of the structures in the 1800 and 1900 block of Los Griegos Road and the 1500 and 1600 block of Guadalupe Trail may have surviving segments that date from the Mexican or early American-Territorial era.[101]

Today, what remains of old Los Griegos lies within the boundaries of the Los Griegos Historic District, added to the National Register in 1984. Los

Griegos Chapel, at 1838 Griego Road NW, was built in the 1840s as a simple, box-like adobe building. In 1885, it was remodeled in the Gothic Revival style with a steeply pitched metal roof, bell towers, and pointed crowns. It was originally dedicated to San Isidro but was later called Our Lady of Guadalupe Church. The chapel has been restored and renovated in the late twentieth century and now serves as a private residence.[102] Other properties in the district are built from fragments of older structures or bear a resemblance to the styles of the nineteenth century.

Los Griegos Chapel, now a private residence, in the heart of Los Griegos Historic District.

Los Ranchos de Albuquerque

From Los Griegos, the Camino Real de Tierra Adentro continued north to *Los Ranchos de Albuquerque*, the Ranches, a continuation of small farms settled during the eighteenth century. In 1694, Captain Diego Montoya applied for a 70,000 acre land grant between the Rio Grande and the crest of the Sandia Mountains, extending from today's Griegos Road north to El Pueblo Road.

Twelve years later, Antonio Montoya, Diego's brother, conveyed the grant to Elena Gallegos, a family member, and it became known as the Elena Gallegos Grant. When Elena Gallegos died in 1731, her only child, Antonio Gurulé, became the sole heir to her estate and lived on the property until his death in 1761. During the remainder of the century, the descendants of Elena Gallegos, and her son, Antonio, divided the land into small ranchos, narrow strips of land that fronted the river and ran eastward to the mountains. Much of the grant remained open common land used by all the settlers. Over time, these lands were further divided and became known by extended family names such as Los Gallegos or Los Montoyas.[103]

In the 1780s, three plaza settlements, Los Poblanos, Los Gallegos, and Plaza de Señor de San José de los Ranchos, became collectively known as *Los Ranchos* and were located along today's Rio Grande Boulevard. The first hamlet was *Los Poblanos*, named for a family who came from Puebla, Mexico, in the eighteenth century, and settled near today's Montano Road. *Los Gallegos* was named for the Gallegos family, and was located east of Los Poblanos, near today's Grecian Avenue.[104] The largest of the three sites was *Plaza de Señor de San José de los Ranchos*, listed in church records by 1783, and located along today's Rio Grande Boulevard, between Chaves and Green Valleys Roads. Later, it became known simply as Los Ranchos. Another settlement, *Los Garcías*, named for the García family, was founded further north in the 1850s, closer to El Pueblo Road. In the early nineteenth century, Los Ranchos remained the largest of the plaza settlements north of Albuquerque with 330 people.[105]

After the Mexican-American War, Los Ranchos profited from United States military activity in the region, and some landowners accumulated considerable wealth. Juan Cristóbal Armijo, a member of the Albuquerque Armijo family, owned thousands of acres in the area, especially around Los Poblanos and Los Gallegos. After the Civil War, Union troops helped control Navajo raids, and the North Valley's common grasslands were once again open to large flocks of sheep. Freight wagons helped transport wool along the old trail. When the railroad arrived, Los Ranchos prospered and had access to even greater markets in the eastern United States.[106] In 1874, a major flood destroyed most of the homes at Los Ranchos. Some stayed and rebuilt, but others moved north, closer to today's village center and Ranchitos Road. In 1884 and 1891, flooding damaged many of the new, rebuilt houses and weakened the church. The church survived until 1904, when it, and the remaining homes in the hamlet, were completely destroyed. This time, the last residents of the village of Los Ranchos abandoned the site, leaving it deserted.[107]

Later floods, and the leveling of land for farming, removed any traces of Los Ranchos from the surface by the mid-twentieth century. In 1996 and 1997, an archaeological survey was conducted at the site of the old Los Ranchos Plaza. The partial excavation and survey revealed a linear village, about one-quarter mile wide and one mile long. A large cobblestone patio or plaza, a rare architectural feature in this part of New Mexico, was also uncovered. On the north side of the plaza were the remains of a sizable house, or perhaps an inn, and several much smaller adobe residences were located further north. The ruins of the church were noted northwest of the site.[108]

Los Ranchos was a series of small eighteenth-century farms north of the villa.

Alameda

Alameda is just north of Los Ranchos, near today's Alameda Boulevard, in an area where the Rio Grande makes a sharp bend to the east. Alameda means cottonwood grove in Spanish, and the thick river bosque around the site is probably the origins of the name.[109] It was the site of a Tiwa pueblo and a seventeenth-century Franciscan mission with a church dedicated to Santa Ana, Saint Anne, the mother of Mary.[110] The Alameda Tiwa had a reputation for resisting Spanish rule, and in 1650 they conspired with their Navajo allies to rise up against the colonists. The revolt was quickly put down, and several Tiwa were hanged as traitors. As a result, in 1680, the Alameda Tiwa enthusiastically joined in the Pueblo Revolt, killing residents of the mission, driving the remaining Spaniards from the pueblo, and looting farms and ranches in the general vicinity. When Otermín's forces returned the next year, the Tiwa defiantly resisted. They were driven into the nearby mountains, and the remains of the pueblo and mission were burned.[111] In 1702, about fifty Tiwa who had scattered after the revolt were brought back to Alameda by Franciscan missionaries who attempted to re-build the village. In 1706, a new mission church was built and overseen by the friars from Bernalillo, but after a few years the village was abandoned and the remaining Alameda Tiwa were moved south to Isleta Pueblo.[112]

In 1710, Captain Francisco Montes Vigil received the Alameda Land Grant, a tract of more than 89,000 acres, in today's Bernalillo and Sandoval counties. Within two years he sold it to Captain Juan González Baz II, who had also returned with Vargas's army in 1692, and the González family settled on the grant and built a small chapel.[113] In 1776, Fray Domínguez described Alameda as a predominantly Spanish settlement with sixty-six families and 388 persons.[114] He also mentioned a chapel, dedicated to Our Lady of the Conception, built by Juan González, and cared for by his sons and grandsons. It was a small building, with a modest belfry and two little bells, facing south on to the property. Alongside the chapel was a cemetery. The chapel was apparently destroyed by the early nineteenth century and replaced by a second one, which faced east and survived until a flood in 1903. Today, Alameda is surrounded by the suburban growth of Albuquerque but has been able to preserve much of its rural, agricultural atmosphere, especially close to the river. The seventeenth-century mission was located somewhere near Rio

Grande and Alameda Boulevard, which was later the center of the eighteenth- and nineteenth-century villages, but in 1903, river flooding forced the village to move southeast to its present location.

Corrales

Corrales is just north of Alameda, on the west bank of the Rio Grande. A thirteenth-century Tiwa pueblo stood at the present village site, and there may have been a handful of pioneers there before the 1680 Pueblo Revolt, but Corrales was not formally settled until after 1700. Farmers moved onto a twenty-mile stretch along the Rio Grande where they grazed livestock and herded their horses in an area that became known as *Los Corrales de Alameda*, the Cottonwood Corrals.[115] By the early years of the eighteenth century, the González family acquired title to the west-bank grant and established a series of small farms and ranches along the river. Others moved into the area, expanding the irrigation system and opening up land for cattle and sheep grazing along the Rio Grande. In 1776, Fray Domínguez described two settlements at Corrales, both a series of ranchos along the sandy banks of the river with "not very good" land.[116] By 1805, about 300 people lived at Plaza de Corrales, a community near the river with houses clustered around a defensive plaza and church. Much of the land at Corrales was developed by the González family who intermarried with new settlers, including the Gutiérrez clan, and subdivided long tracts of land that fronted the river.[117] Few eighteenth-or early nineteenth-century travelers crossed over to visit the modest village or made note of it in their journals or reports.

A series of major floods plagued the region in the early nineteenth century and several deluges destroyed much of the original town site in the 1860s, including the central plaza and church. The Gutiérrez homestead, located farthest from the river on an elevated site, was one of the few to survive, so the family donated property for a new church, plaza, and cemetery southwest of the old village. The present Church of San Ysidro was built near the Gutiérrez house after 1865.[118] With the new village plaza and church now adjacent to their home, the Gutiérrez residence became an important gathering place for Corrales residents and enhanced their standing in the community. The period following the Civil War and the arrival of the railroad in the 1880s increased opportunities in Corrales and agricultural markets. The late nineteenth century brought European farmers into the area, especially Italian and French families who cultivated vineyards and orchards. In the early twentieth century, the common grazing-lands west of the village were purchased by cattle ranchers who spread their properties out on to the mesa. After the Second World War, a new bridge connected Corrales with the booming city of Albuquerque, but Corrales still remained agricultural and developed a reputation as a haven for artists and those escaping the new, fast pace of the city.

Casa San Ysidro is located on Old Church Road in the village center. The house is often called a colonial hacienda, but it was actually re-constructed in the Territorial style around a small nineteenth-century home built by the Gutiérrez family in the 1870s. During the 1890s, two large rooms were added later, creating an L-shaped facade. Historian Ward Alan Minge and his wife Shirley purchased the property in 1952 and began a major restoration and expansion of the house. Over the next thirty years, they added twenty-five rooms and storage areas. Following the outline of the foundation ruins, they used traditional construction techniques to expand the house, barn, and adobe walls. Many artifacts recovered from sites in the Rio Abajo were incorporated into the complex. Discarded carved portals, vigas from properties slated for demolition, and flooring (some dating back to the eighteenth century), were blended with contemporary materials to maintain a traditional look. The family collected Spanish and Mexican-era relics and artifacts that were used to furnish the interior. The Minges lived in the home until 1997 when it was opened to the public as an extension of the Albuquerque Museum. The museum, in cooperation with the Village of Corrales, oversees and maintains the site.[119]

Fray Domínguez did not mention a church in his 1776 report, but by 1800 a small adobe chapel was built at Corrales. It was destroyed during the 1864 flood, and today's San Ysidro Church was built on higher ground, further west and away from the river. It was typical of small nineteenth-century New Mexico village chapels; a one-story adobe building in a basic cruciform plan, with a simple bell gable. The church was substantially remodeled in the 1930s when twin bell towers were built on the front façade, a concrete skirting was added, and a pitched tin roof was laid over the old flat adobe one. The San Ysidro Church was deconsecrated in 1961, and it was modified and used as a theater for thirteen years until it was purchased by the Corrales Historical Society and donated to the village. Since the 1970s, the Society has maintained and managed the church, using it for cultural presentations, festivals, council meetings, and musical and artistic events. San Ysidro Church was placed on the National Register of Historic Places in 1980.[120]

Sandia Pueblo

NM 313 follows the path of the Camino Real de Tierra Adentro out of the Albuquerque area and into Sandia Pueblo, also known by its native Tiwa name, *Ná i ad*, meaning a dusty or sandy place. Archaeological evidence indicates that the site has been inhabited since the early fourteenth century. In 1617, the Mission of San Francisco, dedicated to Saint Francis, was established, and the Spanish called the site *Sandia*, or watermelon, probably referring to the reddish appearance of the Sandia Mountains at sunset.[121] Little is known of life at the mission in the mid-seventeenth century, but the Sandia Tiwa ransacked the pueblo and drove the Spanish from the village during the 1680 Pueblo Revolt. Sandia's missionaries escaped, but the church and surrounding structures were vandalized and razed during the revolt.[122] In the August retreat from Santa Fe, Governor Otermín found Sandia Pueblo deserted. The next year, when he attempted to re-conquer New Mexico, Otermín destroyed what little was left.[123]

In September 1742, two Franciscans traveled west into Hopi country to lure some of the Tiwa back to mission settlements in the Middle Rio Grande Valley. Much to their surprise, more than 440 Tiwa and Hopi expressed an interest and, in 1748, Lieutenant Governor Bernardo de Bustamante y Tagle formally granted land at Sandia. Fray Juan Miguel Menchero founded the new mission settlement, and Indian laborers and draft animals from surrounding Keres pueblos were used to re-build the old church in the 1750s.[124] The Hopi minority was soon absorbed and lost many of their cultural traditions, but, to this day, a kachina ceremony is performed at Sandia Pueblo each May 15, keeping a distinct Hopi cultural tradition alive in a Tiwa community.[125] Sandia has traditionally had two patron saints, Saint Anthony, venerated by the Indian community, and Our Lady of Sorrows, preferred by the residents at nearby Bernalillo who were served by the mission.[126] Fray Domínguez portrayed Sandia Pueblo as a poor, primitive settlement where a few Spanish and mostly Indian settlers, numbering less than 300, survived among the ruins.[127] The church was still unfinished, and work resumed in 1777. Materials from the pre-Revolt church were used to build the new one. It appears to have been completed sometime during the following decade and survived seventy years or so until it was destroyed by flooding. In 1864, a new church, with a simple cruciform design and a large bell over the front entrance, was built on a rise a few hundred feet from the old one. The church served the community for more than one hundred years and underwent a series of renovations which modernized its outward appearance. In 1976, it was restored, to more closely resemble its 1864 design.[128]

Captain John Bourke visited Sandia Pueblo in November 1881. He noted that the Tiwa raised corn, wheat, grapes, apples, beets, beans, and onions[129] and had abundant provisions of food stored for the winter. He saw strings of chile, and rooms piled high with blue and red corn, pumpkins, squashes and onions.[130] Horses, burros, mules, cattle, sheep, goats, chickens, dogs, and cats roamed the village. He also saw a variety of crafted goods traded at Sandia including selenite windows, Navajo bridles of silver, Hopi baskets, and American pails and tools.[131] Even so, the pueblo continued to decline, and, by 1900, Sandia was one of the smallest settlements in the area, with fewer than one hundred residents. It recovered somewhat, but even today less than 500 tribal members live on the Sandia Indian Reservation.

The old pueblo lies on an elevated site just east of NM 313. The present-day settlement has few visible remains from its colonial or nineteenth-century past. Sandia Pueblo maintains a traditional social and political organization.[132] The 1864 church and an early twentieth-century schoolhouse are near the western entrance to the village. The Sandia Tiwa operate the *Bien Mur* (or Big Mountain), Indian Market Center in northeast Albuquerque, the largest commercial Indian market in the American Southwest. It sells a large variety of Native-American arts and crafts and promoting Indian artists and designers. A festival for Saint Anthony takes place on each June 13 and is open to the public.

Bernalillo

The Camino Real de Tierra Adentro continued north along the path of NM 313 to Bernalillo, settled during the seventeenth century by descendants of Pascuala Bernal and her husband Juan Griego, who came north with the Oñate expedition in 1598. *Bernalillo*, or Little Bernal, probably refers to a member of the Bernal-González family who established a hacienda there before 1680. After the revolt, some of the family returned to the area, and three years later Bernalillo was listed as a *real*, or camp and headquarters,[133] established by Governor Vargas in 1695 as a defensive bulwark. Small land grants were given to families who worked the land and became self-sufficient farmers or ranchers. This replaced the seventeenth-century encomienda system that often harnessed Pueblo Indians as laborers. Colonists laid out a plaza and built a church dedicated to Saint Francis at the site. The first alcalde mayor was Fernando Durán y Chaves II who oversaw the entire Middle Rio Grande Valley and dispersed land grants to homesteaders who set up small farms and ranches in the area.[134] Although the new system of land tenure was designed to reduce tensions between Indians and settlers, in 1696 rumors circulated that a second rebellion was being planned. Durán y Chaves sensed trouble and moved his family and other settlers from Bernalillo to San Felipe Pueblo, high on the mesa, to be protected in the event of an attack. Once the 1696 rebellion was put down, Durán y Chaves and his people returned to Bernalillo.[135]

In March 1704, Governor Vargas led fifty Spanish soldiers and a contingent of Pueblo warriors through the Middle Rio Grande Valley in pursuit of Apaches who had been raiding settlements in the area. Vargas settled at Bernalillo, and, once again, used the town as his base of operations. During the campaign, an unknown epidemic plagued the troops, and several who became seriously ill were sent back to Santa Fe. A few days later, as Vargas led his men south along the trail, he became ill as well and called off the expedition. He was taken back to the headquarters in Bernalillo where his condition worsened. Durán y Chaves took the governor into his home where Vargas, on the verge of death, wrote his last will and testament. Governor Diego de Vargas died on April 8, 1704. A mass was said in the small Bernalillo church, and his body was returned to Santa Fe for burial.[136]

There was a modest chapel at Bernalillo, built about 1700. It attracted a few settlers in the early eighteenth century, but flooding washed away many of the homes, the church, and a small convent in the 1730s. In the mid-eighteenth century, there were references to both a church of *San Francisco*, or Saint Francis, and *Nuestra Señora de Dolores*, Our Lady of Sorrows. Forty years later, the settlement had only eighty residents.[137] Bernalillo seemed well-placed when plans were first made to bring the railroad to New Mexico. By 1880, there was a brief mining boom in the hills around Placitas, about eight miles east, and Bernalillo soon had mercantiles, inns, saloons, and a newspaper. There was a wild west frontier atmosphere in the town as fortunes were made and lost, and violence occasionally scarred the community. The railroad came, but the great boom never quite materialized. Instead, it moved a few miles south to Albuquerque. Within a few years, the mining also turned to bust.[138] Even so, about 1,000 people lived in Bernalillo by the turn of the century. During most of the twentieth century, Bernalillo has been hemmed in by Pueblo Indian lands and overshadowed by the growth of nearby Albuquerque. In more recent decades, it has grown substantially to more than 7,000 residents.

Camino del Pueblo (NM 313) follows the path of the old Camino Real through central Bernalillo today. The Abencio Salazar Historic District, placed on the National Register of Historic Places in 1979, is east of Camino del Pueblo in the northern end of the town. The district includes a rapidly dwindling number of examples of nineteenth-and early twentieth-century architecture. The structures are known for their straight walls, square corners, and generally massive construction. The Salazar family built major adobe building in the area from the 1860s until the 1940s.[139] Our Lady of Sorrows Church, located on Camino del Pueblo, is a large, cruciform-shaped church, made of adobe bricks and covered with brown stucco. It was constructed in 1857 and served the community for more than one hundred years. The church was renovated in 1892 with modifications typical of the day, including a metal roof, wooden brackets, round windows, and scored plastering to resemble brick. Our Lady of Sorrows has massive twenty-foot-high adobe walls, in some places more than four feet thick, resting on a stone foundation. It remained in use until 1971 when a new church, just to the south, was completed. Our Lady of Sorrows was added to the National Register in 1977.[140]

A popular story handed down over the centuries is that after returning to New Mexico, Governor Diego de Vargas made a holy vow to San Lorenzo and promised that his people would never forget that the 1680 Pueblo Revolt erupted on the August 10 feast day. The saint was thanked for saving the Spanish from destruction, allowing them to return to the north, and protecting them as they re-established the province. Over the years, ritual celebrations and dances have been held to honor Saint Lawrence, and each August 9–11 the town of Bernalillo holds a Fiesta de San Lorenzo, which they claim to be the "oldest continuous community celebration" in the state.[141]

Just west of Bernalillo, on US 550 across the river, is Coronado State Monument, named for Spanish conquistador Francisco Vásquez de Coronado, whose expedition camped near the site in the winter of 1540. The site contains a reconstruction of the pueblo of *Kuaua*, which means evergreen in ancient Tiwa.

Kuaua is typical of a pre-historic Pueblo village, a part of the Classical Period of the Anasazi Culture, which spanned the period 1325–1600 CE in northern New Mexico.

The Abencio Salazar Historic District has several prominent examples of late nineteenth-century adobe construction.

8

The Northern Pueblos

*T*he early Camino Real de Tierra Adentro continued north from Bernalillo and passed through the Eastern Keres pueblos of Santa Ana, San Felipe, Santo Domingo, and Cochiti. Keres-speaking people were part of a migration of Ancestral Pueblo sometime around the first millennium, migrating south and east toward the lower Jemez basin, the Pajarito Plateau, and into the Rio Grande Valley. There may have been several migrations, from the San Juan Basin, Mesa Verde through Chaco Canyon, and areas further west.[1] The Keresan language appears to have emerged by the fifteenth century and is not linguistically related to the Tanoan family of languages spoken by most Pueblo Indians.[2] The Keres cut a large wedge between the Tiwa and Tewa, and occupied an area that spread from today's Bernalillo north to Cochiti Dam. Like the Piro and Tiwa, Keresan Pueblo were agricultural and lived in multi-stored adobe dwellings, sharing similar cultural and social traditions with neighboring tribes.

Santa Ana Pueblo

Ranchos de Santa Ana is located along NM 313, about four miles northwest of Bernalillo. The Santa Anans first lived near today's San Felipe Pueblo at a site they named *Tamayá*, visited by the Oñate expedition in 1598.[3] Franciscans renamed Tamayá Pueblo *Santa Ana*, in honor of Saint Anne, who, according to Christian tradition, was the mother of the Virgin Mary.[4] Little is known about relations between the Spanish and Santa Anans in the seventeenth century, but its Indian residents joined in the 1680 Pueblo Revolt. Santa Ana warriors joined the natives of San Felipe in the march to Santo Domingo Pueblo and in the siege of Santa Fe.[5] When Otermín's refugees made their way south along the Camino Real, they found all of the area pueblos, including Santa Ana, deserted.[6] Governor Otermín returned the next year and ordered his men to set fire to what was left of the pueblo.[7] In 1692, Vargas negotiated a truce with the

Santa Anans, and they were re-settled at a site along the Jemez River, which they continued to call Tamayá, honoring their old pueblo. They became Vargas allies and fought in campaigns against Cochiti Pueblo, Jémez, and Tewa Indians.[8] Friars built a small chapel at new Tamayá, and, by the late seventeenth century, the pueblo was once again called Santa Ana.[9]

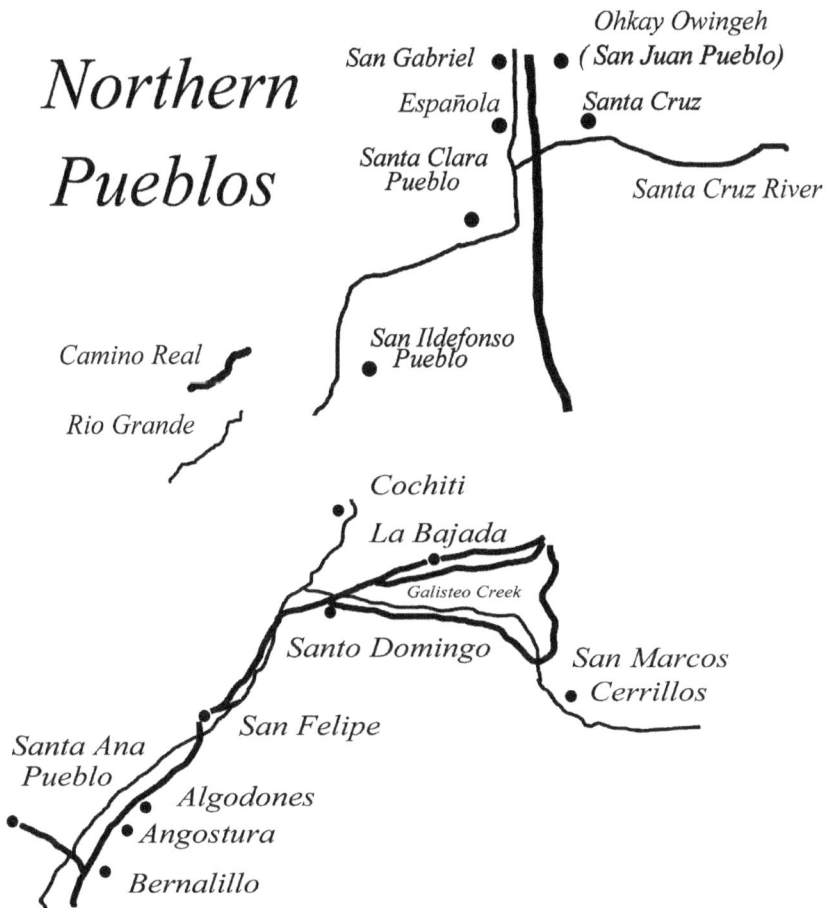

Northern Pueblos

San Gabriel •

Ohkay Owingeh
• (San Juan Pueblo)

Española

Santa Cruz

Santa Clara
Pueblo

Santa Cruz River

San Ildefonso
Pueblo

Camino Real

Rio Grande

Cochiti

La Bajada

Galisteo Creek

Santo Domingo

San Marcos
• Cerrillos

San Felipe

Santa Ana
Pueblo

Algodones

Angostura

Bernalillo

The Camino Real through the Northern Pueblos.

Santa Ana Church, 1900. New Mexico Department of Tourism Photograph Collection, Image 2802, Courtesy of the New Mexico State Records Center and Archives.

In 1776, Fray Domínguez counted 384 people living in nine large room blocks alongside the church at Santa Ana Pueblo. He noted that the Jemez River was an unreliable source of water and described how some Santa Anans had moved southeast of the pueblo, along the banks of the Rio Grande, where they were growing substantial quantities of wheat and corn.[10] They also grew cotton and produced textiles. They made most of their own clothing and ceremonial garments but manufactured baskets, pottery, and leather goods that were traded with settlements along the Camino Real. By the mid-eighteenth century, Santa Anans were cultivating more land south along the river, and the large array of fields on the path of the Camino Real became known as *Ranchos de Santa Ana*, the agricultural heart on the community. People continued to live in the old pueblo during the winter months, but in spring they moved south to the Ranchos. Eventually they built homes there and the old village of Tamayá was abandoned.[11] Tamayá was never a major mission center and was neglected in the Mexican era. In 1846, Lieutenant. Abert found the pueblo "almost entirely deserted" and noted that most of the residents lived at Ranchos de Santa Ana where they were tending their crops.[12] The old pueblo of Tamayá continued to decline during the nineteenth century. In 1890, a Special Indian Agent for the New Mexico Territory reported that, during most of the year, only one or two men, and many stray cats, guarded the empty pueblo. Santa Anans were prospering but were still quite isolated. Only one spoke English; many were fluent in Spanish, and Kersesan was the still the common language in the pueblo.[13]

Today, Tamayá lies on a remote site on the northwest bank of the Jémez River. It is closely guarded and protected, opened to visitors only once a year for the annual feast. Tamayá is one of the best preserved Pueblo villages in New Mexico, with few signs of contemporary life. There are two plazas, two ceremonial kivas, a series of one-and two-story adobe homes, and the old mission church. The 1706 church, with its bell tower and balcony, is the largest and most prominent structure in the abandoned village, used for ceremonial occasions and feast days. The circular Turquoise kiva is southeast of the church; the Pumpkin kiva is further east, closer to the river.[14] The old village of Tamayá is only opened to the general public on Saint Anne's Day, July 26 of each year.

Ranchos de Santa Ana, a few miles south near the Rio Grande on the Camino Real de Tierra Adentro, remains the agricultural and residential center of the community, although much of Santa Ana Pueblo's economy today is based on revenues from its casino, entertainment center, golf course, and mail order distribution center for native and regional goods. The pueblo experienced a revival of traditional crafts in the mid-twentieth century and has a number of local artisans who continue to produce fine-quality pottery and woven goods.[15]

Angostura and Algodones

In the seventeenth century, there was an area just north of Bernalillo called *La Angostura*, the Narrow Pass, referring to a gap in the Rio Grande Valley. Fernando Durán y Chaves claimed to have lived on a west bank site known as *San Antonio de la Angostura*, the Narrows of Saint Anthony, prior to the 1680 revolt, which he described as lying between the mouth of the Rio Santa Ana and the place where the Rio Grande enters a restricted canyon as it heads north toward Santa Fe. In 1692, he was granted two tracts of land, one at Angostura and one further south at Atrisco. [16]Durán y Chaves moved his family back to Angostura, but, when Indian attacks plagued the settlement, they moved south to Atrisco.[17] By 1745 the land grant had been transferred to Andrés Montoya, the alcalde of San Felipe Pueblo, but it is unclear if anyone settled the site. In the 1820s, Mexican homesteaders returned to Angostura.[18] A New Mexico Highway Department Camino Real marker on NM 313 near the railroad tracks describes Angostura and tells the story of the small agricultural village near the narrows.

Algodones, a small village of several hundred residents, lies along NM 313, just north of Angostura. It is named for *algodón*, the Spanish word for cotton, and most likely refers to the cottonwood trees found along the river, or cotton fields that were once common in the area.[19] Algodones does not appear in any colonial documents or travelers' accounts. It may have been settled during the Mexican era, probably around the same time that people moved to nearby Angostura. There are a few remains of adobe structures along the road and some crumbling mounds in the surrounding fields near a nineteenth-century church, located east of the highway. A bed and breakfast establishment on the west side of the road is built around the Montoya-Gallegos house, an eighteenth-century placita-style structure that has undergone substantial renovation over the years.

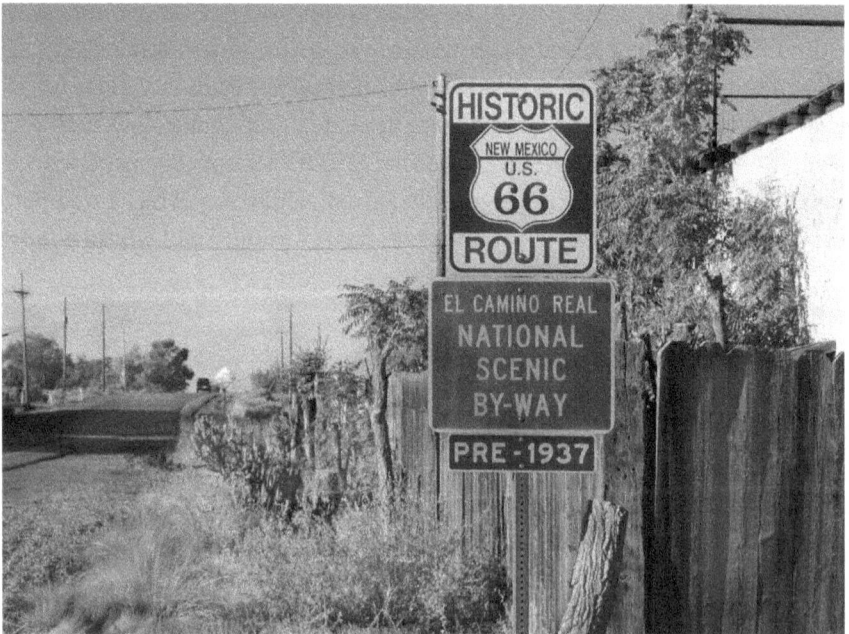

Historic Route 66 followed a segment of the original Camino Real de Tierra Adentro through Algodones.

San Felipe Pueblo

Beyond Algodones, NM 852 parallels the path of the Camino Real de Tierra Adentro and leads into the San Felipe Indian Reservation.[20] San Felipe is known as *Katishtya* to its Keres-speaking people who are culturally tied to the pueblos of Cochiti and Zia. Fifteenth-century conflicts with the Tewa Indians may have driven them south to the present locations.[21] By 1609, Franciscans established a church and convent and named the mission[22] San Felipe, for Saint Philip the Apostle, one of the twelve disciples of Jesus.[23] San Felipeans were outraged by Spanish attempts to end their religious practices and destroy their ceremonial kivas. When the revolt broke out in 1680, San Felipe Pueblo joined in the attacks on the Spanish and sacked the mission.[24]

By the end of 1680, the pueblo and mission were in ruins. Many San Felipeans moved west, to the base of Santa Ana Mesa, where they were joined by natives of Cochiti and San Marcos. Over the next ten years, conflicts divided the tribes, and, when Vargas returned in 1692, he negotiated a peace with the San Felipeans. They were re-settled north of the old village site and became allies in the fight against other natives.[25] In 1696, a new chapel was consecrated on the west bank of the river, high atop the mesa. A few years, later the San Felipe Indians came down from the mesa and settled at the present site, where new dwellings and an entirely new church were built.[26] The San Felipeans cultivated land in the rich soils on the east bank of the river and produced a variety of crops, including several fruits. They grazed livestock, processed wool, and became known for their woolen goods and cotton textiles.[27] Eighteenth-century Spanish engineer Captain Don Bernardo Miera y Pacheco, who dabbled in religious arts, carved a large statue of St. Philip the Apostle and sold it to the pueblo.[28]

Zebulon Pike passed through San Felipe in 1807 and observed a large wooden bridge (one of the few along the entire trail), that led across the Rio Grande to the village. He enjoyed dinner at the home of the local priest, where he and his escorts were entertained by a small quartet, playing drums, French horns, violins, and cymbals.[29] When Colonel Abert visited San Felipe in October 1846, he noted that Pike's bridge was gone, entirely swept away by the river.[30] San Felipe Pueblo regularly traded with Indian, Hispanic, and Anglo-American communities nearby, and the north and south sides of the plaza had wide wooden gates that opened for wagon traffic.[31] Captain Bourke visited San Felipe in 1881 and observed plentiful foodstuffs and livestock. Corn, wheat, chile, tomatoes, peaches, apples, beans, beets, plums, and apricots were produced.[32]

San Felipe Pueblo Church, 1897. New Mexico Department of Tourism Photograph Collection, Image 2806, Courtesy of the New Mexico State Records Center and Archives.

Today, San Felipe is one of the larger pueblos in the region, tucked between the mesa and the river, with two roads passing along the east and west edge of the village. The ruins of the 1696 church are still visible today, on the mesa overlooking the pueblo. The historic village center remains much as it was in the eighteenth and nineteenth centuries with Pumpkin and Turquoise kivas near an immense central plaza, which sinks to a depth of almost three feet. The San Felipe church, just south of the kiva, faces east toward the river and has not changed dramatically since the colonial period, although there have been modifications over the years. Sometime after 1800, the nave was extended and two bell towers were added to the front façade. The extension of the church is even more impressive when viewed from the side, and the low lengthened nave has an almost ship-like appearance. The front façade has a series of bright, colorful designs and images. Inside, the San Felipe church maintains a spartan interior, but the Miera y Pacehco carving of San Felipe is still one of the more prominent icons.

San Felipe is a culturally conservative pueblo but visitors are allowed to tour the pueblo throughout the year. The village is most accommodating during its two major celebrations, the Feast of San Felipe on May 1 and the San Pedro Feast Day in late June. During the May celebrations, hundreds of traditionally dressed locals take part in the great Corn Dance in the large central plaza. A revival of crafts in the 1970s incorporated designs and colorings from other pueblos, especially Zia and Cochiti.[33] The tribe has also gone to great lengths to preserve the Keresan language which can still be heard spoken throughout the pueblo.

Santo Domingo Pueblo

Parrot Road, an unpaved road east of the railroad tracks, leads north from San Felipe and closely follows the path of the old Camino Real de Tierra Adentro for eight miles to Santo Domingo, the largest of the eastern Keres-speaking pueblos. Santo Domingo Pueblo, known as *Gipuy*, was originally about two miles east of the present village, near the confluence of Galisteo Creek and the Rio Grande.[34] Gipuy was destroyed by floodwaters sometime before 1590, and a new pueblo, known as *Huashpa Tzena*, was built by the time Gaspar Castaño de Sosa visited in 1591 and christened the settlement *Santo Domingo*, Saint Dominic, for the Spanish founder of the Order of Preachers, or the Dominican friars. In early July 1598, Juan de Oñate arrived at Santo Domingo Pueblo with his advance party and was met by two Christian Indians, Tomás and Cristóbal, who had come north with Castaño de Sosa and had stayed behind to live at Santo Domingo, taking Indian wives and settling in the pueblo. With Spanish-speaking translators now in his service, Oñate began organizing the new colony. He summoned tribal leaders from the nearby pueblos and arranged a formal ceremony to mark Spanish authority over the region. On July 7, a grand council of Indian representatives gathered at the central kiva in Santo Domingo and listened to Oñate, through his new interpreters. Each native emissary was asked to kneel and kiss the hand of a Franciscan father, thus becoming vassals of the crown and surrendering authority to Oñate. It is unlikely that any of the delegates understood the greater meaning of the ceremony, or how it would impact their lives in the months and years to come. After six days at Santo Domingo Pueblo,

Oñate and his advance party continued north along Galisteo Creek, and east toward San Marcos Pueblo, a route that became the main seventeenth-century corridor of the Camino Real de Tierra Adentro.[35]

Santo Domingo Pueblo was a centrally located site for the Spanish and served as the provincial headquarters for the Keres pueblos and a regional archives for the Franciscans. By the mid-1600s, the mission at Santo Domingo was noted as one of the best in New Mexico.[36] Initially the Spanish presence offered protection from nomadic raids by Navajos and Apaches, but the use of Indian labor, the forced conversion to Catholicism, along with epidemics and drought, caused many in Santo Domingo Pueblo to doubt the powers of the Spanish. By the 1670s, there was a revival of native religious practices and the Spanish responded by cracking down on "sorcery." In 1675, several Santo Domingo residents, including a mestizo Keres leader named Alonso Catití, were arrested, taken to Santa Fe, and charged with heresy.

Carretta and plow, Santo Domingo Pueblo, n.d. New Mexico Department of Tourism Photograph Collection, Image 1562, Courtesy of the New Mexico State Records Center and Archives.

When the Pueblo Revolt erupted in 1680, Catití led his people against the Spaniards at Santo Domingo. They ransacked the mission, killed Franciscans, several soldiers, and a few sympathetic Indian authorities. The assaulting party continued down the Camino Real de Tierra Adentro toward San Felipe and Santa Ana. When Governor. Otermín returned the next year, many of the Keres Pueblo, including Catiti, fled to Cochiti Pueblo and took refuge on the nearby mesa.[37]In 1692, Vargas used his Pueblo allies to subdue the Keres. Some joined in the 1696 revolt, but, by the next year, the mission was re-established and many returned to Santo Domingo.[38]

The present pueblo was built after a major flood in the late 1690s and then served as the Spanish mission headquarters for New Mexico.[39] A new church was constructed in 1706 and expanded in the 1740s. Fray Domínguez visited in 1776 and described a settlement of 136 Keres families, living in six major housing-blocks arranged around a beautiful plaza. High adobe walls with two gates surrounded the entire pueblo, offering protection from enemy Indian raids. Santo Domingo Pueblo had good farmland that produced an abundance of crops, especially peaches, apricots, melons, and watermelons.[40]

Although Santo Domingo Pueblo appears to be an ancient Indian village today, it was actually rebuilt several times in the late nineteenth and early twentieth centuries.[41] In the 1870s, much of the west end of the pueblo was lost to river flooding, and by 1884 the waters wore away the dirt cliffs alongside the church and seeped into the remaining residences. Attempts were made to build up the levies, but two years later the Rio Grande reached record levels. Residents gathered their belongings, removed doors and fixtures, herded animals, and climbed onto higher ground east of the village. By early June, they began dismantling sections of the church, carrying icons, statues, paintings, and fixtures up to the new town. On June 3, 1886, the church and old convent collapsed under the rising waters of the river, the vigas gave way, and the walls dropped.[42] In the 1890s, Father Noel Dumarest supervised the building of an entirely new church on an elevated site far east of the old settlement. Instead of the Gothic-style construction taking place at many nearby villages, he chose to maintain the basic mission-design, and created a replica of the old church. Today's Santo Domingo church, like its predecessors, is a long, single-nave structure. Two towers, with a balcony between, are along the façade, similar to the churches at nearby San Felipe and Cochiti. The church is entered through a small, walled cemetery in front of the building. The Santo Domingo Church is painted a bright white and has many colorful features. Painted patterns and decorations adorn the large wooden beams and balcony. Two large horses are painted on the front of the church, a traditional image that has been present since the early twentieth century.[43]

Today, the pueblo lies east of the main road, and a small footbridge crosses the acequia and leads to the village center. A wide street through the pueblo functions as a plaza. Numerous housing blocks made of adobe and concrete, and two circular ceremonial kivas, are along the central street. After the new pueblo was built and stabilized in the early twentieth century, the railroad brought travelers to Santo Domingo, and a revival of traditional crafts and cultural practices, and a new tourist trade, followed. The Bernalillo Mercantile Company, located a few miles east at Domingo Station, a stop on the Atchison, Topeka, and Santa Fe Railway, became a major trading center for area pueblos. Tourists regularly visited the village as it became especially well-known for its corn dances on August 4th of each year, the feast day of Saint Dominic. Santo Domingo Pueblo continues to welcome visitors and has a lively trade in native crafts, especially since the recent restoration of some of the mercantile company buildings.[44]

Cochiti Pueblo

Cochiti, the last Keres-speaking pueblo on the trail, is located on the west bank of the Rio Grande, about ten miles north of Santo Domingo on NM 22, below Cochiti Dam.[45] Oral tradition places the pueblo's ancestors at Frijoles Canyon by the fourteenth century and a move to the present site probably took place about one hundred years later. Another Keres settlement, Old Cochiti, located high atop a mesa about seven miles northwest of today's pueblo, consisted of two villages, the larger one having six roomblocks grouped around two plazas and kivas. A second, smaller village nearby was scattered among cultivated fields. It appears that Old Cochiti and the present-day village site were occupied just prior to the sixteenth-century arrival of the Spaniards.[46] The Keres called the pueblo *Kotyete*, which means stone kiva. In 1598, Oñate called the pueblo Cochiti, a Spanish rendering of its native Keres name. *San Buenaventura de Cochiti Mission* was established by the mid-seventeenth century, named for Saint Bonaventure, a pioneer Franciscan, who, as an infant, was held by Saint Francis who predicted *buenaventura*, good fortune, for the young boy.[47]

Cochiti also joined in the 1680 revolt, but little is known about what happened in the pueblo.[48] When Vargas surveyed the area in 1692, he found Cochiti abandoned and rebel Indians, from Cochiti, San Marcos, and San Felipe, defending the nearby mesa. It took two years of skirmishes and negotiations, but by 1694 the Cochiti Pueblo made peace with the Spaniards, and many later served in Vargas's armies.[49] The mission at Cochiti was re-established,[50] and the present church was built after 1706 on the site of the original seventeenth-century mission chapel. Bishop Tamarón visited in 1760 and found a resident Franciscan overseeing an Indian population of 450 and a Hispanic one of 140.[51] Fray Domínguez later described the pueblo as lying on a low plain in full view of the river where several acequias drew waters to irrigate the surrounding fields. Wheat, corn, fruits, and green vegetables were grown in the surrounding fields.[52] Livestock grazed along the river and wool and cotton textiles were produced in the village.[53]

Nineteenth-century Cochiti Pueblo was a small, self-sufficient agricultural community. Several Hispanic families had moved into the area by the late nineteenth century and operated trading posts and mercantile establishments in the pueblo.[54] Captain Bourke toured Cochiti Pueblo in November 1881 and was impressed by the wide variety of crops, which included corn, chile, pumpkins, and onions, that were stocked in the home, as well an assortment of gourds, tortoise rattles, and tin picture frames.[55] He also noted wheat, pumpkins, peaches, apples, plums, apricots, beans, onions, and squashes. Horses, mules, burros, oxen, cows, dogs, cats, pigs, chickens, and turkeys wandered through the pueblo.[56]

Today, San Buenaventura Church is located in the historic center of Cochiti Pueblo. Governor Vargas ordered that a new church be built in 1696. Whether this was a re-construction of the old church or an entirely new one is unclear but in either case, San Buenaventura Church was completed in the early 1700s. Father Domínguez was unimpressed with the church, calling it the plainest one he had seen throughout the province.[57]In 1819, skilled masons were brought in from Santa Cruz de la Cañada, and the church was repaired and extensively remodeled. The nave was narrowed, towers were built, and a choir loft and balcony were also added. Despite the attention, the church had returned to its dilapidated state by mid-century. In the early twentieth century, it underwent the usual neo-Gothic renovations with a high pointed steeple, metal roof, and arched portal being added to the exterior. In the 1960s, a major renovation project essentially "re-missionized" the church.[58]

The second half of twentieth century brought great changes to the area around Cochiti Pueblo, impacting the architectural integrity and landscape of the community. The neat, traditional village, once considered a nearly perfect example of a traditional pueblo, was greatly affected by the building of Cochiti Dam. Detached houses now surround the community, and development along the river and canals has taken its toll. The historic center remains much the same, and the renovations of the 1960s returned a more simple, traditional look to the church. The winding streets of the pueblo pass two round kivas, one of the Pumpkin clan and the other of the Turquoise clan, which are northeast of the church. Some of the homes in the immediate area of the church and kiva date back to the early days of the pueblo, although extensive renovations have been made over the years.[59] The village is still a quiet, somewhat remote settlement, visited by far fewer tourists than nearby pueblos, but it has experienced a revival of traditional crafts in recent decades, especially pottery, jewelry, and drums. Cochiti celebrates the feast day of Saint Bonaventure, July 14, with traditional ceremonies and dances.

The Galisteo Basin and San Marcos Pueblo

From the Santo Domingo-Cochiti area, the early seventeenth-century Camino Real de Tierra Adentro followed Galisteo Creek east about fifteen miles to *Yá atze*, one of eight large Tano Indian pueblos in the western Galisteo Basin. The Tano Pueblo, also known as the Southern Tewa, moved east into the Galisteo Basin and the Santa Fe area sometime after 1100 CE,[60] and like the Tiwa and Keres, they lived in multi-storied adobe dwellings, clustered around plazas or atop mesas for protection. Yá atze was founded about 1300 CE along one of the deeper arroyos and was home to a mixed population of Tano and Keres Indians. By the mid-fifteenth century, it had become a major regional center of trade and may have had several thousand inhabitants spread throughout a settlement of pueblo-style roomblocks.[61] The Rodriguez-Chamuscado expedition appears to have visited the pueblo in 1581. In 1590, Captain Gaspar Castaño de Sosa camped at San Marcos. The Oñate caravan made its way to San Marcos and took some initial sample ores from the nearby hills. In 1612, Fray Alonso de Peinado oversaw the building of a mission church and convent, and missionaries re-named the village *San Marcos*, for Saint Mark the Evangelist, a companion of Saint Peter in the first century. Yá atze became known as San Marcos Pueblo.[62]

Before the Spanish arrived, Yá atze specialized in turquoise and lead-glazed ceramic pottery, which was often traded for obsidian, a black volcanic glass prized by the San Marcans. The Tanos mined turquoise in the surrounding Cerrillos Hills, which they may have shared with the Keres Indians of nearby Santo Domingo and Cochiti pueblos. At San Marcos, mines dating back to about 1000 CE were worked by natives who sold their stones to the peoples of the Chaco Canyon area where it became a prized commodity. Tens of thousands of artifacts uncovered at San Marcos date from the period of 900 to 1150 CE. When *la turquesa*, turquoise, was first introduced to Europe, it was said to come from Turkey and was known in Spain as a precious stone, but not considered of great value. Spaniards saw fine examples of turquoise in the Valley of Mexico, where it had been commonly used since the 600s CE, and encountered it among many natives as they made their way north. When the Spanish arrived in the 1590s, they ridiculed the Indians for revering the blue stones but some of their Tlaxcalan servants recognized the materials for their mystical qualities. The Indians named a small hill on the north side of the Cerrillos range, about two and one-half miles west of San Marcos, *Cerro Chalchihuitl,* Nahuatl for Turquoise Hill.[63]

San Marcos Pueblo also controlled regional lead mines and used the dense metallic element for glazing pottery. Spaniards used lead to cast balls for their muskets and knew that lead was often present near veins of silver, so they organized Indian laborers to extract gold and silver from the nearby Cerrillos Hills and built several smelters in the area. Juan de Oñate surveyed the Galisteo Basin in July 1598 and visited San Marcos. Felipe de Escalante, who had been in the area seventeen years earlier with the Rodriguez-Chamuscado expedition, guided Oñate. By the next year, New Mexico's first silver ore was taken from the Cerrillos Hills and Vicente de Zaldivar opened several mines and small smelters nearby. Some Spanish settlers had experience in the mines of Zacatecas and hoped that the area around the pueblo would produce similar riches, but the San Marcos area never yielded the high quality, or quantity, of silver that many colonists expected. Silver mining appears to have continued on a small scale (there were silversmiths in Santa Fe and several missionary accounts mention silver) but was never an important part of the colonial economy.[64] Even so, before the 1680 Pueblo Revolt, San Marcos remained an important paraje on the Camino Real de Tierra Adentro.[65]

Disease and the use of Indian laborers in the mines took its toll on the native population, and by mid-century there were only about 600 people living in the pueblo. The Tanos divided during the 1680 Pueblo Indian Revolt. On August 9, representatives of San Marcos and La Ciénega pueblos traveled to Santa Fe and informed Governor Otermín of the planned uprising. The next day, when the rebellion erupted, many San Marcans abandoned the pueblo and joined in the fighting. Spaniards gathered to defend themselves against the attack and within a few days were able to reach the Villa of Santa Fe. They later escaped down the Camino Real with Governor Otermín.[66] The pueblo was abandoned and as the Spanish fled the region, San Marcos Tanos joined Keres Indians at Cochiti and San Felipe. The San Marcans, assisted by Indians from Santo Domingo and Cochiti Pueblo, filled in some of the mine shafts and destroyed the smelters as they left the hills. After the revolt, the San Marcos Indians scattered and formed refugee communities among the Apache, Hopi, and Navajo people. A few followed the Spanish south to El Paso del Norte.[67]In October 1692, Governor Vargas returned and visited the ruins of San Marcos, noting that "some of the rooms and walls of its house blocks and dwellings survive, and likewise the walls and nave of the church as well as those of the convento are in good condition." But none of the San Marcans had returned to the pueblo during the Spaniards' twelve-year absence, and San Marcos and the nearby Tano pueblos were never re-settled.[68] By the eighteenth century, the ruins of San Marcos were already being well-obscured, high on the bluff, no longer connected to the main route of El Camino Real de Tierra Adentro.[69]

Some Spaniards returned and used the old pueblo site for grazing and herding and a few Tanos moved back to the Galisteo Basin in the 1690s. In 1754, San Marcos Pueblo was included in a land grant issued to Antonio Urbaño Montaño, who salvaged wood and metal from the site to build a family ranch. Comanche attacks in the 1770s destroyed what remained of the pueblo.[70] The site became known as *Cerrillos*, the Little Hills, and the entire area became known as Los Cerillos. Throughout the eighteenth century, there was some small-scale silver and lead mining in the Cerrillos Hills, a few mine grants were awarded, and prospectors occasionally found substantial-sized nuggets. The Mexican era brought another brief mining revival in the Cerrillos area, especially in the 1830s, but by the 1840s Anglo-American travelers noted that the old mines had closed. There is no record of any regular mining activity until the 1870s when the Territorial government opened tracts in the Cerrillos Hills for public purchase. By the end of the decade, a new era was underway as the American West experienced a great mining boom and silver prices soared. Los Cerrillos Mining District was formed in 1879, and thousands of prospectors came to the area seeking their fortunes, especially as rumors circulated that there was gold in the nearby hills. Few precious minerals were found at the old pueblo site, so nineteenth century prospectors ventured higher into the surrounding hills. By the early 1880s, there were many small silver mining camps throughout the region, but only one, present-day Cerrillos, has survived.[71]

San Marcos Pueblo was located near today's Cerrillos Hills Historic District, on New Mexico's Turquoise Trail.

The ruins of San Marcos remained hidden from view, and well-protected, until archaeologists conducted a few preliminary studies in the early twentieth century.[72] Today, San Marcos Pueblo is an isolated site on a butte overlooking the region, surrounded by cholla and juniper, a large patch of brown earth littered with millions of fragments of ceramics and pieces of turquoise from the nearby hills. The San Marcos Pueblo site, a sixty-acre zone near NM 14 in the Galisteo Basin, is one of the largest ancestral Puebloan ruins in the Southwest. It was added to the National Register of Historic Places in 1982. In the late 1990s and the early years of the twenty-first century, several extensive surveys and excavations took place at the site. They revealed large roomblocks, kiva depressions, and adobe walls. A seventeenth-century mission complex, atop one of the residential room blocks, has also been uncovered. A recent dig exposed parts of the Catholic chapel, remains of the choir loft, and altar.[73]

San Marcos and the surrounding hills are located near a popular tourist route, the Turquoise Trail, which winds south from Santa Fe along NM 14 through Cerrillos and Madrid, but the ruins of the abandoned pueblo are not generally open to the public. In 1978, Mount Chalchihuitl was entered in the New Mexico State Register of Cultural Properties. The village of Cerrillos lies within Cerillos Hills Historic District, and north of the village is the Cerrillos Hills Historic Park, an area of hiking trials, historic sites, and recreational spaces. The cone-shaped Cerrillos Hills rise about 1,000 feet above the valley floor and are the remains of ancient volcanoes. Along the trails through the hills are the remnants of mines and mining operations dating back to a time well before the Spanish arrived in the region.

Tewa Country and the First Provincial Capital

Keres and Tewa Pueblo Indians trace their ancestral migration through the Pajarito Plateau, located in today's Bandelier National Monument, a site named for pioneer archeologist and ethnologist Adolph A. F. Bandelier (1840–1914), who specialized in North American Indian cultures and visited Frijoles Canyon in the 1880s, studying the ancient ruins and cliff dwellings.[74] The site was officially designated a monument in 1916 and is administered by the National Park Service. Most of the 32,000-plus acre site is a wilderness area, but it is best known for its restored Ancestral Pueblo ruins and kivas, and a great variety of petroglyphs and rock paintings. Ancestral Pueblo peoples lived in Española Basin villages and cultivated maize by the 600s CE. By 1150 CE, they were building permanent structures around Frijoles Canyon, and, within 200 years, as the population peaked, they constructed larger multi-storied dwellings. A second migration took place after 1300 CE and brought other groups of Ancestral Pueblo from the Mesa Verde area, ancestors of the Keres and Tewa.[75] They developed irrigation systems that improved crop yields and built larger, permanent residential structures. These settlements were fortified and often located higher on the mesas to protect against Ute and Navajo attacks. There appears to have been two distinct areas of Frijoles Canyon inhabited at the time. The southern settlers were Keresan speakers, ancestors of today's pueblos of Cochiti, Santo Domingo, and San Felipe. Northern settlers spoke Tewa and later established the pueblos of San Ildefonso, Santa Clara, and San Juan. Tewa country extended from the Rio Grande Valley, near its confluence with the Rio Chama, down to the area north of Santa Fe.[76] By the time the Spanish arrived in the sixteenth century, the mesa top villages were abandoned and population had declined noticeably.[77]

San Ildefonso Pueblo

From San Marcos Pueblo, the early seventeenth-century Camino Real de Tierra Adentro headed north between the Rio Grande and today's US 84/285. A branch trail, roughly parallel to County Road 84, led west through several Tewa communities to San Ildefonso Pueblo. In July 1598, the Oñate expedition made its way north, and just beyond Santo Domingo Pueblo they encountered a deep canyon carved out by the Rio Grande. An advance party proceeded north looking for a pass through the region, and, leaving the river, they climbed an escarpment and crossed a plateau that led toward the Sangre de Cristo Mountains. Their route paralleled the Rio Grande, several miles to the west, and took them into the Tewa country of the Española Valley. It is not entirely clear why Juan de Oñate chose to establish the provincial capital among the Tewa. Oñate's chroniclers claimed that the Tewa invited them into their pueblos, encouraged them to stay, and eagerly assisted as they established their capital in the north. The Tewa also had better harvests and stockpiled large quantities of corn. The surrounding mountains might have continued to inspire hopes for finding precious metals.[78]

San Ildefonso Pueblo is known as *Pohwoge*, Where the Waters Cut Through, in Tewa. It is one of six surviving Tewa pueblos in northern New Mexico and the first of three Tewa communities along El Camino Real de Tierra Adentro National Historic Trail.[79] *Pohwoge* was founded around 1300 CE, just south of today's village. A second settlement, *Perage*, was located just across the river. When the Spanish entered the region in the late sixteenth century, this was the largest of nine Tewa settlements.[80]

The Spanish re-named Pohwoge *San Ildefonso*, or Saint Ildephonse, for the seventh-century Spanish monk who became Archbishop of Toledo.[81] The Tewa nation was the first to be formally baptized by the Franciscans, and San Ildefonso soon became an important center of missionary activity.[82] But relations were often strained in the mid-seventeenth century, and in 1680 San Ildefonso played an important role in the Pueblo Revolt as hundreds of Tewa living in the vicinity rallied behind the insurrection's leaders. They killed two resident missionaries, destroyed the church, and drove the remaining Spanish from the settlement. After the revolt, many Tewa fled the pueblo and lived in the surrounding countryside.[83] When the Spanish returned twelve years later, they found the site deserted, but received reports that as many as 1,000 Indians from San Ildefonso, Tesuque, Santa Clara, and others had sought refuge atop Black Mesa, a nearby landmark and sacred Tewa site. They held out for almost two years, but in late February 1694 Governor Vargas organized Spanish troops and Indian allies to re-take the area, remove the Indians from the mesa, and re-settle the pueblo below.[84] Vargas established a field headquarters at the abandoned pueblo and unsuccessfully attempted to take the mesa.[85] In September they returned, but by then the mesa was crowded with as many as 2,000 Indians, from nine Tewa and two Tano pueblos. Although they were greatly outnumbered, Vargas, his Spanish troops, and Indian allies laid siege and were able to draw the native warriors down into a series of skirmishes, weakening the resistance, and exhausting their food supply. A peace was finally negotiated, and the Indians agreed to come down from Black Mesa, rebuild their pueblos, and allow the Spanish to once again oversee the region.[86]

San Ildefonso Mission was re-established and a second church was built, but within a year there were renewed conflicts. In 1696, the Tewa participated in a second revolt against the Spanish and killed two Franciscan friars. Vargas's troops, who made a two-day inspection of the Tewa region after the revolt had been brought under control, discovered the bodies and saw that they were properly buried. In retaliation, several nearby Tewa pueblos, Nambe, Cuyamungue and Jacona, were laid waste.

By the end of the seventeenth century, rebellions among the Tewa had subsided and the Spanish were once again in control.[87] Fray Juan de Tagle arrived in San Ildefonso in 1701 and spent the next twenty-five years serving the pueblo. He oversaw the construction of a new church and convent and was able to acquire generous donations for the mission, elaborate artworks for the main altars, and the construction of a "porter's lodge" or open chapel, an enclosed and roofed area of worship alongside the church. New Mexico Governor Antonio Valverde y Cosío paid for much of the work.[88] The eighteenth century brought more Hispanics into the Española Basin, and their small farms soon surrounded the pueblo and dotted the river valley.[89] The farmland around San Ildefonso was quite productive, yielding good quantities of wheat and corn.[90] The native population declined during the eighteenth and nineteenth centuries,[91] and Spanish, Mexican, and Anglo-American pioneers reduced tribal lands as settlers occupied abandoned sites, or bought them cheaply. By the 1870s, only 156 people lived at San Ildefonso.[92] The community also suffered from internal divisions, and the dual organization of the pueblo, based on a division of Summer and Winter people, added to problems.

In the early twentieth century, the Santa Fe tourist trade brought a revival of traditional crafts, and the pueblo became known for its pottery, once actively traded along the Camino Real de Tierra Adentro.[93] Today, the San Ildefonso Pueblo Museum exhibits many examples of its traditional black-on-black pottery, made famous by San Ildefonso's best known ceramics artist, María Martínez (1887–1980). Members of her family continue the tradition, making San Ildefonso Pueblo a popular tourist attraction, the most frequently visited of the northern pueblos. A few craft shops around the plaza exhibit the works and occasionally offer visitors demonstrations of this ancient craft.

The basic layout of San Ildefonso has undergone few changes, and its historic core is comprised of flat-roofed adobe houses, some with segments dating to the fourteenth century, centered around two plazas. They are generally modest, with viga-supported roofs, several small interior rooms, and corner fireplaces. Two plazas were once located directly in front of the church, but they have been merged into a very large one. The church survived until 1904 when it was demolished and replaced with a small, tin-roofed building that resembled a rural schoolhouse. In 1958, plans were made to replace the schoolhouse with today's church, a replica of the 1711 mission church that stood at San Ildefonso for almost 200 years. In 1968, the new church at San Ildefonso Pueblo was dedicated, standing on the exact same site as the previous ones,[94] at the northwest end of the pueblo, alongside the plaza. A traditional circular ceremonial kiva is located nearby. During ritual or ceremonial events, dancers rise from the kiva and enter the plaza, symbolizing how the Tewa came from the underground into this world. The streets of the pueblos are generally unpaved. Beehive-shaped ovens are found throughout, along with a mix of traditional and nineteenth-century Territorial architecture. South of the plaza are several nineteenth-century structures including a church and schoolhouse. San Ildefonso Pueblo was added to the National Register of Historic Places in 1975.

Bow and arrow dancers on kiva steps, San Ildefonso Pueblo, New Mexico, c. 1925–1945. T. Harmon Parkhurst, Courtesy Palace of the Governors Photo Archives (NMHM/DCA), Neg. No. 003608.

The pueblo is a popular tourist destination and is accustomed to regular visitors. Photography permits are available at the welcome center, and a walking tour guides guests through the village. The kachina cult, a tradition more associated with the Hopi, survives in some of today's Tewa pueblos, including San Ildefonso. The kachina are the spirits of the dead, and people who devote their life to traditional religious practices are believed to join the kachina after their death. The masked dancers embody a particular spirit, one that visits the pueblo for a part of each year. Spirits are revered, though not necessarily worshipped, by the pueblo. Masks, dolls, and drawings often represent the kachina tradition in northern New Mexico.[95] January 23 is the feast day of San Ildefonso, when visitors can experience traditional Indian dances on the plaza. The nearby villages of Pojoaque, Jacona, and Nambe were Tewa settlements destroyed after the 1696 rebellion. Today, each has a small Tewa population.

Santa Clara Pueblo

Santa Clara Pueblo lies about eleven miles beyond San Ildefonso on NM 30, which follows the path of the original Camino Real de Tierra Adentro. In the 1300s CE, migrants from the eastern slopes of the Jemez Mountains began to congregate in larger settlements such as Puye Pueblo, on the Pajarito Plateau. The Indians at Puye lived in dwellings carved out of the side of the mesa and farmed the land around the plateau. After 200 years of occupation, their descendents, the Santa Clara Tewa, migrated about ten miles east and settled near the Rio Grande. In the sixteenth century they established the village of Kha'po', the Valley of the Wild Roses, today's Santa Clara Pueblo.[96]

In July 1598, Franciscan friars renamed Kha'po' *Santa Clara*, for St. Clare, who, along with St. Francis, founded the order of nuns called *clarisas* in Spanish, or the Poor Clares.[97] A chapel was built in 1617, and when Benavides arrived in the 1620s he founded a monastery. For much of the seventeenth century, Santa Clara was a *visita*, or mission, of San Juan Pueblo, so there was no resident friar.[98] During the Pueblo Revolt, the small church was destroyed, and Santa Clara Pueblo became a central gathering point for the Tewa and rebels from Jemez. Indian sentries were stationed along the Camino Real, and branch trails were sealed off in preparation for the assault on Santa Fe.[99] After the revolt, some Santa Clara Tewa fled west and joined Hopi and Navajo settlements. Other scattered among the remaining Tewa villages of the region. When the Spanish returned in 1692, the Santa Clarans gathered with other Tewa at Black Mesa and resisted the re-conquest. They held out until September 1694 when the region was pacified, and many of the old Tewa mission sites, including Santa Clara, were re-established.[100]

A few Tewa who returned from western settlements introduced customs from the Hopi and Navajo into Santa Clara culture. Santa Clara Pueblo, by then well off the main track of the Camino Real to Santa Fe, was still connected to the capital and its environs, and as the pueblo was rebuilt, European influences became more evident. Rectangular, above-ground kivas appeared in the village, and detached, colonial adobe-style homes were built near the older, large housing blocks.[101] Domínguez visited Santa Clara in 1776 and described four housing blocks, five small houses outside of the plaza, and a fortified tower at the end of the village. North of the pueblo were ranches inhabited by Spaniards, mestizos, and genízaros, spread out along the Rio Grande.[102]

In the early nineteenth century, Santa Clara Pueblo remained a quiet agricultural settlement along the Rio Grande with several hundred residents living within the traditional boundaries of the village. By the 1870s Santa Clara had been impacted by Anglo-American development and became more involved in the new commercial economy of the region. United States government agency policies emphasized the individual over the tribe, and some Santa Clarans, especially younger tribal members, traveled outside the region, attended Indian schools, and were greatly influenced by Anglo-American culture.[103] As the threat of Navajo raids lessened, the defensive design of the settlement disappeared. Towers were razed, and walled segments were torn down. The village spread outward, beyond its original boundaries, and new architectural influences were seen, incorporating lumber, pitched roofs, and territorial features. Modernization sparked divisions within the Tewa community, especially between generations and the Summer and Winter people. The clans divided their traditions and territory within the village. A second plaza was built west of the village center with a second ceremonial kiva.[104]

In 1881, the narrow gauge Denver and Rio Grande Railroad arrived with its right-of-way passing within a quarter mile of the pueblo. The small nearby settlement of *Plaza Española* became a railroad town, with a population of more than 150 people by the next year. The original name of the camp was derived from its "Spanish" settlement, separate from the surrounding Indian communities. Española soon drew Anglo-American settlers and immigrant workers, and brought new commercial influences to the pueblo.[105]

Today, Santa Clara Pueblo is a small community on the west bank of the Rio Grande, about two miles south of Española. The tribal offices and community center are along the main road into the village. The twentieth-century church at

Santa Clara stands on an elevated site and is somewhat set off from the village center. The church that existed prior to 1680 did not survive the revolt, but remaining segments may have been used to construct a new one as the pueblo was re-settled in the early eighteenth century. By the 1750s, it was badly damaged by flooding and was nothing more than a mound of rubble. Services were held in a small chapel built alongside the remains. In 1756, Fray Mariano Rodríguez de Torre began the construction of a new church.[106] Fray Domínguez described the new structure as extremely long and narrow, merely fourteen feet wide. It reminded him of a cannon. He noted that it had forty-seven vigas, a very large number, holding up a thick earthen roof. The interior was rather plain, without a choir loft, and the front façade had a small arch with a single church bell. In the 1780s, years after Domínguez's visit, a large altarpiece and side altar screens were painted and became the most impressive artwork in the church. Nineteenth-century visitors commented on the poor condition of the church, and in 1909 a powerful storm collapsed the structure.[107]

By the 1910s, plans were underway for a replacement. The new structure, completed in 1918, followed the same general design of the old one, flat with two peaks, and a simple bell arch. It stood near the site of the old church, at the northern end of the pueblo, away from the plaza. The old, weathered doors of the 1756 church were saved and used in the new structure. Since 1918, the church has been remodeled, and the old doors replaced. Its grey-beige earth tones, simple door and window frames, and limited ornamentation give it a distinctly modern Southwest look. A single tower stands on the southeast end, and minor exterior modifications were made in the 1970s and 1980s.[108]

The historic center of the pueblo is organized around two loosely outlined plazas, southwest and southeast of the church. Adobe-based residential structures surround the plazas. Many of their basic foundations date from the colonial and Mexican era. Several homes have small artisan centers and shops where traditional crafts and pottery are displayed and sold. Throughout the village center are examples of ovens, corrals, and pens. There are two rectangular kivas in Santa Clara, for the Summer and Winter moieties. A second plaza, originating from a factional dispute between the Summer and Winter people of the pueblo in the late nineteenth century, is located west of the first. The western Winter kiva was built in the early twentieth century on the site of the old circular one. Along the southern edge of the village are later residences, corrals, pens, and fields.[109]

Cloud Dance, Santa Clara Pueblo, New Mexico, c.1925–1945. T. Harmon Parkhurst, Courtesy Palace of the Governors Photo Archives (NMHM/DCA), Neg. No. 04220.

Santa Clara has a long tradition of pottery making, noted by both Bourke and Bandelier. The pueblo is best known for its wedding jars, double-necked vessels with two mouths connected by a handle. The main festivities and ceremonies at Santa Clara Pueblo take place on August 12 each year and include buffalo, harvest, and corn dances. Other celebrations follow in the winter months. Santa Clara Pueblo was added to the National Register of Historic Places in 1974. The Puye Cliff Dwellings, about ten miles west of Santa Clara, are owned and operated by Santa Clara Pueblo, and, according to tribal tradition, were the Tewa's ancestral home. The ruins are extensive, with an outline of dwellings several stories high and at least 700 rooms carved into the high cliff ridge. The Puye Cliff Dwellings were added to the National Register of Historic Places in 1966 and can only be visited by special arrangements with Santa Clara Pueblo.

Santa Cruz de la Cañada

Santa Cruz de la Cañada is northeast of Santa Clara Pueblo, off US 285/84, near the Santa Cruz River. Santa Cruz de la Cañada was once a Spanish *villa*, an administrative center for the northern part of the province, and while seventeenth-century colonial authorities may have had high hopes for the town, it developed slowly; it was never as prominent as El Paso del Norte or Santa Fe, and declined in the American Territorial era. Today, it is simply known as Santa Cruz[110] and is often cited as New Mexico's "forgotten" villa. It is not clear how many Spaniards lived in the Santa Cruz area at the time of the Pueblo Revolt. The valley, commonly known as La Cañada, had scattered farms, but there was no central hacienda or mission in the immediate area. As the rebellion erupted in August 1680, settlers hid near the river, hoping to defend themselves against the attacks, but were instead forced to flee.[111] They were gathered by local authorities and marched to Santa Fe, about twenty-five miles south along the Camino Real. After the Spanish were gone, Tano Indians, who had been driven west during inter-tribal rivalries with Pecos Indians, moved into La Cañada. When the Spanish returned in the 1690s, Tanos were living at San Lázaro and San Cristóbal, two small pueblos on the south bank of the Santa Cruz River. Vargas formally re-took possession of Santa Fe on the Feast of the Exaltation of the Holy Cross, September 14, 1692, and *Santa Cruz*, the Holy Cross, became the patronal title of troops in New Mexico for the rest of the Spanish Colonial period.[112]

Good arable land was in short supply beyond Santa Fe so when a group of new colonists arrived from Zacatecas in 1694, Vargas decided to offer them homesteads in the north, near the old settlements of La Cañada. The next year, Vargas moved the Tano Indians further up the valley to Chimayó, and made land grants to settlers around the old pueblo of San Lázaro. It was officially named *La Villa Nueva de la Santa Cruz de la Cañada*, the New Town of the Holy Cross of the Gentle Valley, the third villa established in New Mexico.[113] Pioneer settlers were provided pack mules, horses, grains, seeds, and rations of corn and beef. Spring flooding created havoc along the banks of the river, so the colonists soon moved to higher ground at the present-day site of the town.[114] For years, the new villa grew slowly and suffered several major setbacks. The first few winters brought disease and food shortages, demoralizing many of the residents. When Vargas inspected the villa in 1704, he found the plaza abandoned and only six families living in the immediate vicinity.[115]

Within a few years people returned to Santa Cruz, and a new church was constructed. It was adequate, but not well-built, and by the early 1730s it was in ruins. The parishioners were granted permission to build a new church, and in 1733 work began on a larger, more permanent structure. The new church was a parish church, not a mission, so residents of the community had to supply the materials and labor.[116]With limited funds and few workers, the project continued well into the 1740s, taking fifteen years to complete. Unlike El Paso del Norte or Santa Fe, Santa Cruz lacked a formal layout and design. Even though its location offered defensive advantages, many families preferred to live outside of its limits in the farmlands surrounding the villa. In 1760, Bishop Tamarón found "no semblance of a town" and "the settlers scattered over a wide area."[117] Fray Domínguez was also disappointed when he visited the villa sixteen years later. He noted only eight small houses near the church, "to keep it company."[118] The rest of the settlement was nothing more than a series of ranches spread out along the old Camino Real. He counted 680 people at the villa, and scattered up La Cañada, away from the main road, were the communities of Chimayó, Quemado, and Truchas, which added another 700 or so to the total population.[119] Sometime after the Domínguez visit, Santa Cruz de La Cañada was modified into a fortified plaza with new defensive arrangements around the church. As a colonial administrative center, the parish expanded, overseeing ten additional area chapels and churches by the 1780s. During the Mexican era it remained a primary destination on the road from Santa Fe, linked to the Santa Fe Trail and the Old Spanish Trail which headed west to Los Angeles. Even so, Santa Cruz never developed into a major regional center.[120]

Santa Cruz had a contentious political history and played a central role in the Revolt of 1837, also known as the Chimayó Revolt. After Mexican independence, there were concerns that New Mexicans were being unfairly treated by the new republican government; overly regulated, cheated by Mexican officials, and subject to higher taxes. In 1835, President López de Santa Anna appointed Albino Pérez governor, and many in northern New Mexico feared his arrival as an extension of the central government's power. Pérez led what many considered to be a luxurious and decadent life in Santa Fe and was greatly resented by the poor New Mexican farmers who lived in the Rio Arriba. He was also friendly with corrupt officials who often harassed traders on the Santa Fe Trail. Rumors of new taxes further inflamed the controversy.[121] In the summer of 1837, the local alcalde, Juan José Esquibel, protected several area residents against criminal charges, in defiance of Governor Pérez. Esquibel was promptly arrested, and, after an angry mob freed him, he organized a rebellion against the Pérez government. In August, Esquibel's army of local farmers, merchants, Indians from nearby pueblos, and militiamen marched south toward Santa Fe.

When they encountered Pérez near San Ildefonso, many of the governor's troops deserted and joined in the rebellion. Pérez fled back toward the provincial capital but was captured and killed. His head was displayed in the central plaza in Santa Fe after the rebels triumphed. A new governor, José Gonzáles, assumed control, but his government was soon plagued with scandals. Local uprisings continued, and the fighting finally came to an end when former governor Manuel Armijo commandeered a new army from the south and secured the province.[122]

Ten years later, when New Mexico was occupied by United States troops, Taos residents rose up against their American rulers in the Taos Rebellion. A broad cross-section of New Mexicans, including merchant elites, Indians, and poor Hispanics, resented the American invasion. The loss of sovereignty, isolation from the Mexican Republic, and the superior attitudes of Anglo-Americans all added to the tensions. On January 14, in an uprising organized by Pablo Montoya, a Hispanic resident of Taos, and Tomás Romero, a Taos Pueblo Indian, a small contingent of rebels murdered the appointed governor of New Mexico, Charles Bent, and five others during an attack on his home. The insurgent army grew and raided other settlements in the area, making their way south toward Santa Fe. United States Army Colonel Sterling Price, with 300 well-armed men, marched north to break up the rebel army at Santa Cruz. With superior weapons and better organization, Price forced the rebels to retreat, and, after a brief skirmish, scattered them into the countryside. Price followed the remnants of the insurgent force to Las Trampas and on to Taos. At Taos, more than 150 Indians and Hispanic New Mexicans were killed during the siege. The rebellion was finally put down, and Montoya and Romero were captured. Romero was killed while being held for trial, and Montoya was court-martialed and executed. Other trials and executions followed, and by April the Taos Rebellion had ended.[123]

Within a few years, Santa Cruz benefited from projects undertaken by the United States Army in the 1850s, as improvements were made to branch roads that reached north to Abiqui and Taos, and eventually extended to Colorado. It was still situated on the main road to Santa Fe and experienced an increase in commercial traffic. New stagecoach routes passed through the town, but Santa Cruz lost out when railroads replaced the old trails in the 1880s. By the end of the century, Santa Cruz de la Cañada was in decline, losing much of its its commercial and political influence.[124]

Today, the most prominent building in Santa Cruz is the Holy Cross Church, which towers over the hilly landscape of La Cañada. Work began on the church in the 1730s and continued for ten years as the villa grew. Fray Domínguez described the Holy Cross Church as a large structure with a typical cruciform design. He noted the work of Fray Andrés José García de la Concepción (one of the few Franciscan artists of the colonial era whose work has been identified), who made many of the wood carvings at Santa Cruz, including the altar screen and rails, several carved santos, and a *Santo Entierro*, the body of Christ, which is still located along the south wall of the church."[125] During the 1790s, several improvements were made to the church, including a new pulpit, replacement vigas, and the addition of a choir loft. By then, the church at Santa Cruz oversaw smaller chapels at Chimayo, Quemado, and Truchas along the road to Taos. By the early years of the nineteenth century, the Santa Cruz church was a prominent sight, towering over the few residences nearby.[126] Sometime during mid-century, a second tower was added, and in the 1870s major changes were made to the church, typical of those throughout the Territory. A central pediment was erected, and two wooden towers with iron crosses rose across the façade.[127]

Holy Cross Church faces east and still dominates the old villa site as it overlooks the open, unlandscaped plaza.

In the early twentieth century a shingled, pitched roof was laid over the old flat one. A wood floor, pews, and electric lighting were installed. Although the interior was remodeled, much of the church's elaborate artworks were neglected. By mid-century, the church was once again in need of major repair, and in the late 1970s the Church of Santa Cruz was meticulously restored. The outside walls were strengthened and re-surfaced, exterior details and roofing were cleaned and replaced, and the area surrounding the church was made to appear as it had in photographs from the 1870s. Inside, hard plaster was stripped from the walls, the flooring was removed and lowered, and the paintings, statues, and altar screens were cleaned and refurbished. In the colonial era, the church was noted as one of the wealthiest in the province, and during the restoration the cross on the main altar screen was found to be silver, rather than bronze.[128]

Today, the colonial villa of Santa Cruz is a neighborhood within the city limits of Española. Holy Cross Church faces east and still dominates the old villa site, overlooking the open, unlandscaped plaza, scattered adobe ruins, and modern businesses and residences. It is an exceptionally well-preserved example of New Mexican colonial architecture. Its massive adobe walls have been cement-plastered beige, and a broad metal roof gleams in the bright sunlight. Twin square bell towers stand at the church's front corners framing the main entrance.[129] Several adobe ruins lie on properties along the south and east side of the plaza. Most are the remains of nineteenth-century buildings, but some may date from the original founding of the villa. The plaza is crisscrossed by several narrow roads, the remnants of regional trails that once led through the villa.

Ohkay Owingeh (San Juan Pueblo)

Ohkay Owingeh, until quite recently known by the Spanish name of San Juan Pueblo, is located about eight miles north of Santa Clara, in the Española Valley, near the confluence of the Rio Grande and the Rio Chama. *Ohkay Owingeh*, "the place of the strong people," was the first Spanish capital of New Mexico and the administrative center of the colony for more than ten years until the founding of Santa Fe. This Tewa village became the northern terminus of the Camino Real de Tierra Adentro, linked to Mexico City, more than 1,600 miles to the south, and later served as a junction for other regional trade routes. San Juan Pueblo was also the Tewa village farthest away from Keres influence, and as one of six surviving Tewa settlements, is seen as the "mother village," a more conservative community where traditional cultural and political practices have been better preserved and protected.[130]

By the early sixteenth century, Tewa Indians were living at two thriving pueblos where the Rio Grande met the Rio Chama, Ohkay Owingeh, and Yungue.[131] On July 11, 1598, Juan de Oñate led an advance party into the first pueblo, proclaiming it the provincial capital of New Mexico. The Franciscan friars promptly named the site *San Juan Bautista*, Saint John the Baptist, but it was soon renamed *San Juan de los Caballeros* to honor both Saint John the Baptist and the caballeros, or explorer-knights, who had led the expedition up the Rio Grande.[132] In late July, Oñate toured other northern pueblos and explored the lands east and west of the valley. By August 10, he was back at San Juan, organizing Indian labor and beginning construction of the acequia system and a new Spanish town. It is not entirely clear where the first Spaniards settled. They were probably at San Juan, but as the main caravan arrived they laid out the first capital at *Yungue*, Mockingbird Place, a partially abandoned settlement, on the west bank of the river. The friars renamed Yungue for Saint Gabriel, one of the Archangels.[133]

The New Mexican capital had a rough start. A few days after the caravan arrived, forty-five soldiers and officers (almost one-third of the expeditionary force), rebelled. Unimpressed with New Mexico, disappointed with the lack of gold and silver, and frustrated with having to settle in a poor, remote Tewa pueblo, the colonists planned to desert and return south to Santa Bárbara. Oñate had the lead mutineers arrested and condemned to death. He insisted that an example be made, to maintain order at the new capital. Under pressure, he backed down from the execution order and allowed leniency for the rebels. A few days later a ceremony of atonement took place.[134]

A new church was hastily constructed at San Gabriel. It was a large, open chapel, dedicated to San Juan Bautista, and able to accommodate the entire camp. There was a weeklong celebration, similar to the one that had taken place in April near El Paso, with re-enactments, a play, tilting matches, and bullfights. The new colony appeared stable, but within a few days there were more problems. On September 12, four colonists stole horses and fled south along the trail. A search party followed, led by Captain Gaspar Pérez de Villagrá, who pursued the men into the Chihuahuan Desert and followed them almost all the way back to Santa Bárbara. Two men escaped, and two were executed under orders from Villagrá.[135] The early days at San Juan Pueblo continued to be fraught with factional disputes and challenges to Oñate's authority. Don Juan tried to maintain order, but the loss of control over his colonists eventually led to his recall. In 1609, Pedro de Peralta was appointed royal governor of New Mexico and began plans for a new villa at Santa Fe, formally founded the next year. San Juan Pueblo never became the major capital city that Oñate envisioned, but Spanish settlers remained there for years, and the mission church continued its duties among the Tewa.[136] As a small, regional outpost north of Santa Fe, well off the main route of the Camino Real de Tierra Adentro, San Juan Pueblo lost its administrative status but remained an important center of religious and commercial activity.

As the seventeenth century continued, conflicts between natives and Spaniards became more common. In the 1670s, Spanish officials began a crackdown on traditional spiritual practices among the Indians, accusing them of heresy and sorcery. Equating Indian spiritualism with witchcraft, the Spanish made a sweep of the Tewa pueblos in 1675; they accused forty-seven residents of sorcery, and brought them to Santa Fe to face charges. Popé (c.1630–c.1688), a Tewa religious leader from San Juan, was one of the accused. The heretics were specifically charged with bewitching Fray Andrés Durán of San Ildefonso, and killing seven friars and three Spaniards through sorcery. Three were sentenced to death by hanging. Each was to be executed in a different pueblo, as an example to the Indian residents. One captive committed suicide and the rest were sentenced to servitude, corporal punishments, or imprisonment. The crackdown by Spanish officials created an uproar throughout the pueblos and Indians from surrounding communities descended on Santa Fe demanding the prisoners' release. Governor Juan Francisco Treviño, sensing the potential threat, agreed to let the prisoners go on the condition that they "forsake idolatry" and abandon their heathen ways. One of the freed prisoners was Popé, who had been branded a sorcerer, publicly flogged, and humiliated by the Spanish. Shortly after his release, he moved to Taos, where he began planning a major uprising against the colonials.[137]

Popé's 1680 Pueblo Indian Revolt drove the Spanish out of northern New Mexico. It is not clear exactly what happened at Popé's pueblo of San Juan, but the mission priest was killed during the uprising. As Popé oversaw the revolt in the north, his role was probably that of a religious, rather than a military leader. It is unlikely, as a priest, that he would have been involved in warfare or the killing of Spaniards. As the rebellion spread, homes and haciendas in the area were sacked and destroyed, and thirty Spaniards living in the general vicinity of San Juan were killed.[138] Popé temporarily unified the various Pueblo and Apache tribes against the Spanish and freed northern New Mexico from the colonial yoke. He toured the surrounding pueblos ordering the remaining churches and convents destroyed, Christian icons burned, and any traces of Spanish colonialism erased. But after the Spanish were gone, old rivalries resurfaced, and Popé's allied armies often wreaked havoc on Indian settlements, looting and pillaging the very communities they had helped free. Popé held the fragile alliance together for a few years but had lost control of the north by the mid-1680s. By the time the Spanish returned in 1692, rival factions were at war for territory, and Popé was dead.[139] San Juan Pueblo was abandoned during the revolt. When Vargas returned, most of the Tewa resisted and for almost two years the Spanish fought for control of the region. In late 1693, a truce was negotiated and San Juan Pueblo was re-settled. Early the next year, missionaries were back at the village.[140]

A new church was completed by 1706, probably built on the same site as the original chapel, and expanded and renovated in the 1740s. In 1776, Domínguez described it as a large, square structure, with a substantial choir loft and convent.[141] The pueblo extended north from the church, with three residential structures that formed a street through the settlement. Domínguez observed a series of homesteads beyond San Juan, Rio Arriba, La Hoya, Canoa, and Embudo, with small family farms along the river and acequia channels. About 200 people lived in the pueblo itself and another 700 to 800 Indians, mestizos and Spaniards, in the surrounding communities.[142]

Although San Juan had lost many of its people during the revolt, suffered from epidemics and disease, and was no longer in a prominent position along the Camino Real de Tierra Adentro, it remained an important mission center and was linked to regional trade routes in the Española Valley.[143] Processed wool and textiles became the village's major crafts, sold along the trail. After Mexican Independence, San Juan Pueblo lost its mission status, but the pueblo remained much the same as it was in the late colonial era. Photographs taken in the 1880s show the church, courtyard, and nearby buildings as Domínguez had described them, one hundred years before.[144] In 1881, Captain Bourke called San Juan Pueblo "picturesque," built on a bluff overlooking a broad expanse of fertile land along the Rio Grande.[145] Overall, Bourke found San Juan to be "among the first of the Pueblos in cleanliness, good order, industriousness and progressive qualities."[146]

Women winnowing wheat, San Juan Pueblo, New Mexico, c.1925–1945? T. Harmon Parkhurst, Courtesy Palace of Governors Photo Archives (NMHM/DCA), Neg. No. 003966.

In 1865, Father Camilo Seux arrived in New Mexico from France and became an important influence in the religious organization and re-design of the community. During his long tenure at San Juan, he introduced a French-Gothic style of architecture to the village. Father Seux made slow, subtle changes at first but eventually redesigned and rebuilt the entire religious center of the village, constructing some of San Juan's most prominent buildings. Under his guidance, and often despite great resistance from the native population, Father Seux moved the cemetery away from the church courtyard, and added modern windows, pitched roofs and chimneys, and new facades to the surrounding structures. The eighteenth-century church underwent substantial renovations. The interior was cleaned and whitewashed. Wooden santos and colonial ornaments were replaced by plaster statues and a new altarpiece. The exterior was changed to reflect the French and Anglo-American styles popular at the time. A new pitched roof and steeple were added, along with a simulated stone masonry façade. In the 1880s, Father Seux brought a life-sized bronze statue of the Virgin Mary, a replica of the famous one at Lourdes, and had a chapel constructed for pilgrims who had begun to visit San Juan. In 1890, the Gothic stone structure was blessed by the archbishop. As renovations continued into the twentieth century, the old eighteenth-century mission church was eventually demolished, with only the most basic structural components left as a shell for the new brick church, built opposite the chapel, and completed in 1913.[147] Today, Father Seux's architectural influence can still be seen in the village center, where the brick-and-stone church and chapel tower over, and stand in stark contrast to, the surrounding adobe residential dwellings, many that have elements dating back to the colonial era and before.

San Juan Pueblo lies along NM 74, off NM 68, north of Española. Parallel one and two-story adobe housing blocks surround a plaza area behind the chapel, and a rectangular ceremonial kiva lies at the east end of the pueblo. The twentieth-century cemetery, which replaced the one located in front of the church, is further east, toward NM 68. The main street through the village center leads to the church, chapel, tribal offices, and craft center. Saint John the Baptist Church (Father Seux's 1913 Gothic church), is an imposing, brick structure on the west side of the center, with a large bell tower and modern windows and fixtures. Our Lady of Lourdes Pilgrimage Shrine, a chapel one-fifth the size of the Saint Chapelle at Paris, with its red stone buttressed exterior, is on the opposite side of the street facing the church and statue. The shrine underwent a major restoration in 2004.[148] San Juan Pueblo is still the largest of the northern pueblos, with almost 2,000 residents, and is active in many efforts to maintain its culture and traditions. It is the headquarters of the Eight Northern Indian Pueblos Council and the Ohkay Owingeh Arts and Crafts Cooperative which highlights the decorative arts and features several prominent local artisans. The pueblo's annual San Juan Fiesta is held each June 23 and 24 when traditional native dances are performed in the village plaza. An arts and crafts fair takes place each July. Matachines dances, originating in the Spanish colonial era, take place on December 24 and 25.[149] The Popé Run celebrates the Pueblo runners who carried the message to the various pueblos that the 1680 revolt had begun. The pueblo has tried to inventory, preserve, and protect much of its history. San Juan was added to National Register of Historic Places in 1974 and in recent years has conducted inventories of historic properties. Agricultural has long been an important part of the local economy, and a cooperative grows and packages tomatoes, corn, chili, squash, beans, and melons.

In 1991, a non-profit organization was founded to commission a statue honoring the central leader of the 1680 Pueblo Revolt, San Juan Pueblo's Popé. New Mexico and Arizona Native-American organizations, many of whom credit Popé with allowing some of their traditional spiritual practices to be preserved, helped with the planning. A statuary commission was formed in 1997 and Jemez Pueblo artist Clifford Fragua was contracted to create a lasting memorial to the Tewa leader. The statue was designated to be the 100th and final statue in the National Statuary Hall in Washington, D.C. The seven-foot three-and- one-half ton marble statue was completed in 2005, and a delegation of New Mexico tribal delegates, the state's congressional members, and representatives from Texas and Arizona tribes attended the unveiling in the nation's capitol building. Today, a small replica of the statue is kept in the tribal council offices.[150] In 2007, after more than 400 years, San Juan Pueblo officially changed its name back to Ohkay Owingeh, the original Tewa name of the village.[151]

There is a monument marking the site of Yungue Pueblo and San Gabriel de Yungue, the first capital of New Mexico, off of Yungue Road, which heads south towards the old bridge just across the Rio Grande. It is located on a mound which is part of the old pueblo. Southwest of the mound was the site of the Spanish settlement San Gabriel. While the first capital of New Mexico was remembered by the Tewa, it was essentially forgotten by New Mexico scholars until the 1940s when a small excavation renewed interest in the site. Surveys conducted in the early 1960s revealed a surprising amount of information about the site and confirmed much of the documentary record. Testing indicated that the pueblo had been constructed and occupied around 1300 CE and remained in use for centuries, at least until the mid-1500s. Work in the Eastern Mound revealed many signs of European occupation and renovation after 1598, suggesting that the Tewa had settled the Spaniards in an abandoned, unused area of their pueblo. Evidence of doorframes, windows, ovens, and tables revealed that the Spanish made use of much of the old residential blocks and modified them with European fixtures. Spanish debris around the site included the remains of cooking jars, colonial era pottery, and brass and iron pieces. The nave of the old church was also located at the site. In 1966, San Gabriel de Yungue was listed on the National Register of Historic Places.[152]

9

On to Santa Fe

*B*eyond Santo Domingo Pueblo, three branch roads of the Camino Real de Tierra Adentro led north. The original 1598 trail took travelers through the Galisteo Basin, east to San Marcos Pueblo, and then up toward Tewa country. After Santa Fe was established as the provincial capital in 1610, the new road passed through *Las Bocas*, the mouth of the Santa Fe River Canyon, up to La Ciénega, and on to the new villa. Both roads remained in use for centuries, but Las Bocas often flooded during the spring and summer months, and when the waters receded, there was considerable debris along its path. Sometime during the seventeenth century, a third branch of the trail ascended La Bajada Hill and Mesa and continued onto the open grassland plains below Santa Fe. This was the shortest and most direct route, but it was a steep, treacherous road and only travelers on foot or horseback, or herds of livestock, could make their way up the escarpment. All three roads left the wide floodplain of the Rio Grande and climbed to the brown uplands of the Santa Fe River Basin, a land of desert grasses and scattered trees, bushes, and stray junipers, with elevations reaching 7,000 feet.[1]

Santa Fe Area

El Camino Real through the Santa Fe Area.

La Bajada Village and Mesa

La Bajada escarpment and mesa are geological formations, major breaks in the landscape that separate the Rio Grande rift from the Santa Fe plateau. The escarpment slopes gently up from the river basin and then abruptly rises 600 feet to the mesa above. The sharp rise is the result of a volcanic cap, basalt that has compressed the clay and sandstone over the eons. Massive boulders are scattered throughout the area. Below the mesa is an open grassland known as *La Majada*, the Shepherd's Camp. The mesa is atop the escarpment, which extends across the plains toward Santa Fe. La Bajada was also a major administrative, cultural, and economic divide in colonial New Mexico. Traditionally, it separated the province into two districts, the *Rio Arriba*, or Upper River, and the *Rio Abajo*, or Lower River. The Rio Arriba comprised the capital region of Santa Fe and areas north, including the original Camino Real route through the northern pueblos. The Rio Abajo included everything to the south, reaching El Paso del Norte and into the Chihuahuan Desert. New Mexico's colonial governors oversaw the Rio Arriba, while lieutenant governors usually tended to matters in the Rio Abajo.[2]

The small village of San Miguel de la Bajada, more commonly known as *La Bajada*, or the Descent, lies below the hill and mesa, alongside the Santa Fe River. A modest Indian pueblo was located near the site and a few seventeenth-century pioneers may have lived there prior to the 1680 Pueblo Revolt, but it does not appear that anyone returned immediately after the rebellion. Vargas passed by the escarpment when he re-conquered New Mexico in the 1690s, but it was not until the late eighteenth century that pioneer settlers returned to La Bajada. They dug an acequia to the Santa Fe River and established a small village of clustered farming homesteads. Sometime after 1800 a tiny church was built to serve the small agricultural hamlet. La Bajada is seldom mentioned in early travelers' accounts. While some adventurous traders may have attempted to climb or descend La Bajada, it is unlikely that there was any regular traffic until the 1860s when the United States Army cleared much of the debris and opened the road for wagon trains. The first description of stagecoaches using the road was in 1869 when one traveler wrote that they:

> came to "La Bajada" a very severe grade, having an overhanging vertical wall of hundreds of feet on one side and a sheer precipice of 500 on the other. The descent was so risky that stage passengers always alighted and

made their way down on foot, while the driver found abundant occupation in taking care of his train and slowly creeping down with a "heavy break on…"[3]

By the early 1870s La Bajada had become an overnight coach stop on the road to Santa Fe with a freight depot and post office. After 1903, the Territorial Highway Commission improved the La Bajada wagon road and it became part of an important automobile route through northern New Mexico. After extensive grading, removal of debris, and the building of retaining walls, the roadway became a segment of the Ocean to Ocean Highway. The La Bajada section was regarded as an engineering marvel and was later designated as a part of New Mexico 1, the first major north-south automobile highway through the new state. In the 1920s further improvements were made and La Bajada road became part of the first federal highways through the region, US 66 and US 85. After 1926, as automobile travel became more common, La Bajada had a tourist camp, service station, and travel center. The road became an attraction in itself, celebrated in brochures and postcards. Tourists marveled at the hairpin turns, the steep ascent, and the spectacular views of the Rio Grande Valley and surrounding mountain ranges. But La Bajada's fame was short-lived, and by 1932 a new road was constructed about three miles east, close to where Interstate 25 climbs the mesa today. La Bajada no longer drew the attention of tourists, and people simply bypassed the village on their way to Albuquerque or Santa Fe.[4]

Today, San Miguel de La Bajada is located off NM 16, northeast of Santo Domingo Pueblo, near the Cochití Lake exit of Interstate 25. A New Mexico Highway Department Camino Real Marker stands at the entrance to the village, which is home to about one hundred people. The isolation of La Bajada for most of the last eighty years has preserved segments of the old roadbed and assorted historic structures from the nineteenth century and early automobile age. Portions of the old wagon road, and the Camino Real de Tierra Adentro, have also been identified near the escarpment. A small nineteenth-century adobe chapel, dedicated to Saint Michael, is located in the village center and several structures nearby may be built around early nineteenth-century adobe walls and foundations.[5] The former tourist camp is a private residence, and the old cabins are now used for storage. The remains of an early twentieth-century service station are evident, and a timber bridge, typical of those constructed in New Mexico during the early automobile era, is located just east of the village. Much of the land around La Bajada is public land, and there are currently projects underway to protect segments of the old roads and develop it for hiking and heritage tourism projects, especially in light of recent attempts to open the area to mining. The mesa and village of La Bajada remain one of the most dramatic and scenic areas along the National Historic Trail, and in 2002 both were added to the National Register of Historic Places.[6]

The village and church of La Bajada stand in the shadow of the basaltic escarpment and mesa, on a branch trail to Santa Fe.

La Cieneguilla

From the summit of La Bajada Mesa, Camino Real travelers continued northeast to La Cieneguilla, a small agricultural settlement further along the Santa Fe River. A Keres pueblo once stood at the site, established in the fourteenth century, and occupied for about 300 years. By the 1660s a few Spaniards had moved into the area, and Francisco de Anaya Almazán was the local alcalde. He traced his lineage back to a prominent family in Salamanca, Spain, had come north in the mid-seventeenth century, and held grants of encomienda in New Mexico at Picuris, Cuarac, and La Ciénega. His son, Francisco II, also held grants of encomienda and served as the alcalde mayor of the Tanos pueblos. His son's wife and child were killed in the Pueblo Revolt, and when he escaped to Santa Fe, he helped defend the villa, and then fled with Governor Otermín's refugee party to El Paso del Norte.[7]

Governor Vargas mentions the pueblo ruins in his journal and may have tried to re-settle some of the Tano Pueblo Indians there after re-conquering the province. Within a few years he opened the area for land grants. In 1693, Francisco II returned north with a new wife and reclaimed the land. He was awarded more than 3,000 acres by the end of the year. Although they were sometimes called haciendas, these Rio Arriba ranchos were fairly self-sufficient, with little reliance on the outside world. The Anaya Almazán family made adobe bricks and *terrones*, cut from the marshy sod, to build homes, defensive structures, and storage facilities. Irrigation systems tapped into the Santa Fe River when possible, but creeks and perennial springs usually provided much of the water. Sheep and cattle grazed on the grassy uplands, providing wool, meat, and hides. Spinning and weaving turned the wool into yarns and textiles. Other common animals included chickens, turkeys, goats, and pigs. Basic field crops (corn, beans, and wheat) fed the pioneers and kept their livestock healthy. Fruit trees produced apples, peaches, pears, plums, and apricots. Some fruits were consumed as they were harvested, but many were dried and stored for future use. Wines and brandies were made from grapes in the colonial period.

The Anaya Almazán family sold much of the land in the 1740s, and many new settlers moved to the site. A small, compact village grew up on the west bank of the Santa Fe River, and villagers farmed the land across the river on the opposite bank. By the end of the century, members of the Anaya, Romero, Montoya, and Mora clans lived at Cieneguilla. In 1776, Fray Domínguez counted twenty-five families, a total of 185 persons. It continued to draw a few new homesteaders in the early nineteenth century but never developed into a sizable town or caught the attention of trail travelers.[8]

The San Antonio Chapel at La Cieneguilla.

Today, La Cieneguilla is a small crossroads settlement, located on land identified as La Cieneguilla Land Grant, on County Road 56, southeast of Santa Fe. Modern houses and a few early twentieth-century remains are clustered along the highway. Paseo de San Antonio, an unimproved road off of County Road 56, leads a few thousand feet west to a small hillside chapel named *Capilla de San Antonio de Cieneguilla*, for Saint Anthony, the only remaining structure from the Spanish Colonial or Mexican era. It was built after 1818 by members of the Mora and Romero families. The chapel, listed as a New Mexico Registered Cultural Property, is a small white stuccoed-adobe church, which sits atop the hillside, overseeing modern housing. It is a flat-roofed rectangular structure with a small belfry. Inside, pine vigas support the simple frame. A wrought-iron fence surrounds several graves near the entrance. According to Mora family descendants, a colonial pioneer brought a statue of Saint Anthony from Portugal to La Cieneguilla in the late eighteenth century. Sporadic wars developed between Hispanic ranchers and nomadic Comanches. In 1776 alone, nine shepherds were killed in attacks at La Cieneguilla and La Ciénega. After several truces, Comanche raiders returned in the early nineteenth century. According to the Moras, the community made a promise to Saint Anthony that if the attacks ceased, they would build a chapel in his honor. They constructed the chapel in 1818–20, and the statue was placed at the altar to protect the village from further assaults. Today, the volcanic rock of the escarpment is seen on the ridge behind the historic landmark, and below, the hill slopes down to farmland watered by the river. Pueblo Indians lived in the area for hundreds of years and several hiking trails lead through the Bureau of Land Management's La Cieneguilla Petroglyph Site along the escarpment nearby. From La Cieneguilla, the Camino Real de Tierra Adentro followed County Road 56, climbing several hundred feet along the Santa Fe River to the area of Airport Road, and into the villa.

La Ciénega

After 1610, the main branch of the Camino Real de Tierra Adentro entered *Las Bocas*, the Mouth of Santa Fe River Canyon, and continued northeast, gently climbing alongside the escarpment. A later variant of the trail followed close to the path of today's Interstate 25. Today, the landscape bears little resemblance to nineteenth-century writers' descriptions of groves of large cottonwoods and duck ponds filled with trout. The Santa Fe River Basin has undergone extensive changes in the past one hundred years as river water, mostly run-off from the Sangre de Cristo Mountains, has been used for farmland irrigation. Today, the flow of water has declined noticeably, and the area is drier with much less vegetation.[9] The Las Bocas branch of the Camino Real de Tierra Adentro led to the settlement of La Ciénega, the last paraje before reaching the Villa of Santa Fe. Colonial La Ciénega was located about halfway between the modern community and the confluence of Ciénega Creek and the Santa Fe River. The immediate area served as a border between two major Pueblo Indians groups, the Keres and the Tanos. Keres-speaking Pueblo Indians called the site *Tziguma*, the Lone Cottonwood, a name that was later applied to the nearby Spanish settlement of El Alamo. The Oñate expedition visited the pueblo in 1598 and called the site *La Ciénega*, named for the valley marshlands where underground springs feed area depressions and allow water to pool. After a mission was established at nearby San Marcos Pueblo, La Ciénega was visited by friars who built a small chapel at the site. Sometime in the first half of the seventeenth century, members of Juan Victoria Carvajal's family moved to La Ciénega. They lived near the pueblo ruins and made use of the marsh's waters to irrigate their fields. By the mid-seventeenth century, some Pueblo Indians returned to the site. In 1680, they helped leaders from nearby Tano Pueblos alert the Spanish of the impending rebellion. During the revolt the natives fled the area and when the Spanish returned in 1692, they found the old pueblo abandoned. Vargas referred to the ruins as *La Cieneguilla*, the Little Marshlands, which was often confused with a later Spanish settlement further north.

Vargas was unimpressed with La Ciénega and suggested that an area further north be opened to re-settlement, so pioneer land grants were made at nearby El Alamo and La Cieneguilla in the mid-1690s. There is no evidence of a formal La Ciénega land grant at the time, but after 1700, Miguel Vega y Coca, a soldier who came to New Mexico with the re-colonizing forces, purchased the land and moved his family, which included seven daughters and their husbands, to La Ciénega. By the 1710s, they were farming land around the old pueblo ruins and several of the daughters had married into the Baca family, who had also settled on the grant. Colonial La Ciénega never developed into a major village; it was merely a small cluster of homes, an extended agricultural community. One of Vega y Coca's daughters, María, married Diego Manuel Baca. He died in 1727, and his will stated that a house and land at La Ciénega was a merger of his property and land brought to the marriage by his wife. This was the first formal reference to the Baca ranch, the largest in the area. The earliest dwellings were built around a defensive square, with solid protective walls, watchtowers, and gated entrances. A central gateway with massive wooden doors opened into the placita, or courtyard, area. Farmers and ranchers spent most of their time in the fields, but when any unusual activity was detected, they headed for the protection of the placita. Later, in the early nineteenth century, as the threat of Comanche attacks subsided, people moved outside of the walls.[10]

As a large hacienda, near the village of La Ciénega, the Baca property became a paraje on the Camino Real de Tierra Adentro. Presidial soldiers stayed at the Baca ranch while scouting areas south of the villa. There may have been a small chapel at the site, and priests routinely visited to perform rituals such as marriages, baptisms, burials, and celebrations of feast days. Fray Domínguez stopped there in 1776 and remarked on the ancient ruins but did not describe the village or hacienda. He counted sixteen families, with more than one hundred people, living around La Ciénega.[11] Four years later, Juan Bautista de Anza, who was searching for a more direct route into Sonora, brought his expedition of fifty-one soldiers and Indians to La Ciénega. Anza was the first to note the ranch's name as *Las Golondrinas*, the Swallows.[12]

El Rancho de Las Golondrinas, a premier living history museum, on El Camino Real de Tierra Adentro National Historic Trail.

The ranch was overlooked by most trail travelers who headed directly into Santa Fe. Zebulon Pike may have stopped at La Ciénega in 1807. In October 1846, as part of their charting of the Rio Grande, Lieutenants Abert and Peck visited mining sites in New Mexico, including the hills around La Ciénega. Abert described the valley as well-populated, with abundant water and an impressive irrigation system. In 1853, Lieutenant Amiel W. Whipple conducted a railroad survey and noted well-cultivated fields, numerous fresh springs, houses, and a church. The village still had a stone tower, or *torreón,* which had served as a defense against Comanche raids. Locals directed his party to a wagon trail just beyond the arroyo which they called the Camino Real. In the late nineteenth century, much of Las Golondrinas Ranch had been divided and sold to Baca family descendants. Other tracts were transferred to members of the González and Delgado families who often intermarried with the Bacas. One descendant, Elfego Pino, consolidated a great deal of acreage, and by the 1930s owned much of La Ciénega and the Golondrinas site, but he was forced to sell out during the Great Depression. Leonora F. Curtin, daughter of a California folklorist, became heir to the property. When she married A.Y. Paloheimo, a Finnish consul for the western United States, they often spent their summers at Las Golondrinas. Encouraged by prominent New Mexico architect John Gaw Meem, they acquired more property around the site and rebuilt the Baca house. After retiring in the 1960s, the couple began envisioning the historic site as a museum, and in 1972 Old Ciénega Village Museum (today El Ranchos de las Golondrinas) opened its doors. As New Mexico's only living history museum, it is the best preserved colonial hacienda along the Camino Real de Tierra Adentro, a restored complex of structures typical of the colonial and Mexican era. The heart of the museum is a fortified hacienda and out buildings grouped around a placita. A defensive tower stands near one of the *zaguanes* or covered entrances. Many historic buildings were moved to the site. A nineteenth century home and all of its outbuildings; a molasses mill, a threshing ground, several primitive water mills, a blacksmith shop, a wheelwright shop, a winery and vineyards, depict many of the essential elements of Spanish Colonial culture. The entire complex has been reconstructed on the original site, overseen by descendants of the Baca family, and meticulously designed and built to capture the spirit and atmosphere of an eighteenth-century agricultural settlement in the Rio Arriba. The eastern boundary of many of the properties around La Ciénega was the Camino Real de Tierra Adentro, a common line in colonial and Mexican land grants.[13]

Agua Fría

Whether travelers followed the Las Bocas road or ventured up La Bajada, the trail eventually took them to a spot near today's NM 599 Loop and Airport Road. From there, the Camino Real followed Agua Fría Street along the river and into the Villa of Santa Fe. The Santa Fe River area was home to many small scattered agricultural Indian hamlets during the 1100s CE, and over the next 200 years these settlements consolidated and larger, more extensive residential pueblos were built. Two major villages, Pindi Pueblo and the Agua Fría Schoolhouse Pueblo, once stood on opposite sides of the river in today's Agua Fría, and their ruins became trail landmarks in the Spanish Colonial era. Both attracted settlers during the Coalition Period (1200–1325 CE), a time when Pueblo Indians moved south from the Four Corners area into the Rio Grande and Santa Fe Basins. By the 1200s CE, Keres, Tanos, and Tewas had established villages throughout the region. Pindi Pueblo appears to have been built during the 1100s, expanded for more than 200 years, and occupied until the early fourteenth century. Most early pueblos along the Santa Fe River were small one-story structures, with a few dozen rooms. They were expanded as the population increased, especially as small pueblos were abandoned and people sought refuge in larger farming villages. Pindi means "turkey" in Tewa and referred to the large turkey pens found at the site. Turkeys, along with corn, beans, and squash, became an important part of the indigenous diet and useful products for trade. Pindi became a large pueblo of two-and three-story structures with as many as 200 rooms, two plazas, and five kivas. Excavations in the 1930s revealed that Pindi Pueblo was a substantial site and regional trade center well into the 1300s, when river flooding badly damaged the village.

On the opposite side of the river stood the Agua Fría Schoolhouse pueblo, named for a nearby district school that existed at the time of the 1930s excavations. Agua Fría was settled around 1200 CE and prospered for about one hundred years, but it too was damaged by river flooding and finally abandoned by about 1420 CE. Somewhere between 1,500 and 2,000 people lived in the two pueblos during their peak occupation in the fourteenth century. The residents of Pindi and Agua Fría appear to have cornered the regional pottery market, controlling area trade in the black-on-white vessels that were extensively bartered throughout the Rio Arriba. Documents indicate that this is where the Spanish camped when they returned to Santa Fe with Vargas in 1692, and the old Camino Real passed through a large open plaza in the pueblo.[14]

Agua Fría was first settled by Spaniards around 1730 when Cristóbal Baca established a small farm along the Camino Real. The Bacas burned part of Pindi Pueblo as they cleared the land for farming along the river, and the settlement became known as *Pueblo Quemado*, the Burnt Village. Much of the land between Cieneguilla and Quemado was essentially grazing land, and during

the eighteenth century several other farms were sited in the vicinity of today's
Agua Fría village. Long rectangular plots of land fronted the river. Fields were
cultivated and livestock roamed the outer reaches of the grants. Some of the
eighteenth-century farms in the area were substantial. The Baca estate included
450 sheep, ten horses, mules and plows, two yoke of oxen, and assorted tools
and farming equipment. Baca's seven children, their spouses, and descendants
divided the complex and continued ranching and farming during the remainder
of the century. Other properties were also settled in the eighteenth century near
Quemado. El Pino, Los Palacios, and the Montoya and Pacheco grants were all
cited as large agricultural operations. The Roybal, Noriega, Pacheco, Montoya,
Padilla, and Hernández families received land grants and continued the pattern
of long narrow plots that fronted the irrigation canals or river. Livestock grazed
on the grassy plains and uplands.

**Agua Fria was the last stop on the Camino Real de Tierra Adentro as it entered the Villa of
Santa Fe.**

By the nineteenth century, these large estates had been subdivided among several generations and smaller, more specialized farms were common. Little is known about the village in the late colonial era. It was the last stop on the trail before entering Santa Fe, and, being only a few miles from the villa's center, it was unlikely that many travelers spent time at the small clusters of modest adobe farmhouses. Fray Domínguez merely noted a place called *Quemado*, the Burnt Site, in 1776, referring to charred pueblo ruins of Pindi alongside the river.[15] In the nineteenth century, the central village became known as *Agua Fría*, named for the chilled waters that flowed from perennial springs and wells in the area. By the Mexican era, Agua Fría was used as a campsite and light grazing area for livestock. Caravans often rendezvoused near the village rather than continue the few miles into the center of the villa. By the 1850s, the Territorial village had a more diversified economy, including weavers, merchants, shoemakers, blacksmiths, and a schoolteacher.

Agua Fría still has some of the atmosphere of a small traditional agricultural community, even though Santa Fe development and traffic often congests Agua Fría Road (the old Camino Real). The heart of the nineteenth-century settlement lies near the San Isidro Church at 3552 Agua Fría Road, a long, rectangular, tan-stuccoed adobe building with a central bell tower and cross. It was built on property donated by the Gallegos family sometime after 1835 and dedicated to Saint Isidore the Laborer, the patron saint of farmers and protector of crops. The Gallegos were very active in church activities, and one family member, Celso Gallegos, became a renowned maker of religious art in the early twentieth century. He carved santos and altar pieces, wooden grave markers, and small works for the interior of the San Isidro Church. In the mid-1920s, his works were featured in Santa Fe galleries and he had established a following among collectors. By the time of his death, the church interior and surrounding cemetery were an open gallery of Gallegos's works. But during the 1960s, landscaping and renovation work at the church led to the removal of most of Gallegos's artworks. Today's gravemarkers are mostly stone and iron, and the church interior features more modern fixtures. Fortunately, some of Gallegos's works have been preserved at other sites and in regional galleries.

Several homes near the church have been built around early adobe structures. Agua Fría was designated as a Traditional Historic Community, the first in New Mexico, by Santa Fe County, marking its significant cultural heritage but without providing any legal protection. In 2004, Agua Fría village was listed as one of New Mexico's Most Endangered Places. There are several adobe buildings that date back to the nineteenth century, scattered throughout the historic core of the village. Near San Isidro Church is a single-lane, unpaved stretch of the old Camino Real which extends about one block through the historic center of the community.

Santa Fe

After 1610, Santa Fe became the northern terminus of El Camino Real de Tierra Adentro, connecting Mexico City with the new provincial capital. It remained the end of the trail for the rest of the colonial era, but several important branch roads soon reached to Taos, the Pecos region, and western New Mexico. For much of the twentieth century there was confusion about when the first Spaniards lived at the villa site, but it now appears that some had settled there in the early years of the new colony. Among the first was Captain Juan Martínez de Montoya who arrived in New Mexico in 1600 and served on the town council of San Gabriel. Although he received a grant of encomienda, the title of hidalgo, and had served in several campaigns and expeditions, Martínez de Montoya became affiliated with a faction of settlers who were increasingly uncomfortable with Oñate's leadership. They were tired of the military exploits and the search for riches, and hoped instead to build an agricultural base in the north, and develop trade with communities in the interior. They also had influence in Mexico City. After Oñate resigned as governor in 1607, the viceroy asked Martínez de Montoya to take charge, but the local *cabildo*, or municipal government, dominated by Oñate supporters, was suspicious and refused the appointment. They asked Don Juan to reconsider, and when he refused, they appointed Oñate's son Cristóbal to assume the office.[16] After the controversy subsided, sometime in early 1608, Martínez de Montoya established a private residence along the Santa Fe River, below the Sangre de Cristo Mountains, near the ruins of an abandoned Tewa pueblo, and named the site the *Plaza de Santa Fe*, the Plaza of the Holy Faith. The next year, Cristóbal Oñate was replaced by Pedro de Peralta. By then, Martínez de Montoya and the Oñates had left the colony. In 1610, Governor Peralta formally founded a new provincial capital, the *Villa Real de Santa Fe de San Francisco de Asís*, The Royal Villa of the Holy Faith of Saint Francis of Assisi, on the site of the Martínez de Montoya homestead.[17]

The original 1598 Camino Real to San Juan Pueblo remained an important link to the northern Indian settlements, and Spanish missionaries and settlers continued working at the old capital site, but with the founding of Santa Fe, the Royal Road veered east near La Bajada, and led into the villa. Early Santa Fe was better fortified than the old capital at San Gabriel. The inner core of the settlement was completed during 1610, and within a few years adjoining military and government structures were built. Their outer walls formed a defensive barrier, and a trench separated the walls from the surrounding fields. There were two towers positioned on the walls with sentries at the north and south end, overseeing the main roads that led into the villa. A large wooden gate served as the only entrance to the villa in its early years. Highways to Taos, Galisteo, Pecos, and the Royal Road of the Interior radiated from the villa.[18] Outside of the walls, cultivated fields and residential areas, including a Mexican Indian settlement called Analco, surrounded the villa. Sometime after 1610 they built a temporary church of mud and thatch. In 1613 some type of permanent structure was begun, and thirteen years later, *La Parroquia*, the parish church and convent of Saint Francis, had been enlarged and remodeled.[19]

For much of the seventeenth century, the Villa of Santa Fe, on the northern edge of the Spanish frontier, was an unstable environment, the scene of repeated conflicts between the provincial government, central authorities in the interior, and the Catholic Church. The capital grew during Peralta's administration but like his predecessor Juan de Oñate, the governor faced numerous challenges and remained in power only a short time. He was ultimately undermined by the Franciscan friars who questioned his authority and exercised the power of the Inquisition to remove him from office and have him imprisoned.[20] In 1680, Santa Fe became a refuge for survivors of the Pueblo Indian Revolt. Those who escaped attacks throughout the Rio Arriba fled to the safely-walled settlement, and within hours of the outbreak, the villa, under the command of Governor Antonio de Otermín, prepared for an assault. The *casas reales*, today's Palace of the Governors, became the central command post where Otermín dispatched patrols to survey the surrounding region and report on the fighting. When the siege began, Indian raiders swarmed into Analco.[21] Many Indian residents fled to the safety of the villa, while others joined in the rebellion. The Spaniards attempted to drive them out but were quickly outnumbered by re-enforcements from nearby pueblos. With the villa cut off from water, and much of its agricultural stores and livestock out of reach, Governor Otermín's troops became desperate. On August 20, they stormed the rebel Indian forces and brought an end to the siege. They found the outlying areas in ruins and homes and fields sacked. Governor Otermín decided to abandon Santa Fe and head south down the Camino Real to the safety of El Paso del Norte, more than 300 miles away.

In early 1691, after several failed attempts to re-conquer the north, a new governor, Diego de Vargas, assumed command at El Paso del Norte. The next year he led a force of one hundred men, comprised of soldiers, citizens, and Indians, back to Santa Fe. During the Spaniards' absence, various Pueblo Indians had occupied the villa, living in the old government buildings, churches, and residences. On September 13, Vargas and his men camped on the outskirts and negotiated a settlement with Pueblo leaders. Optimistic about his "bloodless" re-conquest, he quickly returned south to recruit settlers and urge refugees to move back to the Rio Arriba. When he arrived at Santa Fe in the fall of 1693, however, conditions had changed. His poorly provisioned band of colonists, facing a severe, early winter, soon learned that whatever agreements had been made before were now being re-negotiated. The governor and his troops held out for two weeks but then decided to storm the villa. They charged in and by afternoon secured much of the old settlement. Over the next few days, they gained a stronger foothold and found their Indian adversaries, weary from thirteen years of in-fighting, divided. Vargas negotiated new alliances, and, despite several years of continued conflict, the villa was secure.[22]

Eighteenth-century Santa Fe was stabilized, but it remained a poor, remote frontier outpost, with limited commerce or trade. Population increased, and travel along the old Camino Real resumed, but nomadic Indian attacks remained a problem until late in the century. The compact walled seventeenth-century villa prospered and expanded as farms and ranches spread out from the plaza area, following the waters and irrigation systems of the Santa Fe River. The tight, compact design of the old villa faded, and many of the military functions declined. In 1760, Bishop Tamarón was surprised to find that there was no actual fortress at Santa Fe, only a garrison of eighty mounted soldiers. He described the villa as a "very open place" with houses spaced far apart and few defenses, and during his stay, there were threats of Comanche attacks. He was told that there were 1,285 people living in the villa, but he counted several hundred more and estimated that the population was at least double.[23] In 1776, Fray Domínguez offered a disappointing description of Santa Fe. He found the setting quite impressive, but the villa itself he described as "mournful." He explained that the appearance, design, arrangement, and plan did not "correspond to its status as a villa…" Domínguez compared the provincial capital to a "rough stone set in fine metal" and noted that it lacked every basic necessity. Traveling into the villa on the Camino Real from Agua Fría, he saw a series of "small ranchos at various distances from one another, with no plan as to their location…" He found only the slightest "semblance of a street" running through the villa.[24]

Even so, several streets that radiated from the plaza area were highways into the villa. Engineer Joseph de Urrutia's 1766 map of Santa Fe shows the Camino Real de Tierra Adentro entering the city center along the Camino de Álamo, leading in from Agua Fría. Camino de la Cañada heads northwest toward Santa Cruz de la Cañada and linked the capital with the old trail north to San Juan Pueblo. The Camino de Pecos led east to the Pecos missions and became the route of the Santa Fe Trail into the city by the 1820s. The Acequia Madre, also shown on the Urrutia map, was the main irrigation canal through the colonial villa and is still in use, running along today's Acequia Madre Street six miles through the city to Agua Fría. The acequia headgate is located in the east end, where it draws from the Santa Fe River, to water homes, fields, parks, and public areas.[25] The 1790 census counted 2,500 residents, close to Tamarón's estimate thirty years earlier, most listed as farmers and laborers. Twenty-five *obrajeros*, or workshops, produced basic crafts, often using Indian laborers. Only one person was identified as a schoolteacher, and only one was listed as a fulltime merchant. But living in a villa did influence social status and sixty-six per cent of the residents identified themselves as *españoles*.[26]

In the Mexican era, Santa Fe remained a remote provincial capital in the northern reaches of the republic. When Mexican troops took over the old Spanish presidio, the number of men at the post was greatly reduced. The structures themselves were neglected and dilapidated, and the presidio walls had been dismantled by locals who used the mud blocks for new construction. Santa Fe continued to be described as a dirty, dusty town of broken-down adobe structures. The open plaza was a campsite, filled with wagons and pack animals, and Indian traders. Low adobe buildings closed in on the plaza, reducing its size by half. The Palace of the Governors was smaller as well, with a few offices for civil authorities, a customhouse, and a jail.[27]

One major change occurred in 1821 as the Mexican Republic sought to break its ties with the Spanish commercial system and establish new trading relations with other nations, especially the United States. William Becknell, a Missouri adventurer, arrived at the old villa in November with a small mule train loaded with commercial goods from the east and began trading with local merchants. The governor's office declared the beginning of a new era when Americans could openly transport goods into New Mexico, conduct business with communities along the old Camino Real, and set up their own operations, living and working in the Republic. Becknell had followed a route opened in the early 1790s by Pedro Vial, a Frenchman who had explored, traded, and built rapport with nomadic Indian tribes and blazed several trails east from Santa Fe. Becknell helped develop an overland route that connected commercial outlets along the river with northern New Mexico. Goods from the east came up the river and were carried by mule and wagon trains across the Great Plains. The Santa Fe Trail quickly changed commercial patterns in the west as Anglo-American merchants replaced the colonial caravans and supplied many of the Rio Arriba's consumer goods. In the 1820s, Santa Fe was soon saturated with imports, and trade moved down the old Camino Real, reaching Chihuahua City, twice the size of (and much more prosperous than) Santa Fe. Wagon trains and pack mules were led down the trail, visiting communities along the old Royal Road on their way to the interior. Hispanic New Mexican merchants invested in the emerging commercial system. They outfitted wagon trains that went east to buy goods and organized their own caravans. Native New Mexican traders paid substantially lower duties and offered vigorous competition to their American counterparts. Eventually, much of the trade was conducted through locals who served as middlemen, organizing caravans and wagon trains back to Chihuahua City and Missouri, through Santa Fe.[28]

Santa Fe surrendered to American forces early in the Mexican-American War. On August 18, 1846, the 1,500 soldiers in the United States Army of the West marched into the city under the command of Brigadier General Stephen Watts Kearny and within days, they began changing the old villa. They chose an elevated site a few thousand feet northeast of the plaza for a new American citadel, Fort Marcy. The American flag was hoisted above the plaza, and American merchants converged on the town center. A nineteenth-century Territorial architecture began to take root, blending Spanish Colonial traditions with Anglo-American styles popular in the east.

Stagecoaches ran along the old Camino Real through American territory and linked to new routes that ran east and west of the city. While Santa Fe remained an important crossroads during the 1850s and 1860s, developments later in the century reduced its role as a major traffic hub in the American West. In the late 1870s, Santa Fe was unable to work out agreements with the Denver and Rio Grande Railroad and the Atchison, Topeka, and Santa Fe Railway for a right-of-way and service facilities in the city. As a result, neither line entered the old villa. The Denver and Rio Grande fell on hard times and delayed its expansion in New Mexico, and the Atchison, Topeka, and Santa Fe's surveyors plotted an alternate route through the Galisteo Basin, eighteen miles south of Santa Fe. Even though a spur was built to meet up with the main line in 1880, the rails diverted traffic south. As the Atchison, Topeka, and Santa Fe headed down the Rio Grande Valley, Albuquerque began to surpass Santa Fe as the Territorial population and commercial center. In 1926, one of the first federal highways, US 66, entered Santa Fe along the Pecos Trail and continued south to La Bajada Hill where it followed the old Camino Real and the Rio Grande down to Albuquerque. For the next eleven years this roadway served as the main automobile route through the region and helped link the capital with interstate commerce, travel, and trade. In 1937, US 66 was re-routed. The new highway bypassed Santa Fe and left the old Camino Real de Tierra Adentro. Instead it entered Albuquerque along a path parallel to today's Interstate 40.[29]

As Santa Fe became more isolated and lost its status as a major regional center, some recognized its unique cultural and artistic traditions and began to promote the old villa and preserve its traditional, eclectic blend of architecture. Many structures in the historic core of the city were refurbished and remodeled to reflect this blend of Spanish and Indian traditions. By the time of statehood in 1912, Spanish Pueblo Revival architecture became the official style of the City Different. By the 1930s, American Territorial-architecture styles were also preserved and encouraged. These efforts led to a distinctive Santa Fe style, a blend of earth tones, less formal lines, and roughhewn structures. Rather than the remote, dilapidated town described by Fray Domínguez and early Anglo-American visitors, Santa Fe developed a reputation as a quaint, charming backroads settlement. In the early twentieth century, it became a cultural oasis, attracting artists, intellectuals, and their fellow travelers from all over the world. East coast artists such as John Sloan, Robert Henri, Carlos Vierra, and Randall Davey moved into the old villa, drawn to the exciting mix of New Mexico's Anglo-American, Hispanic, and Native-American cultures, and the region's unique blend of shapes, colors, and light. By mid-century, there was a thriving artists' colony and numerous small galleries that featured the new regional art of the Southwest. Santa Fe also became a literary Mecca. D.H. Lawrence, Mary Austin, Mabel Dodge Luhan, and Paul Horgan spent time in the old villa, published works about the region, and received international acclaim.[30] Santa Fe was still a small, compact community in the 1940s with a population of about 25,000, and most residents lived within walking distance of the central plaza, but the 1950s brought considerable growth. Along with its Bohemian residents, Santa Fe became a popular retirement community and developed a thriving summer tourism trade. Large residential tracts were opened south of the city, and commercial growth spread along its major highways, especially south on Cerrillos Road. As the city changed, officials attempted to capture its unique, eclectic ambience. Much of the city's appearance is the result of efforts in the mid-twentieth century to preserve its historic center. In 1957, the Santa Fe City Council adopted a zoning ordinance that required new construction to conform to Pueblo or Territorial revival styles. Three years later, the Santa Fe Plaza and the Palace of the Governors were designated as National Historic Landmarks. Many sites have been entered in the National Register of Historic Places. Although today's Santa Fe does not look much as it did in the Colonial or Mexican era, it is one of the best preserved sites on the Camino Real de Tierra Adentro and has developed a thriving tourist industry by emphasizing the confluence of Native-American, Hispanic, and Anglo-American cultures. By the 1980s, the state capital and its 74,000 residents had become one of the premier tourist destinations in the Americas, drawing visitors from all over the world.[31]

Palace of the Governors

The Palace of the Governors is one the nation's oldest public buildings and has been in continuous use since the 1610s. It is a long one-story building with a series of rooms that enclose an interior courtyard. The oldest section is a two-room-deep expanse which extends along the entire north side of the Santa Fe Plaza. In front is a long *portal*, or open porch, with exposed boards and vigas, supported by fifteen massive posts and carved corbels. The Palace of the Governors dates from the earliest years of Santa Fe and was probably built when the new capital was first established in 1610. It was originally a *casa real*, or royal government building, and was part of a complex that included a fort, armory, council hall, chapel, and residential quarters. While the first stone and wooden buildings at Jamestown or Plymouth vanished long ago, the Palace remains in use, more than 400 years after it was originally constructed.

Palace of the Governors, Santa Fe. Library of Congress, Prints and Photographs Division, Historic American Buildings Survey, March 21, 1934, HABS NM, 25–SANFE, 2–2.

When the Palace was abandoned during the 1680 Pueblo Revolt, Indians from San Marcos, Ciénega, and the Galisteo Basin moved in and dug storage pits, built hearths, and enlarged adobe segments of the walls. They also added a second story to part of the building and constructed a pueblo-style dwelling. The Palace was hastily rebuilt after New Mexico was re-conquered by the Spanish, and by the 1710s it was in poor condition and required extensive renovation. By the 1730s, the second story had been removed, the south side was rebuilt, and the governor's residence refurbished. It was then a long one-story, one-room deep building, extended along the north side of the plaza. In the 1780s, after the defensive walls around the villa had been removed, the *presidio*, or fortress, was rebuilt on land north and west of the plaza. The Palace remained the government and military headquarters for New Mexico after Mexican independence. Inside were offices, a council hall, the governor's study and family residence, officers' and soldiers' quarters, and a jail. In the 1820s, the Palace was designated as a customhouse where duties were collected, especially from goods traded on the Santa Fe Trail. Furnishings and fixtures from the east, such as window glass and cloth, were brought in on the trail and became common in the Palace.

In 1846, Stephen Kearny's forces occupied Santa Fe and made it the seat of the new American Territorial government. The Palace became the Territorial governor's residence. It also housed a library, the Office of Indian Affairs, the United States Depository, and the United States Land Office. By the 1880s various federal offices had moved to the new capitol south of the river, and the United States military gave up all claims to the Palace. A historical society set up exhibits in some of the old legislative halls. In 1909, the Museum of New Mexico was established as a department of the School of American Archaeology, and the New Mexico Territorial legislature designated the Palace as the home for its historical documents, artifacts, and exhibits. Much of today's exterior is the result of a major renovation from 1910–1913 when Territorial features of the building were preserved, and Spanish-Pueblo Revival styles were incorporated into the structure. Tons of trash and debris that had accumulated behind the building were removed, and interior areas were cleared for exhibits, laboratories, and research facilities. The Palace was officially added to the National Register of Historic Places in 1966 and received a second major overhaul in the 1980s as its entire roof was replaced, and new heating, cooling, and security systems were installed. During the renovations areas were meticulously restored to their nineteenth-century appearances.

Behind the Palace of the Governors is the New Mexico History Museum. This new 96,000 square-foot museum with extensive storage facilities for collections, a large auditorium, two-small theaters, archives, and electronic services opened its doors in 2009. The History Museum is a bilingual facility with multi-media exhibits that seeks to expand the interpretation of the state's history by using a broader cultural perspective that includes contributions by the many indigenous peoples of the region as well as the Spanish, Mexican, and Anglo-American settlers. The museum houses and displays a multitude of artifacts, images, and depictions of life along the trail over the centuries.

La Castrense (Nuestra Señora de la Luz)

Nuestra Señora de la Luz Chapel, Our Lady of the Light, no longer exists, but its most striking iconic feature, a large stone altar screen, has survived. Francisco Antonio Marín del Valle served as New Mexico's governor from 1756 to 1760, and during his brief term of office he financed the construction of a large chapel on the central plaza of the villa, opposite the Palace of the Governors. It was a typical nave-and-transept design and fronted the plaza. The basic mud-plastered façade, with little ornamentation, concealed an elaborate interior, well-furnished and decorated. Mexican stone carvers, some from as far down the trail as Zacatecas, were brought in to create a massive altar screen that filled the rear wall of the chapel. The church faced the plaza and became associated with colonial officers and troops, hence the name *La Castrense,* the Military Chapel. According to Bishop Tamarón, who visited during construction of the church, a vein of white stone, large enough to fill much of the high altar wall, was discovered outside of the villa and brought to the site where it was carved into an elaborate altar screen. Fray Domínguez, visiting sixteen years later, was impressed with the carvings and likened the stone fresco to those "facades which are now used in famous Mexico." Unfortunately, Marín left Santa Fe in 1760, not even staying long enough to attend the church's consecration.[32]

Early nineteenth-century accounts described the structure as neglected and in poor condition, but even so, it remained in use, and governors sometimes marched garrison soldiers in full uniform to attend services at the site. In 1847, Doniphan's troops looted the chapel, and for years the United States Army used the old church for storage. It was briefly made a chapel once again, but by 1856, the diocese lost interest in the property and sold it to a private owner. Fragments of the old chapel building remained until 1955. The front of the structure was razed and the stone altarpiece was dismantled and re-assembled at La Parroquia, the main parish church in Santa Fe. There, it continued to be neglected, and by the 1880s it was placed behind a new wall, in an area used for storage. For years few people even caught a glimpse of the carvings. In the 1930s, money was raised to restore the altarpiece and move it to a more appropriate setting. In 1939, renowned architect John Gaw Meem's new Cristo Rey Church, a massive structure on upper Canyon Road, became the new home for the eighteenth-century stoneworkers' altarpiece, where it remains today.

San Miguel Chapel

The San Miguel Chapel dates from the early decades of the villa, at least as far back as 1628.[33] It is unique among colonial churches in New Mexico in that it was not built for Spanish settlers or local natives. Instead, it served Indian laborers who had come north from Mexico with the earliest colonizing expeditions. San Miguel Chapel, named for Saint Michael, lies in an area that was known as the *Barrio Analco*, the riverside district, an area that had been settled by Pueblo Indians as early as the fourteenth century, but was abandoned by the 1590s. Although there is little documentary evidence, Analco is traditionally believed to have been inhabited by Tlaxcalan Indians from central Mexico. Because of their role in helping Hernán Cortés defeat the Aztecs, the Tlaxcalans were exempt from certain taxes and were often included in the armed forces of the Spanish military. Some may have come north with the Oñate expedition in 1598 as soldiers. Others worked as laborers or servants on supply caravans accompanying Franciscan missionaries along the Camino Real.[34] Tlaxcalans had a special status, but they were still regarded as Indians and, accordingly, were settled in a community *analco*, in Nahuatl, "across from," the Santa Fe River. No doubt the Tlaxcalans were represented in the barrio of Indians "from Mexico" that developed at Analco, outside of the official limits of the villa. Some type of primitive chapel existed in the earliest years of the settlement, and in 1626, when Fray Benavides lived in Santa Fe, a new church was built in Analco. It was in use until 1640 when a dispute between Governor Luís de Rosas and the Franciscans ended with the dismantling of the church, and a second one, called an *ermita*, or an outlying chapel, was built later, at the same site, but was lost during the 1680 Pueblo Revolt. Vargas visited the ruins when he returned to the villa in 1693, and slowly, the new colonial government attempted to re-construct San Miguel. The remaining walls were repaired and strengthened, a new roof was added, and Vargas asked that a Marían image known as *La Conquistadora*, the Lady of the Conquest, be placed in the chapel. But by the early eighteenth century the church was still incomplete, and in 1709 Agustín Flores Vergara, an official in the governor's office, arranged a fundraising project. He toured a wooden statue of San Miguel throughout the colony asking for donations and during the next year San Miguel was finished, with a simple, single nave constructed with new adobe bricks, hefty vigas, crossbeams, and corbels, and a new interior. Much of the work was done by Indian craftsmen, masons, stoneworkers, woodcarvers, and painters, who had come north after the re-establishment of the villa.[35]

Although evidence supporting the claim is slender, this building in the Analco Historic District is known as the Oldest House in the United States.

Additional artworks were produced for San Miguel over the next few decades including a canvas image of San Miguel, painted by royal engineer Don Miera y Pacheco, sometime before 1760. Although there are numerous references to the Indian community of Analco in the seventeenth century, after the re-conquest the area attracted more Spaniards and mestizo residents. It lost its distinction as a native settlement, and a parish church and the military chapel drew worshippers away from San Miguel. Still, Bishop Tamarón described the church as "fairly decent," but Fray Domínguez noted it was merely a chapel, some distance from the main parish church.[36] Later visitors described San Miguel as a small site, occasionally used by Indians, mesitzos, and genízaros on feast days. In the 1790s, the interior was refurbished, and an elaborate painted altar screen was added, but by the mid-nineteenth century the church was neglected. The upper section of its tower collapsed, the adobe walls cracked, and its outward appearance became increasingly dilapidated. During the Territorial period, much of the exterior was re-designed, and distinctly Anglo-American and Gothic features were added. A single massive tower replaced the older one, stone buttresses strengthened the façade, and a pitched metal roof was added.[37]

In the first half of the twentieth century, San Miguel Chapel had a strange architectural appearance, with its mix of styles and eras. The last major renovation of the church came in 1955 with a return to a simpler appearance, re-introducing some of the mission features of the Colonial era. Even today, after many renovations, San Miguel Chapel still has a somewhat awkward, clumsy outward look. The large single tower seems disproportionate, and the buttresses, now plastered over with adobe, seem out of place. Inside, the church has a more classic, elegant look even though many of the fixtures and furnishings date from the late nineteenth and twentieth centuries. Much of the front altar dates from the eighteenth century and features a series of religious icons and paintings, including the statue of Saint Michael from Mexico City that toured the province earlier in the century.[38] One controversial artifact which was preserved at the San Miguel Chapel is commonly known as the Oñate Medallion, a portion of a cloth banner, believed to be from the 1598 expedition. The fragile, tattered fabric bears the image of the Spanish royal coat of arms during the reign of King Felipe II. On the other side is a badly faded image of the Virgin Mary, depicted as Our Lady of Remedies. Strong circumstantial evidence links the medallion to Oñate. It appears to date from the late sixteenth century and resembles descriptions of banners carried by the original colonists. In his journals, Governor Vargas described how a banner from the Oñate expedition was saved from destruction during the Pueblo Revolt, closely guarded for twelve years, and then returned to Santa Fe after the re-conquest. Vargas' description of the banner closely matches the medallion, the coat of arms, and the depiction of the Virgin Mary. Vargas did have San Miguel Chapel rebuilt, where the banner was preserved for centuries, but not everyone agrees on this particular banner's authenticity. Some scholars have pointed out that even though all the descriptions match, many banners were brought with the colonizing expedition. Whether this particular one belonged to Oñate and was used to lead the entrada may never be known for sure. The medallion is now housed in the collections of the New Mexico History Museum.[39]

The San Miguel Chapel dates from the early decades of the villa.

Trails from the Villa

Missouri wagon trains entered town along today's Old Santa Fe Trail which joined Old Pecos Trail and continued northwest into the central plaza. In the early twentieth century, the Daughters of the American Revolution marked 170 sites along the trail, from New Franklin, Missouri, to Santa Fe, and on the southeast corner of the plaza is the End of the Trail Monument, a historic granite stone marker, the last in the series. Missouri traders camped in the area and sold their wares from their wagons. Later, they occupied several adobe buildings around the plaza and opened retail outlets for the many products they imported from the east. From the plaza, Chihuahua Trail traffic followed Agua Fria Street southwest out of the city and down the old Camino Real. Santa Fe artist William Penhallow Henderson painted a mural depicting a wagon train arriving in Santa Fe from the eastern mountains. The mural was a New Deal federal art project and is located in the United States Courthouse on Paseo de Peralta. Many structures in the immediate area of the Palace and plaza became commercial outlets in the nineteenth century as trade extended east, west, and north of the villa, building off the foundation established by the Camino Real de Tierra Adentro hundreds of years before. A small stone monument, facing the Palace of the Governors, honors General Stephen W. Kearny and his triumphant march into Santa Fe and down the old Camino Real in 1846.

Reynaldo Rivera's *Journey's End,* a massive bronze sculpture depicting a Santa Fe Trail wagon train as it approaches the old villa, stands on Museum Hill.

Notes

Introduction

1. The classic study of the Camino Real is Max L. Moorhead's *New Mexico's Royal Road: Trade and Travel on the Chihuahua Trail* (Norman: University of Oklahoma Press, 1958). Other works include Cleve Hallenbeck, *Land of the Conquistadores* (Caldwell: Caxton Printers, 1950); U.S. National Park Service, *El Camino Real de Tierra Adentro National Historic Trail: Draft Comprehensive Management Plan* (Santa Fe: New Mexico 2004); Gabrielle Palmer, ed., *El Camino Real de Tierra Adentro* (Santa Fe: Bureau of Land Management, 1993); Gabrielle G. Palmer and Stephen L. Fosberg, comps., *El Camino Real de Tierra Adentro: Volume Two* (Santa Fe: Bureau of Land Management, 1999); Michael P. Marshall, "El Camino Real de Tierra Adentro: An Archaeological Investigation" (unpublished ms, Santa Fe, 1990); Hal Jackson, *Following the Royal Road: A Guide to the Historic Camino Real de Tierra Adentro* (Albuquerque: University of New Mexico Press, 2006). Joseph P. Sánchez and Bruce A. Erickson, *From Mexico City to Santa Fe: A Historical Guide to El Camino Real de Tierra Adentro* (Los Ranchos: Rio Grande Books, 2011); Enrique R. Lamadrid, "*Rutas del Corazón*: Pilgrimage and Cultural Commerce on the Camino Real de Tierra Adentro," *New Mexico Historical Review* 83, no. 4 (2008): 423–450.

2. María Luisa Pérez-González, "Royal Roads in the Old and New World: The Camino de Oñate and its Importance in the Spanish Settlement of New Mexico," *Colonial Latin American Historical Review* 7, no. 1 (1998): 196–97.

3. Alexander von Humboldt, *Political Essay on the Kingdom of New Spain. With Physical Sections and Maps founded on Astronomical Observations and Trigonometrical and Barometrical Measurements.* John Black, trans. 4 vols. (New York: AMS Press, 1970), 2: 8. Camino Real de Tierra Adentro seldom appears on maps or documents but was the commonly used name for the road.

4. Dan Scurlock, "Floods, Fords, and Shifting Sands," in Palmer and Fosberg, comps., *El Camino Real*, 41–43; Michael P. Marshall, "Journal of a Reconnaissance, " in Palmer and Fosberg, comps., *El Camino Real*, 15–17; Moorhead, *New Mexico's Royal Road*, 3–5.

5. Carroll L. Riley, "The Pre-Spanish Camino Real," in Palmer, ed., El Camino Real, 15–16; Carroll L. Riley, *Rio del Norte: People of the Upper Rio Grande from Earliest Times to the Pueblo Revolt* (Salt Lake City: University of Utah Press, 1995), 83–85, 99, 104.

6. Jason S. Shapiro, *Before Santa Fe: Archaeology of the City Different* (Santa Fe: Museum of New Mexico Press, 2008), 92–94; Riley, *Rio del Norte*, 98.

7. Riley, "The Pre-Spanish Camino Real," 15–16; Riley, *Rio del Norte*, 99, 104.

8. Albert H. Schroeder and Daniel S. Matson, eds., *A Colony on the Move: Gaspar Castaño de Sosa's Journal, 1590–1591* (Santa Fe: School of American Research, 1965).

9. David J. Weber, *The Spanish Frontier in North America* (New Haven: Yale University Press, 1992), 77–80.

10. Marc Simmons, *The Last Conquistador: Juan de Oñate and the Settling of the Far Southwest* (Norman: University of Oklahoma Press, 1991), 91–98; George P. Hammond and Agapito Rey, eds., *Don Juan de Onate: Colonizer of New Mexico, 1595–1628* (Albuquerque: University of New Mexico Press, 1953), 1: 220-226; Marc Simmons, "Carts on the Camino Real," in Simmons, *Coronado's Land: Essays on Daily Life in Colonial New Mexico* (Albuquerque: University of New Mexico Press, 1991), 82-83.

11. Wilbert H. Timmons, *El Paso: A Borderlands History* (El Paso: Texas Western Press, 1990), 127; George D. Torok "El Camino Real de Tierra Adentro through the Pass of the North, I" *Password* 50, no. 4, (2005): 169-88.

12. Simmons, *Last Conquistador*, 91-111.

13. Simmons, *Last Conquistador*, 134-38, 144-46; Miguel Encinias, Alfred Rodriguez, and Joseph Sánchez, eds., *Historia de la Nueva Mexico, 1610* (Albuquerque: University of New Mexico Press), 1992.

14. Elizabeth Archuleta, "History Carved in Stone: Memorializing PóPay and Oñate, or Recasting Racialized Regimes of Representation," *New Mexico Historical Review* 82, no. 2 (2007): 317-42; Yolanda Leyva, "Monuments of Conformity: Commemorating and Protesting Oñate on the Border," *New Mexico Historical Review* 82, no. 2 (2007): 343-68.

15. Scurlock, "Floods, Fords, and Sands," 44-47; Marshall, "Journal of Reconnaissance," 15-18; Moorhead, *New Mexico's Royal Road*, 15-23.

16. Weber, *Spanish Frontier*, 124-26; Michael Bletzer, "Pueblos without Names: A Case Study of Piro Settlements in Early Colonial New Mexico" (PhD diss., Southern Methodist University, 2009).

17. James E. Ivey, "Seventeenth Century Mission Trade on the Camino Real," in Palmer, ed., *El Camino Real*, 42-43; Moorhead, *New Mexico's Royal Road*, 47-49.

18. Simmons, "Carts on the Camino," 83; Mrs. Edward E. Ayer, trans., *The Memorial of Fray Alonso de Benavides, 1630* (Chicago: R.R. Donnelley and Sons Company, 1916); Anne E. Hughes, *The Beginnings of Spanish Settlement in the El Paso District* (El Paso: Press of El Paso Public Schools, 1935).

19. France V. Scholes, "The Supply Service of the New Mexican Missions in the Seventeenth Century," *New Mexico Historical Review* 5, no. 1 (1930): 93, 97, 111-13.

20. Ayer, trans., *Benavides Memorial*, 1-3.

21. Ivey, "Seventeenth Century Mission Trade," 46-48; J. Paul Taylor y Romero, "La Caravana," in Palmer and Fosberg, comps., *El Camino Real*, 293-95.

22. Charles Wilson Hackett and Charmion Clair Shelby, eds., *Revolt of the Pueblo Indians of New Mexico and Otermín's attempted Reconquest, 1680–1682* (Albuquerque: University of New Mexico Press, 1942), 2: xix-xxviii; John L. Kessell, *Kiva, Cross, and Crown: The Pecos*

Indians and New Mexico, 1540–1840 (Tucson: Southwest Parks and Monuments Association. 1987); David J. Weber, ed. *What Caused the Pueblo Revolt of 1680?* (Boston: Bedford/St. Martin's Press, 1999); Andrew L. Knaut, *The Pueblo Revolt of 1680: Conquest and Resistance in Seventeenth Century New Mexico* (Norman: University of Oklahoma Press, 1995), 9-14; J. Manuel Espinosa, *Crusaders of the Río Grande: The Story of Don Diego de Vargas and the Reconquest and Refounding of New Mexico* (Chicago: Institute of Jesuit History, 1942), 244-71, 60

23. Timmons, *El Paso*, 53-56; Elizabeth Cunningham and Skip Miller, "Trade Fairs in Taos," in Palmer and Fosberg, comps., *El Camino Real*, 87-89.

24. Pekka Hamalainen, *The Comanche Empire* (New Haven: Yale University Press, 2008), 1,3,9.

25. Hamalainen, *Comanche Empire*, 73, 92-93.

26. Cunningham and Miller, "Trade Fairs," 88.

27. Hamalainen, *Comanche Empire*, 157, 204.

28. Janet R. Fireman, *The Spanish Royal Corp of Engineers in the Western Borderlands: Instruments of Bourbon Reform, 1764 to 1815* (Glendale: A.H. Clark Company, 1977), 55-58, 71-77, 74-78; Moorhead, *Royal Road*, 34; Eleanor B. Adams, ed. *Bishop Tamarón's Visitation of New Mexico, 1760* (Albuquerque: University of New Mexico Press, 1954); Eleanor B. Adams and Fray Angelico Chávez, eds. *The Missions of New Mexico, 1776: A Description by Fray Francisco Atanasio Domínguez with Other Contemporary Documents* (Albuquerque: University of New Mexico Press, 1956); George Kubler, *Religious Architecture of New Mexico in the Colonial Period and since the American Occupation* (Albuquerque: University of New Mexico Press, 1973); John L. Kessell, *The Missions of New Mexico Since 1776* (Albuquerque: University of New Mexico Press, 1980. New Edition, Santa Fe: Sunstone Press, 2012); Rick Hendricks, ed., *New Mexico in 1801: The Priests' Report* (Los Ranchos: Rio Grande Books, 2008); Hamalainen, *Comanche Empire*, 113-14.

29. Donald Jackson, ed., *The Journals of Zebulon Montgomery Pike: With Letters and Related Documents* (Norman: University of Oklahoma Press, 1966).

30. Joseph P. Sánchez, "Under the Mexican Eagle: A Historical Overview of the Camino Real de Tierra Adentro in New Mexico, 1821–1848," *Chronicles of the Trail* 4, no. 3 (2008): 18-19.

31. Moorhead, *Royal Road*, 86, 91; Josiah Gregg, *Commerce of the Prairies or the Journal of a Santa Fé Trader* (New York: Henry G. Langley, 1844).

32. George Wilkins Kendall, *Narrative of the Texan Santa Fé Expedition* (New York: Harper and Bros., 1844), 2:13.

33. Moorhead, *Royal Road*, 80-81, 119-20.

34. John James Abert, *Abert's New Mexico Report, 1846–47* (Albuquerque: Horn & Wallace, Publishers, 1962. New Edition, Santa Fe: Sunstone Press, 2012); Ralph P. Bieber, ed., *Marching with the Army of the West, 1846–1848* (Philadelphia: Porcupine Press, 1974); Bieber, ed., *Journal of a Soldier under Kearny and Doniphan, 1846–47* (Glendale: Arthur H. Clark Co., 1935); George F. Ruxton, *Adventures in Mexico and the Rocky Mountains* (London: John Murray, 1849); Frederich Adolph Wislizenus, *Memoir of a Tour to Northern Mexico connected with Colonel Doniphan's Expedition in 1846 and 1847* (Washington: Tippin and Streeper, 1848); Stella M. Drumm, ed., *Down the Santa Fe Trail and into Mexico: The Diary of*

Susan Shelby Magoffin, 1846–1847 (New Haven: Yale University Press, 1926).

35. Charles M. Haecker, "The Brazito Battlefield: Once Lost, Now Found," *New Mexico Historical Review* 72, no.3 (1997): 229-38; Mark L. Gardner, "The Mexican War and the Chihuahua Trail," in Palmer and Fosberg, comps., *El Camino Real*, 247-62; K. Jack Bauer, *The Mexican War 1846–1848* (New York: Macmillan Company, 1974), 152-53; John D. Eisenhower, *So Far from God: The U.S. War with Mexico, 1846–1848* (New York: Random House, 1989),240; John Russell Bartlett, *Personal Narrative of Exploration and Incidents in Texas, New Mexico, California, Sonora, and Chihuahua connected with the United States and Mexican Boundary Commission during 1850, '51, '52, and '53* (London: G. Routledge, 1854); William H. Emory, *Report on the United States and Mexican Boundary Survey made under the Direction of the Secretary of the Interior* (Washington: Cornelius Wendell, Printer, 1857).

36. W.W.H. Davis, *El Gringo or New Mexico and Her People* (New York: Harper and Brothers, 1857).

37. Roscoe P. and Margaret B. Conkling, *The Butterfield Overland Mail, 1857–1869; Its Organization and Operation over the Southern Route to 1861; Subsequently over the Central Route to 1866; and under Wells, Fargo and Company in 1869* (Glendale: A.H. Clark Company, 1947); Wayne R. Austerman, *Sharps Rifles and Spanish Mules: The San Antonio-El Paso Mail, 1851–1881* (College Station: Texas A&M University Press, 1985).

38. Conkling and Conkling, *Butterfield Overland Mail*, 2: 92, 94-95.

39. Donald H. Couchman, *Cooke's Peak: Pasaron por Aquí : A Focus on United States History in Southwestern New Mexico* (Las Cruces: U.S. Bureau of Land Management, 1990), 3-9; Lyle Henry Wright and Josephine Bynum, eds., *The Butterfield Overland Mail: Only through Passenger on the first Westbound Stage* (San Marino: The Huntington Library), 1954.

40. John M. Taylor, *Bloody Valverde: A Civil War Battle on the Rio Grande, February 21, 1862* (Albuquerque: University of New Mexico Press, 1995), 6-9; Don E. Alberts, "Civil War along the Camino Real," in Palmer, ed., El Camino Real, 195-204.

41. Vernon J. Glover, "Rails on the Camino Real," in Palmer, ed., *El Camino Real*, 205-11; Lansing B. Bloom, ed., "Bourke on the Southwest, X." *New Mexico Historical Review* 11, no. 2 (1936): 245-282.; Bloom, ed., "Bourke on the Southwest, XI." *New Mexico Historical Review* 12, no. 1 (1937): 41-77; Bloom, ed., "Bourke on the Southwest, XIII." *New Mexico Historical Review* 13, no. 2 (1938): 192-238.

42. John W. Murphey, "A New King's Highway," *Chronicles of the Trail* 7, no.2 (2011): 18-20.

43. Jaime José Fushille, "Trail to El Paso: La Jornada de Cantarrecio" (master's thesis, University of Texas at El Paso, 1990), 2-3; Herbert C. Morrow, *The Mission Trail: History, Architecture, Cultural Heritage, and Historic Preservation of the Lower Valley of El Paso, Texas: A Historic Preservation Plan* (El Paso: West Texas Council of Governments, 1981), 4-5; David Kammer, "Route 66 and National Old Trails Road Historic District at La Bajada" (National Register of Historic Places Inventory-Nomination Form, Albuquerque, 2000), 7:7-8, 8:8.

44. One of the few exceptions was the survey of the Butterfield Overland Mail route by Roscoe P. and Margaret B. Conkling who traveled the trail in the 1930s and made references to the colonial roadway in their work. See Conkling and Conkling, *Butterfield Overland Mail*, 2: 92+.

Chapter 1: North through the Chihuahuan Desert

1. Simmons, *Last Conquistador*, 50, 58, 91.

2. Roy Bernard Brown, "Arqueología Colonial en Chihuahua: El Caso de El Carrizal," in Pacheco and Sánchez, eds., *Memorias del Coloquio*, 50-51.

3. Rex E. Gerald, "An Introduction to Missions of the Paso del Norte Area," *Password* 20, no.2 (1975): 47-58; Rex. E. Gerald, *Spanish Presidios of the Late Eighteenth Century in Northern New Spain* (Santa Fe: Museum of New Mexico Press, 1968); Herbert C. Morrow, *The Mission Trail*, 1-3; John A. Peterson, *Archaeological Survey of the San Elizario High School Site, San Elizario, Texas* (El Paso: J.A. Peterson, 1995); John A. Peterson, Timothy B. Graves, and David V. Hill, eds., *The 1995 San Elizario Plaza Archaeological Project* (Austin: Texas Department of Transportation, 2002).

4. Bieber, ed., *Journal of a Soldier*, 335.

5. Michael P. Marshall, "Journal of a Reconnaissance of the Camino Real," in Palmer and Fosberg, comps., *El Camino Real*, 25-26.

6. Moorhead, *Royal Road*, 16; Marshall, "Journal of a Reconnaissance," 22-23.

7. Marshall, "Journal of a Reconnaissance," 18.

8. Hammond and Rey, eds., *Don Juan de Oñate*, 1: 314; Moorhead, *Royal Road*, 18.

9. Gerald, "Introduction to Missions," 52; Fushille, "Trail to El Paso," 2.

10. Fushille, "Trail to El Paso," 5.

11. Patrick H. Beckett and Terry L. Corbett, *The Manso Indians* (Las Cruces: COAS Publishing and Research, 1992), 3-6.

12. Hammond and Rey, eds., *Don Juan de Oñate*, 1: 315.

13. Gerald, "Introduction to Missions," 49; Ayer, trans., *Benavides Memorial*, 212n.

14. Rick Hendricks and W. H. Timmons, *San Elizario: Spanish Presidio to Texas County Seat* (El Paso: Texas Western Press, 1998), 11-13.

15. Moorhead, *Presidio*, 167; Peterson, Graves and Hill, eds., *San Elizario Plaza*, 66, 77.

16. Coues, ed., *Expeditions of Zebulon Pike*, 2: 648-49.

17. Hendricks and Timmons, *San Elizario*, 54.

18. Hendricks and Timmons, *San Elizario*, 43, 57.

19. Conkling and Conkling, *Butterfield Overland Mail*, 2: 47-48, 52.

20. Harry Wilson Clark, "The History, Archaeology, and Oral Traditions of the San Elizario Jail: An Interdisciplinary Study" (master's thesis, University of Texas at El Paso, 2002), 9-10; Hendricks and Timmons, *San Elizario*, 94-95.

21. Peterson, Graves, and Hill, eds., *San Elizario Plaza*, 74, 75.

22. Hendricks and Timmons, *San Elizario*, 54; C.L. Sonnichsen, *Pass of the North: Four Centuries on the Rio Grande* (El Paso: Texas Western Press, 1968), 1: 110.

23. Drumm, ed., *Down the Santa Fe Trail*, 224.

24. Sonnichsen, *Pass of the North*, 1: 207.

25. *Herald-Post*, (El Paso, Texas), June 19, 1959; William W. Lockhart, "Casa Ronquillo," *Password* 41, no.2 (1996): 84.

26. Several essays and commentaries about the Thanksgiving story can be viewed at the Plimoth Plantation website.

27. Miguel Encinias, Alfred Rodríguez, and Joseph P. Sánchez, trans.,eds., *Historia de la Nueva México, 1610* (Albuquerque: University of New Mexico Press, 1992), 130.

28. Joseph P. Sánchez, "The First Thanksgiving," *New Mexico Magazine*, November 2004, 34-36.

29. Rick Hendricks, "Camino Real at the Pass: The Economy and Political Structure of the Paso del Norte Area in the Eighteenth Century," *Password* 44, no.1 (1999): 8; Sonnichsen, *Pass of the North*, 1: 74.

30. Rebeca A. Gudiño Quiroz, *Don Antonio Valverde y Cossío, Gobernador de Nuevo México: Una Aproximación a su Vida Pública y Privada* (Cd. Juárez.: Universidad Autónoma de Ciudad Juárez, 1994), 7-8; Hendricks, "Camino Real at the Pass," 18-19.

31. Hadley, Naylor, and Schuetz-Miller, eds., *Presidio and Militia*, 2: 242. Hendricks, "Camino Real at the Pass,"19; Hendricks and Timmons, *San Elizario*, 12-13.

32. Hendricks and Timmons, *San Elizario.*, 11-12;Peterson, Graves, and Hill, eds., *San Elizario Plaza*, 31, 35; Kessell, *Kiva, Cross, and Crown*, inside cover.

33. Sonnichsen, *Pass of the North*, 1:78; Rick Hendricks, "New Light on an old Mystery: Locating Santa María de Las Caldas and the Hacienda de San Antonio," in Kathryn Weedman, Rick López, David O. Brown, and John A. Peterson, eds., *Cultural Resources Survey in Socorro and San Elizario, El Paso County, Texas: Phase II Architectural Studies* (El Paso: Archaeological Research Inc., 1994), 405; *Herald-Post*, (El Paso, Texas), Oct. 13, 1979.

34. John A. Peterson, "Lost Missions and Other Spanish Colonial Sites in the Lower Valley of El Paso" (unpublished paper, El Paso, 1995), 9.

35. Ayer, trans., *Benavides Memorial*, 18; Charles L. Nieman, *Spanish Times and Boom Times: Toward an Architectural History of Socorro, New Mexico* (Socorro: Socorro County Historical Society, 1972), 2.

36. Hackett and Shelby, eds., *Revolt of the Pueblo*, 1: cxxvii; Nieman, *Spanish Times and Boom Times*, 3.

37. Katherine H. White, *The Pueblo de Socorro Grant* (El Paso: Katherine Hope Huffman White Memorial Trust, 1986), 36.

38. Marshall and Walt, *Rio Abajo*, 285; Ernest J. Burrus, "An Historical Outline of the Socorro Mission," *Password* 29, no.4 (1984): 145-6; Rex E. Gerald, "The Old Socorro Mission Site Test Excavations, 1981–83," *The Artifact* 28, no.1 (1990): 1-29; Timmons, *El Paso*, 20-21.

39. White, *Pueblo de Socorro*, 44, 55-56.

40. J. Walter Fewkes, "The Pueblo Settlements near El Paso, Texas," *American Anthropologist* 4, no.1 (1902): 72.

41. David Ewing Stewart, ed., *The Gold Rush Diary of William P. Huff* (Van Vleck: n.p., 2000), July 20, 1849 entry.

42. Conkling and Conkling, *Butterfield Overland Mail*, 2: 53-54.

43. Helen Simons and Cathryn A. Hoyt, eds., *Hispanic Texas: A Historical Guide* (Austin: University of Texas Press, 1992), 322.

44. Terri Myers, Diane Williams, and Laurie A. Marder, eds., *Property Descriptions, Significant Assessments, and National Register Eligibility Determinations, Socorro and San Elizario* (Austin: Hardy, Heck, Moore Inc., 1995), 171-72.

45. Myers, Williams, and Marder, eds., *Property Descriptions, National Register Eligibility*, 173.

46. Jean Fulton, "The Texas Socorro Mission Preservation Project," *Chronicles of the Trail* 2, no.2 (2006): 3.

47. Lois Stanford, "Local Devotion to St. Michael: Examining Expressions of Popular Catholicism in Socorro, Texas," in Thomas J. Steele, Paul Rhetts, and Barb Awalt, eds., *Seeds of Struggle/Harvest of Faith: The Papers of the Archdiocese of Santa Fe Catholic Cuatro Centennial Conference* (Albuquerque: LPD Press, 1998), 124-26.

48. Marta Estrada, "The Cemetery Trail: A Tour of History and Traditions in the El Paso Valley," *Password* 34, no.3 (1989): 141.

49. Simons and Hoyt, eds. *Hispanic Texas*, 278; Nicholas P. Houser, "The Tigua Settlement of Ysleta del Sur," *The Kiva* 36, no.1 (1970): 25-27; Nicholas P. Houser, "La Entrada Por El Alto: The Entrance by the High Bridge" (unpublished draft, El Paso, 1999), 16-17.

50. Kessell, *Missions Since 1776*, 215.

51. Hackett and Shelby, eds., *Revolt of the Pueblo*, 1: i-li.

52. Hackett and Shelby, eds., *Revolt of the Pueblo*, 1: xcv.

53. Hackett and Shelby, eds., *Revolt of the Pueblo*, 1: cxxi, cxxx, cxxxi.

54. Kessell, *Missions Since 1776*, 216.

55. W.H. Timmons, "Ysleta: The Oldest Town in Texas," *Password* 37, no.2 (1992): 80-81.

56. Herbert C. and Karen Morrow, "The Ysleta Historic District: A Historical and Architectural Perspective," *Password* 36, no.3 (1991): 162.

57. W.H. Timmons, "The Spanish Census of Ysleta in 1790," *Password* 37, no.4 (1992):137-40.

58. Ralph P. Bieber and Averam B. Bender, eds., *Exploring Southwest Trails, 1846–1854* (Glendale: Arthur H. Clark Company, 1938), 316-17.

59. Bloom, ed., "Bourke on the Southwest, XIII," 206.

60. Bloom, ed., "Bourke on the Southwest, XIII," 205, 206, 209.

61. Tom Diamond, ed., "J. Walter Fewkes' Diary Notes, 1901," in Beckman, comp., *Ysleta del Sur Pueblo Archives*, 3: 189,195.

62. Conkling and Conkling, *Butterfield Overland Mail*, 2: 55-56.

63. Bloom, ed., "Bourke on the Southwest, XIII," 206.

64. Houser, "Tigua Pueblo," 340.

65. Morrow and Morrow, "Ysleta Historic District," 164.

66. Morrow and Morrow, "Ysleta Historic District," 163-64.

67. Metz, *Guided through Time*, 240.

68. Estrada "Cemetery Trail,"139.

69. Conkling and Conkling, *Butterfield Overland Mail,* 2: 410.

Chapter 2: Ciudad Juárez

1. Bud Newman, "Fray García de San Francisco, Founder of El Paso: A Syllabus of Errors," *Password* 24, no.4 (1984): 179-186.

2. Jacques Lafaye, *Quetzalcóatl and Guadalupe: The Formation of Mexican National Consciousness, 1531–1813* (Chicago: University of Chicago Press, 1976), 231-99.

3. Adair W. Margo, "Nuestra Señora de Guadalupe del Paso del Norte: Its Foundation, Construction, and Decoration" (master's thesis, New Mexico State University, 1982), 14.

4. Timmons, *El Paso*, 14, 15; Gerald, "Introduction to Missions," 55.

5. Adams, ed., *Tamarón's Visitation*, 34-5.

6. Rex E. Gerald, "Portrait of a Community: Joseph de Urrutia's Map of El Paso del Norte," *American West* 3, no.2 (1966): 38-39; The Urrutia map is also reproduced in Moorhead, *Presidio*, 150-51.

7. Oscar J. Martinez, *Border Boom Town: Ciudad Juárez since 1848* (Austin: University of Texas Press, 1975), 10; Timmons, *El Paso*, 81.

8. Moorhead, *Presidio*, 148-49; Bieber, ed., *Journal of a Soldier*, 312.

9. Davis, *El Gringo*, 383.

10. Davis, *El Gringo*, 384.

11. Timmons, *El Paso*, 128, 155.

12. Timmons, *El Paso*, 227-28.

13. Martinez, *Border Boom Town*, 83-85.

14. *Herald-Post*, (El Paso, Texas), May 18, 1939.

15. Sonnichsen, *Pass of the North*, 1:231; Martinez, *Border Boom Town*, 159.

16. Marshall and Walt, *Rio Abajo*, 252; Ayer, trans., *Benavides Memorial*, 215-16.

17. The eastern edge of the original Senecú settlement was about one to two miles northwest of Ysleta. An historical marker at Alameda and Valdespino is probably within range of the original mission lands. Simons and Hoyt, eds., *Hispanic Texas*, 276; Cleofas Calleros, "Original Senecú Mission Founded in New Mexico," *Times*, (El Paso, Texas), June 15, 1952.

18. Francisco Ochoa Rodríguez, "Ordenanzas de la Cédula Real en tres pueblos del Valle del Paso del Norte," *e.nnova* I, no.1 (2009): 90; The San Antonio de Senecú cemetery, located off of Blvd. Francisco Villarreal Torres, is often said to have been a part of Old Senecú but little historical or archaeological evidence supports this claim.

19. Cited in Gerald, "Introduction to Missions," 55; Adams, ed., *Tamarón's Visitation*, 39.

20. Rex E. Gerald and Olympia Caudillo, "Bravo 1795: An Inventory of the Missions of Senecú, Ysleta, and Socorro by Fray José Bravo in the Year 1795," *Password* 33, no.2 (1988): 21-22.

21. Gerald and Caudillo, "Bravo 1795," 23, 24, 26.

22. Bartlett, *Personal Narrative*, 1:148.

23. Fewkes, "Pueblo Settlements," 72-73.

24. Hughes, *Beginnings of Settlement*, 322-23.

25. Ochoa Rodríguez, "Ordenanzas de la Cédula Real," 91; Timmons, *El Paso*, 18, 19; Gerald, "Introduction to Missions," 54; Cleofas Calleros, "San Lorenzo Mission In Mexico First

Erected North of River," *Times*, (El Paso, Texas), May 25, 1952; Author conversation with John A. Peterson, April 1999. Peterson believes that the original settlement may have been near the end of Viejo Calle de San Lorenzo, on the grounds of a nearby housing project.

26. Gerald, "Introduction to Missions," 54.

27. Adams, ed., *Tamarón's Visitation*, 38.

28. *Times*, (El Paso, Texas), June 1, 1952.

29. Gerald, "Introduction to Missions," 54.

30. Lamadrid, "Rutas del Corazón," 432.

31. *Times*, (El Paso, Texas), June 1, 1952.

32. Torok, "Camino Real de Tierra Adentro I," 185.

33. Margo, "Nuestra Señora de Guadalupe," 45, 47-48.

34. Guadalupe Santiago and Miguel Ángel Berumen, *La Misión de Guadalupe* (Cd. Juárez: Cuadro por Cuadro, 2004), 108, 115.

35. Santiago and Berumen, *Misión de Guadalupe*, 73-75.

36. Martinez, *Border Boom Town*, 22-23.

37. Hughes, *Beginnings of Settlement*, 364-65.

38. Hendricks and Timmons, *San Elizario*, 14; Timmons, *El Paso*, 58.

39. Gerald, "Portrait of a Community," 40; Adams, ed., *Tamarón's Visitation*, 34; Moorhead, *Presidios*, 21; Armando B. Chávez M., *Sesenta Años de Gobierno Municipal* (Mexico: Gráfico Cervantina, 1959), 366.

40. Ruxton, *Adventures in Mexico*, 165.

41. Wislizenus, *Memoir of a Tour*, 43.

42. Quoted in Marshall, "Journal of a Reconnaissance," 18.

43. Marshall, "Journal of a Reconnaissance," 19, 21; John Roney, "Tracing the Camino Real: The Chihuahua Section," in Palmer, ed., *El Camino Real*, 91-92; Moorhead, *Royal Road*, 31.

44. *Times*, (El Paso, Texas), Aug. 28, 1998; José Leodegario Vázquez Reyes, *Por qué se llama así la calle donde vivo?* (Cd. Juárez: Ayuntamiento de Juárez, 1998), 235, 178; Ignacio Esparza Marín, *Monografia Historica de Ciudad Juárez* (Cd. Juárez: s.n., 1991), 129-30; The church is located near the intersection of Avenida Reforma and Perimetral Carlos Amaya.

45. Mary D. Taylor, "Cura de la Frontera: Ramón Ortiz," in Palmer and Fosberg, comps., *El Camino Real*, II, 275.

46. Samuel E. Sisneros, "El Paseño, Padre Ramón Ortiz: 1814–1896," *Password* 44, no. 2 (1999): 107.

47. Quoted in Sonnichsen, *Pass of the North*, I: 108; Sisneros, "El Paseño," 108.

48. Taylor, "Cura de la Frontera," 268-69; Sonnichsen, *Pass of the North*, I: 118.

49. Taylor, "Cura de la Frontera," 274-75.

50. *Herald*, (El Paso, Texas), Mar. 12, 1896; *Times*, (El Paso, Texas), Dec. 28, 1952.

51. Sonnichsen, *Pass of the North*, I: 380; Manuel G. Gonzáles, "Dr. Mariano Samaniego (1831–1905) Citizen of the El Paso Valley," *Password* 35, no. 4 (1990): 162-63; Timmons, *El Paso*, 163; *Times*, (El Paso, Texas), Oct. 4, 1905.

52. Timmons, *El Paso*, 163; *Times*, (El Paso, Texas), May 20, 1909.

53. Esparza Marín, *Monografia historica* , 130.

54. Ralph Roeder, *Juárez and his Mexico* (New York:Viking Press, 1947), 4-8.

55. Sonnichsen, *Pass of the North*, I: 164.

56. Sonnichsen, *Pass of the North*, I: 164-66.

57. *Herald-Post*, (El Paso, Texas), Sept. 25, 1945.

58. Torok, "El Camino Real de Tierra Adentro I," 184.

Chapter 3: American El Paso

1. Torok, "El Camino Real de Tierra Adentro II," 11-14.

2. Timmons, *El Paso*, 107; Metz, *Guided through Time*, 258.

3. Conkling and Conkling, *Butterfield Overland Mail*, 1: 11; Sonnichsen, *Pass of the North*, 1: 140,141.

4. Austerman, *Sharps Rifles*, 35-38.

5. Timmons, *El Paso*, 126-27.

6. Timmons, *El Paso*, 129-30.

7. Sonnichsen, *Pass of the North*, 1: 249, 258, 288; Timmons, *El Paso*, 209-308.

8. Sonnichsen, *Pass of the North*, 1: 105-06.

9. James Magoffin Dwyer Jr., "Hugh Stephenson," *New Mexico Historical Review* 29, no. 1 (1954): 2-3; Rex W. Strickland, *Six Who Came to El Paso: Pioneers of the 1840s* (El Paso: Texas Western Press, 1963), 35.

10. Strickland, *Six Who Came*, 36-37.

11. Deen Underwood, *Concordia Cemetery: A Walking Tour* (El Paso: Concordia Heritage Association, 1997).

12. Wilbert H. Timmons, *James Wiley Magoffin: Don Santiago-El Paso Pioneer* (El Paso: Texas Western Press, 1999), 11, 20-21.

13. Timmons, *Magoffin*, 27, 29, 40, 41, 45, 49.

14. Davis, *El Gringo*, 376.

15. Timmons, *Magoffin*, 88-89.

16. Simons and Hoyt, eds., *Hispanic Texas*, 276; Metz, *Guided through Time*, 176.

17. Sonnichsen, *Pass of the North*, 1: 107; J.J. Bowden, *The Ponce de León Land Grant* (El Paso: Texas Western Press, 1969), 3; Timmons, *El Paso*, 79.

18. Stephen K. Mbutu and John A. Peterson, *The Union Plaza Downtown El Paso Development Archaeological Project: Overview, Inventory and Recommendations*, (El Paso: Anthropology Research Center, 1998), 40.

19. Timmons, *El Paso*, 79.

20. Bowden, *Ponce de León Grant*, 44n; Mbutu and Peterson, *Union Plaza Archaeological Project*, 40.

21. León Metz, *Guided through Time,* 20.

22. Mbutu and Peterson, *Union Plaza Archaeological Project*, 44; Metz, *Guided Through Time*, 51.

23. Timmons, *El Paso*, 141.

24. Anson Mills, *My Story*, ed. C.H. Claudy (Washington: Press of Byron S. Adams, 1921), 53.

25. Metz, *Guided through Time*, 51; Timmons, *El Paso*, 142.

26. Mills, *My Story*, 54.

27. Bowden, *Ponce de León Land Grant*, 31, 33, 43.

28. Hammond and Rey, eds., *Don Juan de Oñate*, 1: 315. This is the first reference to the site as "el paso."

29. Hammond and Rey, eds., *Don Juan de Oñate*, 1: 315; Simmons, *Last Conquistador*, 101; Timmons, *El Paso*, 14.

30. Strickland, *Six Who Came*, 37-38; Metz, *Guided through Time*, 228-29.

31. Strickland, *Six Who Came*, 39.

32. Davis, *El Gringo*, 376.

33. Metz, *Guided through Time*, 230.

34. Harriot Howze Jones, "Heritage Homes of El Paso: Hart's Mill-La Hacienda Cafe," *Password* 21, no. 3 (1976):115-18.

35. Metz, *Guided through Time*, 8-9.

36. Bartlett, *Personal Narrative*, 1: 198.

37. Conkling and Conkling, *Butterfield Overland Mail*, 2: 90. (All quotes).

38. The Butterfield Overland Trail ran north from Hart's Mill along the old Camino Real.

39. Adams, ed., *Tamarón's Visitation*, 40.

40. Gregg, *Commerce of the Prairies*, 241. The flooding of the river made it impossible for Gregg's party to use the upper crossing. Instead they located another ford further south. At times, cargo and wagons were floated across the river on canoes.

41. Wislizenus, *Memoir of a Tour*, 40; Santiago Nieves, "El Camino Real," *Password* 26, no. 3 (1981): 126.

42. Scurlock, "Floods, Fords, and Shifting Sands," 50.

43. Timmons, *El Paso*, 104; Tim B. Graves, Stephen F. Schlett, and John A. Peterson, *The Canutillo-El Paso Upper Valley Water Transmission Facilities Project: Survey Results and Recommendations* (El Paso: Archaeological Research, 1997), 15.

44. Wislizenus, *Memoir of a Tour*, 25-26.

45. Strickland, *Six Who Came*, 11-12.

46. Nancy Hamilton, "The Frontera Settlement," *Password* 30, no. 2 (1985):57.

47. Strickland, *Six Who Came*, 11.

48. Strickland, *Six Who Came*, 12.

49. Hamilton, "Frontera Settlement," 60.

50. Graves, Schlett, and Peterson, *Canutillo-El Paso Upper Valley*, 17.

51. Thomas C. O'Laughlin, *The Keystone Dam and Other Archaic and Formative Sites in Northwest El Paso, Texas* (El Paso: University of Texas at El Paso, 1980).

52. Sonnichsen, *Pass of the North,* 1: 32; Timmons, *El Paso,* 18.

53. Marshall, "El Camino Real de Tierra Adentro," 179-80.

54. Dan Scurlock, "Floods, Fords, and Shifting Sands," 47; Edward Staski, "Some of What We Have Learned," *Chronicles of the Trail* I, no. 2 (2005): 7; Staski, "An Archaeological Survey of El Camino Real de Tierra Adentro Las Cruces-El Paso," *International Journal of Historical Archaeology* 8, no. 2 (2004), 231-3.

55. Staski, "An Archaeological Survey," 242-43: Scurlock, "Floods, Fords, and Shifting Sands," 50.

Chapter 4: The Mesilla Valley

1. Nancy G. Stotz, *Historic Reconstruction of the Ecology of the Rio Grande/Río Bravo Channel and Floodplain in the Chihuahua Desert* (Las Cruces: Desert Scribes, 2000), 5-9.

2. Maude Elizabeth McFie, Lansing Bloom, ed., Jo Tice Bloom, ed. and annotations, *A History of Mesilla Valley-1903* (Las Cruces:Yucca Tree Press, 1999), 2; Jon Hunner and Peter Dean *The Mesilla Valley: An Oasis in the Desert* (Santa Fe: Sunstone Press, 2008), 6.

3. Timmons, *El Paso,* 79-80.

4. Bowden, *Spanish and Mexican Land Grants,* 97-99.

5. Timmons, *James Wiley Magoffin,* 50-51.

6. Waterman L. Ormsby, *The Butterfield Overland Mail* (San Marino: Huntington Library, 1954), 79; Conkling and Conkling, *Butterfield Overland Trail,* 2: 92-93.

7. Conkling and Conkling, *Butterfield Overland Mail,* 2: 92, 94-95.

8. Mark L. Gardner, "The Mexican War and the Chihuahua Trail: The Doniphan and Price Expeditions," in Palmer and Fosberg, comps., *El Camino Real,* 247-48.

9. Gardner, "The Mexican War," 249.

10. Gardner, "The Mexican War," 249.

11. K. Jack Bauer, *The Mexican War 1846–1848* (New York: Macmillan Company, 1974), 152-53; John D. Eisenhower, *So Far from God: The U.S. War with Mexico, 1846–1848* (New York: Random House, 1989), 240.

12. McFie, *Mesilla Valley,* 59; Bowden, *Spanish and Mexican Land Grants,* 87-89.

13. Strickland, *Six Who Came,* 34-35; Bowden, *Spanish and Mexican Land Grants,* 89.

14. Jackson, *Following the Royal Road,* 76-78; Haecker, "Brazito Battlefield," 231-32.

15. Francis Stanley, *The Fort Fillmore, New Mexico Story* (Pantex: F. Stanley, 1961), 3-5; Richard Alan Powder, "Research Design for Fort Fillmore, New Mexico" (master's thesis, New Mexico State University, 1988), 4.

16. Edward Staski and Joanne Reiter, "Status and Adobe Quality at Fort Fillmore, New Mexico: Old Questions, New Techniques," *Historical Archaeology* 30, no.1 (1996), 1; Stanley, *Fort Fillmore,* 3-4.

17. Lydia Spencer Lane, *I Married a Soldier,* 99-100.

18. Powder, "Design for Fort Fillmore," 7; Stanley, *Fort Fillmore,* 6.

19. Staski and Reiter, "Status and Adobe," 3; Conkling and Conkling, *Butterfield Overland Mail*, 2: 100, 98 (quote).

20. Timmons, *El Paso*, 126.

21. Conkling and Conkling, *Butterfield Overland Mail*, 2: 101.

22. Timmons, *El Paso*, 129, 131.

23. Couchman, *Cooke's Peak*, 111-12.

24. McFie, *History of the Mesilla Valley*, 34.

25. Conkling and Conkling, *Butterfield Overland Mail*, 2: 102-03; Linda G. Harris, *Las Cruces: An Illustrated History* (Las Cruces: Arroyo Press, 1993), 47.

26. Couchman, *Cooke's Peak*, 141; Powder, "Design for Fort Fillmore," 6-7.

27. Gordon R. Owen, *Las Cruces, New Mexico, 1849–1999: Multi-Cultural Crossroads* (Las Cruces: Red Sky Publishing Company, 1999), 39.

28. Mary M. Steeb, Michael Romero Taylor, and Anthony C. Pennock, *The Las Cruces Historic Buildings Survey* (Las Cruces: Doña Ana County Historical Society, 1982), 65.

29. "Dedication of the Taylor-Barela-Reynolds Mesilla State Monument," *Chronicles of the Trail* 2, no.3 (2006): 2-6.

30. Michael Taylor and Ellen Threinen, "La Mesilla Historic District Multiple Resource Area" (National Register of Historic Places Inventory-Nomination Form, Las Cruces, 1980), 2-3.

31. Robert Julyan, *The Mountains of New Mexico*, 211.

32. Wesley R. Hurt, "Tortugas, An Indian Village in Southern New Mexico," *El Palacio* 59, no.4 (1952): 108.

33. Beckett and Corbett, *Tortugas*, 1. Although the neighborhood is named for Saint John of God, the village actually celebrates the June 24th feast day of Saint John the Baptist.

34. *Western Catholic Reporter*, Dec. 11, 2006; Beckett and Corbett, *Tortugas*, 3-4.

35. Beckett and Corbett, *Manso Indians*, 2-3.

36. McFie, *History of the Mesilla Valley*, 40; Owen, *Las Cruces*, 30-32.

37. Owen, *Las* Cruces, 34-35; Steeb, Taylor, and Pennock, *Las Cruces Historic Buildings*, 97.

38. Harris, *Las Cruces Illustrated*, 62, 66-67.

39. Owen, *Las Cruces*, 66-67, 118; Harris, *Las Cruces Illustrated*, 78, 86.

40. Anthony Pennock, "Mesquite Original Town Site District of Las Cruces" (National Register of Historic Places Inventory-Nomination Form, Las Cruces,1980), 2-4; Sandra L. Marshall and John R. Versluis, *Historic Architectural Styles, Las Cruces, N.M.: Celebrating 150 Years* (Las Cruces: Doña Ana Historical Society, 2000), 26-27.

41. Bartlett, *Personal Narrative*, 1: 211: Adams, ed., *Tamarón's Visitation*, 41.

42. Julyan, *Place Names*, 112.

43. Bowden, *Spanish and Mexican Land Grants*, 70; Neal W. Ackerly and Chris Wilson, "Doña Ana Village Historic District" (National Register of Historic Places Registration Form, Albuquerque, 1998)8: 2-3; Mary Jane García, *An Ethnohistory of Doña Ana Village: Hispanic Catholics versus Hispanic Methodists* (Las Cruces: Rosetta Printing, 1986), 12-14.

44. Bowden, *Spanish and Mexican Land Grants*, 70-71.

45. Ackerly and Wilson, "Doña Ana Village Historic District," 7:1.

46. Bieber, ed., *Journal of a Soldier*, 298, 298n.

47. Joseph G. Dawson, *Doniphan's Epic March: The 1st Missouri Volunteers in the Mexican War* (Lawrence: University Press of Kansas, 1999), 109.

48. Steeb, Taylor, and Pennock, *Las Cruces Historic Buildings Survey*, 21; Bartlett, *Personal Narrative*, 1: 212.

49. Timmons, *El Paso*, 88.

50. García, *Ethnohistory of Doña Ana*, 81-84.

51. "Doña Ana's Matanza," *Cornerstones Community Partnerships* 5, no.1 (1999): 6.

52. "Doña Ana's Matanza," 7.

53. Frank Thayer, "Doña Ana: Historic Village tries to stop the Clock," *New Mexico Magazine*, July 1990, 64-65.

54. Ackerly and Wilson, "Doña Ana Village Historic District," 7:3; Steeb, Taylor, and Pennock, *Las Cruces Historic Buildings*, 23.

55. Harvey Fergusson, *The Conquest of Don Pedro* (New York: Morrow, 1954); William T. Pilkington, *Harvey Fergusson* (Boston: Twayne Publishers, 1975), 132-37.

56. Fergusson, *Conquest of Don Pedro*, 33-34, 81.

57. Ackerly and Wilson, "Doña Ana Village Historic District," 8:5, 14.

58. Loring Sitler, "Churches of the Valley along the Southern Rio Grande," *Journal of the Southwest* 45, no.2 (2003): 31. García, *Ethnohistory of Doña Ana*, 44.

59. Marshall and Walt, *Rio Abajo*, 243; Simmons, *Last Conquistador*, 103.

60. Kinnaird, ed., *Frontiers of New Spain*, 85.

61. Moorhead, *Presidio, 65*; Adams, ed., *Tamarón's Visitation*, 41.

62. Timothy Cohrs and Thomas J. Caperton, *Fort Selden, New Mexico* (Santa Fe: Museum of New Mexico Press, 1974), 16, 26-28.

63. Noble, *Pueblos, Villages and Forts,* 249-50; Cohrs and Caperton, *Fort Selden*, 16.

64. Couchman, *Cooke's Peake*, 170; Cohrs and Caperton, *Fort Selden*, 27.

65. Cohrs and Caperton, *Fort Selden*, 28-29.

66. Jackson, *Royal Road*, 72.

67. Jackson, *Royal Road*, 71.

68. Moorhead, *New Mexico's Royal Road*, 20.

69. James E. Ivey, "Seventeenth-Century Mission Trade on the Camino Real," in Palmer, ed., *El Camino Real*, 42-43.

70. John Roney, "About Paraje San Diego," in *Portrait in Sound of an Ancient Road*, produced by Jack Loeffler (2004; Santa Fe: Peregrine Arts Sound Archives), audio CD; Snow, "A Headdress of Pearls," in Palmer, ed., *El Camino Real*, 70.

71. Staski, "Change and Inertia on the Frontier," 31.

Chapter 5: The Jornada del Muerto

1. Douglas K. Boyd, "Paraje (de Fra Cristobal): Investigations of a Territorial Period Hispanic Village Site in Southern New Mexico" (master's thesis, Texas A&M University, 1986), 8-11.
2. Brodie Crouch, *Jornada del Muerto: A Pageant of the Desert* (Spokane: Arthur H. Clark Company, 1987), 47.
3. Simmons, *Last Conquistador,* 104; Crouch, *Jornada del Muerto,* 56; Riley, *Rio del Norte,* 248.
4. Riley, *Rio del Norte,* 120; Crouch, *Jornada del Muerto,* 77-78.
5. Crouch, *Jornada del Muerto,* 43; Joseph P. Sánchez, "Bernard Gruber and the New Mexican Inquisition," in Palmer, ed., *El Camino Real,* 121-132.
6. Sánchez, "Bernard Gruber," 130.
7. George Wilkins Kendall, *Narrative of the Texan Santa Fé Expedition* (New York: Harper and Bros., 1844), 2:13.
8. Point of Rocks may also refer to a low outlier of rocks nearby. See Jackson, *Royal Road,* 69.
9. Simmons, *Last Conquistador,* 104.
10. Marshall and Walt, *Rio Abajo,* 242.
11. Hallenbeck, *Land of the Conquistadores,* 361; Crouch, *Jornada del Muerto,* 85-86.
12. Marshall, "El Camino Real de Tierra Adentro," 47.
13. Jean Fulton, "Disintegrating Boots," *Chronicles of the Trail* 5, no. 4 (2009): 3-4.
14. Gibbs, Chávez, and Reynolds, "Spaceport Recovery Plan," 37-40.
15. Crouch, *Jornada del Muerto,* 86.
16. Marshall and Walt, *Rio Abajo,* 242.
17. Austerman, *Sharps Rifles,* 29, 315, 38 (quote).
18. Marshall and Walt, *Rio Abajo,* 244.
19. Crouch, *Jornada del Muerto,* 52, 136.
20. Crouch, *Jornada del Muerto,* 132-36, 143-49, 142(quote).
21. Boyd, "Paraje," 42; Hallenbeck, *Land of the Conquistadores,* 361.
22. Mike Marshall, "Contadero Mesa," in *Portrait in Sound of an Ancient Road,* produced by Jack Loeffler (2004; Santa Fe: Peregrine Arts Sound Archives), audio CD.
23. Torrez, "Governor Allende's Instructions," in Palmer and Fosberg, comps., *El Camino Real,* 112.
24. Boyd, "Paraje," 62.
25. Boyd, "Paraje," 70-71.
26. Boyd, "Paraje," 101-110.
27. Marshall and Walt, *Rio Abajo,* 293.
28. Marshall and Walt, *Rio Abajo,* 240.
29. John O. Baxter, *Las Carneradas: Sheep Trade in New Mexico 1700–1860* (Albuquerque: University New Mexico Press, 1987), 9, 31, 42.
30. Baxter, *Las Carneradas,* 90-91.
31. Marshall and Walt, *Rio Abajo,* 270.

32. Hendricks and Timmons, *San Elizario*, 44.

33. Marshall and Walt, *Rio Abajo*, 286.

34. Marshall and Walt, *Rio Abajo*, 237.

35. Marshall and Walt, *Rio Abajo*, 287.

36. Timmons, *El Paso*, 86.

37. Boyd, "Paraje," 71.

38. Alberts, "Civil War," 195-96.

39. Marshall and Walt, *Rio Abajo*, 287.

40. Jackson, *Royal Road*, 63.

41. Durwood Ball, " Fort Craig, New Mexico, and the Southwest Indian Wars, 1854–1884," *New Mexico Historical Review* 73, no. 2 (1998): 153-55.

42. Ball, "Fort Craig, New Mexico," 157, 159, 163.

43. Francis Stanley, *The San Marcial, New Mexico Story* (Pantex: F. Stanley, 1960?), 5-7.

44. Marshall and Walt, *Rio Abajo*, 282, 272; Stanley, *San Marcial*, 6.

45. Stanley, *San Marcial*, 8-9.

46. Richard Melzer, "Floods Haven't Washed Away Memories of Railroad Town," *New Mexico Magazine*, July 1990, 98.

Chapter 6: The Socorro Valley

1. Marshall and Walt, *Rio Abajo*, 135.

2. Ayer, trans., *Benavides Memorial*, 16-17.

3. Michael P. Marshall, *Qualacú: Archeological Investigation of a Piro Pueblo* (Albuquerque: U.S. Fish and Wildlife Service, 1987), 126, 125.

4. Some estimates are as high as forty pueblos. Kantner, *Protohistoric Puebloan World*, 267.

5. Marshall and Walt, *Rio Abajo*, 137, 139, 140.

6. Riley, *Rio del Norte*, 271.

7. Riley, *Rio del Norte*, 45; Steven LeBlanc, "San Felipe Pueblo Ruin" (National Register of Historic Places Inventory-Nomination Form, Santa Fe, 1980), 4.

8. Ayer, trans., *Benavides Memorial*, 202, 269n.

9. Hackett and Shelby, eds., *Revolt of the Pueblo*, 1: xxvii; Barrett, *Conquest and Catastrophe*, 68.

10. Hackett and Shelby, eds., *Revolt of the Pueblo*, 1: lxxxii.

11. Hackett and Shelby, eds., *Revolt of the Pueblo*, 1: lxxiii-lxxiv.

12. Hackett and Shelby, eds., *Revolt of the Pueblo*, 1: cxxviii.

13. Marshall and Walt, *Rio Abajo*, 253.

14. Marshall and Walt, *Rio Abajo*, 182-85.

15. Hackett and Shelby, eds., *Revolt of the Pueblo*, 1: cxxvii.

16. Adams, ed., *Tamarón's Visitation*, 42.

17. Marshall and Walt, *Rio Abajo*, 251-52, 182-85.

18. Marshall, *Qualacú*, 27.

19. Hammond and Rey, eds., *Don Juan de Oñate*, 1: 318.

20. Marshall, *Qualacú*, 127-28.

21. Julyan, *Place Names*, 310.

22. Ruxton, *Adventures in Mexico*, 183.

23. Varney, *New Mexico Ghost Towns*, 85; Thomas E. Dabney, *The Man Who Bought the Waldorf: The Life of Conrad N. Hilton* (New York: Duell, Sloan and Pierce, 1950).

24. Howard B. Nickelson, "The History of the Carthage Coal Mine," in Charles Carroll and Lynn Sebastian, eds., *Fort Craig: The United States Fort on the Camino Real* (Socorro: New Mexico Bureau of Land Management, 2000), 235; Dorothy A. Zamora, Jack Bertram, Kenneth J. Lord, and Yvonne R. Oakes, *Excavations at the Coal Mining Community of Carthage, Socorro County, New Mexico* (Santa Fe: Museum of New Mexico, 1997), 5-7.

25. Nickelson, "Carthage Coal Mine," 236-37; Zamora, et al., *Excavations at Carthage*, 15-16.

26. Peggy A. Gerow and Patrick Hogan, *They Called it Home: An Architectural and Historical Assessment of San Pedro, Socorro County, New Mexico* (Albuquerque: Office of Contract Archaeology, 1994), 19, 22.

27. Marshall and Walt, *Rio Abajo*, 284-85.

28. Gerow and Hogan, *They Called it Home*, 99; Spitler, "Churches of the Valley," 20.

29. Marshall and Walt, *Rio Abajo*, 240.

30. Marshall and Walt, *Rio Abajo*, 277.

31. Wislizenus, *Memoir of a Tour*, 37; Marshall and Walt, *Rio Abajo*, 303.

32. Marshall and Walt, *Rio Abajo*, 303-04; Spitler, "Churches of the Valley," 18.

33. Hammond and Rey, eds., *Don Juan de Oñate*, 1: 318.

34. Amy C. Earls, "Las Huertas, Old Socorro, Teypama" (National Register of Historic Places Inventory-Nomination Form, Santa Fe, 1982), 1-2.

35. Information about Teypana and Plaza Montoya provided from several unpublished papers by Dr. Michael Bletzer, Southern Methodist University.

36. Hammond and Rey, eds., *Don Juan de Oñate*, 1: 319; *El Defensor Chieftain*, (Socorro, New Mexico), Aug. 4, 2007; Marshall and Walt, *Rio Abajo*, 248.

37. Ayer, trans., *Benavides Memorial*, 7, 9; Bruce Ashcroft, *The Territorial History of Socorro, New Mexico* (El Paso: Texas Western Press, 1988), 2; Charles L. Nieman, *Spanish Times and Boom Times: Toward an Architectural History of Socorro, New Mexico* (Socorro: Socorro County Historical Society, 1972), 2.

38. Ayer, trans., *Benavides Memorial*, 18; Nieman, *Spanish Times and Boom Times*, 2.

39. Hackett and Shelby, eds., *Revolt of the Pueblo*, 1: cxxvii; Nieman, *Spanish Times and Boom Times*, 3.

40. Adams, ed., *Tamarón's Visitation*, 42.

41. Ashcroft, *Territorial History of Socorro*, 4.

42. Nieman, *Spanish Times and Boom Times*, 5; Ashcroft, *Territorial History of Socorro*, 6.

43. John P. Conron and Anthony Alofsin, *Socorro: A Historic Survey* (Albuquerque: University

of New Mexico Press, 1980), 10-12.

44. Walter K. López, "San Miguel Mission: Spirit of Socorro," *New Mexico Magazine*, June 1998, 41-42; Bartlett Gilbert and Charles Quinlan, "El Torreón, Socorro: A Case History," *New Mexico Architecture* 5, no.1 (1963): 21-22.

45. López, "San Miguel Mission," 42-44.

46. Conron and Alofsin, *Socorro*, 49.

47. "García Nepomucero House" (National Register of Historic Places Registration Form, Socorro, 1990), 2-3.

48. Conron and Alofsin, *Socorro*, 49-50.

49. Abert, *New Mexico Report*, 132.

50. Michael Marshall, "Parida (LA 31718)" (National Register of Historic Places Inventory-Nomination Form, Santa Fe, 1986), 2-3; Marshall and Walt, *Rio Abajo*, 276, 278, 290-91.

51. Dan Scurlock, "A Cultural Resource Investigation of Two Historic Sites in Lemitar, New Mexico" (unpublished report for the Bureau of Land Management, Socorro, 1982), 7, 9.

52. Gonzáles, *Hispanic Elite*, 13-14.

53. Davis, *El Gringo*, 363.

54. Scurlock, "Lemitar," 9, 11.

55. Scurlock, "Lemitar," 12, 13.

56. Scurlock, "Lemitar," 12, 13.

57. Scurlock, "Lemitar," 15, 16-7, 19.

58. Terry Sanchez, "The Manuel Armijo House in Lemitar, New Mexico" (unpublished paper, BLM files, Socorro, n.d.), 2.

59. Scurlock, "Lemitar," 20-31.

60. Marshall and Walt, *Rio Abajo*, 280.

61. Hackett and Shelby, eds., *Revolt of the Pueblo*, 1: cxxvii.

62. Marshall and Walt, *Rio Abajo*, 254-55.

63. Marshall and Walt, *Rio Abajo*, 265.

64. Riley, *Rio del Norte*, 230. The expedition's notes called the site "La Hoya."

65. Hammond and Rey, eds., *Don Juan de Oñate*, 1: 319.

66. Ayer, trans., *Benavides Memorial*, 17.

67. Marshall and Walt, *Rio Abajo*, 203; Ayer, trans., *Benavides Memorial*, 17.

68. Hackett and Shelby, eds., *Revolt of the Pueblo*, 1: cxxix.

69. Adams, ed., *Tamarón's Visitation*, 42.

70. Hackett and Shelby, eds., *Revolt of the Pueblo*, 1: lxxi.

71. Hackett and Shelby, eds., *Revolt of the Pueblo*, 1: 377; Ramona Rand-Caplan, "The History of the Sevilleta Land Grant in the First Person: Oral Histories from La Joya de Sevilleta" (master's thesis, University of New Mexico, 2006), 23.

72. Jackson, ed., *Journals of Zebulon Pike*, 1: 407.

73. Rand-Caplan, "History of the Sevilleta Grant," 26-27; Gilberto Espinosa and Tibo J. Chávez, *El Rio Abajo* (Portales: Bishop Publishing Company, 1974), 4,7.

74. Quaife, ed., *Commerce of the Prairies*, map insert.

75. Rand-Caplan, "History of the Sevilleta Grant," 28, 37.

76. Jackson, *Royal Road*, 58; Marshall and Walt, *Rio Abajo*, 275, 298-99.

Chapter 7: Tiwa Country

1. Kantner, *Protohistoric Puebloan World*, 266.

2. Adams and Chávez, eds., *Missions of New Mexico*, 254.

3. Julyan, *Place Names*, 371.

4. References use both the Colorado and Colorada spelling.

5. Adams, ed, *Tamarón's Visitation*, 43.

6. Adams, ed., *Tamarón's Visitation*, 43.

7. Wislizenus, *Memoir of a Tour*, 35.

8. Julyan, *Place Names*, 67.

9. Schaafsma, "Spanish Contact Indian Pueblos," 72.

10. Marshall and Walt, *Rio Abajo*, 257.

11. Jackson, *Royal Road*, 55.

12. F. Stanley, *The Tome, New Mexico Story*, (Pep: F. Stanley, 1966), 4-5; Kessell, *Missions Since 1776*, 149; Dan Scurlock, "The Camino Real at Cerro and Plaza Tomé," in Palmer and Fosberg, comps., *El Camino Real*, 231-33.

13. Scurlock, "Camino Real at Cerro," 233.

14. Scurlock, "Camino Real at Cerro," 234-35.

15. Marc Simmons, *Taos to Tomé: True Tales of Hispanic New Mexico* (Albuquerque: University of New Mexico Press, 1978), 37-9. A more recent study of relations between the Comanche and New Mexican settlers has raised questions about the attack. See Thomas W. Kavanagh, "Los Comanches: Pieces of an Historic, Folkloric Detective Story, Part I," *New Mexico Historical Review* 81, no.4 (2006): 1-37.

16. Scurlock, "Camino Real at Cerro," 236.

17. Kessell, *Missions Since 1776*, 151-52; Kubler, *Religious Architecture*, 114.

18. Julyan, *Place Names*, 368; Espinosa and Chávez, *Rio Abajo*, 63.

19. Patty Baratti-Sallani, "Valencia Church, Sangre de Cristo, La Precosa Sangre" (National Register of Historic Places Inventory-Nomination Form, Socorro, 1982), 1.

20. Julyan, *Place Names*, 368.

21. Abert, *New Mexico Report*, 100.

22. Espinosa and Chávez, *Rio Abajo*, 66.

23. Baratti-Sallani, "Valencia Church," 1.

24. John M. Taylor, "Perseverance and Renewal: The Missions of Tomé," in Steele, Rhetts, and Awalt, eds., *Seeds of Struggle*, 154.

25. Baratti-Sallani, "Valencia Church," 1-2.

26. Julyan, *Place Names*, 263; Taylor, "Missions of Tomé," 160.

27. Taylor, "Missions of Tomé," 161.

28. Abert, *New Mexico Report*, 100.

29. Wislizenus, *Memoir of a Tour*, 35.

30. Drumm, ed., *Diary of Susan Magoffin*, 153-54.

31. Davis, *El Gringo*, 356.

32. Simmons, *Albuquerque*, 166.

33. Simmons, *Albuquerque*, 186-88.

34. Taylor, "Missions of Tomé," 162.

35. Julyan, *Place Names*, 306; Marshall and Walt, *Rio Abajo*, 280.

36. Julyan, *Place Names*, 176.

37. Adams and Chávez, eds., *Missions of New Mexico*, 208, 208n.

38. Margaret Espinosa McDonald, "Vamos Todos a Belén: A Cultural Transformation of the Hispanic Community in the Rio Abajo Community of Belén, New Mexico from 1850–1950" (PhD diss., University of New Mexico, 1997), xx, xxv-xxvi.

39. Espinosa and Chávez, *El Rio Abajo*, 201-02.

40. Hendricks, ed., *New Mexico in 1800*, 124.

41. McDonald, "Vamos Todos a Belén," 5-6.

42. Espinosa and Chávez, *El Rio Abajo*, 81, 84-85.

43. McDonald, "Vamos Todos a Belén," 30-31, 35-36.

44. In numerous documents and accounts of the region the name appears as Chaves, Chávez, or Chávez.

45. Joseph P. Sánchez, *Between Two Rivers: The Atrisco Land Grant in Albuquerque History, 1692–1968* (Norman: University of Oklahoma Press, 2008), 20.

46. Espinosa and Chávez, *El Rio Abajo*, 42-43.

47. Espinosa and Chávez, *El Rio Abajo*, 44.

48. John Taylor and Patty Gallegos, "Our Lady of Guadalupe, Los Chaves," *Tradición* 10, no.1 (2005): 31-32.

49. Julyan, *Place Names*, 210.

50. Abert, *New Mexico Report*, 100.

51. Patty Guggino, "La Capilla de San Antonio de Los Lentes" (National Register of Historic Places Registration Form, Los Lunas, 2003), 1-2.

52. Julyan, *Place Names*, 209-10.

53. Espinosa and Chávez, *Rio Abajo*, 53.

54. Guggino, "La Capilla de San Antonio," 11.

55. Julyan, *Place Names*, 174; Florence Hawley Ellis, "Isleta Pueblo," in Ortiz, ed., *Handbook of North American Indians*, 351.

56. Julyan, *Place Names*, 174.

57. Treib, *Sanctuaries of New Mexico*, 256.

58. Kessell, *Missions Since 1776*, 215.

59. Hackett and Shelby, eds., *Revolt of the Pueblo*, 1: i-li.

60. Weber, ed., *Pueblo Revolt of 1680*, x.

61. Hackett and Shelby, eds., *Revolt of the Pueblo*, 1: xcv.

62. Hackett and Shelby, eds., *Revolt of the Pueblo*, 1: cxxi, cxxx, cxxxi.

63. Kessell, *Missions Since 1776*, 216.

64. Adams, ed., *Tamarón's Visitation*, 42, 43.

65. Adams and Chávez, eds., *Missions of New Mexico*, 206-07.

66. Wislizenus, *Memoir of a Tour*, 26.

67. Bloom, ed., "Bourke on the Southwest, XIII," 193.

68. Bloom, ed., "Bourke on the Southwest, XIII," 196.

69. Treib, *Sanctuaries of New Mexico*, 264.

70. Ellis, "Isleta Pueblo," 360.

71. Ellis, "Isleta Pueblo," 358.

72. Brian Luna Lucero, "Old Towns Challenged by the Boom Town: The Villages of the Middle Rio Grande Valley and the Albuquerque Tricentennial," *New Mexico Historical Review* 82, no. 1 (2007): 43, 44.

73. Susan Dewitt, *Historic Albuquerque Today: An Overview Survey of Historic Buildings and Districts* (Albuquerque: Historic Landmarks Survey of Albuquerque, 1978), 58.

74. Julyan, *Place Names*, 255.

75. Sánchez, *Between Two Rivers*, 14.

76. Luna Lucero, "Old Towns Challenged," 42-43.

77. Sánchez, *Between Two Rivers*, 11; Espinosa and Chávez, *El Rio Abajo*, 12.

78. Joseph P. Metzgar, "The Atrisco Land Grant," *New Mexico Historical Review* 52, no. 3 (Oct. 1977): 269-70.

79. Sánchez, *Between Two Rivers*, 28.

80. Metzgar, "Atrisco Land Grant," 272, 274.

81. Sánchez, *Between Two Rivers*, 154.

82. Metzgar, "Atrisco Land Grant," 277-83.

83. Sánchez, *Between Two Rivers*, 264-68.

84. *Journal* (Albuquerque, New Mexico), Dec. 19, 2006.

85. Luna Lucero, "Old Town Challenged," 39.

86. There is some scholarly debate about whether a west bank branch of the Camino Real de Tierra Adentro connected the area from Los Padillas north to Corrales. If it did, it was not commonly used and does not appear in early travelers'accounts. By the mid-nineteenth century a west bank trail probably did exist.

87. Simmons, *Albuquerque*, 168-69.

88. Luna Lucero, "Old Town Challenged," 52, 63; Simmons, *Albuquerque*, 228.

89. Dewitt, *Historic Albuquerque Today*, 54, 56.

90. Simmons, *Albuquerque*, 40; Adams and Chávez, eds., *Missions of New Mexico*, 145n.

91. Marc Simmons, "The Founding of Albuquerque: Another Look," in Simmons, *Spanish*

Pathways, 39-41.

92. Simmons, *Albuquerque*, 82-86.

93. Adams and Chávez, eds., *Missions of New Mexico*, 151.

94. Simmons, *Albuquerque*, 276, 361, 369-72.

95. Adams and Chávez, eds., *Missions of New Mexico*, 146, 362.

96. Treib, *Sanctuaries of New Mexico*, 235.

97. Byron A. Johnson, *Old Town, Albuquerque, New Mexico: A Guide to its History and Architecture* (Albuquerque: Albuquerque Museum, 1980), 64-73.

98. Johnson, *Old Town Albuquerque*, 103-10.

99. Dewitt, *Historic Albuquerque Today*, 50-51.

100. Dewitt, *Historic Albuquerque Today*, 46; Luna Lucero, "Old Town Challenged," 38.

101. Dewitt, *Historic Albuquerque Today*, 46-47.

102. Cynthia Sue Bruce, Los Griegos Historic District" (National Register of Historic Places Inventory-Nomination Form, Albuquerque, 1981), 7:120-25.

103. Carol J. Condie, ed., "Los Ranchos Plaza (LA 46638)" (unpublished report for the Maxwell Museum of Anthropology (Albuquerque, New Mexico 2007), 14-15.

104. Julyan, *Place Names*, 211.

105. Condie, ed., "Los Ranchos Plaza," 18.

106. Condie, ed., "Los Ranchos Plaza," 19.

107. Condie, ed., "Los Ranchos Plaza," 20.

108. Condie, ed., "Los Ranchos Plaza," 106, 108.

109. Julyan, *Place Names*, 6-7.

110. Adams and Chávez, eds., *Missions of New Mexico*, 367.

111. Hackett and Shelby, eds., *Revolt of the Pueblo*, I: xlix, clvii, clxii.

112. Simmons, *Albuquerque*, 87, 103.

113. Westphall, *Mercedes Reales*, 126; Adams and Chávez, eds., *Missions of New Mexico*, 344.

114. Adams and Chávez, eds., *Missions of New Mexico*, 152.

115. Julyan, *Place Names*, 97-98.

116. Adams and Chávez, eds, *Missions of New Mexico*, 144, 154.

117. Julyan, *Place Names*, 97-98.

118. Two major river floods in 1864 and 1868 disrupted life in Corrales. It is not known which one actually destroyed the village plaza.

119. Steve Larese, "Corrales' Casa San Ysidro," *New Mexico Magazine*, May 1999, 65-66.

120. Ellen Threinen, "San Ysidro Church" (National Register of Historic Places Inventory-Nomination Form, Santa Fe, 1980), 2.

121. Julyan, *Place Names*, 322; Elizabeth A. Brandt, "Sandia Pueblo," in Ortiz, ed., *Handbook of North American Indians*, 343.

122. Hackett and Shelby, eds., *Revolt of the Pueblo*, I: xlix.

123.Simmons, *Albuquerque*, 42; Hackett and Shelby, eds., *Revolt of the Pueblo*, I: xciii.

124. Kessell, *Missions Since 1776*, 136. Eighteenth century Spaniards referred to the Hopi as

Moqui.

125. Simmons, *Albuquerque*, 37; Adams and Chávez, eds., *Missions of New Mexico*, 138.

126. Kessell, *Missions Since 1776*, 139.

127. Adams and Chávez, eds., *Missions of New Mexico*, 143.

128. Kessell, *Missions Since 1776*, 139.

129. Bloom, ed., "Bourke on the Southwest, XIII," 199-200.

130. Bloom, ed., "Bourke on the Southwest, XIII," 199.

131. Bloom, ed., "Bourke on the Southwest, XIII," 200.

132. Brandt, "Sandia Pueblo," 347-48.

133. Adams and Chávez, eds., *Missions of New Mexico*, 144; Julyan, *Place Names*, 36.

134. Simmons, *Albuquerque*, 45.

135. Sánchez, *Fernando Durán y Chaves*, 11.

136. Espinosa, *Crusaders of the Rio Grande*, 356; Simmons, *Albuquerque*, 46-47.

137. Adams and Chávez, eds., *Missions of New Mexico*, 144.

138. F. Stanley, *The Bernalillo, New Mexico Story* (Pep: F. Stanley, 1964), 15.

139. Ellen Threinen, "Abencio Salazar Historic District" (National Register of Historic Places Inventory-Nomination Form, Santa Fe, 1979), 3-4.

140. Ellen Threinen, "Our Lady of Sorrows Church" (National Register of Historic Places Inventory-Nomination Form, Santa Fe, 1977), 2-3.

141. Lamadrid, "Pilgrimage and Cultural Commerce," 432.

Chapter 8: The Northern Pueblos

1. Kantner, *Protohistoric Puebloan World*, 261, 264.

2. Riley, *Rio del Norte*, 97, 102.

3. Hammond and Rey, eds., *Juan de Oñate*, 1: 319.

4. Ayer, trans., *Benavides Memorial*, 20.

5. Leslie A. White, *The Pueblo of Santa Ana, New Mexico* (Menasha: American Anthropological Association, 1942), 25.

6. Hackett and Shelby, eds., *Revolt of the Pueblo*, 1: xciv.

7. Espinosa, *Crusaders of the Rio Grande*, 32.

8. Kessell, *Kiva, Cross and Crown*, 267, 271; Espinosa, *Crusaders of the Rio Grande*, 32.

9. Adams, ed., *Visitation of Tamarón*, 66.

10. Adams and Chávez, eds., *Missions of New Mexico*, 170-71.

11. James Purdy, "Pueblo of Santa Ana" (National Register of Historic Places Inventory-Nomination Form, Santa Fe, 1974), 7.

12. Abert, *New Mexico Report*, 71.

13. Quoted in White, *Pueblo of Santa Ana*, 29.

14. Purdy, "Pueblo of Santa Ana," 3.

15. Strong, "Santa Ana Pueblo," 403.

16. Sánchez, *Between Two Rivers*, 21.

17. Sánchez, *Between Two Rivers*, 21.

18. Julyan, *Place Names*, 16.

19. Julyan, *Place Names*, 12.

20. Jackson, *Royal Road*, 35.

21. James Purdy, "Pueblo of San Felipe" (National Register of Historic Places Inventory-Nomination Form, Santa Fe, 1972), 2; Riley, *Rio del Norte*, 97.

22. Hammond and Rey, eds., *Don Juan de Oñate*, 1:365; Pauline Turner Strong, "San Felipe Pueblo," in Ortiz, ed., *Handbook of North American Indians*, 392.

23. Adams and Chávez, eds., *Missions of New Mexico*, 361.

24. Hackett and Shelby, eds., *Revolt of the Pueblo*, 1:cl.

25. Espinosa, *Crusaders of the Rio Grande*, 161.

26. Adams and Chávez, eds., *Missions of New Mexico*, 161n.

27. Adams and Chávez, eds., *Missions of New Mexico*, 165; Hendricks, ed., *New Mexico in 1801*, 24.

28. Adams and Chávez, eds., *Missions of New Mexico*, 160.

29. Jackson, ed., *Journals of Zebulon Pike*, 1:399.

30. Abert, *New Mexico Report*, 65-66.

31. Bloom, ed., "Bourke on the Southwest, XIII," 213; Strong, "San Felipe Pueblo," 394.

32. Bloom, ed., "Bourke of the Southwest, XIII," 212; Purdy, "Pueblo of San Felipe," 4.

33. Strong, "San Felipe Pueblo," 397.

34. Charles H. Lange, "Santo Domingo Pueblo," in Ortiz, ed., *Handbook of North American Indians*, 379.

35. Treib, *Sanctuaries of New Mexico*, 226; Simmons, *Last Conquistador*, 108.

36. Adams and Chávez, eds, *Missions of New Mexico*, 131.

37. Hackett and Shelby, eds., *Revolt of the Pueblo*, 1:xlv.

38. Espinosa, *Crusaders of the Rio Grande*, 213; Kessell, *Kiva, Cross, and Crown*, 241.

39. James Purdy, "Pueblo of Santo Domingo" (National Register of Historic Places Inventory-Nomination Form, Santa Fe, 1973), 2.

40. Adams and Chávez, eds. *Missions of New Mexico*, 132.

41. Purdy, "Pueblo of Santo Domingo," 2.

42. Purdy, "Pueblo of Santo Domingo," 3; Kessell, *Missions Since 1776*, 131.

43. Kessell, *Missions Since 1776*, 133.

44. Treib, *Sanctuaries of New Mexico*, 231.

45. James Purdy, "Pueblo of Cochiti" (National Register of Historic Places Inventory-Nomination Form, Santa Fe, 1974), 2.

46. Wilcox, *Pueblo Revolt*, 212-14.

47. Julyan, *Place Names*, 89; Charles L. Lange, "Cochiti Pueblo," in Ortiz, ed., *Handbook of*

North American Indians, 366.

48. Hackett and Shelby, eds., *Revolt of the Pueblo*, 1: xliii.

49. Rick Hendricks, "Pueblo-Spanish Warfare in Seventeenth Century New Mexico," in Preucel, ed., *Archaeologies of the Pueblo Revolt*, 189-91.

50. Espinosa, *Crusaders of the Rio Grande*, 220.

51. Adams, ed., *Visitation of Tamarón*, 65.

52. Adams and Chávez, eds., *Missions of New Mexico*, 156.

53. Hendricks, ed., *New Mexico in 1801*, 56.

54. Charles H. Lange, *Cochiti: A New Mexico Pueblo, Past and Present* (Austin: University of Texas Press, 1959), 11, 12, 16.

55. Bloom, ed., "Bourke on the Southwest, XIII," 234.

56. Bloom, ed., "Bourke on the Southwest, XIII," 236.

57. Adams and Chávez, eds., *Missions of New Mexico*, 156-57.

58. Kessell, *Missions Since 1776*, 157.

59. Lange, "Cochiti Pueblo," 367.

60. Riley, *Rio del Norte*, 102.

61. Walter Wait, "History of Our District," *San Marcos Association Newsletter* 4, no. 7 (2006): 1-3.

62. Lippard, *Down Country*, 175-76.

63. Stuart A. Northrup, "Turquoise," *El Palacio* 79, no.1 (1973), 18.

64. *New Mexican*, (Santa Fe, New Mexico), June 1, 2008; Simmons, *Last Conquistador*, 150.

65. R.B. Brown, "El Camino Real: The Route of Power," *Chronicles of the Trail* 4, no. 4 (2008): 6-7.

66. Hackett and Shelby, eds., *Revolt of the Pueblo*, 1: xxxviii-xxxxix.

67. Lippard, *Down Country*, 123, 253.

68. Riley, *Rio del Norte*, 96, 271.

69. Kessell, *Kiva, Cross, and Crown*, 253.

70. Ann F. Ramenofsky and Christopher Pierce, "Proposal to Conduct Archaeological Research at San Marcos Pueblo (LA98)" (unpublished proposal, University of New Mexico Collections, Albuquerque, 1999), 1-4.

71. Homer Milford, "History of the Los Cerrillos Mining Area" (New Mexico Abandoned Mine Land Bureau Reports, Santa Fe, 1996), 1-3.

72. Cordelia Thomas Snow, "A Brief History of Mission San Marcos" (unpublished paper, Office of the State Historian, Santa Fe, n.d.), 2.

73. *New Mexican*, (Santa Fe, New Mexico), June 1, 2008; Ramenofsky and Pierce, "Proposal," 11.

74. Robert P. Powers, ed., *The Peopling of Bandelier: New Insights from the Archaeology of the Pajarito Plateau* (Santa Fe: School of American Research Press, 2005), xiv-xv.

75. Kurt F. Anschuetz, "Tewa Fields, Tewa Traditions," in V.B. Price and Baker H. Morrow, eds., *Canyon Gardens: The Ancient Pueblo Landscapes of the American Southwest* (Albuquerque: University of New Mexico Press, 2006), 61, 68.

76. Florence Hawley Ellis, "The Long Lost "City" of San Gabriel de Yungue," in *When Cultures Meet: Remembering San Gabriel de Yungue Oweenge* (Santa Fe: Sunstone Press, 1987), 11-12.

77. Riley, *Rio del Norte*, 90-92.

78. Simmons, *Last Conquistador*, 109.

79. San Ildefonso, Santa Clara, and San Juan pueblos lie along the trail while Tesuque, Pojoaque and Nambé are nearby. Anschuetz, "Tewa Fields," 61.

80. Ortiz, *Tewa World,* 12-14.

81. Adams and Chávez, eds, *Missions of New Mexico*, 360n.

82. Ayer, trans., *Benavides Memorial*, 23-4.

83. Hackett and Shelby, eds., *Revolt of the Pueblo*, 1: xxxv.

84. Espinosa, *Crusaders of the Rio Grande*, 164.

85. Hendricks, "Pueblo-Spanish Warfare," 187-88.

86. Hendricks, "Pueblo-Spanish Warfare," 195-96.

87. Kessell, *Kiva, Cross and Crown,* 287; Adams and Chávez, eds., *Missions of New Mexico*, 64n.

88. Ayer, trans., *Benavides Memorial*, 239n.

89. Westphall, *Mercedes Reales*, 20.

90. Adams and Chávez, eds., *Missions of New Mexico*, 71, 69.

91. Hendricks, ed., *New Mexico in 1801*, 7.

92. Ayer, trans., *Benavides Memorial*, 239n.

93. Bloom, ed., "Bourke on the Southwest, XII," 66.

94. Kessell, *Missions Since 1776*, 78-79.

95. Ortiz, *Tewa World*, 70-72, 18.

96. Willard W. Hill, *An Ethnography of Santa Clara Pueblo, New Mexico*, ed. Charles H. Lange (Albuquerque: University of New Mexico Press, 1982), 5-7; Nancy S. Arnon and W.W. Hill, "Santa Clara Pueblo," in Ortiz, ed., *Handbook of North American Indians*, 296-97.

97. Adams and Chávez, eds., *Missions of New Mexico*, 360.

98. Ayer, trans., *Benavides Memorial*, 45, 360n.;Treib, *Sanctuaries of New Mexico*, 136.

99. Hackett and Shelby, eds., *Revolt of the Pueblo*, 1: xxxv.

100. Espinosa, *Crusaders of the Rio Grande*, 164, 208.

101. Rina Swentzell, "An Architectural History of Santa Clara Pueblo" (PhD. diss., University of. New Mexico, 1976), 25-26.

102. Adams and Chávez, eds., *Missions of New Mexico*, 118-19.

103. Swentzell, "Architectural History," 43-48.

104. Swentzell, "Architectural History," 43-45.

105. Julyan, *Place Names*, 126.

106. Adams, ed., *Visitation of Tamarón*, 64.

107. Adams and Chávez, eds., *Missions of New Mexico*, 114-15; Treib, *Sanctuaries of New Mexico*, 137-38.

108. Treib, *Sanctuaries of New Mexico*, 139.

109. Arnon and Hill, "Santa Clara Pueblo," 297; Swentzell, "Architectural History," 63-68.

110. Julyan, *Place Names*, 324.

111. Hackett and Shelby, eds., *Revolt of the Pueblo*, 1: xxxvi.

112. Adams and Chávez, eds., *Missions of New Mexico*, 322.

113. Westphall, *Mercedes Reales*, 19.

114. Kessell, et al., eds., *Blood on the Boulders*, 2: 644-45.

115. Espinosa, *Crusaders of the Rio Grande*, 354.

116. Corinne P. Sze, "La Iglesia de Santa Cruz and the Site of the Plaza of Santa Cruz de la Cañada" (National Register of Historic Places Registration Form, Santa Fe, 1994), 8:33-35.

117. Adams, ed., *Visitation of Tamarón*, 63.

118. Adams and Chávez, eds., *Missions of New Mexico*, 82.

119. Adams and Chávez, eds., *Missions of New Mexico*, 84.

120. Sze, "Iglesia de Santa Cruz," 8:33.

121. Janet Lecompte, *Rebellion in the Rio Arriba* (Albuquerque: University of New Mexico Press, 1985), 15.

122. Lecompte, *Rebellion in the Rio Arriba*, 59.

123. Lecompte, *Rebellion in the Rio Arriba*, 71.

124. Sze, "Iglesia de Santa Cruz," 8:34.

125. Adams and Chávez, eds., *Missions of New Mexico*, 73.

126. Treib, *Sanctuaries of New Mexico*, 157.

127. Bloom, ed., "Bourke on the Southwest, XIX," 251.

128. *Journal*, (Albuquerque, New Mexico), Dec. 24, 1995; *New Mexican*, (Santa Fe, New Mexico), Dec. 3, 1999; Sze, "Iglesia de Santa Cruz," 7:4.

129. Sze, "La Iglesia de Santa Cruz," 8:34.

130. Ortiz, *Tewa World*, 12, 13.

131. Ortiz, *Tewa World*, 14-15.

132. Simmons, *Last Conquistador*, 120-21.

133. Myra Ellen Jenkins, "Oñate's Administration and Pueblo Indians," in *When Cultures Meet*, 63-64.

134. Simmons, *Last Conquistador*, 115-16.

135. Simmons, *Last Conquistador*, 116-18.

136. Simmons, "Spaniards of San Gabriel," 44.

137. Alfonso Ortiz, "Popay's Leadership: A Pueblo Perspective on the 1680 Revolt," in Weigle, ed., *Telling New Mexico*, 110-11; Kessell, *Kiva, Cross and Crown*, 232-34.

138. Hackett and Shelby, eds., *Revolt of the Pueblo*, 1: xxxv.

139. Kessell, *Kiva, Cross and Crown*, 237-38, 241.

140. Espinosa, *Crusaders of the Rio Grande*, 77, 216; Ortiz, "Popay's Leadership," 112.

141. Adams and Chávez, eds., *Missions of New Mexico*, 84-85.

142. Hendricks, ed., *New Mexico in 1801*, 64.

143. Adams and Chávez, eds., *Missions of New Mexico*, 90-92.

144. Kessell, *Missions Since 1776*, 90.

145. Bloom, ed., "Bourke on the Southwest, XIX," 260, 263.

146. Bloom, ed., "Bourke on the Southwest, XIX," 267.

147. Kessell, *Missions Since 1776*, 93-94.

148. Trieb, *Sanctuaries of New Mexico*, 147-48.

149. Sweet, *Dances of the Tewa*, 83.

150. *New Mexican*, (Santa Fe, New Mexico), Mar. 4, 2005.

151. *Rio Grande Sun*, (Española, New Mexico), July 26, 2007.

152. Ellis, "Lost City," 11, 32.

Chapter 9: On to Santa Fe

1. Marshall, "El Camino Real de Tierra Adentro," 132-36.

2. Marshall, "El Camino Real de Tierra Adentro," 145-47.

3. David Kammer, "Route 66 and National Old Trails Road Historic District at La Bajada" (National Register of Historic Places Inventory-Nomination Form, Albuquerque, 2002), 7:7-8, 8:8.

4. Kammer, "Route 66 and National Old Trails," 7:7-8, 8:8.

5. Kubler, *Religious Architecture of New Mexico*, 105.

6. Kammer, "Route 66 and National Old Trails," 8:11.

7. Melissa Payne, "Valley of Faith: Historical Archeology in the Upper Santa Fe River Basin" (PhD diss., University of New Mexico, 1999), 133.

8. Adams and Chávez, eds., *Missions of New Mexico*, 43.

9. Marshall, "El Camino Real de Tierra Adentro," 142.

10. Sandra K. Schackel, "Resurrected Rancho: Old Ciénega Village Museum" (master's thesis, University of New Mexico, 1982); John O. Baxter, "The Acequia System of El Rancho de las Golondrinas" (National Register of Historic Places Inventory-Nomination Form, Santa Fe, 1979), 2-3.

11. Adams and Chávez, eds., *Missions of New Mexico*, 41, 42.

12. Louann Jordan, *El Rancho de las Golondrinas*, (Santa Fe: Colonial New Mexico Historical Foundation, 1977), 5-6.

13. Schackel, "Resurrected Rancho," 18.

14. *New Mexican*, (Santa Fe, New Mexico), Aug. 30, 2009.

15. Adams and Chávez, eds., *Missions of New Mexico*, 41.

16. Simmons, *Last Conquistador*, 180-81.

17. James Ivey, "The Viceroy's Order Founding the Villa Santa Fe: A Reconsideration, 1605–1610," in *All Trails Lead to Santa Fe*, 101-03.

18. Joseph P. Sánchez, "The Peralta-Ordóñez Affair and the Founding of Santa Fe," in Noble, ed., *Santa Fe*, 30-32.

19. Cordelia Thomas Snow, "A Window to the Past: The San Miguel and La Conquistadora Chapels and their Builders, 1610–1776," in *All Trails Lead to Santa Fe*, 148-49.

20. Sánchez, "The Peralta-Ordóñez Affair,"30-32.

21. Arnold Vigil, "Barrio de Analco," *New Mexico Magazine*, December 2006, 63-64.

22. John L. Kessell, "By Force of Arms: Vargas and the Spanish Restoration of Santa Fe," in Noble, *Santa Fe*, 54-60.

23. Adams, ed., *Tamarón's Visitation*, 46,47.

24. Adams and Chávez, eds., *Missions of New Mexico*, 39-40.

25. Jackson, *Royal Road*, 7-8.

26. Adams, ed., *Tamarón's Visitation*, 47.

27. Janet Lecompte, "When Santa Fe was a Mexican Town: 1821–1846," in Noble, ed., *Santa Fe*, 81-83.

28. Lecompte, "When Santa Fe was a Mexican Town,"83.

29. Simmons, *Albuquerque*, 214, 223.

30. Kay Aiken Reeve, *Santa Fe and Taos, 1898–1942: An American Cultural Center* (El Paso: Texas Western Press, 1982), 3-6.

31. *New Mexican*, (Santa Fe, New Mexico), Oct. 27, 2007.

32. Adams and Chávez, eds., *Missions of New Mexico*, 34; Treib, *Sanctuaries of New Mexico*, 113-14.

33. Snow, "A Window to the Past," *151-52*.

34. Treib, *Sanctuaries of New Mexico*, 78.

35. Snow, "A Window on the Past," 151-52.

36. Adams, ed., *Tamarón's Visitation*, 47; Adams and Chávez, eds., *Missions of New Mexico*, 38.

37. Adams and Chávez, eds, *Missions of New Mexico*, 38; Treib, *Sanctuaries of New Mexico*, 81.

38. Treib, *Sanctuaries of New Mexico,* 83-84.

39. Diana Del Mauro, "Both Sides Now," *New Mexico Magazine,* June 2009.

Bibliography

Articles:

Apodaca, Heather. "Places of the Strong People." *New Mexico Magazine*, January 2009.

Archuleta, Elizabeth. "History Carved in Stone: Memorializing PóPay and Oñate, or Re-casting Racialized Regimes of Representation." *New Mexico Historical Review* 82, no. 2 (2007): 317-42.

Austerman, Wayne R. "Ben Coons' Santa Fe Passage." *Password* 30, no. 1 (1985): 40-43.

Ball, Durwood. "Fort Craig, New Mexico, and the Southwest Indian Wars, 1854–1884." *New Mexico Historical Review* 73, no. 1 (1998): 153-55.

"Big Force at Work on Road." *El Paso Herald*, Feb. 22, 1916.

Bloom, Lansing B. "Alburquerque and Galisteo: Certificate of their Founding, 1706." *New Mexico Historical Review* 10, no. 1 (1935): 48-50.

———. "Bourke on the Southwest, X." *New Mexico Historical Review* 11, no. 2 (1936): 245-282.

———. "Bourke on the Southwest, XI." *New Mexico Historical Review* 12, no. 1 (1937): 41-77.

———. "Bourke on the Southwest, XIII." *New Mexico Historical Review* 13, no. 2 (1938): 192-238.

———. "The Chihuahua Highway." *New Mexico Historical Review* 12, no. 2 (1937): 209-16.

Brockmoller, Janet Y. "A Music of Two Spheres: The Story of Margaret Conkling." *Password* 30, no. 3 (1985): 143-48.

Bronitsky, Gordon. "Indian Assimilation in the El Paso Area." *New Mexico Historical Review* 62, no. 2 (1987): 151-62.

Brown, R.B. "El Camino Real: The Route of Power." *Chronicles of the Trail* 4, no. 3 (2008): 3-12+.

Burrus, Ernest J. "An Historical Outline of the Socorro Mission." *Password* 29, no. 3 (1984): 145-150.

Calleros, Cleofas. "Writer Describes Father Ortiz' Kindness." *Times* (El Paso, Texas), Dec. 21, 1952.

———."San Lorenzo Mission in Mexico Erected North of River." *Times* (El Paso, Texas), May 25, 1952.

———."Thousands Thronged Juárez for Funeral of Father Ortiz." *Times* (El Paso, Texas), Dec. 28, 1952.

———."Governo Otermín established San Lorenzo as Center for Southwest Missionary Work." *Times* (El Paso, Texas), June 1, 1952.

———."Thousands Thronged Juárez for Funeral of Father Ortiz." *Times* (El Paso, Texas), Dec. 28, 1952.

Colligan, John B. "Early Owners of the Nestor Armijo Home." *Southern New Mexico Historical Review* 1, no. 1 (1994): 11-17.

Cordoba, James M. "Colonial New Mexico Santos and their Makers." *El Palacio* 109, no. 3 (2001): 26-30.

Crimmins, M.L. "Fort Fillmore." *New Mexico Historical Review* 6, no. 3 (1931): 327-33.

Cross, Jack L. "Wagons Roads across New Mexico, 1846–1860." *Password* 7, no. 1 (1962): 16-34.

Daniel, James M., ed. and trans. "Diary of Pedro José de la Fuente." *Southwestern Historical Quarterly* 60, no. 3 (1956): 260-281.

Davila, Erika. "A Faithful Restoration." *New Mexican* (Santa Fe, New Mexico), Dec. 3, 1999.

"Dedication of the Taylor-Barela-Reynolds Mesilla State Monument." *Chronicles of the Trail* 2, no. 3 (2006): 2-6.

Del Mauro, Diana. "Time Exposure." *New Mexico Magazine*, June 2009.

Dwyer, James Magoffin Jr. "Hugh Stephenson." *New Mexico Historical Review* 29, no. 1 (1954): 2-4.

Edwards, John. "Lost Parish Resurfaces Downriver." *Herald Post* (El Paso, Texas), Oct. 13, 1979.

Estrada, Marta. "The Cemetery Trail: A Tour of History and Traditions in the El Paso Valley." *Password* 34, no.3 (1989): 137-44.

"Father Ortiz' Funeral." *Herald* (El Paso, Texas), March 12 1896.

Fewkes, J. Walter. "The Pueblo Settlements near El Paso, Texas." *American Anthropologist* 4, no. 1 (1902): 57-75.

Fulton, Jean. "Disintegrating Boots." *Chronicles of the Trail* 5, no. 1 (2009): 3-5.

Garrett, Rebecca T. "An El Paso Historic Preservation Venture: El Paso Landmarks, Inc." *Password* 41, no. 3 (1996): 107-12.

Gerald, Rex E. "An Introduction to Missions of the Paso del Norte Area." *Password* 20, no. 2 (1975): 47-58.

———. "The Old Socorro Mission Site Test Excavations, 1981–83." *The Artifact* 28, no.1 (1990): 3-6.

———. "Portrait of a Co mmunity: Joseph de Urrutia's Map of El Paso del Norte, 1766." *American West* 3, no. 3 (1966): 38-41.

Gerald, Rex E. and Olympia Caudillo. "Bravo 1795: An Inventory of the Missions of Senecú, Ysleta, and Socorro by Fray José Bravo in the Year 1795." *Password* 33, no. 2 (1988): 19-40.

Gilbert, Bartlett and Charles Quinlan. "El Torreón: A Case History." *New Mexico Architecture* 5, no. 1 (1963): 21-25.

New Mexico Historical Review 39, no. 1 (*1964*): 1-15.

Gomez, David. "Place of the Strong People." *New Mexico Magazine* , January 2009.

Gonzales, Manuel G. "Dr. Mariano Samaniego (1831–1905): Citizen of the El Paso Valley." *Password* 35, no. 4 (1990): 159-190.

Greenleaf, Richard E. "Atrisco and Las Ciruelas, 1722–1769." *New Mexico Historical Review* 52, no. 1 (1967): 5-25.

———. "The Founding of Albuquerque, 1706: An Historical Problem."

Fulton, Jean. "The Texas Socorro Mission Preservation Project." *Chronicles of the Trail* 2, no.2 (2006): 2-4.

Hamm, Ron. "Socorro's Old San Miguel Mission." *New Mexico Magazine*, February 1983.

Haecker, Charles M. "Brazito Battlefield: Once Lost now Found." *New Mexico Historical Review* 72, no. 3 (1997): 229-238.

Hamilton, Nancy. "The Frontera Settlement." *Password* 30, no. 3 (Summer 1985): 175-177.

Hamm, Ron. "Socorro's Old San Miguel Mission." *New Mexico Magazine*, February 1983.

Hendricks, Rick. "Camino Real at the Pass: The Economy and Political Structure of the Paso del Norte Area in the Eighteenth Century." *Password* 44, no.1 (1999): 2-16.

———. "Santa María de las Caldas and the Hacienda de San Antonio." *Nuestras Raices* 6, no. 3 (1994): 2-4.

Hoover, Sandra S. "Mission Landscaping." *Password* 31, no. 3 (1986): 147-51.

Houser, Nicholas P. "The Tigua Settlement of Ysleta del Sur," *The Kiva* 36, no.1 (1970): 23-27.

Hurt, Wesley R. *"Tortugas, an Indian Village in Southern New Mexico,"* *El Palacio* 59, no. 4 (1952): 104-122.

Jones, Harriot Howze. "Heritage Homes of El Paso: Hart's Mill-Hacienda Café." *Password* 21, no. 3 (1976): 115-118.

Jones, Oakah L. "San José del Parral: Colonial Trade of Parralenses with Nuevo México and El Paso del Río del Norte." *Journal of Big Bend Studies* 13 (2001): 11-25.

Kavanagh, Thomas W. "Los Comanches: Pieces of an Historic, Folklore Detective Story." *New Mexico Historical Review* 81, no. 1 (2006): 1-37.

"La Iglesia de San Ysidro." *Preservation New Mexico* 5, no. 3 (1988): 1-2.

Lamadrid, Enrique R. *"Rutas del Corazón*: Pilgrimage and Cultural Commerce on the Camino Real de Tierra Adentro." *New Mexico Historical Review* 83, no. 4 (2008): 423-450.

Larese, Steve. "Corrales' Casa San Ysidro." *New Mexico Magazine*, May 1999.

Leach, Joseph. "Stage Coach through the Pass: The Butterfield Overland Mail Comes to El Paso." *Password* 3, no. 3 (1953): 130-137.

Leyva, Yolanda. "Monuments of Conformity: Commemorating and Protesting Oñate on the Border." *New Mexico Historical Review* 82, no. 2 (2007): 343-68.

Lopez, Walter K. "Spirit of Socorro rooted in Historic Church." *New Mexico Magazine*, June 1998.

Lucero, Brian Luna. "Old Towns Challenged by the Boom Town: The Villages of the Middle Rio Grande Valley and The Albuquerque Tricentennial." *New Mexico Historical Review* 82, no. 1 (2007): 37-70.

Melzer, Richard. "Floods Haven't Washed Away Memories of Railroad Town," *New Mexico Magazine*, July 1990.

Metzgar, Joseph V. "The Atrisco Land Grant, 1692–1977." *New Mexico Historical Review* 52, no. 3 (1977): 269-296.

Miles, Bob. "Early Roads to El Paso." *Password* 31, no. 2 (1986): 75-92.

Morrow, Herbert C. and Karen. "The Ysleta Historic District: A Historical and Architectural Perspective." *Password* 36, no. 4 (1991): 159-167.

Murphey, John W. "A New King's Highway," *Chronicles of the Trail* 7, no.2 (2011): 18-20.

Newman, Bud. "Fray Garcia de San Francisco, Founder of El Paso: A Syllabus of Errors." *Password* 29, no. 4 (1984): 179-190.

Nieves, Santiago. "El Camino Real." *Password* 26, no. 3 (1981): 126.

Nigro, Fred W. "La Capilla de San Antonio in La Cieneguilla." *La Herencia* 58, no. 2 (2008): 30-32.

Noble, David Grant. "Fort Craig: Yanks and Rebs met at Frontier Outpost." *New Mexico Magazine*, January 1995.

Ochoa Rodríguez, Francisco. "Ordenanzas de la Cédula Real en tres pueblos del Valle del Paso del Norte." *e.nnova* 2, num. 1 (2009): 85-94.

Ortiz, Alfonso. "Popay's Leadership: A Pueblo Perspective." *El Palacio* 86, no. 1 (1980–81): 18-22.

Payne, Melissa. "Lessons from the Rio Abajo: A Colonial Patron's Contested Legacy." *New Mexico Historical Review* 80, no. 3 (2005): 397-415.

Pérez-González, María Luisa. "Royal Roads in the Old and the New World: The *Camino de Oñate* and Its Importance in the Spanish Settlement of New Mexico." *Colonial Latin American Historical Review* 7, no. 2 (1998): 191-218.

Pérez López, David. "Calles que Cuentan Historias." *El Diario* (Cd. Juarez, MX), 20 de Junio, 1999.

Poole, Lauren K. "Historic San Felipe Church Enlivens Spirit of Old Town." *New Mexico Magazine*, June 1991.

Porter, Eugene O. "Down the Chihuahua Trail with Wislizenus. Part One" *Password* 18, no. 1 (1973): 21-32.

———. "Down the Chihuahua Trail with Wislizenus. Part Two." *Password* 18, no. 2 (1973): 66-74.

———. "Down the Chihuahua Trail with Wislizenus. Part Three." *Password* 18, no. 3 (1973): 114-15.

———. "Down the Chihuahua Trail with Wislizenus. Part Four." *Password* 18, no. 4 (1973): 169-180.

Post, Stephen. "Archaeology behind the Palace of the Governors: A New Look at History and Cartography." *El Palacio* 108, no. 2 (2003): 6-11.

Price, Paxton. "Martin's Well at Aleman." *Southern New Mexico Historical Review* 2, no. 1 (1995): 24-29.

Putman, G.P. "Padre Aided Friend and Foe Wounded in War with Mexico." *Times* (El Paso, Texas), Sept. 8, 1953.

Ramenofsky, Ann F, Fraser Neiman, and Christopher D Pierce. 2009. "Measuring Time, Population, and Residential Mobility from the Surface at San Marcos Pueblo, North Central New Mexico". *American Antiquity.* 74, no. 3 (2009): 500-10.

Ramenofsky, Ann F, C David Vaughan, and Michael N Spilde. "Seventeenth-Century Metal Production at San Marcos Pueblo, North-Central New Mexico". *Historical Archaeology.* 42, no. 4 (2008): 101-109.

Rubin, Gail. "Barelas: Explore a Duke City Gem." *New Mexico Magazine*, October 2004.

Sánchez, Joseph P. "The Founding of Santa Fe." *Chronicles of the Trail* 6, no. 3 (2010): 12-15.

———. "Introduction: Juan de Oñate and the Founding of New Mexico, 1598–1609."
Chronicles of the Trail 7, no.2 (1998): 3-6.

Scholes, France V. "Documents for the History of the New Mexican Missions in the Seventeenth Century." *New Mexico Historical Review* 1, no. 1 (1929): 45-58.

———. "The Supply Service of the New Mexico Missions in the Seventeenth Century." *New Mexico Historical Review* 5, no. 1 (1930): 93-115.

———. "The Supply Service of the New Mexico Missions in the Seventeenth Century." *New Mexico Historical Review* 5, no. 2 (1930): 186-210.

———. "The Supply Service of the New Mexico Missions in the Seventeenth Century." *New Mexico Historical Review* 5, no. 4 (1930): 386-404.

Scholes, France V. and Lansing B. Bloom. "Friar Personnel and Mission Chronology, 1598–1629." *New Mexico Historical Review* 20, no. 1 (1945): 58-75.

Sharpe, Tom. "Santa Cruz celebrates church's 250th anniversary with Book." *New Mexican* (Santa Fe, New Mexico), May 16, 1983.

Silva, Guadalupe. "Hidden History: Centuries-Old Mission still Packs Them In." *Times* (El Paso, Texas), Aug. 28, 1998.

Sisneros, Samuel E. "El Paseño, Padre Ramón Ortiz: 1814–1896." *Password* 44, no. 2 (1999): 103-08.

Snow, David H. "The Prehistoric Southwestern Turquoise Industry." *El Palacio* 79, no.1 (1973): 11-16.

Spencer, Wilson. "El Contadero." *Rio Grande History* 6 (1978): 6-7.

Spitler, Loring W. "Churches of the Valley along the Southern Rio Grande," *Journal of the Southwest* 45, no. 1 (2003): 9-32.

Staski, Edward. "An Archaeological Survey of El Camino Real de Tierra Adentro, Las Cruces-El Paso." *International Journal of Historical Archaeology* 8, no. 4 (2004): 231-245.

———. "Change and Inertia on the Frontier: Archaeology at the Paraje de San Diego, Camino Real, in Southern New Mexico." *International Journal of Historical Archaeology* 2, no. 1 (1998): 21-44.

———. "Some of What We Have Learned." *Chronicles of the Trail* 1, no. 2 (2005): 4-5.

Staski, Edward and Paul S. Johnston. "Munition Artifacts from Fort Fillmore, New Mexico." *Historical Archaeology* 26, no. 1 (1992): 66-73.

Staski, Edward and Joanne Reiter. "Status and Adobe Quality at Fort Fillmore, New Mexico: Old Questions, New Techniques." *Historical Archaeology* 30, no. 1(1996): 1-18.

Steele, Thomas J. "Albuquerque in 1821: Padre Leyva's Descriptions." *New Mexico Historical Review* 70, no. 2 (1995): 159-178.

Strykowski, Jason. "The Founding of Santa Fe." *New Mexican* (Santa Fe, New Mexico), Jan. 2, 2009.

Taylor, John and Patty Gallegos. "Our Lady of Guadalupe, Los Chávez." *Tradición* 10, no. 1 (2005): 30-32.

Taylor, John and Patty Gallegos. "The Churches of San Clemente Parish." *Tradición* 10, no. 2 (2005): 44-46.

Timmons, W.H., ed. "The Benavides *Memorial.*" *Password* 37, no. 1 (1992): 38-40.

———. "Bicentennial El Paso." *Password* 21, no. 3 (1976): 99-100.

———. "Defending Spain's Northern Frontier: The El Paso Area." *Password* 26, no. 3 (1981): 78-81.

————. "Geographic Description of New Mexico by Fray Juan Agustín de Morfi." *Password* 21, no. 1 (1976): 153-54.

————. "A Map of the El Paso Area in the 1770s." *Password* 21, no. 2 (1976): 47-52.

————. "The Arrival of the Pueblo Revolt Refugees at the Pass of the North." *Password* 26, no. 2 (1981): 29-31.

————. "The Significance of the Oñate Expedition in El Paso History." *Password* 25, no. 4 (1980): 159-61.

————. "The Spanish Census of Ysleta in 1790." *Password* 37, no. 3 (1992): 137-40.

Thayer, Frank. "Doña Ana: Historic Village tries to stop the Clock," *New Mexico Magazine*, July 1990.

Torok, George D. "El Camino Real de Tierra Adentro through the Pass of the North." *Password* 50, no. 4 (2005):169-188.

————. "El Camino Real de Tierra Adentro through the Pass of the North, Part II." *Password* 51, no. 1 (2006): 3-20.

Vigil, Arnold. "Barrio de Analco." *New Mexico Magazine*, December 2006.

Voynick, Steve. "Turquoise Motherlode: Jeweler Strives to Preserve Cerillos Mines." *New Mexico Magazine*, July 2004.

Wait, Walter. "History of Our District." *San Marcos Association Newsletter* 2, no. 2 (2006): 1-5.

Wallace, William S. "Stagecoaching in Territorial New Mexico." *New Mexico Historical Review* 32, no. 2 (1957): 204-211.

Wilson, John P. "Excavations at Fort Fillmore." *El Palacio* 74, no. 3 (1967): 27-41.

Wilson, Spencer. "El Contadero." *Rio Grande History* 6 (1976): 6-7.

————. "The Ocean to Ocean Highway or New Mexico's other Historic Highway." *La Crónica de Nueva México,* July 2010.

"Ynocente Ochoa." *Times (El Paso, Texas),* May 20, 1909.

Dissertations, Theses, Pamphlets, and Unpublished Papers:

Ackerly, Neal W. and Chris Wilson. "Doña Ana Village Historic District." National Register of Historic Places Registration Form. Albuquerque: 1998.

Baratti-Sallani, Patty. "Valencia Church, Chapel Sangre de Cristo, La Precosa Sangre." National Register of Historic Places Inventory-Nomination Form. Socorro: 1982.

Baxter, John O. "The Acequia System of El Rancho de las Golondrinas." National Register of Historic Places Inventory-Nomination Form. Santa Fe: 1979.

————. "El Rancho de las Golondrinas." National Register of Historic Places Inventory-Nomination Form. Santa Fe: 1975.

————. "Old Ciénega Village Museum." National Register of Historic Places Inventory-Nomination Form. Santa Fe: 1975.

————. "The Tomé Jail." National Register of Historic Places Inventory-Nomination Form. Santa Fe: 1977.

Bletzer, Michael. "Forgotten Pueblos: A Summary Overview of Piro History and Archaeology." Unpublished paper. Dallas: Southern Methodist University, 2005.

———. *Pueblos Arruinados*: an Archaeological assessment of Colonial-Period settlement abandonment among the Piros of south central New Mexico." Unpublished paper. Dallas: Southern Methodist University, 2008.

———. 2009. "Pueblos without Names A Case Study of Piro Settlement in Early Colonial New Mexico." PhD dissertation, Southern Methodist University, 2009.

Boyd, Douglas Kevin. "Paraje (De Fra Cristobal): Investigations of a Territorial Period Hispanic Village Site in Southern New Mexico." Master's thesis, Texas A&M University, 1986.

Brown, David O, Timothy B. Graves, John A. Peterson, and Mark Willis. "El Paso County Lower Valley Water District Authority Phase II Water Supply and Wastewater Project: Archaeological Testing." El Paso, Texas: Archaeological Research Inc., 1995.

Bruce, Cynthia Sue. "Los Griegos: Nomination to the National Register of Historic Places and Design Guidelines." Master's thesis, University of New Mexico, 1982.

Castillo-Wilson, Larry. "The New Mexico Trail: Las Vueltas de Socorro." Socorro: unpublished paper, 1980.

Cerrillos Hills Park Coalition. "History of the Los Cerrillos Mining Area." Santa Fe: unpublished paper, New Mexico Abandoned Mine Land Bureau Santa Fe, 1994.

Clark, Harry Wilson. "The History, Archaeology, and Oral Traditions of the San Elizario Jail: An Interdisciplinary Study." Master's thesis, University of Texas at El Paso, 2002.

Condie, Carol, ed. "Los Ranchos Plaza (LA 46638): Test Excavations at a Spanish Colonial Settlement in Bernalillo County, New Mexico, 1996–1997." Albuquerque: Maxwell Museum Technical Series No. 4, 2007.

Cook, Sylvia. "Our Lady of Sorrows Church." National Register of Historic Places Inventory-Nomination Form. Santa Fe: 1970.

Espinosa-McDonald, Margaret. "Vamos Todos a Belén: A Cultural Transformation of the Hispanic Community in the Rio Abajo Community of Belén, New Mexico from 1850 to 1950." PhD dissertation, University of New Mexico, 1997.

Garcia, Mary Jane. "An Ethnohistory of Doña Ana: Hispanic Catholics vs. Hispanic Methodists in the Village."Master's thesis, New Mexico State University, 1986.

Gibbs, Victor, Christina Chavez, and David H. Reynolds. "Archaeological Data Recovery Plan for Four Sites along the Spaceport America Entrance Road, Sierra County, New Mexico." Las Cruces: New Mexico Spaceport Authority, 2009.

Earls, Amy C. "Teypama." National Register of Historic Places Inventory-Nomination Form. Santa Fe: 1982.

Fritz, Scott Edward. "Mesilla Valley Merchants, 1870–1881: History of Anglo and Hispanic Involvement in the Santa Fe Trade of Southern New Mexico." Master's thesis, New Mexico State University, 1997.

Guggino, Patty. "La Capilla de San Antonio de Los Lentes." National Register of Historic Places Inventory-Nomination Form. Los Lunas: 2003.

Harper, Tom. "Aerial Photography of El Camino Real de Tierra Adentro on Sevilleta National Wildlife Refuge." Socorro: 2010.

Houser, Nicholas P. "La Entrada Por El Alto: The Entrance by the High Bridge" Unpublished draft, El Paso: 1999.

Kammer, David. "El Cerro Tomé (Tomé Hill) Site." National Register of Historic Places Inventory-Nomination Form. Santa Fe: 1995.

———. "San Elizario Historic District." National Register of Historic Places Registration Form. Albuquerque: 1996.

LeBlanc, Steven. "San Felipe Ruin (L.A. 597)." National Register of Historic Places Inventory-Nomination Form. Santa Fe: 1980.

Lent, Stephen C. and Linda J. Goodman. "Archaelogical Testing and a Brief Ethnohistory of San Gabriel de Yungue Owinge, San Juan Pueblo, New Mexico." Santa Fe: 1992.

"Los Duranes Chapel." National Register of Historic Places Inventory-Nomination Form. Santa Fe: 1984.

Margo, Adair W. "Nuestra Señora de Guadalupe del Paso del Norte: Its Foundation, Consctruction, and Decoration, 1668–1982." Master's thesis, New Mexico State University, 1982.

Marshall, Michael. "Casa Colorado." National Register of Historic Places Inventory-Nomination Form. Santa Fe: 1985.

———. "El Camino Real de Tierra Adentro: An Archaeological Investigation." Unpublished Report for New Mexico State Historic Preservation Office, 1990.

———. "A Cultural Properties Assessment for the Camino Real De Tierra Adentro National Historic Trail System: Identification of Linked Historic Properties, Evaluation of Properties Condition and Potential Risk Factors, and Provisional Recommendations for Continued Research and Cultural Resource Management." Santa Fe: Bureau of Land Management, 2005.

———. "Parida (LA 31718)." National Register of Historic Places Inventory-Nomination Form. Santa Fe: 1981.

Marshall, Michael P. and Henry J. Walt. "A Cultural Resources Survey for the Proposed Sunland Park Drive Extension Project, Dona Ana County, New Mexico and El Paso County." Santa Fe: Cibola Research, 1995.

———. "Spanish Contact Indian Pueblos and Spanish Colonial and Mexican Settlements in the Rio Medio District of New Mexico. National Register of Historic Places Inventory-Nomination Form. Santa Fe:1985.

McCachren, Michael. "The Garcia Opera House." National Register of Historic Places Inventory-Nomination Form. Santa Fe:1974.

———. "Garcia, Juan Nepomuceno House." National Register of Historic Places Registration Form. Santa Fe: 1980.

Milford, Homer. "History of the Los Cerrillos Mining Area." Santa Fe: New Mexico Abandoned Mine Land Bureau Reports, 1996.

Pennock, Anthony. "Mesquite-Original Townsite District of Las Cruces." National Register of Historic Places Inventory-Nomination Form. Las Cruces: 1980.

Peterson, John A. "Lost Missions and Other Spanish Colonial Sites in the Lower Valley of El Paso." Unpublished paper. El Paso: University of Texas at El Paso, n.d.

Pioneer Savings and Trust. "History of the Armijo House." Las Cruces: Pioneer Savings, 1982.

Powder, Richard Alan. "Research Design for Fort Fillmore, New Mexico." Master's thesis, New Mexico State University, 1988.

Purdy, James. "Pueblo of Cochití." National Register of Historic Places Inventory-Nomination Form. Santa Fe: 1974.

———. "Pueblo of San Felipe (Katishtya)." National Register of Historic Places Inventory-Nomination Form. Santa Fe: 1973.

———. "Pueblo of Santa Ana." National Register of Historic Places Inventory-Nomination Form. Santa Fe: 1973.

———. "Pueblo of Santo Domingo." National Register of Historic Places Inventory-Nomination Form. Santa Fe: 1972.

Ramenofsky, Ann F. and Christopher Pierce. "Proposal to Conduct Archaeological Research at San Marcos Pueblo (LA98)." Unpublished proposal. Albuquerque: 1999.

Rand-Caplan, Ramona L. "The History of the Sevilleta Land Grant and in the first person: Oral histories from La Joya de Sevilleta,"the Jewel of the Sevilleta." Master's thesis, University of New Mexico, 2006.

Romero, Brenda Mae. "The Matchines Music and Dance in San Juan Pueblo and Alcalde, New Mexico: Context and Meaning." PhD dissertation, University of California at Los Angeles, 1993.

Sanchez, Terry. "The Manuel Armijo House in Lemitar, New Mexico." Unpublished seminar paper, Socorro: New Mexico Tech University, 1980.

Schackel, Sandra Kay. "Resurrected Rancho: Old Cienega Village Museum." Master's thesis, University of New Mexico, 1982.

Scurlock, Dan. "A Cultural Resource Investigation of Two Historic Sites in Lemitar, New Mexico." Socorro: Bureau of Land Management, 1982.

———. "Sagrada Familia de Lemitar Church, Los Dulces Nombres." National Register of Historic Places Inventory-Nomination Form. Socorro: 1981.

Snow, Cordelia Thomas. "A Brief History of Mission San Marcos."unpublished paper, Santa Fe: Office of the State Historian, n.d.

Swanson, Betsy. "Mesquite Street Original Townsite Historic District." National Register of Historic Places Inventory-Nomination Form. Las Cruces: 1984.

Swentzell, Rina. "An Architectural History of Santa Clara Pueblo." PhD dissertation, University of New Mexico, 1976.

Sze, Corinne P. "La Iglesia de Santa Cruz and the Site of the Plaza of Santa Cruz de la Cañada." National Register of Historic Places Registration Form. Santa Fe: 1994.

———. "Palace of the Governors." National Register of Historic Places Registration Form. Santa Fe: 2003.

Taylor, Michael R. and Ellen Threinen. "La Mesilla Historic District Multiple Resource Area." National Register of Historic Places Inventory-Nomination Form. Las Cruces: 1980.

"Templo y Panteón de San José." Cd. Juárez: San José Parish, n.d.

Threinen, Ellen. "Our Lady of Sorrows Church." National Register of Historic Places Inventory-Nomination Form. Santa Fe: 1977.

———. "Abenicio Salazar Historic District." National Register of Historic Places Inventory-Nomination Form. Santa Fe: 1979.

———. "Felipe Chaves House." National Register of Historic Places Inventory-Nomination Form. Santa Fe: 1980.

———. "Gutiérrez House." National Register of Historic Places Inventory-Nomination Form. Santa Fe: 1978.

———. "San Ysidro Church." National Register of Historic Places Inventory-Nomination Form. Santa Fe: 1979.

Walker, James B. "San Jose de Las Huertas." National Register of Historic Places Registration Form. Santa Fe: 1990.

Whitmore, Jane. "The Traditional Village of Agua Fria." Santa Fe: Landmark Preservation Consultants, 1983.

Books:

Abbink, Emily. *New Mexico's Palace of the Governors: History of an American Treasure*. Santa Fe: Museum of New Mexico, 2007.

Abert, John James. *Abert's New Mexico Report, 1846–47*. Albuquerque: Horn & Wallace, Publishers, 1962. New Edition, Santa Fe: Sunstone Press, 2012.

Adams, Charles E. and Andrew I. Duff, eds. *The Protohistoric Pueblo World, A.D. 1275–1600*. Tucson: University of Arizona Press, 2004.

Adams, Eleanor B., ed. *Bishop Tamarón's Visitation of New Mexico, 1760*. Albuquerque: University of New Mexico Press, 1954.

Adams, Eleanor B. and Fray Angelico Chavez, eds. *The Missions of New Mexico, 1776: A Description by Fray Francisco Atanasio Dominguez with Other Contemporary Documents*. Albuquerque: University of New Mexico Press, 1956. New Edition, Santa Fe: Sunstone Press, 2012.

Adler, Michael, ed. *The Prehistoric Pueblo World, A.D. 1150–1350*. Tucson: University of Arizona Press, 1996.

All Trails Lead to Santa Fe: An Anthology Commemorating the 400th Anniversary of the Founding of Santa Fe, New Mexico in 1610. Santa Fe: Sunstone Press, 2010.

Ashcroft, Bruce. *The Territorial History of Socorro, New Mexico*. El Paso: Texas Western Press, 1988.

Austerman, Wayne R. *Sharps Rifles and Spanish Mules: The San Antonio-El Paso Mail, 1851–1881*. College Station: Texas A&M Press, 1985.

Bandelier, Adolph. *The Southwestern Journals of Adolph F. Bandelier*. Charles Lange, Carroll Riley, and Elizabeth Lange, eds. 4 vols. Albuquerque: University of New Mexico Press, 1970. New Edition, Santa Fe: Sunstone Press, 2012.

Barrett, Elinore M. *Conquest and Catastrophe: Changing Rio Grande Pueblo Settlement Patterns in the Sixteenth and Seventeenth Centuries*. Albuquerque: University of New Mexico Press, 2002.

Barrick, Nona and Mary Taylor. *The Mesilla Guard, 1851–61*. El Paso: Texas Western Press, 1976.

Bartlett, John Russell. *Personal Narrative of Exploration and Incidents in Texas, New Mexico, California, Sonora, and Chihuahua connected with the United States and Mexican Boundary Commission during 1850, '51, '52, and '53*. 2 vols. London: G. Routledge, 1854.

Bauer, K. Jack. *The Mexican War 1846–1848*. New York: Macmillan & Co., 1974.

Baxter, John O. *Las Carneradas: Sheep Trade in New Mexico, 1700–1860*. Albuquerque: University of New Mexico Press, 1987.

Beckett, Patrick H. *Las Cruces, New Mexico 1881: As Seen by Her Newspapers*. Las Cruces: COAS Publishing and Research, 2003.

Beckett, Patrick H. and Terry L. Corbett. *The Manso Indians*. Las Cruces: COAS Publishing and Research, 1992.

———. *Tortugas*. Las Cruces: COAS Publishing and Research, 1990.

Bieber, Ralph P., ed. *Marching with the Army of the West, 1846–1848*. Philadelphia: Porcupine Press, 1974.

———. *Journal of a Soldier under Kearny and Doniphan, 1846–47*. Glendale: Arthur H. Clark Co., 1935.

Bolton, Herbert E. *Spanish Exploration in the Southwest, 1542–1707*. New York: Charles Scribner's Sons, 1916.

Borah, Woodrow W. *Early Colonial Trade and Navigation between Mexico and Peru*. Berkeley: University of California Press, 1954.

Bowden, J.J. *The Ponce de León Land Grant*. El Paso: Texas Western Press, 1969.

———. *Spanish and Mexican Land Grants in the Chihuahua Acquisition*. El Paso: Texas Western Press, 1971.

Calleros, Cleofas. *El Paso: Then and Now*. El Paso: American Print Company, 1954.

Campa, Arthur L. *Hispanic Culture in the Southwest*. Norman: University of Oklahoma Press, 1979.

Carie, Rev. Giles. *The Guadalupan Triduum in Tortugas*. Las Cruces: Rev. Giles Carie, 1997.

Carroll, Charles and Lynn Sebastian, eds. *Fort Craig: The United States Fort on the Camino Real*. Socorro: New Mexico Bureau of Land Management Field Office, 2000.

Castleman, Bruce A. *Building the King's Highway: Labor, Society, and family on Mexico's Caminos Reales, 1757–1804*. Tucson: University of Arizona Press, 2005.

Chávez M., Armando B. *Sesenta Años de Gobierno Municipal...1897–1960*. Mexico: Gráfico Cervantina, 1959.

Cohrs, Timothy and Thomas J. Capeton. *Fort Selden, New Mexico*. Santa Fe: Museum of New Mexico, 1974.

Conkling, Roscoe P. and Margaret B. Conkling *The Butterfield Overland Mail, 1857–1869: Its Organization and Operation over the Southern Route to 1861; Subsequently over the Central Route to 1866; and under Wells, Fargo and Company in 1869*. 3 vols. Glendale: A.H. Clark Co., 1947.

Conron, John P. and Anthony Alofsin. *Socorro: A Historic Survey*. Albuquerque: University of New Mexico Press, 1980.

Couchman, Donald H. *Cooke's Peak, Pasaron por Aquí: A Focus on United States History in Southwestern New Mexico*. Las Cruces: New Mexico Bureau of Land Management Field Office, 1990.

Coues, Elliott, ed. *The Expeditions of Zebulon Montgomery Pike to the Headwaters of the Mississippi River, through Louisiana Territory, and in New Spain, during the Years 1805-6-7*. 3 vols. Minneapolis: Ross & Haines, 1965.

Cramaussel, Chantal, ed. *Rutas de Nueva España*. Zamora: El Colegio de Michoacán, 2006.

Crouch, Brodie. *Jornada del Muerto: A Pageant of the Desert*. Spokane: A.H. Clark Co., 1989.

Davis, W.W.H. *El Gringo or New Mexico and Her People*. New York: Harper and Brothers, 1857. New Edition, Santa Fe: Sunstone Press, 2012.

Dawson, Joseph G. *Doniphan's Epic March: The 1st Missouri Volunteers in the Mexican War*. Lawrence: University Press of Kansas, 1999.

Dewitt, Susan. *Historic Albuquerque Today: An Overview Survey of Historic Buildings and Districts*. Albuquerque: Historic Landmarks Survey of Albuquerque, 1978.

Dozier, Edward P. *The Pueblo Indians of North America*. New York: Holt, Rinehart, and Winston, Inc., 1970.

Drumm, Stella M., ed. *Down the Santa Fe Trail and into Mexico: The Diary of Susan Shelby Magoffin, 1846-1847*. New Haven: Yale University Press, 1926.

Eisenhower, John D. *So Far from God: The U.S. War with Mexico, 1846-1848*. New York: Random House, 1989.

Emory, William H. *Report on the United States and Mexican Boundary Survey made under the Direction of the Secretary of the Interior*. 2 vols. Washington: Cornelius Wendell, Printer, 1857.

Encinias, Miguel, Alfred Rodriguez, and Joseph Sanchez, eds. *Historia de la Nueva Mexico, 1610*. Albuquerque: University of New Mexico Press, 1992.

Esparza Marín, Ignacio. *Monográfia histórica de Ciudad Juárez*. Cd. Juárez: Imprenta Lux, 1991.

Espinosa, Gilberto and Tibo J. Chavez. *El Rio Abajo*. Portales, New Mexico: Bishop Publishing Company, 1967.

Espinosa, J. Manuel. *Crusaders of the Rio Grande: The Story of Don Diego de Vargas*. Chicago: Institute of Jesuit History, 1942.

Fergusson, Harvey. *The Conquest of Don Pedro*. New York: W. Morrow Co., 1954.

Fireman, Janet R. *The Spanish Royal Corp of Engineers in the Western Borderlands: Instruments of Bourbon Reform, 1764 to 1815*. Glendale: A.H. Clark Company, 1977.

Frazer, Robert W. *Forts of the West: Military Forts and Presidios, and Posts commonly called Forts, West of the Mississippi River to 1898*. Norman: University of Oklahoma Press, 1972.

Garcia, Mary Jane. *An Ethnohistory of Doña Ana Village: Hispanic Catholics versus Hispanic Methodists*. Las Cruces: Roseta Press, 1986.

Gerald, Rex E. *Spanish Presidios of the Late Eighteenth Century in Northern New Spain*. Santa Fe: Museum of New Mexico Press, 1968.

Gerhard, Peter. *The North Frontier of New Spain*. Norman: University of Oklahoma Press, 1993.

Gerow, Peggy A. and Patrick Hogan. *They Called it Home: An Architectural and Historical Assessment of San Pedro, Socorro County, New Mexico*. Albuquerque: Office of Contract Archaeology, 1994.

Goetzmann, William H. *Army Exploration in the West, 1803-1863*. New Haven: Yale University Press, 1959.

———. *Exploration and Empire: The Explorer and the Scientist in the Winning of the American West*. New York: Knopf, 1966.

Gonzales, Manuel G. *The Hispanic Elite of the Southwest*. El Paso: Texas Western Press, 1989.

González Díaz, Falia, and Diana Jiménez Gil. *The Threads of Memory :El hilo de la Memoria*. Santa Fe: New Mexico History Museum, 2010.

Greene, A.C. *900 Miles on the Butterfield Trail*. Denton: University of North Texas Press, 1994.

Gregg, Josiah. *Commerce of the Prairies or the Journal of a Santa Fe Trader*. New York: Henry G. Langley, 1844.

Gudiño Quiroz, Rebeca A. *Don Antonio Valverde y Cosío, Gobernador de Nuevo México: Una Aproximación a su Vida Publica y Privada*. Cd. Juárez: Universidad Autónoma de Ciudad Juárez, 1994.

Hackett, Charles W. and Charmion Clair Shelby, eds. *Revolt of the Pueblo Indians of New Mexico and Otermín's Attempted Reconquest, 1680–1682*. 2 vols. Albuquerque: University of New Mexico Press, 1942.

Hadley, Diana, Thomas Naylor and Mardith K. Schuetz-Miller, eds. *The Presidio and Militia on the Northern Frontier of New Spain: A Documentary History*. 2 vols. Tucson: University of Arizona Press, 1997.

Hallenbeck, Cleve. *Land of the Conquistadores*. Caldwell: Caxton Printers, 1950.

Hamalainen, Pekka. *The Comanche Empire*. New Haven: Yale University Press, 2008.

Hammond, George P. and Agapito Rey, eds.*Don Juan de Oñate: Colonizer of New Mexico, 1595–1628*. 2 vols. Albuquerque: University of New Mexico Press, 1953.

Hammond, George P. and Agapito Rey, eds. *The Rediscovery of New Mexico, 1580–1594: The Explorations of Chamuscado, Espejo, Castaño de Sosa, Morlete, Leyva de Bonilla and Humana*. 2 vols. Albuquerque: University of New Mexico Press, 1966.

Hammond, George P. and Agapito Rey, eds. *Narratives of the Coronado Expedition, 1540–1542*. Albuquerque: University of New Mexico Press, 1940.

Harlow, Francis H. *Modern Pueblo Pottery, 1880–1960*. Flagstaff: Northland Press, 1977.

Hendricks, Rick. *New Mexico in 1801: The Priests' Report*. Los Ranchos: Rio Grande Books, 2008.

Hendricks, Rick and W. H. Timmons. *San Elizario: Spanish Presidio to Texas County Seat*. El Paso: Texas Western Press, 1998.

Harris, Linda G. *Houses in Time: A Tour through New Mexico History*. Las Cruces: Arroyo Press, 1997.

Hill, Willard Williams. *An Ethnography of Santa Clara Pueblo New Mexico*. Albuquerque: University of New Mexico Press, 1982.

Humboldt, Alexander von. *Political Essay on the Kingdom of New Spain with Physical sections and maps founded on astronomical observations and trigonometrical and barometrical measurements*. 4 vols. New York, New York: AMS Press, 1966–70.

Hunner, Jon and Peter Dean. *The Mesilla Valley: An Oasis in the Desert*. Santa Fe: Sunstone Press, 2008.

Jackson, Donald. *The Journals of Zebulon Montgomery Pike: With Letters and Related Documents*. 2 vols. Norman: University of Oklahoma Press, 1966.

Jackson, Hal. *Following the Royal Road: A Guide to the Historic Camino Real de Tierra Adentro*. Albuquerque: University of New Mexico Press, 2006.

Johnson, Byron A. *Old Town, Albuquerque, New Mexico: A Guide to its History and Architecture.* Albuquerque: Albuquerque Museum, 1980.

Jones, Oakah L. *Nueva Vizcaya: Heartland of the Spanish Frontier.* Albuquerque: University of New Mexico Press, 1988.

Jordan, Louann. *El Rancho de Las Golondrinas: Spanish Colonial Life in New Mexico.* Santa Fe: Colonial New Mexico Historical Foundation, 1977.

Julyan, Robert H. *The Mountains of New Mexico.* Albuquerque: University of New Mexico Press, 2006.

———. *The Place Names of New Mexico.* Albuquerque: University of New Mexico Press, 1996.

Kendall, George Wilkins. *Narrative of the Texan Santa Fé Expedition comprising a description of a Tour through Texas.* 2 vols. New York: Harper and Brothers, 1844.

Kessell, John L. *Kiva, Cross, and Crown: The Pecos Indians and New Mexico, 1540–1840.* Tucson: Southwest Parks and Monuments Association, 1987.

———. *The Missions of New Mexico since 1776.* Albuquerque: University of New Mexico Press, 1980. New Edition, Santa Fe: Sunstone Press, 2012.

———. *Pueblos, Spaniards, and the Kingdom of New Mexico.* Norman: University of Oklahoma Press, 2008.

———. *Spain in the Southwest: A Narrative History of Colonial New Mexico, Arizona, Texas, and California.* Norman: University of Oklahoma Press, 2002.

Kinnaird, Lawrence, ed. *The Frontiers of New Spain: Nicolas de Lafora's Description, 1766–1768.* Berkeley: The Quivira Society, 1958.

Knaut, Andrew L. *The Pueblo Revolt of 1680: Conquest and Resistance in Seventeenth-Century New Mexico.* Norman: University of Oklahoma Press, 1995.

Kubler, George. *Religious Architecture of New Mexico in the Colonial Period and since the American Occupation.* Albuquerque: University of New Mexico Press, 1973.

Lane, Lydia Spencer. *I Married a Soldier.* Albuquerque: University of New Mexico Press, 1987.

Lange, Charles H. ed. W.W. Hill. *An Ethnography of Santa Clara Pueblo New Mexico.* Albuquerque: University of New Mexico Press, 1982.

Lange, Charles H. *Cochití: A New Mexico Pueblo, Past and Present.* Austin: University of Texas Press, 1959.

Lecompte, Janet. *Rebellion in the Rio Arriba, 1837.* Albuquerque: University of New Mexico Press, 1985.

León G., Ricardo. *Chihuahua: Las Epocas y Los Hombres, Mariano Samaniego: Medio Siglo de Vida Fronteriza.* Cd. Juárez: Meridiano 107 Editores, 1991.

Lippard, Lucy R. *Down Country: The Tano of the Galisteo Basin, 1250–1782.* Santa Fe: Museum of New Mexico Press, 2010.

Marshall, Sandra L. and John R. Versluis. *Historic New Mexico Styles, Las Cruces, N.M.: Celebrating 150 Years.* Las Cruces: Doña Ana County Historical Society, 2000.

Marshall, Michael P. *Qualacú: Archeological Investigation of a Piro Pueblo.* Albuquerque: U.S. Fish and Wildlife Service, 1987.

Marshall, Michael P. and Henry J. Walt. *Rio Abajo: Prehistory and History of a Rio Grande Province.* Santa Fe: New Mexico Historic Preservation Program, 1984.

Martinez, Oscar J. *Border Boom Town: Ciudad Juárez since 1848*. Austin: University of Texas Press, 1975.

Mbutu, Stephen K. and John A. Peterson, *The Union Plaza Downtown El Paso Development Archaeological Project: Overview, Inventory and Recommendations*. El Paso: Anthropology Research Center, 1998.

McFie (Bloom), Maude Elizabeth and Lansing Bloom, ed., annotations by Jo Tice Bloom. *A History of the Mesilla Valley, 1903*. Las Cruces: Yucca Tree Press, 1999.

Metz, Leon. *El Paso: Guided through Time*. El Paso: Mangan Books, 1999.

Meyers, Terry, Diane Williams, and Laurie A. Marder, eds., *Property Descriptions, Significant Assessments, and National Register Eligibility Determinations, Socorro and San Elizario*. Austin: Hardy, Heck, Moore Inc., 1995.

Milford, E. Homer and Mike E. Swick. *Cultural Resources Survey for Real de los Cerrillos Project, Santa Fe County, New Mexico*. Vol.1. *Historic Survey of the Los Cerrillos Area and Its Mining History*. *New Mexico Abandoned Mine Land Bureau Report*. Santa Fe: Mining and Minerals Division, 1995.

Mills, Anson. *My Story*. Washington: Press of Byron S. Adams, 1921.

Mills, W. W. *Forty Years at El Paso, 1858–1898*. El Paso: Carl Hertzog, 1962.

Montoya, Joe L. *Isleta Pueblo and the Church of St. Augustine*. Isleta Pueblo: St. Augustine Church, 1978.

Moorhead, Max L. *New Mexico's Royal Road: Trade and Travel on the Chihuahua Trail*. Norman: University of Oklahoma Press, 1958.

———. *The Presidio: Bastion of the Spanish Borderlands*. Norman: University of Oklahoma Press, 1975.

Morrow, Herbert C. *The Mission Trail*. El Paso: West Texas Council of Governments, 1981.

Mullin, Robert N. *Stagecoach Pioneers of the Southwest*. El Paso: Texas Western Press, 1983.

Nieman, Charles L. *Spanish Times and Boom Times: Toward an Architectural History of Socorro, New Mexico*. Socorro: Socorro County Historical Society, Inc., 1972.

Noble, David Grant, ed. *Santa Fe: History of an Ancient City*. Santa Fe: School of American Research Press, 1989.

O'Laughlin, Thomas C. *The Keystone Dam and Other Archaic and Formative Sites in Northwest El Paso, Texas*. El Paso: University of Texas at El Paso, 1980.

Ormsby, Waterman L. *The Butterfield Overland Mail: Only through Passenger on the first Westbound Stage*. San Marino: The Huntington Library, 1954.

Orozco, Victor. *Historia General de Chihuahua: Tierra de Libres: Los Pueblos del Distrito de Guerrero en el Siglo XIX*. Ciudad Juárez: Universidad Autónoma de Ciudad Juárez, 1995.

Ortiz, Alfonso, ed. *Handbook of North American Indians*. Vol. 9. Southwest. Washington: Smithsonian Institution, 1979.

———. *New Perspectives on the Pueblos*. Albuquerque: University of New Mexico Press, 1972.

———. *The Tewa World: Space, Time, and Becoming in a Pueblo Society*. Chicago: University of Chicago Press, 1969.

Owen, Gordon R. *Las Cruces, New Mexico, 1849–1999: Multi-Cultural Crossroads*. Las Cruces: Red Sky Publishing Company, 1999.

Pacheco, José de la Cruz and Joseph P. Sánchez, eds. *Memorias del Coloquio Internacional El Camino Real de Tierra Adentro*. Mexico: Instituto Nacional de Antropología e Historia, 2000.

Palmer, Gabrielle, ed. *El Camino Real de Tierra Adentro*. Santa Fe: New Mexico Bureau of Land Management, 1993.

Palmer, Gabrielle and Stephen L. Fosberg, comps. *El Camino Real de Tierra Adentro: Volume II*. Santa Fe: New Mexico Bureau of Land Management, 1999.

Pescador, Juan Javier. *Crossing Borders with the Santo Niño de Atocha*. Albuquerque: University of New Mexico Press, 2009.

Peterson, John A. Timothy B. Graves, and David V. Hill, eds., *The 1995 San Elizario Plaza Archaeological Project*. Austin: Texas Department of Transportation, 2002.

Picazo, Father Luis, comp. *La Iglesia de Santa Cruz de la Cañada*. Santa Cruz: Santa Cruz Parish, 1983.

Pilkington, William T. *Harvey Fergusson*. Boston: Twayne Publishers, 1975.

Porter, Eugene O. *San Elizario: A History*. Austin, Texas: Jenkins Publishing Company, 1973.

Powell, Philip W. *Soldiers, Indians, and Silver: The Northward Advance of New Spain, 1550–1600*. Berkeley: University of California Press, 1952.

Powers, Robert P., ed. *The Peopling of Bandelier: New Insights from the Archaeology of the Pajarito Plateau*. Santa Fe: School of American Research Press, 2005.

Price, Vincent B. and Baker H. Morrow, eds., *Canyon Gardens: The Ancient Pueblo Landscapes of the American Southwest*. Albuquerque: University of New Mexico Press, 2008.

Prince, L. Bradford. *Spanish Mission Churches of New Mexico*. Cedar Rapids: Torch Press, 1915. New Edition, Santa Fe: Sunstone Press, 2012.

Quaife, Milo M., ed. *Six Years with the Texas Rangers, 1875–1881*. New Haven: Yales University Press, 1925.

Reeve, Agnesa Lufkin. *From Hacienda to Bungalow: Northern New Mexico Houses, 1850–1912*. Albuquerque: University of New Mexico Press, 1988.

Reps, John W. *The Forgotten Frontier: Urban Planning in the American West before 1890*. Columbia: University of Missouri Press, 1981.

Riley, Carroll L. *Rio del Norte: People of the Upper Rio Grande from Earliest Times to the Pueblo Revolt*. Salt Lake City: University of Utah Press, 1995.

Ruxton, George F. *Adventures in Mexico and the Rocky Mountains*. London: John Murray, 1849.

Sánchez, Joseph P. *Between Two Rivers: The Atrisco Land Grant in Albuquerque History, 1692–1968*. Norman: University of Oklahoma Press, 2008.

Sánchez, Joseph P. and Bruce Erickson, eds. *From Mexico City to Santa Fe: A Historical Guide to El Camino Real de Tierra Adentro*. Los Ranchos: Rio Grande Books, 2011.

Sanchez, F. Richard. *White Shell Water Place: An Anthology of Native American Reflections on the 400th Anniversary of the Founding of Santa Fe, New Mexico*. Santa Fe: Sunstone Press, 2010.

Santiago Quijada, Guadalupe. *Propiedad de la tierra en Ciudad Juárez, 1888–1935*. Tijuana: El Colegio de la Frontera Norte, 2002.

Santiago, Guadalupe and Miguel Ángel Berumen, *La Misión de Guadalupe*. Cd. Juárez: Cuadro por Cuadro, 2004.

Sargeant, Kathryn and Mary Davis. *Shining River, Precious Land: An Oral History of Albuquerque's North Valley*. Albuquerque: Albuquerque Museum, 1986.

Schroeder, Albert H. and Donald S. Matson, eds. Castaño de Sosa, Gaspar. *A Colony on the Move: Gaspar Castaño de Sosa's Journal 1590–1591*. Santa Fe: School of American Research Press, 1965.

Schlett, Stephen F., and John A. Peterson, *The Canutillo-El Paso Upper Valley Water Transmission Facilities Project: Survey Results and Recommendations*. El Paso: Archaeological Research, 1997.

Shapiro, Jason S. *Before Santa Fe: Archaeology of the City Different*. Santa Fe: Museum of New Mexico Press, 2008.

Simmons, Marc. *Coronado's Land: Essays on Daily Life in Colonial New Mexico*. Albuquerque: University of New Mexico Press, 1991.

———. *The Last Conquistador: Juan de Oñate and the Settling of the Far Southwest*. Norman: University of Oklahoma Press, 1991.

———. *Spanish Pathways: Readings in the History of Hispanic New Mexico*. Albuquerque: University of New Mexico Press, 2001.

———. *Taos to Tomé: True Tales of Hispanic New Mexico*. Albuquerque: Adobe Press, 1978. New Edition, Santa Fe: Suntone Press, 2013.

Simmons, Marc and Hal Jackson. *Following the Santa Fe Trail: A Guide for Modern Travelers*. Santa Fe: Ancient City Press, 1984.

Simons, Helen and Cathryn A. Hoyt, eds. *A Guide to Hispanic Texas*. Austin: University of Texas Press, 1996.

Sonnichsen, Charles L. *Pass of the North: Four Centuries on the Rio Grande*. 2 vols. El Paso, Texas: Texas Western Press, 1968.

Spears, Beverley. *American Adobes: Rural Houses of Northern New Mexico*. Santa Fe: Ancient City Press, 1986.

Stanley, Francis. *The Belen, New Mexico Story*. Pantex: F. Stanley, 1962.

———. *The Bernalillo, New Mexico Story*. Pep: Panther Press, 1964.

———. *The Fort Fillmore, New Mexico Story*. Pantex: F. Stanley, 1961.

———. *The San Marcial, New Mexico Story*. White Deer: F. Stanley, 1960.

———. *The Sandia New Mexico Story*. Pep, Texas: Panther Press, 1968.

———. *The Tome, New Mexico Story*. Pep: F. Stanley, 1966.

Steeb, Mary M., Michael Romero Taylor, and Anthony C. Pennock. *The Las Cruces Historic Buildings Survey*. Las Cruces: Doña Ana County Historical Society, 1982.

Steele, Thomas J., Paul Rhetts, and Barbe Awalt, eds. *Seeds of Struggle, Harvest of Faith: The Papers of the Archdiocese of Santa Fe Catholic Cuarto Centennial Conference on the History of the Church in New Mexico*. Albuquerque: LPD Press, 1998.

Stotz, Nancy G. *Historic Reconstruction of the Ecology of the Rio Grande/Río Bravo Channel and Floodplain in the Chihuahua Desert*. Las Cruces: Desert Scribes, 2000.

Strickland, Rex W. *Six Who Came to El Paso: Pioneers of the 1840s*. El Paso: Texas Western College Press, 1963.

Sturtevant, William C., gen. ed. *Handbook of North American Indians*. 20 vols. Washington, DC: Smithsonian Institution, 1978.

Sweet, Jill D. *Dances of the Tewa Pueblo Indians: Expressions of New Life*. Santa Fe: School of American Research, 1985.

Taylor, John. *Bloody Valverde: A Civil War Battle on the Rio Grande, Feb. 21, 1862*. Albuquerque: University of New Mexico Press, 1995.

Taylor, Mary D. and Nona Barrick. *A Place as Wild as the West ever Was: Mesilla, New Mexico 1848–1872*. Las Cruces: New Mexico State University Museum, 2004.

Thompson, Gerald. *The Army and the Navajo*. Tucson: University of Arizona Press, 1976.

Thonhoff, Robert H. *San Antonio Stage Lines, 1847–1881*. El Paso: Texas Western Press, 1971.

Timmons, W.H. *El Paso: A Borderlands History*. El Paso: Texas Western Press, 1990.

Timmons, Wilbert H. *James Wiley Magoffin: Don Santiago, El Paso Pioneer*. El Paso: Texas Western Press, 1999.

Treib, Marc. *Sanctuaries of Spanish New Mexico*. Berkeley: University of California Press, 1993.

Underwood, Deen. *Concordia Cemetery: A Walking Tour*. El Paso: Concordia Heritage Association, 1997.

United States National Park Service and Bureau of Land Management. *El Camino Real de Tierra Adentro National Historic Trail: Draft Comprehensive Management Plan*. Santa Fe: Long Distance Trails Group, 2002.

United States National Park Service. *Proceedings: Speakers Series, El Camino Real from Mexico City to Santa Fe 1999*. El Paso: Chamizal National Memorial, 1999.

Vázquez Reyes, José Leodegario. *Por qué se llama así la calle donde vivo?* Cd. Juárez: Ayuntamiento de Juárez, 1998.

Weber, David J. *The Mexican Frontier, 1821–1846: The American Southwest under Mexico*. Albuquerque: University of New Mexico Press, 1982.

———. *The Spanish Frontier in North America*. New Haven: Yale University Press, 1992.

———. *What Caused the Pueblo Revolt of 1680?* Boston: Bedford/St. Martin's Press, 1999.

Weedman, Kathryn, Rick López, David O. Brown, and John A. Peterson, eds. *Cultural Resources Survey in Socorro and San Elizario, El Paso County, Texas: Phase II Architectural Studies*. El Paso: Archaeological Research Inc., 1994.

Weedman, Kathryn, David O. Brown and John A. Peterson, eds. *Cultural Resources Survey in Socorro and San Elizario, El Paso County, Texas: Phase III-San Elizario*. El Paso: Archaeological Research Inc., 1994.

Weigle, Marta, ed. *Telling New Mexico: A New History*. Santa Fe: Museum of New Mexico Press, 2009.

Westphall, Victor. *Mercedes Reales: Hispanic Land Grants of the Upper Rio Grande Region*. Albuquerque: University of New Mexico Press, 1983.

White, Katherine H. *The Pueblo de Socorro Grant*. El Paso: Katherine Hope Huffman White Memorial Trust, 1986.

White, Leslie A. *The Pueblo of San Felipe*. Millwood: Kraus Reprint Co., 1974.

White, Leslie A. *The Pueblo of Santa Ana, New Mexico*. New York: Kraus Reprint Co., 1969.

Wislizenus, Frederick Adolph. *Memoir of a Tour to Northern Mexico connected with Colonel Doniphan's Expedition in 1846 and 1847.* Washington: Tippin and Streeper, 1848.

Zamora, Dorothy A. *Excavations at the Coal Mining Community of Carthage, Socorro County, New Mexico.* Albuquerque: Museum of New Mexico, 1997.

Audio Collection:

Loeffler, Jack. *Portrait in Sound of an Ancient Road: Stories and Songs of El Camino Real De Tierra Adentro.* Santa Fe: Peregrine Arts Sound Archive, 2004. Audio CD Series.

Index

Abencio Salazar Historic District, 250, 251

Abert, Lieutenant James William, 32, 189, 198, 210, 254, 257, 297

Abeytas, New Mexico, 211

Acoma Pueblo, 21

Agriculture, 26, 27, 28

Agua Fría, New Mexico, 298-302

Agua Fría Schoolhouse Pueblo, 299, 301

Alameda, New Mexico, 244-45

Alamillo, New Mexico, 193

Alamillo Mission, 193

Albuquerque, New Mexico, 233, 234-38

Alemán, New Mexico, 149, 154

Alemán Ranch, 154

Algodones, New Mexico, 256

Amador, Martin, 132, 135

Amador Hotel, 135

American El Paso (see El Paso, Texas)

Anasazi, 16

Anaya Almazán, Francisco de, 293

Angostura, New Mexico, 255-56

Apaches, 17, 28, 54, 56, 67, 71, 118, 123, 125, 143, 147, 166, 167, 173, 183, 212, 226

Armendáriz, Pedro de, 156, 161-62

Armijo, Ambrosio, 238

Armijo, Governor Manuel, 105, 132, 190, 237, 238

Armijo, José de, 237

Armijo, Juan Cristóbal, 237, 242

Armijo, Nestor, 132, 134-35

Ascárate, Juana María, 102

Atchison, Topeka and Santa Fe Railway, 35, 169, 179, 185, 191, 214, 235, 262, 307

Atrisco, New Mexico, 228

Atrisco Heritage Foundation, 230

Baca, Cristóbal, 299

Baca, Diego Manuel, 296

Baca, Juan José, 187

Bandelier, Adolph, 268

Bar Cross Ranch, 157

Barelas, New Mexico, 231-32

Barrio Analco, 312

Bartlett, Commissioner Russell, 59, 78, 100, 113

Battle of Brazito, 89, 105, 121-22

Battle of Peralta, 211

Bautista de Anza, Juan, 297

Baylor, Lieutenant Colonel John R., 124, 126

Beale, Lieutenant Edward, 47, 210

Bean-Butterfield Building, 127

Becker, John, 214

Becknell, William, 306

Belén, New Mexico, 213-16

Belén Cut-Off, 214

Benavides, Fray Alonso de, 25, 175, 195

Bennett Sackett, Lieutenant Delos, 131

Bernal, Pascual, 248

Bernalillo, New Mexico, 248-51

Bernalillo Mercantile Company, 262

Bien Mur Indian Market Center, 248

Billy the Kid, 52

Black Mesa, 159

Bliss, William Wallace Smith, 106

Bosque del Apache, 23

Bosque del Apache National Wildlife Refuge, 175

Bosque de Pinos, 209

Bosque Farms, New Mexico, 209

Bosquecito, New Mexico, 189

Bourke, Captain John G., 35, 66, 224, 248, 257, 263, 284

braceros, 76

Bravo, Fray José, 77
Brazito, New Mexico, 89, 121-23
Buffalo Soldiers, 143
Butterfield, John, 34
Butterfield Overland Mail, 34, 47, 52, 67, 98, 99, 108, 120, 123, 125

Cabeza de Vaca, Alvar Núñez, 18
California Gold Rush, 98, 115
Camino de los Muleros, 114
Camino Nacional, 30
Campbell, General Thomas, 198
Canby, Colonel Edward R. S., 163
Canutillo, Texas, 119-21
caravans, 24, 25, 26
Carbajal, Juan, 60
Carabajal's Store, 60
Cárdenas, President Lázaro, 76
Carleton, Major James, 231
Carrizal, 39, 105, 160
CARTA (Camino Real de Tierra Adentro Trail Association), 10, 37
Carthage, New Mexico, 179
Carthage Coal Company, 180
Casa Colorada, New Mexico, 202-03
Casa Ortiz, 60
Casa Ronquillo, 51
Casa San Ysidro, 246
Casas Grandes, Chih., 17
Castaño de Sosa, Gaspar, 18, 259, 264
Catití, Alonso, 260
cement plasters, 49
Cerrillos, New Mexico, 266, 267
Cerrillos Hills Historic District, 268
Chaco Canyon, 16
Chamizal Treaty, 110
Chapel of Saint Anthony at Los Lentes, 219, 220
Chaves, José Mariano, 210
Chávez, Felipe, 213, 214-16
Chihuahua City, Mexico, 27, 47, 60, 83, 87, 93, 102, 104, 105, 122, 160, 306

Chihuahua Trail, 30, 31, 73, 185, 190, 206, 208, 214, 235, 316
Chimayo, New Mexico, 280
Church of San Isidro, 245
Cinco de Mayo, 92
Ciudad Juárez, Mexico, 81
Civil War (U.S.), 34, 103, 109, 242
Cochiti Pueblo, 257, 262-64, 291
Coloradas, Mangas, 167
Comanches, 28, 67, 165, 205, 266, 296, 304
Conchos River, 19
Concordia, Texas, 102-04
Concordia Cemetery, 103
Connelly, Doctor Henry, 210
conventos, 25
Coons, Benjamin Franklin, 108
Coronado, Francisco Vásquez de, 250
Coronado State Monument, 250
Corrales, New Mexico, 245-47
Corrales Historical Society, 246
Cortés, Hernando, 18
Cortés Moctezuma, Isabel de Tolosa, 18
Craig, Captain Louis, 165
Cuervo y Valdés, Governor Francisco, 234
Curtin, Leonora F., 298

Daughters of the American Revolution, 315
Davis, Judge William W.H., 33, 74, 106, 112
Denver and Rio Grande Railroad, 35, 307
Díaz, President Porfirio, 95
Domínguez, Fray Atanasio, 29, 201, 212, 222, 244, 245, 254, 263, 274, 275, 278, 280, 284, 293, 296, 301, 304, 305, 307, 311, 312
Domínguez de Mendoza, Tomé, 205
Doña Ana, New Mexico, 105, 118, 122, 123, 136
Doniphan, Colonel Alexander W., 32, 40, 122, 137
Duke of Alburquerque, 234
Dumarest, Father Noel, 261
Durán y Chaves, Nicolás, 216
Durán y Chaves, Pedro Gómez, 228

Durán y Chaves I, Fernando, 228, 255
Durán y Chaves II, Fernando, 228, 229, 249

Eight Northern Indian Pueblos Council, 287
ejidos, 27
El Camino Real de Tierra Adentro, 11, 13, 14, 15, 23, 99, 118, 138, 144, 171, 252, 264, 269, 273, 281, 282, 289, 303, 315, 316
El Camino Real de Tierra Adentro National Historic Trail, 13, 14, 15, 39, 150, 252, 269, 289, 292
El Camino Real International Heritage Center, 167-68
El Contadero, New Mexico, 159-60
El Paso, Texas, 39, 47, 48, 97-117
El Paso Canyon, 96, 97, 113
El Paso del Norte, Mexico, 33, 64, 74, 93, 120
El Ranchos de las Golondrinas, 298
Elena Gallegos Land Grant, 242
Elephant Butte Reservoir, 158
encomienda, 24, 173
Engle, New Mexico, 156
entrada, 19
escoltas, 25
Española, New Mexico, 274, 286
Española Valley, 253, 268, 284
Esquibel, Juan José, 278

Felipe Chávez House, 215
Fergusson, Harvey, 139-40
Fewkes, J. Walter, 67, 78
Flores Vergara, Agustín, 312
Fort Bliss, 34, 102, 106, 108, 111, 123, 126, 163
Fort Conrad, 162, 165
Fort Craig, 34, 165-67, 168, 178, 179, 185, 211
Fort McRae, 185
Fort Selden, 143, 185
Fragua, Clifford, 287
Franciscans, 19, 24, 56, 118, 260, 262, 270, 273, 312
Francisco de Ayeta, Father, 117, 174
Franklin, Texas, 107-10

Franklin Mountains, 113
Fray Cristóbal, New Mexico, 33, 147
Fray Cristóbal Mountains, 23
Frijoles Canyon, 268, 269
Frontera, Texas, 114-16

Gadsden Purchase, 100, 123
Galisteo Basin, 264, 289, 309
Gallegos, Celso, 301
García, Lieutenant Alonso, 27, 64, 184, 195, 234
García, Gregorio N., 50
García Conde, Pedro, 100
García de la Concepción, Fray Andrés José, 280
genízaros, 205
Gibson, George R., 32, 74
Gil de Ávila, Fray Alonso, 174
Gonzáles, José, 279
González, Juan, 244
Gregg, Josiah A., 30, 203
Gruber, Bernardo, 149
Guadalupe Bravo, Mexico, 42
Guadalupe Mission, 26, 71, 72, 80, 81-83, 85, 90, 117, 174
Gutiérrez-Hubbell House, 227, 228

Hacienda San Antonio, 54-55
Hacienda Tiburcios (see Tiburcios)
Hart, Juan, 111
Hart, Simeon, 110-11
Hart's Mill, 111-12
Hilton, Conrad, 179
Hopi Indians, 272, 273
Holy Cross Church, 280, 281
Hubbell, James L., 227-28
Huff, William P., 59

INAH (Instituto Nacional de Antropología y Historia), 95
Isleta Pueblo, 64, 200, 213, 219, 220-25

Jarales, New Mexico, 212

Jornada del Muerto, 23, 144, 147-70
Juan José Baca House, 187
Juan Nepomucero García House, 187
Juárez, Benito, 89, 90, 92
Jumano Indians, 71

Katishtya Pueblo, 257
Kendall, George Wilkins, 31, 89, 150
Kearny, General Stephen W., 32, 235, 306, 316
Keresan, Keres Indians, 252, 257, 259, 264, 265, 268, 295, 299
Keystone Heritage Park, 116
Kha' po' Pueblo, 273
Kotyete Pueblo, 262

La Bajada, New Mexico, 289, 290-92
La Castrense, 310-11
La Ciénega, New Mexico, 295-98, 309
La Cieneguilla, New Mexico, 292-95
La Hacienda Café, 112
La Joya de Sevilleta, New Mexico, 193, 194-99
La Joyita, New Mexico, 198
La Mesilla, New Mexico, 124, 125-29
La Parida, New Mexico, 189
La Salinera, 117
La Salineta, 117
La Toma (the Taking), 19, 80
Lacouture, Felipe, 83
Lafora, Nicolás de, 29
Laguna del Muerto, 147, 155
Land Grants, 229-31
Lane, Lydia Spencer, 124
Las Barrancas, New Mexico, 203-04
Las Cruces, New Mexico, 102, 133
Las Golondrinas, 297
Las Nutrias, New Mexico, 200
Lemitar, New Mexico, 189-93
Los Candelarias, New Mexico, 240
Los Candelarias Chapel, 240
Los Chaves, New Mexico, 216-17
Los Corrales de Alameda, 245

Los Duránes, New Mexico, 238-39
Los Duránes Chapel, 238, 239
Los Gallegos, New Mexico, 242
Los Griegos, New Mexico, 240-41
Los Griegos Chapel, 240
Los Griegos Historic District, 240
Los Lentes, New Mexico, 217-18
Los Lentes Pueblo, 218
Los Lunas, New Mexico, 217-18
Los Padillas, New Mexico, 225
Los Poblanos, New Mexico, 242
Los Portales Museum, 50
Los Ranchos de Albuquerque, New Mexico, 241-43
Luis López, New Mexico, 181-82
Luna, Domíngo de, 217
Lynde, Major Isaac, 124

Magoffin, James Wiley, 104-06, 120-21, 190
Magoffin, Joseph, 106
Magoffin, Susan Shelby, 32, 105, 131
Magoffin Home, 107
Magoffinsville, 104-07
Manso Indians, 19, 43, 45, 53, 56, 71, 80, 110, 118, 122, 129, 130
Marcy, Randolph B., 33
María Costales, José, 136
Martin, John "Jack," 154-55
Martínez, María, 271
Martínez de Montoya, Captain Juan, 302
Matachines, 80, 131
McRae, Captain Alexander, 163
Melendres, Pablo, 131
Menchero, Fray Juan Miguel, 247
Mesilla Guard, 125
Mesilla Valley, 23, 118-46
Mesilla (see La Mesilla, New Mexico)
Mesquite Historic District, 134
mestizaje, 18
Mexican-American War, 32, 118, 121-22, 125, 137, 139, 155, 190, 202, 208

Mexican Central Railroad, 75, 83, 91

Mexican Revolution, 75, 102

Mexico City, Mexico, 16, 23, 24

Miera y Pacheco, Bernardo de, 29, 257

Mills, Anson, 108

Miranda-Bean Building, 126-27

Mission Trail, 42, 44

Mogollon Culture, 200

Montes Vigil, Captain Francisco, 244

Montoya, Captain Diego, 241

Montoya, Pablo, 279

Mount Cristo Rey, 113

Museum of the Revolution (Ciudad Juárez), 94

National Hispanic Cultural Center, 232

Navajo Indians, 17, 162, 165, 167, 190, 242, 248, 273, 274

Nepomucero García, Juan, 187

New Mexico, 18, 173

New Mexico History Museum, 310

Nuestra Señora de la Luz, 310

Ocean-to-Ocean Highway, 36, 291

Ochoa, Inocente, 91, 95

Ohkay Owingeh (See San Juan Pueblo)

Ohkay Owingeh Arts and Crafts Cooperative, 287

Ojo del Muerto, 155

Old Pecos Trail, 315

Old Spanish Trail, 31

Oldest House in the United States, 313

Oñate, Cristóbal (son), 302

Oñate, Juan de, 18-22, 39, 147, 175, 195, 257, 259, 265, 269, 282, 302, 303

Oñate Medallion, 314

Organ Mountains, 23, 119

Ortiz, Father Ramón, 31, 74, 87, 89, 95, 102, 125, 127

Otermín, Governor Antonio, 27, 64, 174, 184, 193, 195, 200, 222, 234, 244, 247, 266, 303

Otero, Antonio José, 208, 215, 218

Our Lady of Guadalupe Mission (See Guadalupe Mission)

Our Lady of Guadalupe Church (Los Chaves), 217

Our Lady of the Immaculate Conception Church, 205, 206

Our Lady of Lourdes Pilgrimage Shrine, 286

Our Lady of Perpetual Help, 183

Our Lady of Purification Church, 137

Our Lady of Sorrows Church (Bernalillo), 249

Our Lady of Sorrows Church (La Joya), 198, 201

Palace of the Governors, 305, 308-10

Palacio Municipal (Ciudad Juárez), 85

Pánuco, Mexico, 18

Pajarito, New Mexico, 226-28

Pajarito Plateau, 252, 268

Paraje, New Mexico, 158-59

parajes, 26

Paraje de Robledo, 141

Parral, Mexico, 26

partido system, 213

Pass of the North, 20, 101, 110

Peinado, Fray Alonso de, 264

Peralta, New Mexico, 209-10

Peralta, Governor Pedro de, 20, 209, 283, 302

Perea, Dolores, 210

Pérez, Albino, 278

Pérez de Villagrá, Captain Gaspar, 282

Perrillo, 147, 151

Petroglyph National Monument, 230

Philip II, King of Spain, 173

Pike, Lieutenant Zebulon Montgomery, 29, 46, 196, 206, 257, 297

Pilabó Mission, 58, 183

Pilgrims (Plymouth, Massachusetts), 52, 53

Pindi Pueblo, 299, 300

Piro Indians, 17, 25, 56, 64, 77, 129, 130, 171, 173, 174, 175, 176, 181, 182, 193, 200, 221

Placitas, New Mexico, 249

Plaza Montoya Pueblo, 182

Plaza de Santa Fe, 302

Plaza de Señor de San José de los Ranchos, New Mexico, 242

Pohwoge Pueblo, 269

Ponce de León, Juan María, 97, 102, 107, 119

Ponce de León Land Grant, 110

Pope, Captain John, 123, 129

Popé, 283-84

Presidio de Nuestra Señora del Pilar del Paso del Rio del Norte, 84

Price, Colonel Sterling, 279

Pueblo Indian Revolt, 26, 27, 117, 158, 208, 216, 221, 247, 252, 261, 270, 303, 309

Pueblo Quemado, 299

Puye Cliff Dwellings, 276

Qualacú Pueblo, 176-77

Ralliére, Father Jean Baptiste, 206

Ranchos de Santa Ana, New Mexico, 254, 255

reducción, 24, 172

Rhodes, Eugene Manlove, 152, 156-57

Rio Abajo, 290

Rio Arriba, 290

Rio Vista Farm Site, 55, 57

Rivera, Reynaldo, 316

Robledo, Pedro de, 141

Robledo Mountain, 141

Rodríguez, Fray Agustín, 18

Rodríguez de Torre, Fray Mariano, 275

Rodríguez-Chamuscado expedition, 18, 173, 194, 264

Roman Empire, 16

Romero, Tomás, 279

Rouiller, August, 158

Royal Road (See El Camino Real de Tierra Adentro)

Royal Road of the Interior (See El Camino Real de Tierra Adentro)

Ruxton, George, 32, 86, 178

Sabinal, New Mexico, 212

Sabino, New Mexico, 193

Sagrada Familia de Lemitar Church, 192

Salazar, Fray Cristóbal de, 157

Salt War, 48, 62

Samalayuca, Mexico, 41

Samalayuca Sand Dunes, 41, 86

Samaniego, Mariano, 91, 95

San Agustín de la Isleta, 222

San Andrés de los Padillas, 225

San Antonio and San Diego Mail, 120

San Antonio, New Mexico, 177-79

San Antonio, Texas, 98

San Antonio Chapel, 294

San Antonio de Sabinal, 212

San Diego, Paraje, 23, 144-45

San Elizario, Texas, 19, 42, 45, 59, 160

San Elizario Genealogical and Historical Society, 50

San Elizario Presidio Chapel, 48

San Felipe Church, 258

San Felipe Neri Church, 236, 237

San Felipe Pueblo, 257-59

San Felipe Pueblo (Socorro Valley), 173

San Francisco, Fray García de, 71

San Gabriel de Yungue Pueblo, 287

San Ildefonso Pueblo, 269-73

San Isidro Church, 302

San José, Mexico, 86-95

San José Chapel, 87

San Juan de los Caballeros, 282

San Juan Pueblo, 20, 196, 281-88, 305

San Lorenzo, Mexico, 72, 79-81

San Luis Obispo Mission, 195

San Marcial, New Mexico, 149, 164, 168-70

San Marcos Pueblo, 257, 266, 267, 289, 295, 309

San Miguel Chapel, 311-15

San Miguel Church, 186

San Miguel de La Bajada, 290

San Pascual, 175

San Pascualito, 175

San Pedro, New Mexico, 177, 178, 179-80

San Pedro Mission Church, 181

San Ysidro de Paxarito, 226

Sandia Pueblo, 200, 247-48

Sangre de Cristo Church, 208

Santa Ana Church, 254

Santa Ana Pueblo, New Mexico, 252-55

Santa Bárbara, Mexico, 19, 282

Santa Clara Pueblo, 273-76

Santa Cruz de la Cañada, New Mexico, 196, 263, 276-81, 305

Santa Cruz River, 276

Santa Fe, New Mexico, 13, 14, 17, 27, 87, 105, 185,, 196, 289, 295, 302-16

Santa Fe River, 289, 295, 298

Santa Fe Trail, 30, 73, 235, 264, 265, 306, 309, 315

Santa María de las Caldas, 55-57

Santo Domingo Church, 261

Santo Domingo Pueblo, 21, 259-62

Santo Niño de Atocha, 140

Selden, Henry H., 143

Senecú, New Mexico, 149, 174

Senecú, Mexico, 73, 77-79, 195

Seux, Father Camilo, 286

Sevilleta (see La Joya de Sevilleta)

Sevilleta National Wildlife Refuge, 198

Sharps Rifle Company, 155

Sibley, Brigadier General Henry H., 34, 163

Skillman, Henry, 33, 99, 155

Socorro, New Mexico, 178, 183-88

Socorro, Texas, 58-63

Socorro del Sur Mission, 184, 195

Socorro Mission (New Mexico) 183

Socorro Mission (Texas) 61

Socorro Valley, 171-99

Southern Pacific Railroad, 101

Southern Tewa (Tanos), 264

Spain, 16-17

stagecoaches, 155

Stephenson, Hugh, 102, 122-23

Suma Indians, 17, 43, 53, 56, 80

Tamarón y Romeral, Bishop Pedro, 29, 72, 77, 80, 114, 141, 175, 203, 263, 278, 304, 305, 313

Tamayá Pueblo, 252, 253, 255

Tano Indians, 264, 277, 293, 295, 299

Taos Pueblo, 28

Taos Rebellion, 279

Taylor-Barela-Reynolds Building, 127-28

Teypana Pueblo, 182

Tewa Indians, 17, 253, 264, 268, 269, 270, 276, 281, 282, 299

Texan-Santa Fe Expedition, 31, 89, 150

Tiburcios, 45, 46

Tigua Indians, 66, 68, 122, 200

Tiwa Indians, 17, 64, 129, 200, 218, 244, 247, 252, 254

Tlaxcalan Indians, 80, 312

Tolosa Cortés Moctezuma, Isabel de, 18

Tomé, New Mexico, 204-07, 220

Tomé Hill, 23, 204, 207

Torres, Captain Diego de, 213

Tortugas, New Mexico, 129-31

Treviño, Governor Juan Francisco, 283

Turn, New Mexico (see Casa Colorada)

Turquoise, 265

United Nations World Heritage Site, 13

United States Bureau of Land Management, 10, 13, 36, 151, 152

United States National Park Service, 10, 13, 36, 151, 152, 230

United States Route 66, 291

Urbaño Montaño, Antonio, 266

Urrutia y de Las Casas, Joseph Ramón de, 29, 73, 305

Ute Indians, 226

Valencia, Blas, 207

Valencia, New Mexico, 207-09

Valverde, New Mexico, 34, 161

Valverde Cosío, Captain Antonio de, 54, 271

Vargas, Governor Diego de, 27, 58, 72, 248, 249, 252, 263, 270, 277, 284, 293, 299, 304, 312, 314

Vega y Coca, Miguel, 296

Veguita, New Mexico, 202

Vial, Pedro, 306

Victoria Carvajal, Juan, 296

villas, 27, 277

Virgin of Guadalupe, 71, 83

Vueltas de Luis López, 181

Wallace, William "Bigfoot," 33

Wertheim, Herman, 139-40

Whipple, Lieutenant Amiel W., 297

White, T. Frank, 114

Whiting, William H.C., 33, 66, 115

Wislizenus, Adolph, 32, 86, 198, 203, 210, 223

Yá atze Pueblo, 264, 265

Yost Escarpment Trail, 152

Ysleta, Texas, 59

Ysleta del Sur Pueblo, 64-70, 200, 222

Ysleta Mission, 66, 68

Yungue Pueblo, 287

Zacatecas, Mexico, 18, 26, 39, 277, 311

Zaldívar, Juan de, 21

Zaldívar, Vicente de, 19, 265

www.ingramcontent.com/pod-product-compliance
Lightning Source LLC
Chambersburg PA
CBHW020821270326
41928CB00006B/393